School Law for the Principal

A Handbook for Practitioners

ROBERT J. SHOOP
Kansas State University

DENNIS R. DUNKLEE
George Mason University

ALLYN AND BACON
Boston London Toronto Sydney Tokyo Singapore

Advisement

This publication and the statements of authorities therein, including the statements of the authors, represent an attempt to respond to the professional needs of the reader. The citations of case law and interpretation and the presentation of scenarios are not designed as statements of final authority. Only a court of law, guided by individual case facts, can be considered as an authority on a specific issue. That issue may be treated differently court to court, state to state. This publication serves a purpose for the education profession and provides only suggested guidelines for the avoidance of litigation. This publication should not be considered an accurate forecaster of impending or future litigation. It should also be noted that any guidelines suggested should be treated with caution in light of the specific subject matter taught and the expected level of personal involvement. There are those administrative and teaching responsibilities that transcend the norm, requiring a higher degree of duty and care, supervision, instruction, and maintenance.

This publication is designed to provide accurate and authoritative information in regard to the subject matter covered. In publishing this book, neither the authors nor the publisher is engaged in rendering legal service. If legal advice or assistance is required, the services of a competent attorney should be sought.

While the scenarios provided in this book are based on actual events, all names (including those of students, parents, teachers, administrators, and school districts) used in the scenarios are fictitious, and any resemblance to real people is coincidental.

Copyright © 1992 by Allyn and Bacon
A Division of Simon & Schuster, Inc.
160 Gould Street
Needham Heights, Massachusetts 02194

Library of Congress Cataloging-in-Publication Data
Shoop, Robert J.
  School law for the principal: a handbook for practitioners/
Robert J. Shoop, Dennis R. Dunklee.
    p. cm.
  Includes bibliographical references and index.
  ISBN 0-205-13447-5 (casebound)
    1. Educational law and legislation—United States. 2. School principals—United States—Handbooks, manuals, etc. I. Dunklee, Dennis R. II. Title.
KF4119.S48   1991
344.73'07—dc20
[347.3047]   91-30298
                                                                              CIP
Printed in the United States of America
10 9 8 7 6 5 4 3 2 1 96 95 94 93 92

Contents

SECTION III
The Legal Relationship of the Principal to the Student 105

SECTION IV
Program Management   *356*

SECTION V
Principal's Tort Liability for Negligence and Risk Management   259

Preface

Once upon a time there was order in our schools and change occurred so benevolently that it was called progress. There was a place and a time for everything. There were authorities, too. The principal spoke without hesitation about what was appropriate behavior. Dad and Mom told their children to go to school and to "mind the teacher," and the students listened and learned and behaved themselves. Teachers and school administrators worked in harmony with each other. Parents left educational decisions up to the schools. The courts rarely got involved with the schools and, when they were asked to make a decision, they tended to side with the schools.

Then something happened. Some say parents failed in their responsibility. Some say schools lost their direction and control. Some say that society became too permissive. Some say the courts started to get involved where they did not belong.

We cannot say for certain whether this once-upon-a-time story is true. This we know: Much that was nailed down suddenly came loose. We also know that the job of being a school principal is vastly different today than it was even ten years ago. Today many principals feel that they are surrounded by a sea of conflicting demands from their school board, central office administration, students, teachers, parents, and community pressure groups. Principals' jobs are further complicated by the seemingly endless and often contradictory statutes, court decisions, and attorney generals' opinions that directly affect the operation of their schools. As a result of these pressures, many principals feel insecure and powerless.

Today's principals face a dilemma as they address the task of balancing the need for order in the schools with the need to respect the legal rights of students, teachers, and parents. Principals are expected to know the laws that relate to special education, bilingual education, and multicultural education, as well as the constitutional and statutory rights of parents, teachers, and students. Many principals have reached a point of frustration and have discarded the illusion that they can continue to operate as they have in the past. There has been a clear shift, and whether we agree with this shift or not, we must admit that legal issues now have a greater impact on the day-to-day operation of the school.

The relationship between the principal and the law has never been easy to define, and it is more complex today than ever before. Although there are a number of good books available on education law, most do not speak directly to the specific needs of the principal. *School Law for the Principal: A Handbook for Practitioners* is written for the building-level administrator. It provides basic information on the current status of law, risk, and site-based management as they relate to the legal rights and responsibilities of principals.

Many principals have only a limited understanding of the legal aspects of school administration. Although most have had a school law course, many of these courses concentrated on broad constitutional and general legal issues. Clearly, these broad principles are important, and principals should have this background. However, most school law courses end without helping the principal translate school law and policy into educational procedures and practice. Most principals know that the law has an impact on almost every facet of education, but they are uncertain regarding exactly how their behavior should respond to these laws.

This book is written to serve as a handbook for practicing principals, both new and experienced; as an alternative to traditional school law texts in courses for pre-service principals; and as a resource for inservice training for principals. It offers the kind of guidance necessary for principals to ensure safe and healthy schools and minimize legal risk.

Principals are expected to know the law. The courts will not accept ignorance of the law as a defense. The majority of legal actions that are brought against school principals are not based on the areas of educational leadership or knowledge of curriculum. Most principals who find themselves defendants in court cases got there as a result of their failure to know the relevant law or to practice sound management based on an understanding of existing court decisions. Not knowing the law results in hardships on teachers, students, parents, and principals, as well as costing school districts countless dollars and precious lost time.

To help the principal "know the law," the material in this book is presented in a nontechnical manner. Whenever appropriate, topics are introduced by reality-based scenarios. Each scenario presents a typical situation that a principal might expect to encounter. The scenarios are based on authentic events and deal with current, relevant, and sometimes controversial topics. The scenarios are followed by "Points to Consider" questions that will stimulate critical thought or discussion. The questions are designed to heighten motivation and reinforce learning. The chapter discussion that follows enlarges upon and summarizes the legal implications presented in the scenarios.

This approach is based on the assumption that confidence and know-how come from successive experience. Each scenario provides the reader with a bridge to travel from legal theory to administrative practice. By vicariously experiencing the situations presented in the scenarios, readers will gain confidence in their ability to cope.

An effective principal must be flexible enough to adjust to a changing environment. By discussing the various decisions involved in the scenarios, readers can increase their ability to adapt to change. They will also gain the ability to recognize and respond appropriately to the early warning signs that often precede conflict. When dealing with controversial issues or critical situations, emotions cannot replace rational thinking. The scenarios provide readers with an opportunity to consider possible courses of action before a situation actually arises. The scenario approach will not only help readers adapt quickly to new situations, but it will also help them develop more trust in their ability to make future decisions that are legally sound.

The organizational basis for this book is the daily activities of the school principal. The book is not intended to explore or even to touch on all areas of school law. Nor is it an attempt at an exhaustive analysis of the legal issues that are presented. Each issue will be treated from the perspective of how it affects the daily life of the principal.

To facilitate the book's use as a desk reference, it is divided into five sections. Section I serves as an overview of education law and schools. Sections II through V describe the legal implications of the principal's relationship to teachers, to students, to program management, and to tort liability and risk management.

The authors of this book believe that the avoidance of education litigation, through the practice of preventive law, requires more than just a knowledge of the law. The determination to practice preventive law and manage risk is an effective administrative mind set. While such a mind set does not enable school administrators to avoid all adjudication, it clearly increases the prospects for rulings that are favorable to school districts and to the education enterprise in total.

The concepts of preventive law and the management of risk, which are woven through the chapters of this book, can be illustrated by six general tenets identified in Figure I-1 and discussed briefly below.

Tenet 1—Substance of Law Limits Educational Organization's Culpability and Exposure. A library of school law books on the shelf and a copy of the State Codes placed strategically on a principal's desk may be impressive. But, while it is important for principals to be generally familiar with the contents of school law books and the provisions of their respective states' codes, it is more important that principals know and understand the substance of the major court rulings that affect principals in the everyday operations of schools. An understanding of the basic tenets of law, bolstered by conscientiously updated knowledge of current education litigation, is the substance of law that forms the foundation for effective principals' day-to-day decision making.

CENTRAL TENETS OF
PREVENTIVE LAW, RISK CONTROL and EDUCATION MANAGEMENT

High

Organization's Culpability and Exposure	Liability Environmental and Personnel Loss	Budget Loss	System Safety and Conflict Resolution	Crisis Management and Motivation	Leadership
				Precedent Knowledge Compliance and Public Information	
			Flexibility		
		Counsel			
	Procedures Judgment Foreseeability				
Substance of Law					
Tenet 1	*Tenet 2*	*Tenet 3*	*Tenet 4*	*Tenet 5*	*Tenet 6*

Low

Risk Factors Diminish
with
Expansion of the Practice of Preventive Law

FIGURE I.1 • *Six Tenets for Reducing Risk Factors*

Tenet 2—Procedures, Judgment, Foreseeability Reduce Liability, Environmental, and Personnel Loss. Case law continues to demonstrate that principals and other school administrators often fail to follow legal procedures and become liable for their commission or omission of required duties or standards of care. While principals may have good intentions in what they do or do not do, the law speaks to nearly every facet of school operations. The duties and standards of care owed by principals to students and adults in the school setting are very specific, and where the law defines procedures and precedent, principals must adhere.

In the absence of specific procedures or precedent, courts will generally uphold principals who exercise reasonable and prudent judgment under the circumstances. When principals make judgments, they must abrogate their personal biases and prejudices in favor of "what is best for all concerned."

Effective principals integrate foreseeability (the art or science of intuitively knowing what might happen) with the practice of preventive law to anticipate potential problems and take appropriate preventive measures.

Tenet 3—Working with Counsel Reduces Budget Loss. Effective school principals seek counsel on issues in question to ascertain that they are following established laws and procedures. Such assistance saves school districts countless hours of work and significant expense in monetary awards by helping to resolve problems before formal legal action becomes necessary.

Tenet 4—Flexibility Endangers System Safety but Enhances Conflict Resolution. Principals cannot demonstrate flexibility with system safety issues. Policies and procedures designed to protect people and property must be strictly adhered to, enforced, and monitored. On the other hand, principals must be flexible when dealing with human values issues. Effective principals recognize that they must accommodate all the people in the school environment, even those who may at times hold ideas different from their own. Principals do not always need to enforce conformity and should see the school as a forum for ideas, values, and viewpoints of many different groups and individuals. Effective principals work to provide a climate in which differing ideas may be tested, allowed to flourish, and channeled toward the good of the school, rather than into conflict.

Tenet 5—Knowledge of Precedent, Constitutional Compliance, and Public Information Needs Enhances Crisis and Motivational Management and Monitoring. Effective principals consult legal precedent in the decision-making process. Principals must understand that court decisions often conflict with each other, though the facts of one case may differ only slightly from those of another. Principals need to understand the specific facts of precedent-setting cases, as well as the courts' final judgments, to make rational decisions.

Students, parents, and school district employees continue to file suits against school personnel and districts on the grounds that their constitutional rights have been violated. As a result of decisions in such cases, some suggest that the courts now run the schools. Effective principals are aware of the extent to which students, teachers, and others have received legal protection under various interpretations of the Constitution. Effective principals also understand that many people do not understand recent court decisions and, therefore, often fail to understand the actions that principals take or do not take. Thus, principals have an ongoing responsibility to inform students, faculty, staff, and parents about court actions that affect the daily operations of their schools.

Tenet 6— Leadership in Education Enterprise Must Be Coupled with Leadership in Preventive Law. Litigation avoidance has been added to the teaching of reading, writing, arithmetic and to all the other societal responsibilities that have been transferred from homes and business to the school. This book for principals is based not only on concrete case law and basic legal theory, but also on practical experience with the daily problems of schools and school districts. The authors have "been there" and have, on occasion, served "under fire." There is nothing like personal threats, police intervention, student injuries, and litigation to convince one that the principal's problems are not all education-related. As surely as preventive medicine may be a "best cure," reasonable, prudent conduct and the practice of preventive law and leadership are the principal's best defenses in the event of litigation. Principals do not want to win lawsuits; they want to avoid them. Effective leadership clearly involves the "taking of risks"; however, such risks should be within the constraints of common sense and the law.

Acknowledgments

The authors are indebted to those persons closest to us for the patience and encouragement so necessary to complete this project. In addition, the authors owe a great deal to our students, our colleagues, and the school principals who all provided ongoing reactions to drafts of the manuscript. Debra Edwards and Jackie Minor deserve special recognition for their work as reader/reactors. A special thank you goes to the SGD writing center for their invaluable help with editing and manuscript preparation.

The School and the Legal Environment

This chapter highlights the several sources of education law and their relationship to the structure and operation of school systems. This overview of the structure of law and operation of the state and federal courts provides the foundation for understanding the manner in which our legal system directs the educational enterprise.

CHAPTER ONE

The Legal Environment

Introduction

The function of law is to regulate human conduct in order to ensure a harmonious society. Legislators and courts are involved in a constant process of attempting to strike a balance that allows individuals as much freedom as possible and, at the same time, allows society to function without unreasonable interference from the conduct of individuals. The United States Constitution provides particular protections of individual rights. Various state and federal statutes protect the general welfare of society and implement the constitutional rights of individuals.

Our system of government provides a structure of laws that protects individual rights and guarantees freedom of religion, speech, press, assembly, and the right of each individual to call upon the courts or government to correct injustices. There are separate legal systems for each of the fifty states, the District of Columbia, and the federal government. For the most part, each of these systems applies its own body of law.

All laws are based on the assumption that for each action there shall be an expected consequence. Laws are society's attempts to ensure that there are consequences that "ought" to result if certain prohibited acts are committed. Our system of laws is based on the assumptions that all citizens should be judged by the same standards of behavior, and for every wrong there follows an inescapable penalty. A law is a rule of civil conduct prescribed by local, state, or federal mandates commanding what is right and prohibiting what is wrong. Laws, then, are simply collections of those rules and principles of conduct that the federal, state, and local community recognize and enforce.

The court system provides the structure that determines the exact relationship between the individual and the law in question. In our legal system the principle of due process of law allows people who have been accused of breaking a law, been harmed by other individuals, or been accused of harming another person to bring their side of the issue before a court for a decision whether they must submit to the force of government or will be protected by it.

Our government is based upon the consent of the governed, and the Bill of Rights denies those in power any legal opportunity to coerce that consent.

Authority is to be controlled by public opinion, not public opinion by authority. This is the social compact theory of government. Because of this, law is not a static set of printed documents, but a living and changing set of precepts that depend on the courts for interpretation.

Laws are divided into two broad classifications: civil and criminal. Criminal law regulates public conduct and prescribes duties owed to society. Civil law regulates relations between individuals.

There are many types of civil law. *Education law* is a generic term that covers a whole class of civil jurisprudence that has been consolidated from traditional legal subject matter areas such as contract, tort, property, constitutional, juvenile, family, and case law. Education law exists to help society, school administrators, teachers, and students to have a generally accepted and mutually understood set of standard practices and procedures.

Sources of Law

In the United States, law is composed of constitutional law, common law, statutory law, and administrative law.

Constitutions

Whether at the federal or state level, a constitution is the basic source of law for the jurisdiction. A constitution specifies the structure of the government and outlines the powers and duties of its principal officers and subdivisions. It also designates the allocation of power between levels of government, between the federal government and the states in the United States Constitution, and between state and local governmental bodies in state constitutions. In addition, constitutions spell out the exact limitations of governmental power. In both the United States Constitution and state constitutions these proscriptions are contained in a bill of rights.

Constitutions are broad philosophical statements of general beliefs. The United States Constitution is written in such broad and general language that it has been amended only twenty-six times in our 200 years. State constitutions are more detailed and specific, with the result that most are frequently amended. Just as the United States Constitution is the supreme law in the United States, state constitutions are the supreme law within each state. State constitutions may not contain provisions, however, that conflict with the United States Constitution.

Because the United States Constitution contains no mention of education, Congress is not authorized to provide a system of education. The Tenth Amendment to the United States Constitution stipulates that "the powers not delegated to the United States by the Constitution, nor prohibited by it to the states, are reserved to the states respectively, or to the people."[1] The United States Supreme

Court has repeatedly and consistently confirmed the authority of states to provide for the general welfare of their residents, including the establishment and control of their public schools. However, the United States Supreme Court has applied various provisions of the United States Constitution to jurisdictions to ensure compliance.

General Welfare Clause

Under article I, section 8 of the Constitution, Congress has the power to "lay and collect taxes, duties, imports and excises, to pay the debts and provide for the common defense and general welfare of the United States. . . ."[2] Congress has often used the general welfare clause as the rationale for the enactment of legislation that directly impacts on the operation of public schools.

First Amendment

The First Amendment states that: "Congress shall make no law respecting an establishment of religion, or prohibiting the free exercise thereof, or abridging the freedom of speech, or of the press; or the right of the people peaceably to assemble, and to petition the Government for a redress of grievances."[3] This amendment affords pervasive personal freedom to the citizens of this country. It has been used as the basis for litigation involving the use of public funds to aid non–public school students, separation of church and state in curriculum matters, students' and teachers' freedom of speech, press censorship, and academic freedom issues.

Fourth Amendment

The Fourth Amendment protects the rights of citizens "to be secure in their persons, houses, papers and effects against unreasonable search or seizure."[4] This amendment emerged in the late 1960's as the basis for litigation concerning the search of students' lockers and personal belongings.

Fifth Amendment

The Fifth Amendment protects citizens from being compelled in any criminal case to be a witness against themselves. Although most due process litigation concerns the Fourteenth Amendment, several self-incrimination issues have been raised in cases concerning teachers being questioned by superiors regarding their activities outside the classroom.[5]

Fourteenth Amendment

The Fourteenth Amendment provides that no state shall "deny to any person within its jurisdiction the equal protection of the laws."[6] This amendment is frequently cited in education cases that deal with race, sex, or ethnic background issues. Recent cases regarding handicaps and school finance issues also have been based on this amendment. As a corollary, this amendment guarantees the right of citizens to due process under the law, and thus has been used to support claims of wrongful discharge by school employees and claims of unfair treatment by students and their parents.

Because education is a state function and responsibility, the state legislature has *plenary,* or absolute, power to make laws governing education. The state legislature also has complete authority to modify the laws regulating education. These laws grow by the accumulation of custom, constitutional provisions, existing laws, moral principles, and community standards. However, statutes cannot override constitutional authority. Whenever legislators consider significant modifications to the law, they must determine whether conditions have changed in such a way as to necessitate a change in the statutes, or whether an amendment to the Constitution is required. Amendments must be approved by the electorate.

Common Law

Many legal experts believe statutes are not law until they are actually tested and adjudicated in a court of law. A court, when confronted with a problem that cannot be solved by reference to pertinent legislation (statutory law), decides that case according to common law. The English common law is defined as those principles, procedures, and rules of action, enforced by courts, that are based on history or custom with modifications as required by circumstances and conditions over time.

Common law is not automatic, but must be applied by a court. Courts decide specific disputes by examining constitutional, statute, or administrative law. When two or more parties are at dispute, the courts become involved in the process when a lawsuit is filed. The court determines the facts of the case and then examines prior judicial decisions to identify legal precedents (if any). This is the doctrine of *stare decisis,* or let the decision stand.

A court is simply an organizational structure that assembles at an appointed time and place to administer law judicially. The primary purpose of courts is to ensure that every person has a fair and unbiased trial before an impartial arbiter. The courts have the power to decide an issue, including the power to decide it wrongly. If a wrong or erroneous decision is made, it is the decision of the losing party to acquiesce to or appeal the decision. The purpose of an appeal is not to dispute the right of the court to make a decision, but to review the trial evidence and the applicable laws to determine whether or not the litigant has been given a fair trial.

It is assumed that there are always conflicting interests and that the courts must weigh one against the other. Often the decision is not between good and bad, but the choice of selecting the greater good or the lesser evil. The courts seek to determine legal liability. For a liability to exist there must be a law and a set of facts that the law defines as illegal.

Statutory and Administrative Law

Statutory laws are laws passed by a legislative body. These laws may alter the common law by adding to, deleting from, or eliminating the law. The courts under our system of government are the final interpreters of legislative provisions.

Administrative laws are regulations promulgated by administrative agencies. An administrative agency is a governmental authority, other than a court or legislative body, that affects the rights of private parties through adjudication or rule making. In many cases the operations of schools are affected more by the administrative process than by the judicial process. It is not uncommon for a state to have several hundred agencies with powers of adjudication, rule making, or both.

Structure of Government

It is the American ideal that the power to control the conduct of people by the use of public will is inherent in the people. This is accomplished by adopting a constitution through which they delegate certain power to the state. Constitutions divide this power and assign it to three branches of government. Although no one branch performs only one function, each has a generally defined area of influence.[7] The responsibilities belong to three separate but equal branches of government. The legislative branch makes the laws. The judicial branch interprets the law. The executive branch enforces the law.

The Legislative Branch

The legislative branch is created constitutionally with the primary function of making laws. It is limited in its function only by the state and federal constitutions. Each state legislature has the absolute power to make laws governing education. It is important to understand that this makes education a state function, makes school funds state funds, and makes school buildings state property.

Although it is an accepted principle of law that the state legislature cannot delegate its law-making powers, it can delegate to subordinate agencies the authority to make the rules and regulations necessary to implement these laws. One such subordinate agency is the state board of education.

State boards of education are the policy-making and planning bodies for the public school systems in most states. They have specific responsibility for adopting policies, enacting regulations, and establishing general rules for carrying out the duties placed on them by state legislatures. Local school districts and local boards are created by the state legislature and have only those powers that are specifically delegated by the legislature or that can be reasonably implied.

The Executive Branch

Although each state has a unique structure, the typical executive branch includes a governor, a lieutenant governor, a secretary of state, a treasurer, and an attorney general. The governor is the chief executive officer of the state and is responsible for the enforcement of the laws of the state. The attorney general is a member of the executive branch of government who often has significant impact on the operation of schools in the state. This person represents the state in all suits and pleas to which the state is a party; gives legal advice to the governor and other executive officers, when requested by them, and performs such other duties as may be required by law.

The attorney general acts as both the defender and the prosecutor of the state's interest. The attorney general acts for the state much as a private attorney acts on behalf of a private client and renders opinions on questions of interest to the state submitted by state officials. In such opinions the attorney general identifies the laws applicable to the question and the set of facts presented. These opinions are not laws or court decisions; they are interpretations of state law that are enforceable in the absence of a contrary court ruling.

The Judicial Branch

Courts interpret law and settle disputes by applying the law. However, a court can decide a controversy only when it has authority to hear and adjudicate the case. Prior to any litigation a lawyer must decide whether to file at the state or federal level, and in which particular court: magistrate, district, or supreme court. The appropriate jurisdiction emanates directly from the law. Court names vary from state to state. For example trial courts are called: (1) supreme courts in New York, (2) circuit courts in Missouri, and (3) district courts in Kansas.

The principal function of the courts is to decide specific cases in light of the constitution and the laws. In each state there are two judicial systems that operate simultaneously: the federal court system and the state courts. Courts in both systems are classified as having either original or appellate jurisdiction.

Original jurisdiction refers to the right of a court to hear a case for the first time. A trial on the facts occurs in a court of original jurisdiction. Once the initial trial is over and a judgment rendered, the appellate process may begin.

Appellate jurisdiction refers to the right of a court to hear cases on appeal from courts of original jurisdiction. In appellate courts, matters of fact are no longer in dispute; instead, questions of law or proceedings from the lower courts serve as the basis for review. The appellate process can proceed to the state's highest court, and, under certain circumstances, to the United States Supreme Court.

The Federal Court System

The federal court system of the United States includes district courts, special federal courts, courts of appeal, and the Supreme Court.

Federal District Courts

There are ninety-seven federal district courts, with at least one in each state, including the Virgin Islands and Puerto Rico. Each district court has a chief judge and other federal judges appointed by the President. These courts have original jurisdiction in cases between citizens of different states where an amount of money over $10,000 is in dispute and in cases involving litigation under federal statutes or the United States Constitution. The district courts have no appellate function. Appeals from the district courts are made to the courts of appeal in the respective circuits.

In some limited circumstances a special three-judge district court can be convened to decide a controversy. This type of tribunal would be used when a state statute is being challenged under the United States Constitution. A special application must be made to the district court and, if granted, the chief judge and at least one other judge must be from the court of appeals. The importance of this type of tribunal lies in the fact that an appeal of its decision goes directly to the United States Supreme Court.

There is a chief judge designated for each federal district court and other judges as authorized by federal law. The judges hold their office for life "during good behavior."

Federal Courts of Appeal

The first level of appeal in the federal court system is in the courts of appeal. These courts provide an intermediate level of appeal between the district courts and the Supreme Court. These courts have only appellate jurisdiction and review the record of the trial court for violations of legal proceedings or questions of law, rather than questions of fact. The courts of appeal operate with several judges. There is no jury; a panel of three or more judges decides the cases before them. In some cases the judges may sit *en banc* (together) to decide the case. There are twelve federal circuits in the United States, each with a court of appeals.

United States Supreme Court

The United States Supreme Court, alone among the federal courts, was created directly by the Constitution, rather than by congressional legislation. This court consists of the Chief Justice and eight Associate Justices. Six justices constitute a quorum. The Supreme Court meets for an annual term beginning the first Monday in October. It has limited original jurisdiction and exercises appellate jurisdiction over federal district courts, federal courts of appeal, and the state supreme courts.

The Supreme Court is the nation's highest court. It is often referred to as "the court of last resort" in that there are no appeals to its decisions. Of course, a constitutional amendment ultimately could be used to reverse this Court's decision; however, this has occurred in only four instances. Since more than 5000 cases are appealed to the Supreme Court each year, the Court most frequently will deny *certiorari* and refuse to review the decisions of the lower courts. The denial of *certiorari* has the effect of sustaining the decisions of the lower courts.

Function of the Courts

Courts have three general functions: deciding controversies, interpreting enacted law, and judicial review.

Deciding controversies consists of determining the facts of the dispute and applying the applicable law. There may be one or more statutes or regulations that apply. If there are none, the court must decide the controversy based on previous decisions of the appellate courts of the state in similar situations. If the case presents a new situation, the court's job is more difficult. When a court does not wait for legislative action and makes a decision, it has in fact made a new law. In this process, *stare decisis,* or the adherence to precedent, creates a new foundational common law.

Interpretation of enacted law occurs when a statute does not provide a clear answer to the question before the court. Because it is not always possible to draft legislation that is unambiguous when applied to specific controversies, the court may be forced to strike down a statute that it feels is vague, ambiguous, or contradictory. The courts tend to use the following four approaches in interpreting legislation:

1. *Literal*—The courts look to the ordinary interpretation of words to determine their meaning.
2. *Purposive*—The courts attempt to ascertain what the legislature intended the law to mean.
3. *Precedent-based*—The courts look to past similar cases and laws to find support for one interpretation of the law.
4. *Policy-based*—The courts interpret the law in relationship to the courts' own view of what is best for society.

The courts often adopt a combination of these approaches in making their decision.

Judicial review is a supreme court's power to declare that a statute is unconstitutional. This power has led some to say that the judicial branch is the first among the three equal branches of government. However, this power is not without its limits. Judges at all levels are expected to base their decisions on precedents under the legal doctrine of *stare decisis*. This means that the court must look to other decisions in similar cases to find direction in dealing with new cases.

Endnotes

1. U.S. Const., amend. X.
2. U.S. Const., art. 1, § 8.
3. U.S. Const., amend. I.
4. U.S. Const., amend. IV.
5. U.S. Const., amend. V.
6. U.S. Const., amend. XIV.
7. R. SHOOP & W. SPARKMAN, KANSAS SCHOOL LAW. (Dubuque, Iowa: Bowers, 1983), 5.

SECTION TWO:

The Legal Relationship of the Principal to the Teacher

INTRODUCTION AND AUTHORITY

As discussed in Chapter 1, the control of public education rests with individual states. The courts have definitively recognized the plenary power of states' legislative bodies to establish, conduct, and regulate the education enterprise. State legislatures, through statutory law, establish the framework within which their school districts operate; however, the actual management of school districts is delegated to state boards of education, state departments of education, and local school boards. These agencies generate rules and regulations, in response to legislative policy, for the administration of public schools.

The establishment of operational policies for public schools is delegated to local school boards. School boards employ superintendents and principals and entrust them with the implementation of board-generated policy and the direct day-to-day management of schools. Such education administration professionals are expected to demonstrate the leadership necessary to manage school districts and individual school units and effectively accomplish the educational objectives identified by local boards. Principals, as the first line of administration in school districts, serve as the critical link between classroom teachers, classified staff, and district administration. This section addresses that linkage by examining the legal relationship between principals and teachers.

While principals' authority to hire and fire personnel is usually limited to recommendation, principals have major responsibilities in personnel or human resources management and are continuously involved with employee relations. Principals recommend teachers and support personnel for employment, evaluate personnel, and document cases for dismissal or nonrenewal. In this pursuit, principals operate in accordance with often confusing federal and state constitutional provisions, statutes, regulations, and local school board policies.

This section examines the role of the principal with respect to the laws of equal employment opportunity, staff selection, contracts, evaluation, nonrenewal and dismissal (including substantive and procedural due process), and other issues directly related to human resources management. This section has been designed to help principals judiciously recruit and interview prospective hirees, recommend for selection, and recommend for termination without encountering legal problems. Failure to recognize and implement nondiscriminatory and appropriate discharge procedures are by far the most common sources of liability in human resources management. In today's litigious society, principals are wise to consider every employment situation as a source of potential litigation and to conduct personnel business in such a way that legal defense will not be needed.

CHAPTER TWO

Constitutional and Statutory Foundations of Staff Selection

Equal Employment Opportunity

The employment process has become more complex each year. The growing complexity of employment relationships can be traced primarily to the enactment of Title VII of the Civil Rights Act of 1964. Title VII established the fundamental concept of equal employment opportunity, which has become the guiding principle of employment practices in the United States today. Subsequent amendment of Title VII and the enactment of other federal laws governing employment practices have broadened the scope of protection for employees and have restricted discriminatory employment practices by employers, includingschool boards and their administrative staffs.

Federal laws prohibiting discrimination in employment are based on both the Thirteenth and Fourteenth amendments to the United States Constitution. These post–Civil War amendments served as the basis for the Civil Rights Acts of 1866, 1870, and 1871, which were enacted by Congress during the Reconstruction period to define and protect the newly established rights of freedmen. These civil rights acts are identified as sections 1981, 1982, and 1983 of Title 42 of the United States Code, commonly cited as 42 U.S.C. § 1981, etcetera.

Section 1981 provides that all persons shall have the right in every state to make and enforce contracts. Section 1982 ensures that full and equal property rights are guaranteed to all citizens in every state, and section 1983 provides for legal remedies when citizens are deprived of civil rights by state actions. Due to its comprehensive (but nearly incomprehensible) language, recent legal activity has focused increased attention on 42 U.S.C. section 1983, which reads:

> *Every person who under color of any statute, ordinance, regulation, custom, or usage, or any State or Territory, subjects, or causes to be subjected, any citizen of the United States or other person within the*

jurisdiction thereof to the deprivation of any rights, privileges, or immunities secured by the Constitution and laws, shall be liable to the party injured in an action at law, suit in equity or other proper proceeding for redress.

Protections against discrimination apply to state actions as well as to the actions of private persons. While state actions denying civil rights on the basis of race are prohibited under the Fourteenth Amendment, the United States Supreme Court has concluded that both sections 1981 and 1982 were based on the Thirteenth Amendment and has held that private persons could not discriminate on the basis of race in the sale of property or in the making of a contract or its enforcement. The importance of this constitutional basis for early civil rights laws is that both state and private actions denying the right to property or to contract, on a discriminatory basis, are prohibited.

Federal legislation in recent years has expanded the protections afforded employees and included job applicants as additional protected persons in the exercise of their constitutional rights to seek and contract for employment. This legislation also recognizes property interest in an employment contract.

School employment decisions are the ultimate responsibility of school boards, who, by law, select and contract with all school district personnel. However, school principals must be aware of the legal constraints on employment practices since they are actively involved in recruiting, interviewing, and recommending teachers and support staff for employment. The following brief descriptions of major federal laws, which affect faculty and staff selection and management, highlight areas in which principals need to exercise knowledge and caution.[1]

Title VII of the Civil Rights Act of 1964

Scenario 2.1:   Rocky Ridge School District advertised for a social studies teacher at the high school. Just prior to interviewing interested applicants, the head football coach, who was also a member of the social studies teaching staff, resigned. The principal then needed a social studies teacher who would also assume a position on the football coaching staff. The principal notified the district personnel office that she wanted to interview only male applicants between the ages of 25 and 45. In addition, since the rest of the football coaching staff were minorities, she preferred to interview only nonminority applicants.

Points to Consider: Is gender a legal selection criteria for a football coach? Can this coaching assignment be added to the social studies position without re-advertising? Is age limitation appropriate? Legal? Can a district legally reserve this position for a nonminority candidate?

Title VII of the Civil Rights Act of 1964 prohibits discrimination in employment by employers or employment agencies and in membership by unions on the basis of race, color, religion, sex, or national origin.[2] Probably the most pervasive federal legislation governing employment practices, this law was amended in 1972 to include state and local governments, governmental agencies, and political subdivisions including school districts. Not only does the law protect employees from discriminatory employment practices, but it also makes it illegal to refuse to hire any individual on the basis of race, color, religion, sex, or national origin. In other words, school districts cannot discriminate in either hiring or employment practices. Title VII and its amendments do provide for several exemptions to its coverage, one of which is an exemption where religion, sex, or national origin is a *bona fide occupational qualification* (BFOQ) reasonably necessary to the normal operation of the particular business or institution. It is unlikely, however, that public schools could justify any discriminatory employment practice as a BFOQ. There are no exemptions for race or color under Title VII, and employers are required to make "reasonable accommodations" for the religious practices of employees and job applicants.

The Equal Pay Act of 1963

Scenario 2.2: Due to rapid enrollment increases, Principal Bill Jones had a vacancy for an additional secretary in the main office of his high school. This was the opportunity that he had been waiting for to extend the main office hours. To handle walk-in inquiries, telephone calls, and other regular secretarial duties, Bill wanted the main office open until 9:00 p.m. each week night. His present secretarial staff (all female) was performance rated into classifications of I, II, and III, with III the highest-paid classification. To reach a III rating, secretaries must have received top merit evaluations over a period of five years. The personnel office sent Bill three applicants, two male, one female, all equally qualified. Because the hours of the job would extend into a time frame in which no administrators would be present in the main office, and personal safety could be a problem, Bill recommended one of the male candidates for the position. In addition, he asked the personnel office to start the new man at the Level III position since he was the "head of household" for his family.

Points to Consider: How will the rest of the secretarial staff in the main office, already working toward achieving a Level III rating and subsequent additional pay, feel about this recommendation if it is accepted by personnel? Is there a BFOQ for gender or pay differential?

The Equal Pay Act of 1963 is an amendment to the Fair Labor Standards Act of 1938, which governs various labor practices including minimum wages and overtime. The Equal Pay Act prohibits wage discrimination, on the basis of gender, among employees who perform equal work in jobs that require equal skill, effort, and responsibility and that are performed under similar working conditions.[3] Legitimate wage rate differences are permissible under certain circumstances; for example, a seniority system or a merit pay plan. However, the practice of a "head of household" pay supplement for male public school teachers would be illegal under the act if the same benefit were not extended to female teachers who were also heads of households.[4]

The Age Discrimination in Employment Act (ADEA)

Scenario 2.3:   The rigorous schedule of a band director is well known. The previous "music man" was forced to retire as the result of a nervous breakdown. The principal wanted to replace him with a "vigorous" younger person to "breathe life" back into a dying program. Because of the night and weekend activities, the principal would feel safer with a male teacher in this job. In addition, the school's faculty had a median age of 52, with no retirements scheduled in the near future. To provide a more balanced age spread and to provide for more "eager" volunteers for extracurricular sponsorship and supervision, the principal had decided to actively promote the hiring of younger teachers for the school in the upcoming years.

Points to Consider: Due to the rigorous schedule of a band director, can a younger person be selected over an older one? Are night activities safer for a male? Is either age or gender a BFOQ in this case? What are the district's rights in attempting to secure a younger faculty for the reasons cited?

The Age Discrimination in Employment Act of 1967 (ADEA) prohibits employment discrimination against individuals between the ages of 40 and 70.[5] Employees as well as job applicants are protected under the terms of the act. Employers are prohibited from hiring, firing, compensating, classifying, referring, or making decisions relative to the terms and conditions of employment based on an individual's age. The act was amended in 1974 to extend coverage to state and local governments including school districts. The original law provided coverage up to age 65, but an amendment in 1978 increased the age limit to 70 years, and in 1986 an additional amendment removed any upper age limit, with certain exceptions for collective bargaining agreements and higher education tenure policies.[6]

Under ADEA, school districts may not establish any policies or practices that limit the employment opportunities of people 40 and older, such as identifying a mandatory retirement age. It is also impermissible for a school district to adopt a policy, or practice, of hiring only beginning teachers, as opposed to those with experience, as part of an effort to control or reducedistrict expenses.[7] When making employment decisions regarding people age 40 and older, principals and others must be certain that their actions are based strictly on the applicant's/ employee's capabilities to adequately perform the required work, and that those actions are clearly documented.

The Age Discrimination Act of 1975 prohibits discrimination on the basis of age in programs and activities receiving federal funds. It specifically provides that ". . . no person in the United States shall, on the basis of age, be excluded from participation in, be denied the benefits of, or be subjected to dis-criminationunder any program or activity receiving Federal financial assis-tance."[8] This 1975 law extended the provisions of ADEA (and its amendments) to all federally funded programs.

The Rehabilitation Act of 1973

Scenario 2.4: John was a recent graduate of State University with a degree in elementary education. John's family and friends had always been amazed at his ability to maintain high grades and to participate in sports. Due to a congenital birth defect, John was legally blind in one eye and had only 20-percent vision in his other eye. John also suffered from seizures that could be only partially controlled by medication. John's record in student teaching was exemplary. The principal liked John in the interview session and was impressed by his achievements; however, she felt that the students at her school would take advantage of John and that he would have discipline problems.

Points to Consider: Is the ability to control students a legitimate BFOQ? If John's past record did not demonstrate such a problem, would the principal's knowledge of her school's population and past experiences be grounds for not recommending John for employment?

Scenario 2.5: Betty Summers was an applicant for a position as an elementary school music teacher. Because the position involved traveling between four schools, the job posting stated that a valid driver's license was required. Betty was an epileptic, but with medication her condition had been stabilized, and she had not experienced a seizure for several years. Nevertheless, she could not legally drive a car, and had never obtained a driver's license. Betty was an experienced teacher and, prior to her husband's job transfer, had successfully taught both vocal and in-strumental music in a large elementary school in another district. When asked in an interview whether she had a driver's license, Betty responded that she did not and voluntccrcd thc information about her epilepsy. She assured the interviewers that she could use public transportation to travel between the assigned buildings. Based on the building principal's concerns about the possible consequences if Betty suffered a seizure in the classroom and about the reliability of public transportation, another candidate was selected for the position.

Points to Consider: Can a driver's license be considered a BFOQ for a traveling elementary school music teacher? Is epilepsy considered a handicap? Can a school district refuse to hire a candidate on the basis of a handicap?

The Rehabilitation Act of 1973 is a comprehensive statute designed to aid the handicapped in securing rehabilitation training and access to federally funded programs, public buildings, and employment. Section 504 of the act provides, in part, that ". . . no otherwise qualified handicapped individual in the United States . . . shall solely by reason of his handicap, be excluded from the participation in, be denied the benefits of, or be subjected to discrimination under any program or activity receiving federal financial assistance."[9]

The law is designed to protect handicapped individuals who are "otherwise qualified" for the particular program or activity; that is, those who can perform the job requirements in spite of their handicapping condition.[10] A handicapped individual is ". . . any person who: Has a physical or mental impairment which substantially limits one or more of such person's major life activities; has a record of such an impairment, or is regarded as having such an impairment."[11]

The term *handicap* covers a wide range of diseases as well as mental and physical conditions. The law at this writing is unclear regarding the protection of active alcoholics or drug abusers who cannot perform the essential functions of their jobs, unless their employment would constitute a direct threat to property or to the safety of others.

Twenty-four states and Washington, D.C., through legislative and administrative action, now specifically include HIV, ARC, or AIDS within the definition of a handicap or a disability in their human rights, civil rights, handicapped rights, or fair employment and housing statutes. Sections 503 and 504 of the Act protect employees of government contractors who are "otherwise qualified" and who suffer from, are regarded as suffering from, or have a record of suffering from HIV, ARC, or AIDS.

Employers are required by the law to make reasonable accommodations for those handicapped persons who are otherwise qualified for the job. This does not mean that employers must make substantial modifications of the job requirements or incur more than minimal costs to reasonably accommodate handicapped persons.

The United States Supreme Court ruled in 1984 that section 504's ban on employment discrimination was applicable to any program receiving federal funds, not just those "programs that receive federal aid the primary purpose of which is to promote employment."[12]

The Americans with Disabilities Act of 1990 (ADA)

Scenario 2.6: Larry was a middle management administrator in his previous position. In a conflict with his immediate superior, Larry lost his temper, struck the superior and "trashed" the office. Larry was fired and sued the company based on the fact that he had a mental condition that caused him, when placed in a position of conflict, to "lose control." Larry presented medical testimony to support his condition and won his case. The court fined the company for not providing "reasonable accommodations" for his disability.

Points to Consider: If Larry, who holds a degree in language arts and is currently certificated in your state, applies for a teaching job in your school, do you have grounds not to recommend him for employment?

The Americans with Disabilities Act (ADA), enacted in 1990, extended comprehensive protection against discrimination in hiring, promotion, discharge, compensation, and training to disabled individuals as well as assuring them access to public buildings, public transportation, and other public services. For most school districts the provisions of ADA become effective in 1992. While the employment provisions may not represent significant new challenges for school officials, the "reasonable accommodation" requirements may entail substantial capital expenditures to provide wheelchair ramps, elevators, telephone devices for the hearing impaired, office equipment for the visually impaired, etcetera.

ADA explicitly covers "mental disabilities," and legal observers are guessing that under this new act it is likely that employers will be obligated to not terminate or discriminate against an applicant or employee with such a disability, and "reasonably accommodate" the disability.[13]

The Veterans' Reemployment Rights Act

Scenario 2.7: In August, John James, a senior high school English teacher, was called up for six to nine months of active duty with his army reserve unit. Because the school year had not yet begun, his teaching position was posted as a vacancy and Mary Jones, a middle school teacher in the same district, was hired to fill the job. Susan Vegas was subsequently hired to fill the vacancy at the middle school created by Mary's transfer. In February, John was released from active duty. He immediately returned to the district and requested reinstatement in the position to which he had been assigned in August.

Points to Consider: Does John have a right to his original position, based on his status as a veteran? If he does, would his right take priority over the rights of Mary and Susan? Does the school district have any responsibility to reemploy John? Because of her Hispanic surname, Susan is classified as a minority. Does this classification provide her with protections that supersede John's or Mary's?

The Veterans' Reemployment Rights Act provides certain protections and benefits to veterans of military service.[14] Individuals who have left employment for the purpose of serving in the military are guaranteed certain reemployment rights. The law provides that veterans, if still qualified, must be restored to their former position, or one of like seniority, status, and pay, upon their return from military service. If a returning veteran is no longer qualified for the former position by reason of a disability, then the veteran is entitled to an offer of reemployment in a position that will provide similar seniority, status, and pay. Employers are exempted from compliance with the law only when the employer's circumstances have so changed as to make it impossible or unreasonable to reemploy the veteran. The law covers private employers as well as federal and state governments, including school districts.

In 1974 the law was expanded to include Vietnam era veterans.[15] One provision of the amended law requires that contractors entering into contracts of $10,000 or more with the federal government are required to take affirmative action on behalf of Vietnam era veterans.

A 1982 amendment to the law established that volunteers who serve as members of the National Guard and Reserve Force of the United States are entitled to various employment rights.[16] Congress requested that employers abide by the provisions of the Veterans' Reemployment Rights Act, grant a leave for military training (exclusive of earned vacation), and provide such employees equal consideration for job benefits and promotions as they would any other employees. More recently, under the same act, reservists called to duty in the Persian Gulf were not only entitled to reclaim their old jobs upon return from active duty, but they were also entitled to all the privileges and benefits that would have accrued had they not left.

The Immigration Reform and Control Act of 1986 (IRCA)

Scenario 2.8:   Chuck Buckley, one of the district's principals, was sent to a local university as a member of the school district's recruitment team. One of the instructions he had received from the personnel office stated: "For those potential candidates that "look foreign" or speak with an accent, add the following question to the list of overall questions you are to ask in the interview. 'Are you authorized to work in this country, and do you hold a valid green card?' Please make note of the candidate's response."

Points to Consider: Is this a legal interview question? Can you be selective (person-specific) in asking such a question? Are physical appearance and accent valid reasons for asking this question?

The Immigration Reform and Control Act of 1986 (IRCA) requires employers to verify the eligibility of every person to work in the United States.[17] The act is designed to protect the employment rights of American citizens and legal aliens (foreign nationals who are authorized to work in this country and possess a valid "green card"). Documents that can verify citizenship include a United States passport, birth certificate, or driver's license (if a photograph is included). It is not recommended, however, that employers ask applicants to verify their citizenship or that they examine documents prior to hiring. Such documents can reveal information about an applicant that an employer has no right to examine under antidiscrimination laws; that is, race, age, gender, etcetera.

IRCA's anti-discrimination provisions make it an unfair employment practice for an employer to discriminate against any individual (other than an unauthorized alien) because of national origin or citizenship status. This means that school officials must make certain that all job offers extended to candidates are understood to be contingent on the candidates' providing proof of their right to work in the United States. School officials should not make the mistake of requiring such proof only for those applicants whom they judge to be foreign looking or to have an accent.

Title IX of the Education Amendments of 1972

Title IX of the Education Amendments of 1972 provides that ". . . no person in the United States shall, on the basis of sex, be excluded from participation in, denied the benefits of, or be subjected to discrimination under any education program or activity receiving federal financial assistance."[18]

In 1975 the Department of Health, Education, and Welfare (HEW) issued regulations governing the operation of federally funded education programs. These regulations were based on HEW's interpretation that the term *person* in Title IX included employees as well as students. Consistent with that interpretation, the regulations included "Subpart E," covering employment practices.[19]

Although the initial focus of compliance with Title IX was on student access to school activities on a gender-neutral basis, female employees soon began to challenge alleged discriminatory employment practices based on gender, opening a series of contradictory federal court rulings regarding the validity of HEW's regulations and whether employees were, in fact, covered by Title IX.[20] It was not until 1982 that the United States Supreme Court clarified the issue. In *North Haven Board of Education v. Bell,* the Court held that the regulations promulgated by HEW interpreting "persons" in Section 901(a) of Title IX to encompass employees was a valid exercise of the department's regulatory authority.[21] However, the Supreme Court also ruled that HEW's authority to make regulations and terminate federal funds was limited to the specific programs receiving the financial assistance. It is clear from the *North Haven* case that employees in federally funded education programs are protected from gender discrimination.

In *Grove City College v. Bell,* the United States Supreme Court held that the receipt of federal financial assistance by some of the college's students did not trigger institutionwide coverage under Title IX, but rather limited coverage to the specific program.[22] Until then the common interpretation had been that it applied to all of the activities at a school that received federal aid for any reason. Congress restored the broader interpretation of Title IX when it passed the Civil Rights Restoration Act in 1988.

The final aspects of Title IX that have direct application to employment practices are the remedies for violation of an individual's rights under the law. The express remedy under Title IX for a violation of its provisions is the termination of federal funds to the specific program. In 1979 the United States Supreme Court held in *Cannon v. University of Chicago* that a private cause of action, though not explicitly provided in Title IX, was an implied remedy under the law.[23] Thus, education institutions that practice employment discrimination based on gender may face both termination of federal funds and private litigation by an aggrieved employee.

Selection of Staff

School districts throughout the United States have developed several methods of staff selection depending on the size and administrative structure of the particular district. The management style of the superintendent determines the degree to which principals are involved in the staffing process. For example, in highly centralized school districts, teachers and support personnel may be assigned to a building with little or no input from the building principal. However, in a decentralized or site-based school district, or in a smaller district, the principal is often involved in all phases of teacher and support personnel selection, from recruitment to recommendation for employment. In some districts the central office maintains a pool of applications and allows principals to review appropriate files, select, and interview candidates prior to making a recommendation to the superintendent.[24]

Regardless of the method of staff selection used, it is imperative that school principals have a working knowledge of the legal aspects of employee selection. As indicated in the previous examination of legislation, a number of federal laws and court cases have instituted constraints on employment decisions in an effort to reduce discrimination in the workplace. Employment decisions must be based on nondiscriminatory factors or factors that can be justified as legitimate exemptions under the law. It is important to remember that equal employment opportunity laws apply to both employees and job applicants, and that all selection criteria and employment decisions must be based on job-related standards. In other words, any criteria used, information required, or interview questions asked must be directly related to required job performance or be justified as a BFOQ for a particular job. Principals, and other interviewers, are faced with the three-pronged task of: (1) recommending the best-qualified teacher or staff person, (2) complying with a multitude of employment laws, and (3) protecting the rights of the prospective hiree.

No one expects to be sued for asking frank questions of a prospective employee. However, litigation in the area of personnel matters continues. This legal activity may be attributed to the public's willingness to go to court, but more likely is based on an increased awareness of equal employment rights by prospective employees.

Before examining the various facets of the selection process, it is important to note that it is impossible to provide unambiguous guidance as to what inquiries or practices are permissible during the preemployment phase. "There are few, if any, categorical rights and wrongs in selection, either legally or professionally. Every employment situation has to be evaluated individually to determine what selection standards are valid and/or legal."[25] This ambiguity, however, does not relieve school officials of the responsibility for ensuring equal employment opportunities in the school system, while legally and ethically securing the services of the best-qualified individuals for particular jobs. Equal employment laws have been, and continue to be, enacted specifically to expand employment opportunities for qualified minorities, females, and others in a protected classification who have been at a disadvantage in the labor market and workplace.

Employment Selection Guidelines

The following information is an outline of the major steps in the selection process. It suggests guidelines that can be used by district-level administrators and school principals to evaluate the process. The material presented has been adapted to fit the education enterprise and was drawn largely from the comprehensive work of Milner and Miner, *Employee Selection Within the Law*, and Panaro, *Employment Law Manual*.[26]

Position Analysis

When a position becomes available:

1. Perform a job analysis to determine the critical work behaviors to be used as criteria for measuring employee performance. Education administrators should not overlook the area of supplemental performance needs, such as those for sponsors, coaches, monitors, etcetera.
2. Develop a job description identifying the skills, knowledge, and abilities needed to perform the job.

    a. Make sure the job standards identify the requirements for satisfactory performance for a beginner in the job.
    b. Every job standard specified must be verifiable as a valid requirement for the job.
    c. For nonteaching positions, every job specification should include levels of skills or abilities necessary for progressively higher-level positions in the same job family (Electrician III, II, I).

3. Evaluate the qualifications for all positions to ensure that there are no excessive or unnecessary requirements that might have the effect of disqualifying a disproportionate number of minorities, women, or others in a protected classification (disparate impact).

Recruitment

Recruitment should include as many potential sources of qualified applicants as possible.

1. Use representatives of protected as well as nonprotected classifications of employees as part of the overall recruitment team.
2. Add colleges and universities with predominately minority or female populations to contact lists of sources of qualified applicants.
3. Maintain records of various recruiting efforts for the purposes of documentation and evaluation.

Initial Applications and Screening

1. Be sure that no preemployment questions have been asked that may lead to a charge of discrimination.

    a. All information required on the application form or asked in an initial interview should be job-related and designed to give information about the applicant's qualifications for a particular job.
    b. All applicants must be asked the same questions.
    c. If an applicant volunteers information that would be illegal to ask for, do not use that information as a basis for rejecting the

applicant. Liability for discrimination exists, regardless of whether the information was solicited or volunteered.

d. If the applicant volunteers information that indicates a problem with the applicant's suitability for the position (e.g., a handicap), the employer may be obligated to investigate further to determine whether the applicant can be reasonably accommodated to perform the job.

2. Be sure that notes or summaries of interviews with job applicants:

a. Refer only to job-related aspects of the position.
b. Are stated in neutral, objective terms.
c. Have no negative inferences. (The interviewer should be sensitive to the negative inferences that can be drawn from seemingly harmless written comments).
d. Do not include coded information (e.g., colored-in circle to indicate black applicant; clear circle to indicate white applicant, etc.).

Interviews

1. Initial interviews should be performed by someone trained in interviewing techniques. An interviewer may ask any questions the interviewer wishes of the applicant, provided that the questions are job-related and do not address prohibited subjects. Case law has demonstrated that the most dangerous questions, from the perspective of legal liability, are questions that the interviewer regards as the most innocent, the "icebreakers" or small-talk questions. Comments from the interviewer can also form the legal basis for alleged discrimination.

2. The person conducting the initial interview should be knowledgeable about the job being filled.

3. The only purposes of the initial interview should be to obtain information that is not provided on the application form and to clarify items on the form that may be difficult to understand. All questions should be limited to those that directly relate to the specified job requirements.

4. Interviews should be documented, including the date of the interview, interviewer's name, and the results—e.g., no job available, application processed further.

5. During subsequent interviews, interviewers should focus only on specific job requirements.

Some examples of prohibited, "better not asked," or "suspect" areas of information that should not be solicited from prospective applicants, unless they can be referenced to a defendable BFOQ, include but are not limited to:

In the area of health: handicapped, mental illness, currently under a doctor's care.

In the area of income: Social Security income; garnishment or bankruptcy record; credit record; pay or receive alimony or child support; charge accounts; own home, furniture, car; method of transportation; lowest salary you will accept; spouse's occupation.

In the areas of marital status or lifestyle: married, intend to marry, engaged, gay, living with someone, divorced, prior married name, maiden name, spouse's name.

In the areas of race, religion, politics: race; ancestral origin; nationality or national origin; place of birth; citizenship; parentage; mother tongue; fluency in English; color of eyes, hair; religion; religious holidays observed; belief in the existence of a Supreme Being[27]; available for Saturday or Sunday work; feelings about Equal Rights Amendment, National Organization of Women, various interest groups.

In personal areas: age, date of birth, height, weight, gender.

In the area of non–work-related issues: arrests, convictions, bondable, type of military discharge and discipline record in service (if applicable), leave job if spouse transferred, friends or relatives working for us (lawful if pursuant to a anti-nepotism policy and there is no adverse impact).

In the area of children: plan to have a family, children under 18, arrangements for care of minor children, intend to become pregnant, time off to have baby, resign or request leave, practice birth control, been pregnant or given birth, abortion, female problems, age (to determine whether of child-bearing age).

Information obtained from questions like the preceding limited examples may not be used as a basis for a selection decision.

Preemployment Testing and Access to Criminal Records

Preemployment tests must not result in a disparate impact on a protected class of individuals. If the use of any preemployment test has an adverse impact on a protected group, the employer must prove that the test is job-related and is a valid measure of the skills and abilities it purports to assess, and the test must be validated properly.

Physical examinations may be used only where the jobs involved clearly require certain physical standards. All applicants for a job requiring a physical examination must be given the same examination. Mandatory screening for drug and alcohol addiction has been challenged and upheld as a violation of privacy rights protected by the Fourth Amendment. However, litigation continues, and a definitive answer to the question of preemployment testing in these areas is not yet available. Fourteen states have enacted laws concerning AIDS testing and confidentiality. In many states, employers may not test present or potential employees for the presence of HIV, ARC, or AIDS.

Many states have permitted school board access to employee criminal records, and some states require fingerprinting and other personal descriptive information that will be forwarded through the Central Criminal Records Exchange to the FBI to obtain criminal history about the applicant. Usually such access is limited by state statute but may, as a common example, require conviction information in the following areas: murder, abduction for immoral purposes or sexual assault, failing to secure medical attention for an injured child and neglect of children, pandering, crimes against nature involving children, obscenity, possession or distribution of drugs, arson, and use of a firearm in the commission of a felony.

Reference Checking

If there are certain personal characteristics known to be important for job performance that might be obtained from references, they should be included in the qualifications listed in the job specification. Examples of such characteristics would include honesty, dependability, ability to work with others, etcetera.

All questions asked in a reference check should relate to the applicant's previous performance. The individual providing the reference should be a person who would have knowledge of the applicant's work performance. There should be a district policy requiring applicants to sign a form authorizing release of the information requested. (Applicant consent is a defense to an action of defamation against a former employer or other referencers.) (See section on defamation and referencing later in this chapter.)

There should be guidelines for evaluating information provided by former employers to make sure that the same information is obtained for all applicants and is used in the same way.

Hiring Decisions

All hiring decisions should be made without regard for race, color, national origin, sex, and religion and should be evaluated to detect any biases that might create an adverse impact on a protected group.

All actions at each stage of the selection process should be documented for purposes of evaluation. Any restrictions related to religion, sex, or national origin must be based on a BFOQ necessary to satisfactory performance in the actual job.

Employment Practices Within the Scope of Title VII, Civil Rights Act of 1964

As indicated previously, the equal employment opportunities provisions of Title VII apply to job applicants as well as employees of the school district.

Proper attention must be given to all employment practices in the school district to ensure compliance with this law, and school administrators should regularly review current federal and state legislation. The following summarizes important federal regulations that govern equal employment opportunities.

Discrimination on the Basis of Gender

Scenario 2.9:   Superintendent Roger Diamond firmly believed that, for all of their fine administrative qualities at the elementary and district levels, women were just not cut out to manage large secondary schools. In executive sessions of the school board, Diamond candidly told the board that he did not believe that the physical safety of women administrators could be guaranteed in a secondary school situation. He did not want to be responsible for the possible consequences of placing a woman in charge of young men who, as Diamond noted, "are constantly testing their strength and virility." Based on Diamond's concerns, the school board adopted the policy that, to protect women from potential physical injury or harm, only male administrators could be assigned to the secondary schools.

Points to Consider: Can gender be considered a BFOQ for secondary school administrative positions? Can a school district legally enforce an employment policy that discriminates against women on the basis of protecting them from potential physical harm?

Scenario 2.10:   The veteran coach of the boy's soccer team at City High School retired at the end of last season after ten years, during which City High's boys won the district championship six times and the state championship twice, and the soccer team had become the source of tremendous pride and school spirit at City High. Principal Clyde Johnson was determined to recruit a new coach who would continue the school's great winning tradition. In addition, the former soccer coach had also served as athletic director and taught health education classes, and Johnson hoped to be able to fill this position without having to reassign the teaching and program coordination responsibilities. One application really caught Johnson's attention. The candidate, Dale Winter, had successfully coached both men's and women's soccer teams and had served as executive director of a well-respected organization that sponsored summer soccer camps nationwide. Johnson thought he had found "his man" until Dale Winter arrived for the interview. Dale Winter, it turned out, was a woman. Though she had an undeniably successful coaching record, and solid experience in program administration as well, Johnson knew he wanted a man in this important position, and he recommended a male candidate for the position.

Points to Consider: Is soccer considered a gender-specific sport? Can gender be construed as a BFOQ for any teaching or coaching position?

An analysis of recent case law, at all levels of the judicial system, suggests the following:

1. The Equal Employment Opportunities Commission (EEOC) believes that the BFOQ exception in regard to gender should be interpreted narrowly.
2. State laws or regulations that prohibit or limit the employment of females, or that constrain salary or wages of females, conflict with and are superseded by Title VII.
3. It is an unlawful employment practice to:

    a. Classify a job as "male" or "female" or maintain separate lines of progression or separate seniority lists based on gender, unless gender is a BFOQ for that job.
    b. Forbid or restrict the employment of married women when such restriction is not applicable to married men.
    c. Phrase help-wanted advertisements to indicate a preference, limitation, specification, or discrimination based on gender unless gender is a BFOQ for the particular job.
    d. Discriminate between men and women with regard to fringe benefits including medical, hospital, accident, life insurance and retirement benefits; profit-sharing and bonus plans; leave; and other terms and conditions and privileges of employment.
    e. Ask questions about pregnancy, childbirth, or related medical conditions that might be used as the basis for excluding any female from employment or promotion opportunities.
    f. Treat a disability due to pregnancy or childbirth differently from any other disability.

Discrimination on the Basis of Religion

Scenario 2.11:   Betty, an experienced fifth-grade teacher in the district, is a member of the African Hebrew Israelites and at times wears a headwrap as an expression of her religious and cultural heritage. During an interview for a position in another school closer to her home, the principal of the prospective school asked her if she would refrain from wearing the headwrap if he recommended her transfer. She agreed and was transferred. During her first year at her new school, Betty attended a districtwide multicultural workshop where she discovered that the district supported multicultural diversity. She resumed wearing the headwrap and was immediately ordered by her principal to stop. She refused and was fired for insubordination.

Points to Consider: If the headwrap issue is grounded in a religious belief, is the wearer protected constitutionally? Can the headwrap be accommodated without undue hardship on the part of the school?

An analysis of recent case law, at all levels of the judicial system, suggests the following:

1. Religious practice is defined by the EEOC to include moral or ethical beliefs as to what is right and wrong that are sincerely held with the strength of traditional religious views, whether or not any group espouses such beliefs or the group to which the individual professes to belong accepts such belief. The definition of religious practices includes religious observances.
2. Employers are required to reasonably accommodate the religious practices of an employee or prospective employee, unless it can be demonstrated that accommodation would result in undue hardship on the conduct of the business of the employer.[28]
3. When there is more than one means of accommodation that would not cause undue hardship, the employer must offer the alternative that least disadvantages the individual with respect to employment opportunities.
4. The duty to accommodate applies to prospective as well as current employees; therefore, an employer may not permit an applicant's need for a religious accommodation to affect, in any way, its decision whether to hire the applicant unless it can demonstrate that it cannot reasonably accommodate the religious practices without undue hardship.

Discrimination on the Basis of National Origin

Scenario 2.12: Based on their particular qualifications, two of the candidates for an English literature vacancy at Central High School were selected for final interview and selection. One was Sara Snow, a second-year teacher from a neighboring district, who had done her student teaching at Central High and had been very successful. Sara had a bachelor's degree in education with an emphasis in language arts. The other candidate was Ali Sadim, a native of Lebanon, who had emigrated to the United States several years earlier when the English-language school in which he taught was forced to close. Ali, who had a master's degree in English literature and nearly ten years of teaching experience, was a naturalized American citizen.

On the surface, Ali seemed to have the stronger credentials; however, the Central High School principal had an aversion to people of Middle

Eastern heritage. While not admitting to this bias, the principal voiced his concern that Ali's heavily accented speech might have a negative effect on the students' ability to learn and recommended, strongly, that the district hire Sara for the position. The Director of Certified Personnel approved the principal's choice and forwarded the recommendation to hire Sara to the Board for approval.

Points to Consider: Can unaccented speech be considered a BFOQ for teaching English literature? Is the principal's comfort level with a prospective teacher a valid basis for making employment decisions? Was Ali discriminated against on the basis of his national origin? If he was, is he protected under Title VII?

An analysis of recent case law, at all levels of the judicial system, suggests the following:

1. National origin discrimination is defined broadly as including, but not limited to, the denial of equal employment opportunity because of an individual's, or his or her ancestor's, place of origin; or because an individual has the physical, cultural, or linguistic characteristics of an ethnic group.
2. It is a lawful employment practice to deny employment opportunities to any individual who does not fulfill the national security requirements of Title VII or the Immigration Reform Act of 1986.
3. The use of a BFOQ exception relating to national origin will be strictly construed.
4. Height and weight requirements must be evaluated to ensure that they do not have a disparate impact based on an ethnic group.
5. A rule requiring employees to speak only English at all times in the workplace is a burdensome term and condition of employment and will be presumed to violate Title VII. However, an employer may have a rule requiring that employees speak only English at certain times where the employer can show that the rule is justified by business necessity.
6. Harassment on the basis of national origin is a violation of Title VII. An employer has an affirmative duty to maintain a working environment free of harassment on the basis of national origin.[29]

Certification

Applicants for employment as teachers must meet eligibility standards that are set by state certification statutes and administered by state and local agencies. In addition, prospective teachers must satisfy the local board of education job qualifications that have been designated for a particular position. Noncertificated personnel must only meet job qualification and, in some cases, licensing requirements like those for plumbers and electricians.

Teachers' eligibility is usually limited to the area of competency that is covered by their certification.[30] Certification, therefore, affects placement and assignment as well as original access to employment as a teacher.

In the absence of explicit statutory exception, the prerequisite of certification cannot be waived by local boards of education.[31] At times, however, states have allowed some exceptions when a critical shortage of teachers in a special curricular area has occurred, and, in some states, previous experience outside of teaching is considered and uncertificated teachers have been allowed to teach on a probationary status.

Certification requirements (laws) serve several purposes. They foster adequate professional training to ensure entry-level competence and continued professional development in the licensed area, and they protect certificated teachers, to some degree, against unfair placement or displacement. Once certificates are issued to qualified individuals, the law recognizes holders of such certification as competent teachers and places the burden of proof in a termination proceeding on local school boards.

The authority of certifying agencies to set the basis for new or renewal certificates includes the power to suspend or revoke certificates for cause, so long as the rationale and regulations are fair in content and fairly applied. Courts will overturn unauthorized and capricious revocation of certificates if the school district that requested the action did not comply with statutory due process procedures.[32] Texas law, cited here as an common example, states that any teacher's certification may be suspended or canceled upon recommendation of a local school board by the state commissioner of education under the following circumstances: satisfactory evidence that the holder is conducting school or teaching activities in violation of the laws of the state; satisfactory evidence that the holder is a person unworthy to instruct the youth of this state; complaint made by the board of trustees that the holder of a certificate, after entering into a written contract with the board of trustees of the district, has without good cause and without the consent of the trustees abandoned the contract.[33]

Related Legal Issues

Prior to the examination of employment terms, evaluation, due process, dismissal, and other issues, two areas need to be discussed beyond their brief introduction earlier in this chapter. As a follow-up to the examination of various civil rights obligations on the part of the employer, the issue of sexual harassment needs to be thoroughly understood. In addition, as a follow-up to the examination of references for employment, a more in-depth discussion of the legal problem areas of referencing is included.

Sexual Harassment

Scenario 2.13: Mary Moore had just returned to the workplace after several years at home caring for her children. She applied for a job as a secretary in the local middle school, and was pleasantly surprised when Principal Paul Brown offered her the job. In addition to a good salary, the job offered Mary a work schedule that matched her children's school schedules and the school was close enough to Mary's home so that she could walk to work. The job was almost too good to be true, and Mary did not want to lose it. When Brown first started flirting with her, Mary was flattered, but a little embarrassed. She did not want Brown to think she had no sense of humor, so she jokingly flirted back at first. However, as Brown's flirting became much more intense, Mary became increasingly uncomfortable. When he attempted to fondle her, Mary finally protested. Brown's response was not what she expected. He angrily asked her why she thought she had gotten the job in the first place, given her out-of-date secretarial skills, and suggested that if she did not "play along" with him, he would find another secretary who would. Mary did not want to lose the job, and she thought she could keep the situation under control without making Brown really angry. Mary tried desperately to complete her secretarial duties efficiently and, at the same time, diplomatically handle Brown's increasingly insistent sexual advances. When Mary could no longer handle the stress her job situation created, she resigned.

Points to Consider: Was Mary the victim of sexual harassment? Did Mary have any recourse other than to resign? If Mary had "given in" to any of Brown's sexual demands, would that have prevented her from seeking legal redress under Title VII? If Mary filed suit for sexual harassment, would the school district have any liability?

Scenario 2.14: Martha Jones, an excellent elementary school teacher, was one of six teachers in the school district who had been selected for the district's leadership development program. After completing the three-year program, which included the completion of graduate work required for certification, participation in a week-long administrative assessment program, and many extra hours spent in workshops and intern assignments, Martha expected to be offered the elementary principalship that would be open next school year. She and her colleagues in the leadership development program had specifically prepared for particular administrative positions in the district. When new administrative assignments were finally announced, Martha was disappointed to find that the elementary school principalship for which she had worked so hard had been awarded to Susan Allen. Martha knew that Susan, a high school English teacher who had not yet completed her certification requirements, was involved in an affair with the deputy superintendent of personnel. Because she knew her own credentials were much stronger than Susan's and that her experience and certification were at the appropriate level, Martha was sure that Susan was awarded the job because of her intimate relationship with the deputy superintendent.

Points to Consider: Did Martha have justifiable reasons to believe that she would be offered an administrative position? Does Martha have grounds to believe that she has been discriminated against? If so, could Martha file a sex discrimination suit against the district under Title VII?

Scenario 2.15:   The air conditioner was being repaired in the elementary school in which Nickie worked. Over a period of several days, John, a repairman working for a private contractor, consistently made sexually explicit and demeaning remarks to Nickie, which included reference to the size of her breasts. On one occasion, he patted her on the buttocks as he passed her in the hall. When Nickie complained to her principal, he told her to "avoid John, but not to worry, because John would be out of the building in a day or two."

Points to Consider: Is a principal responsible for harassing actions of nonschool employees on the school grounds? Can compliments be regarded as sexual harassment?

In 1980 the Equal Employment Opportunity Commission issued guidelines that declared sexual harassment a violation of Title VII of the Civil Rights Act of 1964, established criteria for determining when unwelcome conduct of a sexual nature constitutes sexual harassment, defined the circumstances under which an employer may be liable, and suggested affirmative steps an employer should take to prevent sexual harassment.[34] The EEOC guidelines were reinforced by the United States Supreme Court in *Meritor Savings Bank v. Vinson,* the Court's first decision regarding sexual harassment in the workplace.[35] So effectively did the Supreme Court clarify the nature of sexual harassment and the responsibility employers have for preventing or remedying harassment that in 1988 the EEOC published definitive guidance for employers, victims, EEOC officials, and attorneys.

Sexual harassment is, unfortunately, an all-too-common occurrence in the workplace. According to Bureau of National Affairs data, 40 percent of women are sexually harassed at work, and other studies have reported that the percentage may be as high as 90 percent. In addition, more than 50 percent of respondents to another national study reported that they or someone they knew had terminated employment because of sexual harassment.[36] While men may also be victims of sexual harassment, the vast majority of complaints to date have been filed by women. Therefore, to keep this examination as simple as possible, the female pronoun is used in reference to the victim and the male pronoun is used in reference to the supervisor.

Though specific data regarding the incidence of sexual harassment in school districts is lacking, there is no reason to assume that schools are free of this kind of discrimination. As the on-site representatives of the school district's central administration, principals bear the responsibility for preventing and/or remedying sexual harassment in their schools. Thus, it is important that principals clearly understand what constitutes sexual harassment and what they must do to protect their teachers and other staff from this kind of discrimination.

EEOC guidelines describe sexual harassment as unwelcome sexual conduct that is a term or condition of employment. In *Meritor v. Vinson* the Supreme Court clarified this definition by identifying two kinds of sexual harassment; "*quid pro quo*" (this for that), when submission or rejection of unwelcome sexual advances is implicitly or explicitly made a condition of employment; and "environmental," when sexual conduct unreasonably interferes with an employee's work performance because it creates a hostile or offensive work environment, whether or not there is a tangible economic job consequence. Several other courts have expanded the definition of environmental sexual harassment to include nonsexual conduct (physical or verbal aggression or intimidation) that creates a hostile work environment that would not exist but for the sex of the employee.[37] The EEOC guidelines also identify a third type of sexual harassment, "sexual favoritism." This occurs when a less-qualified applicant receives employment opportunities or benefits as a result of the individual's submission to the employer's sexual advances or requests for sexual favors.[38]

The essential elements of the current position of the EEOC and the courts regarding sexual harassment are as follows.

On the Nature of Sexual Harassment:

Title VII protects the right of all employees to work in an environment that is free from discriminatory intimidation, ridicule, and insult, whether based on sex, race, religion, or national origin. *Quid pro quo* sexual harassment exists whenever a supervisor makes unwelcome sexual advances toward an employee and implicitly or explicitly threatens that the victim's continued employment and/or advancement is contingent upon her submission.

Once the fact of the sexual (or sex-based) conduct of the supervisor is confirmed, the next question to be determined is whether the conduct was unwelcome. In this inquiry the question of whether the victim voluntarily submitted to the supervisor's advances is irrelevant. If the victim has made her protest clear to the offending supervisor, the court will not fault her for submitting rather than face the real or perceived job-related consequences. When an employment opportunity or benefit is granted because of an individual's submission to sexual advances, other employees have grounds to sue on the basis of sexual discrimination under Title VII.

Environmental sexual harassment exists when a pattern of unwelcome and offensive conduct that would be considered abusive by any reasonable person under the same circumstances creates a hostile work environment that inhibits the work performance of an employee. The court views similarly offensive conduct that is sexual in nature and aggressive nonsexual conduct that is focused on an employee because of her sex.

On the Employer's Liability for Sexual Harassment by Supervisors:

The employer is always liable for *quid pro quo* harassment because the employment action (promotion, demotion, transfer, termination) taken by the supervisor is an exercise of authority delegated by the employer. The employer is liable for environmental harassment if the employer has no strong, widely disseminated, and consistently enforced policy against sexual harassment and/or has no effective complaint procedure in place. Without these clear protections in place, employees can reasonably assume that the supervisor has "apparent authority" (tacit approval) to practice sexual harassment. The employer is also liable for environmental harassment if senior management did not take immediate and appropriate steps to terminate the harassing conduct and discipline the offending supervisor or fellow workers. When immediate and appropriate action has not been taken in response to a complaint, employers have also been found liable for sexual harassment by independent contractors.[39]

On Appropriate Remedies to Complaints of Sexual Harassment:

Employers are required to take all steps necessary to prevent sexual harassment. Specifically, they are to formulate and disseminate a strong, clearly stated policy and implement an effective procedure for resolving complaints that does not require the victim to complain first to the offending supervisor. Employers are required to investigate thoroughly every complaint of sexual harassment, deal appropriately with offenders, and make the victim whole.

Negligent Hiring

Scenario 2.16:   As Assistant Director of Certified Personnel, Greg Miller's primary responsibility was the recruitment and placement of elementary school teachers. Bob Smith was one of the nearly 200 candidates Greg interviewed one week. Bob's credentials generally looked very good, but Greg had noticed that there was a two-year gap since the last two employment entries, and that the file contained no recommendations from the last two districts in which Bob was employed. When questioned about this, Bob told Greg that he had taken some time off for travel and study in Europe. In addition, he had only requested recommendations from his previous employers very recently, and perhaps the placement office at his university had just not completed processing the paperwork. Before recommending Bob for hire, Greg contacted the two school districts to verify Bob's employment. Both districts confirmed that Bob had been employed by them and that he had voluntarily resigned. They offered no further details, and Greg asked no additional questions. Two months later, to Greg's shock, Bob Smith was accused of child molesting by the parents of two of his third-grade students. He was subsequently tried and found guilty. During the trial, evidence was produced that Bob had been convicted of a similar offense several years ago and had been sentenced to serve two years in prison in another state. The parents of the victims filed suit against Greg and the school district for the negligent hiring of a convicted child molester.

Points to Consider: Does a school district have either the responsibility or the right to ascertain whether a prospective employee has a criminal record? Are there circumstances under which a school district has a responsibility to investigate a prospective employee's background beyond that which is provided in the application materials? May a school district ask candidates for employment about previous criminal arrests or convictions? Could the school district that formerly employed Bob also be sued for not providing Greg with such critical information?

Negligent hiring, simply defined, is an employer's failure to exercise reasonable care in the selection of applicants relative to the type of position being filled. Most of the litigation in negligent hiring is the result of an employer's failure to screen applicants, conduct thorough background checks, or discover criminal records.

School districts need not conduct criminal background checks on all applicants. The decision should be based on the employee's access to the means or opportunity to commit a crime. "Access" means, among other things: to master keys; money; equipment; drugs or explosives; and, most important in the school setting, to potential victims (children).

One of the best background checks is to review the employment history of the applicant and ask for explanations of inconsistencies. Interviewers should inform all candidates that there will be a follow-up on an individual's work history and educational background. With a systematic mechanism in place for checking applicant backgrounds, school districts add three valuable components to the selection process; additional liability prevention, the avoidance of the embarrassment for selecting an inappropriate applicant, and protection for students from preventable risk of harm.

Defamation and Referencing

Scenario 2.17: As Phil Gorham, Associate Superintendent for Finance and Business for the Sunflower Community School District in Colorado, walked back to his office, he opened a letter from Dr. Craig Lamont, a school superintendent from Vermont that he had met at a national conference last year. He was surprised to read that he was being asked to write a letter of reference for Bill Thorpe. Thorpe was a principal in the Sunflower schools until two years ago when he accepted a similar position in a neighboring school district. Reading on, he discovered that Thorpe had applied for the position of Business Manager in Lamont's district. While Gorham and Thorpe had worked in the same school district for seven years as professional colleagues, they were not personal friends. Gorham remembered that he thought that Thorpe's methods of operation and administration were disorganized and that he spent too much of his time visiting in the community while his faculty ran the school. Some of the community groups that Thorpe had visited with had caused several embarrassing moments for the school district, and Gorham and Thorpe had a number of heated arguments during public presentations of the budget a few years ago. In addition, Gorham recalled that Thorpe had some problems with the district's auditors on occasion.

At first Gorham couldn't understand why Thorpe would ever use his name as a reference. Upon rereading the letter he realized that he had not. Lamont's letter mentioned that he remembered meeting Gorham and wrote because he knew from Thorpe's resume that they had worked in the same district. Lamont was asking Gorham to "tell me the 'real story' about Thorpe."

Gorham knew that Thorpe was not the person anyone would want as a central office administrator. Gorham decided that he had to be honest and included this statement in his reply to Lamont: "Bill Thorpe was one of the weakest school administrators that I have ever worked with. He was disorganized, was not a team player; was not loyal to the district, and was irresponsible. He never was able to get the results that the district expected of him. Bill has a rather odd personality and I had a difficult time having confidence in him. I personally feel that he does not belong in any central office position, especially Business Manager."

When Bill Thorpe was not offered the position, he requested an appointment with Superintendent Lamont. During their meeting he asked why he was not selected. Lamont told him, "After checking around, I decided that you are not the person that we are looking for." When Thorpe challenged this statement, Lamont showed him Gorham's letter.

Points to Consider: Which of Gorham's statements were facts? Which were opinions? Would Gorham's statement that Thorpe has "a rather odd personality" be defamatory?

Principals are frequently asked to write letters of reference or to provide a telephone reference regarding a former employee's qualifications or performance. Whether done to support a staff member's application for transfer or promotion or for inclusion in a professional credential file, agreeing to provide a written or oral reference is not something that should be done lightly. A negative reference can harm a person's reputation and limit or preclude employment opportunities. A person's interest in his or her reputation is protected by laws concerning libel and slander, collectively called defamation.

This area of tort liability is somewhat confusing since it often involves two competing rights: the referencer's right to freedom of expression and the candidate's right to the protection of reputation. When these two rights come into conflict, the courts are often asked to determine whose right is more compelling. Principals and others in a position to provide references or recommendations may open themselves to potential defamation litigation if they include statements that the candidate might consider damaging.

Defamation is generally defined as any language, spoken or written, that tends to lower an individual in the esteem of any substantial and respectable group. Written defamation is called *libel;* spoken defamation is *slander.* Although the elements that make up actionable defamation may vary from state to state, these are the essential elements that are applied in the employment context:

1. The communication must be defamatory. To understand what makes a communication defamatory, it is useful to keep three principles in mind:

   a. No matter how damaging it may be, no statement of factual truth is defamatory.

   b. A false statement is not defamatory unless it damages the reputation of the person about whom it is made.

   c. A statement of pure opinion is never defamatory. Pure opinion, no matter how outrageous it may be, is neither true nor false.

2. The communication must be published, it must reach some third party or parties, and the communication must refer to the plaintiff.

3. The third party or parties must understand the communication to be unfavorable to the plaintiff, and, finally, the plaintiff must have been injured by the communication.

For a referencer's statement to be defamatory, it must be false and must have a tendency to harm the candidate's reputation. It is not necessary that the statement actually demeaned the plaintiff's reputation; it must simply be shown that if the statement were believed, it would have this effect. Courts usually hold that an untrue statement is defamatory if a significant and "respectable" minority of persons would draw an adverse opinion of the candidate after reading or hearing the statement. If the candidate can demonstrate "actual malice," in that the referencer knew that the statement was false or that the statement was made with a "reckless disregard of the truth," punitive damages would likely be awarded in a typical court action.

The following can help principals avoid liability for defamation:

1. Prior to preparing a reference letter or agreeing to be identified as a reference:

   a. Contact the employee to discuss the reference in some detail. Determine to whom the reference information will be given, the specific nature of the position for which the employee is a candidate, and the elements of the employee's work-related qualifications and performance that are relevant to the desired position.

   b. Discuss the key points your reference will address with the employee. Obtain agreement from the employee regarding his or her strengths and weaknesses, and the evidence you intend to cite to support your statements. (While the employee's prior consent to your statement may not protect you from a defamation suit, it can be an important defense against a charge of actual malice.)

   c. If you cannot provide a positive reference for the employee, decline to serve as referencer, or offer the employee the opportunity to select another person to provide the reference.

   d. When you are the only person who can provide the necessary recommendation (e.g., when you have supervised a student teacher's classroom experience), be sure that the information you will provide is objective, factual, and precise and that the student teacher has been fully apprised of your evaluation and understands the contents of the recommendation you will provide.

2. When preparing the reference:

   a. Provide only information that is job-related and relevant to the current situation.

   b. Whether the statement is positive or negative, ensure that the statement of fact is true and provide adequate information to verify its truth.

c. Clearly label statements of your personal opinion.

d. Do not include statements based on rumor or personal hunches.

Summary

In a 1974 New Hampshire case the court said,

> *The employer has long ruled the workplace with an iron hand by reason of the prevailing common law rules. . . . The law governing the relations between employer and employee has evolved over the years to reflect changing legal, social and economic conditions. The courts cannot ignore the new climate prevailing generally in the relationship of employer and employee. . . .[40]*

Discrimination in selection and hiring is a dangerous error for any school district. Principals need to be aware of their vulnerability in litigation when they act as agents of the board in any preemployment matters. This chapter has discussed the problems that school districts and principals have to avoid in the recruitment, selection, and hiring of qualified personnel. The areas examined, and the points stressed, emanate from numerous acts of legislation and mountainous litigation.

Court dicta suggests that all equal rights legislation and litigation have been promulgated "to eliminate existing and continuous discrimination, to remedy lingering effects of past discrimination, and to create systems and procedures to prevent future discrimination."[41] Principals need to be part of the solution to the problem, rather than contributors. Our nation's school districts can only be strengthened by the practice of fairness and equality. Principals must be pro-active in all employment matters.

Endnotes

1. *See generally,* M. McCarthy, Discrimination in Public Employment (Topeka, Kansas: National Organization on Legal Problems of Education, 1983).

2. 42 U.S.C. § 2000e-2 (1976 and Supp. 1981).

3. 29 U.S.C. § 206 (1982).

4. Marshall v. A & M Consolidated Ind. Sch. Dist., 605 F. 2d 186 (5th Cir. 1979).

5. 29 U.S.C. § 206 (1982).

6. Pub. L. 99-592, Cong. Rec. H-11, 280 (October 17, 1986).

7. Geller v. Mackham, 635 F.2d 1027, 1032 (*2d Cir. 1980) *cert. denied,* 451 U.S. 945 (1981).

8. 42 U.S.C. § 6101 (1976 and Supp. V 1981).

9. 29 U.S.C. § 794 (1982).

10. Southeastern Community College v. Davis, 442 U.S. 397 (1979).

11. 29 U.S.C. § 706(7)(B) (1982).

12. Consolidated Rail Corporation v. Lee Ann LeStrange Darrone, 52 U.S.L.W.430 (1984).

13. Adams v. Alderson, U.S. Dist. Ct., D.C. (1989).

14. 38 U.S.C. § 2021 (1976 and Supp. V).

15. Vietnam Era Veterans' Readjustment Assistance Act of 1974, Pub. L. 93-508, 88 Stat. 1578 (1974).

16. Recognition of National Guard and Reserve Forces, Pub. L. 97-252, Title XI, 1130, 96 Stat. 759 (1982).

17. 8 USCA 1324a(b) (WESTLAW PUBLISHING COMPANY 1986).

18. 20 U.S.C. § 1681(a), sect. 901(a),(1982).

19. 34 C.R.F. §§ 105.51–105.61 (1981).

20. M. MCCARTHY & N. CAMBRON-MCCABE, PUBLIC SCHOOL LAW: TEACHERS' AND STUDENTS' RIGHTS (Boston: Allyn and Bacon 1981), 94.

21. 102 S.Ct. 1912 (1982).

22. U.S.L.W. 4283 (1984); 465 U.S. 555 (1984).

23. 99 S.Ct. 1946 (1979).

24. R. J. KRAJEWSKI, J. S. MARTIN, & J. C. WALDER, THE ELEMENTARY SCHOOL PRINCIPALSHIP: LEADERSHIP FOR THE 1990s, (New York: Longman, 1989), 62–63.

25. *See generally,* M. G. MILNER & J. B. MINER, EMPLOYEE SELECTION WITHIN THE LAW (Washington, D.C.: Bureau of National Affairs, 1978).

26. *See generally,* GERARD P. PANARO, EMPLOYMENT LAW MANUAL (Boston: Warren, Gorham & Lamont, 1990).

27. Roe and Doe v. Klein Independent School District, No. H-80-1982 (S. D. Tex. April 30, 1982, *final judgment*).

28. 29 C.F.R. § 1604 (1983).

29. Ambach v. Norwich, 441 U.S. 86 (1979).

30. Steele v. Bd. of Valhalla Union Free School District, 384 N.Y.S. 2d 860 (1976).

31. Bradford Central School District v. Ambach, 436 N.E. 2d 1256 (N.Y. 1982).

32. Alford v. Dept. of Education, 91 CAL. RPTR. 843 (1971); Anonymous v. Board of Education, 318 N.Y.S. 2d 163 (1970); Lehman v. Board of Education, 439 N.Y.S. 2d 670 (1981).

33. Texas Education Code Ann. §13.045(b) (1982).

34. POLICY GUIDANCE ON CURRENT ISSUES OF SEXUAL HARASSMENT, EEOC NOTICE N-915.035 (effective October 25, 1988), 1.

35. 106 S.Ct. 2399 (1986).

36. Maureen P. Woods & Walter J. Flynn, *Heading Off Sexual Harassment,* PERSONNEL, November 1989, 45.

37. Hicks v. Gates Rubber Company, 833 F.2d 1406 (10th Cir. 1987). *See also,* Hall v. Gus Construction Company, 842 F.2d 1010 (8th Cir. 1988).

38. 27 C.F.R. § 1640.11(g).

39. State of New York v. Hamilton, N.Y. Sup. Ct. No. H49647, August 20, 1985.

40. Monge v. Beebe Rubber, 114 H.H. 130 (1974).

41. City of Minneapolis v. Richardson, 239 N.W. 2d 197 (Minn. 1976).

CHAPTER THREE

Contracting and Evaluation

Employment Contracts and Authority

School boards have the statutory authority to make employment decisions for the school system. However, because principals often take an active part in the enforcement of contracts, an examination of various types of employment documents that commonly prevail in a typical school district should be reviewed.

The term *contract* generally describes a document that has signatures, seals, and witnesses for official notarization. Any written document, however, may serve as a contract between individuals if it is sufficiently definite, extends an offer, solicits acceptance, and denotes consideration. *Consideration* is defined as something of value that is exchanged by the parties to the contract. In terms of employment contracts, consideration is the salary and other benefits that the school district is willing to pay in exchange for the teaching services of the professional employee. The terms of the consideration must be specific to enable each party to know and understand any and all obligations required under the contract.

It is important to note that any correspondence between the school district and a prospective employee may constitute an implied contract under law. The same is true of statements made on application forms, job descriptions, or in position postings, distributed within or advertised. Even selected statements in personnel manuals have been found by the courts to constitute a contract.

As discussed in the previous chapter, teacher certification is not a guarantee of employment in any state. Certification merely recognizes the fact that a teacher has met minimum state requirements. A teacher must be certified by the state in order to be a competent party to an employment contract with the school district. Case law and state statutes make it clear that public funds cannot usually be used to pay an uncertified teacher. While the administrative office of a school district typically monitors the status of a teacher's certification upon employment, principals should review the validity of on-site teacher certificates annually. This is particularly true when a teacher is employed under a temporary or probationary certificate.

Decisions to employ, or not to employ, teachers and other school district personnel are among the discretionary powers vested in local school boards. Implicit in such power is the legal obligation that school boards not be arbitrary, capricious, or in violation of a prospective employee's statutory or constitutional rights in the contracting or hiring process. All employment decisions, unless there is a defendable bona fide occupational qualification (BFOQ),[1] must be neutral to race, religion, national origin, and gender. Courts have tended not to review employment decisions made by local school boards unless such decisions have not been made in good faith.

The courts have clearly determined that the duty to hire teachers and other employees is vested in the school board and cannot be delegated.[2] Employment decisions cannot be made by individual board members, the superintendent, or principals. Such decisions must be made by the board of education as a collective body. The principal is never a competent party in any agreements or contracts for the board of education. Even though the prospective teacher has the obligation to know the contractual authority of school districts, the principal, as an interviewer and recommender, must make it clear to prospective employees that the school board has the ultimate authority in employment decisions and that, generally, contracts and employment agreements between teachers and other personnel and the school district can be approved only at legally scheduled meetings of the board of education.

Teacher contracts are governed by the laws of contracts, applicable state statutes, and local school board policies. A typical teaching contract usually includes those elements necessary for an enforceable contract: an agreement including both offer and acceptance, consideration, a description of competent parties, legal subject matter, and proper form.[3]

An *agreement* results from an offer and acceptance between the parties to a contract and refers to the mutual consent by the parties to be bound by the terms specified. When a school district makes an offer to a potential employee, certain characteristics of the offer must exist. The offer must be made with the intent to enter into a contract, communicated to the offeree, definite and certain, and not an invitation to negotiate.

The acceptance of an offer to contract can only be made by the person to whom the offer was made, and must reflect some tangible evidence, either by word or deed, that the person intends to comply with the terms of the offer.[4] The offer may be accepted anytime before the offer is withdrawn or expires according to the terms.

Teachers' contracts are usually straightforward agreements drawn on standard forms specifying only the basic elements of salary, position, and length of employment. In many states these standard employment contracts are supplemented by a "master" contract developed through a collective bargaining process and ratified by the school board and teachers' union. In each case, if all the basic elements of the contract are present, then a valid contract exists. The teacher works in accordance with the contract until the contract expires or until the school board terminates the contract for cause.

While employment contracts have become more specific in terms of responsibilities and duties of the employee, it is not necessary to specify in detail all expectations of employment within the contract document. State laws and regulations, school district policies, and general duties are assumed in the contract. Teachers can be required to perform tasks and duties within their areas of competency and certification, even though they are not delineated specifically in the employment contract. While a teacher's legal rights of employment are derived from the contract, additional rights accrue from any collective bargaining agreement (master contract) in effect at the time of contract issuance. In addition, statutory provisions and rules and regulations of the school district may be considered part of the terms and conditions of any contract.

Types of Employment Contracts

A teacher is generally employed under one of two types of contracts: a term or probationary contract or a continuing/tenure contract. A teacher may also hold a supplementary or an "addendum to" contract. The following is an examination of employment contracts most commonly used in education.

Term or Probationary Contracts

As the name suggests, a *term contract* is valid for a specified period of time, normally one or two years, after which the employee has no guarantee of reemployment. Both parties are released from the contract's obligations at the end of the term specified. Neither party is entitled to reasons at the expiration of the contract, unless mandated by statute, and, generally, a school district is required only to provide notice prior to the expiration date of the contract that the contract will not be renewed.

In a *probationary contract* it is assumed that, with satisfactory evaluations over a specified period of time, the teacher may be entitled to a continuing/tenure contract. Under such a contract a probationary period must be served, during which time school officials must determine whether the teacher merits continuing/tenure status. The maximum length of a probationary period varies, though three years is most common. At the end of the probationary term, the school district must either terminate the teacher's employment or employ the teacher under a continuing/tenure contract.

Although legal debate and court actions continue, it is prudent to assume that teachers employed under probationary contracts have basic due process protections including the right to notice and a hearing. State statutes may require a school district to give notice of its intention to terminate a teacher's probationary contract on or before a predetermined date during the year the contract expires. If the school district fails to provide such notice, then the teacher may be eligible for continued employment.

Tenure or Continuing Contracts

The award of a tenure or continuing contract (hereafter referred to as a *tenure contract*) requires affirmative acts by both the school district and the teacher. Since tenure contracts involve statutory rights, specific procedures and protections vary from state to state. Most tenure statutes specify requirements and procedures for obtaining tenure and identify causes and procedures for the dismissal of tenured personnel. In interpreting tenure laws, courts have attempted to protect teachers' rights, while simultaneously maintaining flexibility for school officials in personnel management.[5] The authority to grant a tenure contract is a discretionary power of a local school board that cannot be delegated.[6] While a tenure contract provides a certain amount of job security, it does not guarantee permanent employment or the right to teach in a particular school or grade. Teachers may be reassigned to positions for which they are certificated and dismissed for causes specified in tenure law. A number of states limit the awarding of tenure to teaching positions and exclude administrative and supervisory positions. Where tenure is available for administrative positions, probationary service and other specified statutory terms must be met.[7] Most courts have concluded, however, that continued service as a certificated professional employee, even as an administrator, does not alter tenure rights acquired as a teacher.[8]

Generally, after a teacher has served the required probationary period and has been reemployed by the school district for the next year, the district must notify the teacher in writing of its decision to award a tenure contract. The teacher then must notify the school district, in writing or by signing the contract, of acceptance of such tenure. If the teacher fails to accept the contract within a specified length of time, the teacher may forfeit the contract.

Tenure contracts provide for continued employment unless the school district terminates the service for specified cause and follows certain procedural guidelines.[9] Once a school district awards tenure status to a teacher, the teacher cannot be terminated or demoted except for cause and after following standard tenets of due process.

Supplementary Contracts

Scenario 3.1:   In the spring of Larry Carter's thirteenth year of teaching, he was informed orally by a district representative that he would not be retained as head basketball coach for the coming year. The implication was clear that if Carter did not resign, he would be released. Carter sent a letter to the board stating, "I hereby resign from duties as head basketball coach, effective the end of this year. I am looking forward, however, to continuing my teaching responsibilities." The board subsequently informed Carter that resigning from one part of the contract was tantamount to voiding the entire contract.

Points to Consider: Is a teacher's contract a single instrument that includes a wide span of duties, both instructional and noninstructional? Is a teacher's contract divisible, even though it contains both primary and supplemental duties? What rights do teachers have in accepting or rejecting extracurricular assignments?

In addition to a term, probationary, or continuing/tenure contract, a teacher may also hold an "addendum to contract," more commonly called a *supplemental contract,* that might include such services as coaching, supervising, sponsoring, directing, monitoring, or other similar activities. Generally, when supplemental contracts are used, the law excludes such contracts from the guarantees inherent in a continuing/tenure contract and from due process requirements.

Public school teachers have traditionally been expected to perform numerous duties in addition to teaching. For example, the nineteenth-century teacher could expect to teach reading, writing, spelling, arithmetic and to perform the following duties: supervise recess and lunch periods, sweep the floors, build the fires, keep the chalk boards clean, and fill the water buckets.[10] Although times have changed, teachers still routinely teach a seven-hour day and then supervise various activities before and after school.

The question of additional pay for supplemental duties is a continuous point of contention between school boards and teacher associations. School boards want to retain the authority to assign teachers additional duties on an "as needed" basis. Teachers' associations generally believe that professional employees should have the right to accept or reject co-curricular or extracurricular assignments; professional employees' acceptance or rejection should in no way affect the employees' teaching contracts; salary for co-curricular and extracurricular activities should relate to the salary schedule for teachers by ratios that reflect differences in assigned responsibility and length of time involved; and professional services required outside of the students' school day should be compensated through supplemental salary or overtime pay.[11]

There is considerable variation among the states regarding how the issue of supplemental duties should be addressed. Because courts are bound by the specific facts of an individual situation and their state statutes, there is wide variation in court decisions. Some states view supplemental duties as independent of teaching assignments; some issue a single contract that includes both teaching and supplemental duties; and some states use both single and separate contracts for supplemental duties.

A number of courts have ruled on the issue of supplemental duties and supplemental contracts. In one case a Connecticut superior court found that additional duties had been assigned to a principal without collective bargaining. The court held that this was a breach of contract and ordered the board of education to begin collective bargaining immediately in order to ensure that the parties could set a proper rate of pay for the duties, in accordance with the contract.[12]

In *Smith v. Board of Education*,[13] the court held that the plaintiffs had suffered no deprivation of property rights when the school board discontinued their employment as coaches. In this case the school board had offered to continue the two teachers' employment as physical education instructors when notification of dismissal from coaching was issued. The teachers argued that they had tenure in their coaching positions and should have been accorded a hearing before being dismissed. The court ruled that the Fourteenth Amendment due process clause does not guarantee a coach continued employment in that capacity.

In a 1980 case in West Virginia, a teacher had taught social studies and physical education classes in addition to being the coach for three sports and the sponsor for the junior/senior prom. When she asked to be released from one of her coaching positions, or to be assigned an assistant, her requests were denied and her name was placed on a list for transfer to another school. The court ruled that, "the board of education's power to assign extracurricular duties to teachers is not unlimited and must be exercised in a reasonable manner. Assignments must be nondiscriminatory, related to a teacher's interest and expertise, and must not require excessive hours beyond the contractual work day."[14]

An examination of three Kansas cases illustrates the impact of courts on teacher contracts. Prior to 1984 it was generally assumed that primary contracts and supplementary contracts were not divisible, and the elimination of one type of duty automatically eliminated the other. Teachers were expected to perform all supplemental duties as a part of their primary contract. This assumption was dispelled by the Kansas Court of Appeals in a 1984 case in which a math teacher was also a head basketball and an assistant football coach.[15] The teacher/coach was told that if he did not resign his basketball position, he would be removed from it. As a result of this conversation, he resigned from coaching, but indicated that he expected to continue as a math teacher. The board responded by stating: ". . . your duties as head basketball coach are an integral and substantial part of your present employment contract. Accordingly, the board has accepted your resignation and nonrenewal of your present employment contract." The court ruled in favor of the teacher.

This decision made it clear that coaching duties must be performed under supplemental contracts, that teachers cannot be required to accept such duties as part of their primary contracts, and that teachers can unilaterally terminate or nonrenew their supplemental contracts without affecting their primary contracts.[16] The Kansas Supreme Court declined to hear this case on appeal and allowed the lower court's decision to stand.

In 1986 the Kansas Court of Appeals ruled that a negotiated contract does not demonstrate authority to require a teacher to accept supplemental duties.[17] In 1988 the Supreme Court of Kansas ruled that supplemental duties, even when conducted during the school day, must not be a part of a teacher's primary contract.[18]

These cases have had considerable impact on Kansas schools and mirror litigation results in many other states. Such decisions have significantly reduced the flexibility of boards of education to assign personnel in a manner that allows maximum use of professional staff in both regular academic and extracurricular activities. Because teachers in some states now have the option of retaining teaching positions while rejecting extracurricular or supervisory activities, many school districts have difficulty attracting teachers who are willing to accept supplemental contracts.

Employment Requirements

School districts possess broad authority in the establishment of job requirements or conditions of employment. Among the most common are continuing education requirements, health and physical requirements, residency requirements, employment outside of the school during the school term, conflict of interest, and nepotism.

Continuing Education Requirements

Though states demand minimum certification requirements for professional educators, such requirements do not preclude individual school districts from requiring personnel to seek and acquire higher professional or academic standards, as long as the requirements are applied in a uniform and nondiscriminatory manner. The right of school districts to dismiss personnel for failing to satisfy continuing education requirements has been upheld by the courts.

Health and Physical Requirements

School districts may adopt reasonable health and physical requirements for professional personnel. The courts have recognized that such requirements are necessary to protect the health and welfare of students and others. Such requirements must not be applied in an arbitrary manner and must not contravene any state or federal laws that protect the rights of the handicapped.

Requiring Teachers to Live Within the School District

Requirements that teachers and other school district employees must live within the school district and requirements prohibiting teachers from holding other jobs during the school term are policies that teachers and others have often found difficult to accept. Both issues have been constitutionally challenged, and the courts have upheld such requirements as district prerogatives as long as the board can provide a rational basis for such policies.

The most frequently cited rationale for teacher in-district residency is that school personnel who live within the district take a more active interest in the schools, students, and communities than do those employees who live outside the district. A school district, then, absent state statutes prohibiting such, can require and enforce residency for school district employees, based on the following assumptions.[19]

1. Such a requirement aids in hiring teachers who are highly motivated and deeply committed to an urban educational system.
2. Teachers who live in the district are more likely to vote for district taxes, less likely to engage in illegal strikes, and more likely to help obtain passage of school tax levies.
3. Teachers living in the district are more likely to be involved in school and community activities bringing them in contact with parents and community leaders and are more likely to be committed to the future of the district and its schools.
4. Teachers who live in the district are more likely to gain sympathy and understanding for the racial, social, economic, and urban problems of the children they teach and are thus less likely to be considered isolated from the communities in which they teach.
5. The requirement is in keeping with the goal of encouraging integration in society and in the schools.

Prohibition of Outside Work During School Term

A school district may adopt a policy prohibiting outside work by school employees during a school term, if the rule is definite, communicated to the employees, and applied in a uniform and consistent manner to all employees.

One court, in reviewing the constitutionality of a second-job prohibition policy incorporated within an employment contact, upheld the board policy, which stated that employees "shall not engage in any other business or profession directly or indirectly, for full or part time, but shall devote [their] entire working time to the performance of . . . duties under this contract."[20]

Conflict of Interest and Nepotism

As evidenced in the preceding contract issues, states and school districts have wide latitude in adopting legislation or policies necessary for the effective administration of schools as long as they are uniformly applied. Additional areas that have been challenged, but upheld by the courts, include board policies prohibiting conflict of interest and, as a separate issue, nepotism.

Employees who enter into a relationship with companies or organizations that conduct business with their school district, either directly (direct sales) or indirectly (consulting or contracting for direct sales), may lose their employment with the school district if prohibited by statute or local policy. In addition, some states or local school districts have strict policies to prevent employment-related favoritism among relatives and family members. In both such relationships, principals should be aware of their individual state and local school district policies on these matters.

Evaluation of Performance

Scenario 3.2: Joan Adams, a middle school language arts teacher with seven years of experience in her school district, had been transferred four times within the district. No principal really wanted Joan, as she was a marginal teacher who had "a difficult rapport with students." When Joan was assigned to Middle Center Middle School, Principal George Hatch watched her carefully through the school year and gathered anecdotal notes in case he ever needed them. At the end of the school term, Hatch shared his notes with the superintendent. Joan was dismissed. Joan and her attorney quickly reminded the superintendent and board that the state had recently passed a law that required all school districts to evaluate all professional employees each year.

Points to Consider: Can the gathering of anecdotal notes, not shared with a teacher, be considered an evaluation?[21] In a state or school district where the evaluation of professional employees is mandated by state or local policy, could Joan successfully challenge her dismissal?[22] Could Hatch be terminated for not evaluating Joan if the gathering of anecdotal notes did not constitute proper evaluation?

Although the primary purpose of employee evaluations is to improve the quality of instruction, from a strictly legal point of view, the purpose of employee evaluations is to provide justification for any action the school district takes in regard to its employees. If done accurately, thoroughly, truthfully, and in a timely fashion, evaluations can be a valuable asset to the education profession and the population it serves, as well as a definitive defensive instrument for employers, in the event their action regarding a particular employee is challenged. If an evaluation demonstrates contemporaneous and early documentation of deficiencies and misconduct, documents repeated instances or patterns of poor performance, and evidences warning or opportunities to improve, an evaluation can be used to refute allegations that the employer acted arbitrarily, inconsistently, without warning, or that the employer's stated reason for any action was a pretext for discrimination. Thus, one important reason for a formal evaluation program is to avoid subjective or arbitrary employment decisions on the part of the school district.

Well-defined evaluation programs benefit employees by providing an opportunity for school district and primary evaluators to formally praise employees for work well done and justify monetary or position advances. At the same time, evaluations provide a warning system by which the employee can be legally advised of any deficiencies and afforded reasonable time and guidance to correct them.

To help ensure accountability and quality teaching, many states, by statute, require periodic appraisal of teaching and principal performance. In states or local districts where formal evaluation is mandated, principals place their jobs in jeopardy if they fail to satisfactorily evaluate their personnel.[23] Though most professional educators assert that the primary reason for evaluation is improvement or remediation based on a "developmental assessment," the results of evaluations are used in a variety of employment decisions including retention, tenure, promotion, salary, reassignment, reduction in force, or dismissal based on "personnel rating." When adverse personnel decisions are the result of evaluations, legal concerns often arise regarding issues of procedural fairness and due process—that is, were established state or local procedures followed; did school officials employ "equitable standards"; was sufficient evidence collected to support the decision; were evaluations conducted in a uniform and consistent manner?

Evaluation Guidelines and Congruence

Scenario 3.3: Mark Groves, a third-year teacher, was notified that he would not be rehired. Mark contested the school district's decision, arguing that he was never honestly and openly evaluated and was denied any opportunity to improve during his third year. Evidence demonstrated that the principal made only two short visits to his class and did not hold a conference with him concerning his teaching performance until after the principal had already recommended that he not be rehired.[24]

Points to Consider: If the state or school district had clear policies on evaluation procedures, and it was evident that the principal had not followed them, would Mark have grounds to successfully challenge his dismissal?[25] Should any deficiencies in teaching be called to Mark's attention?[26] Should time have been given to Mark to correct them?[27]

Courts are generally reluctant to enter into the teacher evaluation process. Judicial reviews are usually limited to procedural issues of fairness and reasonableness. An examination of case law provides principals the following foundation for developing and implementing equitable standards for evaluation, as well as ensuring success of the overall evaluation program:

1. Standards for assessing the effectiveness of teaching must be clearly defined and communicated to teachers.
2. Standards must be applied uniformly and consistently.
3. Opportunity, reasonable time, and support for improvement must be provided.
4. Procedures specified in state statutes or school board policy must be followed.

In addition:

5. Teacher evaluation programs must match the educational goals, management style, concept of teaching, and community values of the school district.
6. Teacher evaluation programs must solicit a strong commitment from district-level administrators, principals, and teachers. All participants must believe that the program is useful, valid, and cost-effective.
7. Successful evaluation programs must allow for adequate resources; the two most critical ones are time to conduct evaluations and evaluator/evaluatee training. Principals have responded in several studies that time and training are the major obstacles in implementing successful evaluation programs.[28] District-level administrators can assist principals by reducing other demands and helping principals manage their time more effectively. Principals need to be trained in the skills of formal evaluation: helping teachers set goals, making accurate observations, evaluating teachers' plans and tests, coaching teachers in specific skills, and conferencing.

Two overall objectives are intrinsic in these guidelines:

1. *Developmental assessment*: The evaluation program must be directed toward the improvement of instruction in the classroom. Developmental assessment is the evaluation of a teacher in order to assist that individual grow professionally. The evaluator does not use distinct evaluative criteria or assign the teacher a formal score or rating. The process spotlights development and improvement. The process is often regarded as a form of clinical supervision.
2. *Personnel rating*: There must be clear strategies for documentation of effectiveness as well as deficiencies in performance that support recommendations for promotion, nonrenewal, or dismissal. Personnel rating is the evaluation of a teacher enabling administrative decisions relative to overall accountability in granting or denying tenure or promotion, renewing contracts, or requesting resignations. This rating process allows for both formative and summative judgments for helping determine the teacher's professional future.

Principals need to distinguish between these two evaluation objectives and formulate standardized methods of observation, documentation, and conferencing. Successful evaluation programs are clear about the purposes of evaluation and match process to purpose. There must be congruence in the evaluation program between purpose and process. When no congruence exists, there is a notable problem when a school district claims that the exclusive goal of evaluation is the improvement of instruction, while the district enforces evaluation procedures that emphasize standardized criteria, numerical scoring, and evaluative labels.

Evaluation Instruments

In past years an informal discussion between the teacher and principal near the end of the school year often constituted a teacher's yearly performance evaluation. Usually such discussions were subjective and focused on behaviors that often did not relate to teaching performance. The most common terms used during such evaluation conferences were "satisfactory" or "no problems noted." If any problems existed, they were usually not noted in writing, but expressed orally to the teacher by the principal, with such corrective comments couched in the concern: "I don't want any of my teachers upset or bad mouthing me to other teachers or to the community."

Today, evaluation instruments are usually formal documents that have been developed through collaborative efforts from the school district, administrators, and teachers. Evaluation programs have greater impact on improved performance when teachers have had viable input into evaluation criteria. A clear mission, coupled with goal-based, results-oriented criteria, fully understood by teachers, is invaluable in the success of the evaluation program. The ideal instrument provides the basis for the assessment of teachers' knowledge, skills, and attitudes and are related directly to effective teaching and professional growth. Such instruments should be periodically validated against realistic job requirements and expectations, and personnel who are subject to formal evaluation should be familiar with the instrument(s) used in the process.

Documentation

Scenario 3.4: Barbara Golden, a secondary math teacher who had been employed in the school district for fourteen years, was dismissed for incompetency based on a single unsatisfactory rating. The evaluation was not supported by any specific data or anecdotal notes. Barbara's past evaluations had always been rated satisfactory.

Points to Consider: If anecdotal notes were considered to be part of any rating procedure, and none were collected for Barbara's dismissal, would such absence of documentation make her rating defective?[29] If anecdotal notes were attached to other teachers' performance ratings, could Barbara claim inconsistency in the application of the evaluation process?[30]

Scenario 3.5: Teacher Steve Steady was observed by several professional colleagues other than the principal. The principal's final rating of Steve was based on the observations of those individuals rather than any observations by the principal. Steve's performance was the subject of extensive discussion between the observers and the principal prior to the final rating. In addition, the principal had received numerous notes about Steve's performance in the classroom from patrons in the community.

Points to Consider: Absent state or local policy against such actions, can the principal delegate teacher performance documentation to other professionals? Can such documentation form a basis for the final evaluation? Can community input from parents, students, etcetera be used as a part of performance documentation?

The evaluation of teachers must be a continuous process. For tenured teachers, formal evaluations may only need to be conducted the number of times required by state or local policy. However, for some teachers, whether they are new to the profession or experienced, more frequent evaluations may be necessary to help identify inadequate performance and provide a rational basis for any employment decision that might be determined concerning the teacher.

Three difficult areas of documentation are often challenged when questions arise about the kinds of documentation that can be used in the evaluation process. The courts in some jurisdictions have held that third-party documentation, shared with the principal, can be grounds for continuing employment decisions.[31] Some courts have also ruled that school districts have the right to base continuing employment decisions on matters outside of a teacher's evaluation. In one such case the court noted that decisions made about the nonrenewal of a nontenured teacher can be made on a "broad basis of input received from a variety of people, including members of the public, parents of students, and a districts member's own knowledge of a teacher even if that knowledge is acquired through having a child in the teacher's class."[32]

Accurate documentation of evaluation findings is necessary for diagnosing strengths and weaknesses in teacher performance and for specifying any necessary remediation. Such documentation serves as a prerequisite for validating an adverse employment decision during due process proceedings or litigation. It is recommended that several types of written memoranda, in addition to actual evaluation instruments, be used to support the documentation process.[33]

1. *Memoranda to the file* should be used to record less significant infractions or deviations by an employee.
2. *Specific incident memoranda* should be used to record conferences with an employee concerning a significant event.
3. *Summary memoranda* should be used to record conferences with an employee in which several incidents, problems, or deficiencies are discussed.
4. *Visitation memoranda* should record observations made on an employee's on-the-job performance.

The use of memoranda, if done appropriately, can provide comprehensive documentation of employee performance. Teachers must be informed of the type of documentation that will be made by the principal as evaluator, how it will be used, and the teacher's right of access to the record. The following provides suggestions in preparing memoranda for general evaluation purposes, but should also withstand judicial scrutiny for possible due process or litigation purposes if necessary.[34]

1. In preparing any memorandum, reliance should be made on the facts; conclusive statements not supported by the facts should be avoided.
2. Directives given in a memorandum should be direct and to the point, and educational jargon should be avoided.
3. The memorandum should be written in the first person and personalized as much as possible. If others are involved, then specific names should be used.
4. Care should be taken to treat all employees similarly and fairly.
5. A memorandum should never be written when the administrator is angry or has become personally involved. In that event the memorandum should be put aside for a day, or an appropriate third party should review it prior to sending it to the employee.

Negative evaluations are never a pleasant experience, particularly when the results will be used to substantiate an adverse employment decision. However, documentation is critical to helping a teacher improve performance or to justify a decision to nonrenew or terminate a contract.

The Evaluation Conference

Scenario 3.6: Gwyn Jacobs, a teacher at Flower Hollow Intermediate School, was notified by the superintendent of deficiencies in her teaching performance. She was advised by the superintendent to visit other teachers. Gwyn was told that she would be visited frequently during the school year by her building principal. Gwyn visited with her principal and was advised, "This is your problem, Gwyn!"

Points to Consider: If Gwyn is terminated at the end of her current contract year, could she reclaim her position on the grounds that she was deprived of the necessary assistance to improve her professional performance? What is the principal's responsibility for assistance?[35]

Evaluation conferences provide the opportunity for the teacher or staff member and the principal to meet professionally to discuss the evaluation. For many principals, this often proves to be the most difficult part of the evaluation process because of the direct, personal contact involved. The purposes of the conference are to review the evaluation findings and to discuss any recommendations. The teacher should be invited to review all the evaluation instruments, any memoranda, or other notes made during the process. If deficiencies are noted, the evaluator should be prepared to offer both specific steps and a reasonable time-frame for improvement. When deficiencies are significant enough that they could lead to a decision to dismiss or nonrenew, the teacher must be advised that failure to demonstrate a specified level of improvement could have such consequences. The teacher must be offered the opportunity to ask questions and seek clarification of all issues discussed during the conference, and the teacher should be given the opportunity to sign the evaluation report. A signature simply attests to the fact that the teacher has been shown the materials and afforded the opportunity to review the contents of the report, not that the teacher agrees with the conclusions. If the teacher refuses to sign the materials, the evaluator should simply make a file memorandum to the effect that the opportunity was offered but declined by the teacher.

The tone of the conference is important, and the principal as evaluator should maintain a professional demeanor at all times. Demonstrations of anger, threats, or attempts to harass or intimidate the teacher have no place. Private remarks made by a teacher in a principal's office, even though made in a hostile manner, are protected by the First Amendment and cannot be a basis for an adverse employment decision.[36]

Summary

The evaluation of personnel is an essential activity of the principal. Just as teachers manage classroom learning by the use of diagnostic prescriptive models, the principal can direct individual and group staff development using evaluation as a diagnostic tool (developmental assessment) and evaluation by objectives (personnel rating) as a prescriptive tool.

The purpose of this chapter is to briefly outline the high points of evaluation programs in order to examine appropriate legal tenets that principals must know and understand. There is much more to be examined in the activity of human development, including the processes of evaluation. Principals are urged to keep current.

Endnotes

1. See Chapter 2 for an examination of the legal tenets of BFOQ.
2. *See* Crawford v. Board of Education, 453 N.E. 2d 627 (Ohio 1983); Fortney v. School District of West Salem, 321 N.W. 2d 225 (Wis. 1982); Walter v. Independent School District, 323 N.W. 2d 37 (Minn. 1982).
3. K. ALEXANDER, SCHOOL LAW (St. Paul, Minn.: West Publishing, 1980), 577–579.
4. *Id.* at 49–50.
5. V. Nordin, *Employees,* THE YEARBOOK OF SCHOOL LAW 1977, PHILIP PIELE (ED.) (Topeka, Kansas; National Organization on Legal Problems in Education, 1977), 177.
6. Board of Education v. Carroll County Education Association, 425 A. 2d 1315 (Md. App. 1982).
7. Wooten v. Alabama State Tenure Commission, 421 So. 2d 1277 (Ala. App. 1982).
8. *See generally,* Berry v. Pike County Board of Education, 488 So. 2d 315 (Ala. 1984); Wolfe v. Sierra Vista Unified School District, 722 P.2d 389 (Ariz. App. 1986).
9. W. HAZARD, EDUCATION AND THE LAW (Columbus, Ohio: Merrill, 1978), 359.
10. Hazel Swarts, "A Descriptive/Statistical Analysis of Supplemental Duties and Supplementary Salary Schedules in Kansas 1984–1986: Effects of *Swager v. U.S.D. 412.*" Unpublished doctoral dissertation, December 1985.
11. KANSAS NATIONAL EDUCATION ASSOCIATION LEADER HANDBOOK AND DIRECTORY 1983–84 (Topeka, Kansas: Kansas NEA, 1984), 113–114.
12. Board of Education of Hartford v. S.B.L.R., Dec. No. 1671 (August 15, 1978); *aff'd* Hartford Board of Education v. Connecticut S.B.L.R., No 22549 (Conn. Super. Ct. Jud. Dist. Hartford/New Britain, June 8, 1979).
13. Smith v. Board of Education, 708 F.2d 258 (7th Cir. 1983).
14. State *ex rel.* Hawkins v. Board of Education, 275 S.E. 2d 908 (W. Va. 1980).
15. Swager v. Board of Education U.S.D. 412, 9 Kans. App. 648, S.Ct. 412 (1984).
16. Id.
17. Ct. App. Kans., No. 58353, Syllabus by the Court, April 17, 1986.

18. Hachiya/Livingston v. U.S.D. 307, Kans. S. Ct. No 59594, Syllabus by the Court, February 19, 1988.

19. Jones v. School District of Borough of Kulpmont, 333 Pa. 581, 3A 2d 914 (1939); Wardwell v. Board of Education of City School District, 529 F.2d (6th Cir. 1976).

20. Wagenblast v. Crook County School District, 707 P.2d 69 (Ore. App. 1985).

21. Witgegenstein v. School Board of Leon City, 347 So. 2d 1069 (Fla. App. 1977).

22. Hyde v. Wellpinit School District No.49, P.2d 1388 (Wash. App. 1980).

23. Schneider v. McLaughlin Independent School District, N.W. 2d 241, N.W. 2d 574 (S.D. 1976).

24. Board of School Trustees v. Rathburn, 536 P.2d 548 (Nev. 1971). *See also,* Vorn v. David Douglas School District No. 401, 562 P.2d (Ore. App. 1980).

25. Lipan v. Board of Education, 295 S.E. 2d 44 (W. Va. 1982).

26. 254 S.E. 2d 561 (W. Va. 1979).

27. Van Horn v. Highline School District No. 401, 562 1 P.2d 641 (Wash. App. 1977). *See also,* Orth v. Phoenix Union High School System No. 210, 613 P.2d 311 (Ariz. App. 1980).

28. R. J. Stiggins & N. J. Bridgeford, Performance Assessment for Teacher Development (Portland, Ore.: Northwest Regional Education Laboratory, 1985).

29. New Castle Area School District v. Blair, 368 A. 2d 345 (Pa. Commw. 1977).

30. Goss v. San Jacinto Junior College, 566 F.2d 96 (5th Cir. 1979).

31. *In re* Feldman, 395 A. 2d 602 (Pa. Commw. 1978). *See also,* Dore v. Dedminster Board of Education, 449 A. 2d 547 (N.J. Super. Ct. App. Div. 1982).

32. Derrickson v. Board of Education, 537 F. Supp. (E.D. Mo. 1989. Opinion written after trial, March 31, 1982).

33. K. Frels and T. Cooper, *Effective Documentation Techniques for Employee Improvement or Termination,* TASB Journal, June 1980, 29.

34. *Id.* at 30.

35. Board of Education v. Merrymeeting Educators' Association, 354 A. 2d 169 (Me. 1976).

36. Given v. Western Line Consolidated School District, 439 U.S. 410 (1979).

CHAPTER FOUR

Teachers' Constitutional Rights, Terms and Conditions of Employment

Introduction

Although education is a state function and the state has the power to enact statutes that regulate the operation of schools and the activities of school employees, such statutes must conform to the significant substantive rights that historically stem from the Magna Charta and are entitled through the United States Constitution. These rights are absolute and cannot be obstructed by state constitutions or by state or federal statutes, except in very limited circumstances. When teachers exercise their constitutional rights, the school principal is often placed in the difficult position of trying to balance such rights against the rights of students, parents, administrators, and school boards.

The past three decades, the period that saw the genesis of the student rights movement, have seen a significant increase in teacher activism. Teachers have continuously challenged school boards' rights to control their lives in the school environment as well as their lives as private citizens. Many of these challenges have been debated in the courts and form the foundation for this chapter.

Although the United States Supreme Court has repeatedly emphasized and affirmed the comprehensive authority of states and local school authorities to control the schools, this authority cannot infringe upon the constitutional rights of teachers or students.[1]

The expansion of individual rights and interests, vested in judicial interpretation of the United States Constitution, has dramatically reshaped the relationship between the principal and the teacher in employment matters. Teachers are protected by due process interests that cannot be arbitrarily denied.

The principal, then, stands as the primary arbiter in problems that require the legal balancing of the interests of the public school as an agency of the state and of teachers as individuals. It is important to keep this concept of balance in mind as this chapter unfolds.

Teachers' Rights

Due Process

Scenario 4.1:   Claude Morris was dismissed from his position as a band and chorus teacher at Forte Middle School. Prior to his dismissal, Claude received a letter from his principal that provided a list of improvements that Claude needed to implement. The list included: "better control of students, more challenges for good students, and special help for less capable students."

Points to Consider: Could this list be considered to be specific reasons for dismissal if Claude did not follow them? If guidance in securing these goals was given and improvement was not forthcoming, would this strengthen the dismissal process? Can the list of improvements alone be considered as guidance? Procedural due process? If Claude had told the principal, in confidence, that "this list is nonsense," could this statement be used in upholding Claude's dismissal?[2]

The Fifth and Fourteenth amendments to the United States Constitution (the Fifth applying to activities of the federal government and the Fourteenth to those of the states) have been the source of the greatest volume of constitutionally based education litigation. The Fourteenth Amendment states that no person shall be deprived of "life, liberty, or property, without due process of law." As courts have interpreted this amendment over time, they have added requirements that procedures must not be arbitrary, unreasonable, or discriminatory in policy or practice. Essentially, then, this amendment demands "fair" procedures including reasonable notice and the right to an unbiased hearing.

Due process is a flexible concept and does not suggest a specific outline that must be followed.[3] Due process, as a concept in the education enterprise, requires fairness in the treatment of teachers by school district officials, including principals. This fairness includes both fairness of procedures used to make decisions and substantive fairness; that is, rules and actions related to educational objectives must be clearly understandable, unbiased, and reasonable.

Courts view due process in two ways: substantive due process and procedural due process. *Substantive due process* is deemed as having been denied if the policies, rules, or regulations are unfair in and of themselves. The basic attributes of substantive due process may be best understood by those features showing its absence. A rule, law, regulation, policy, or action violates substantive due process when it is overly broad or unnecessarily vague, is arbitrary or capricious, invades the protected zone of personal privacy, is unrelated to a valid education objective, or does not use reasonable means to achieve the objective.

Procedural due process means that the policies, rules, and regulations must be carried out in a fair manner. Procedural due process encompasses such basics as the right to timely, clear notification of charges and their basis and the right to an impartial hearing on the charges in which the accused is given an opportunity to defend against them. As the severity of the potential penalty increases, so does the extent of due process procedural protection.

In determining what process is due, courts apply a balancing-of-interest test that weighs the interests of society, as represented by the school, against the rights of the individual—in this chapter, the teacher. This is not a test with complex technical rules, but rather theory about what is fair and just, which allows considerable latitude in judicial examination and judgment.

Interests

Although the United States Constitution does not specifically grant a person a right to employment, the courts have derived a right to work from the Fourteenth Amendment. As early as 1923 the Supreme Court declared that the concept of liberty includes the right of the individual "to engage in the common occupations of life."[4] If the state denies a person the right to work, due process must be provided.

It has been established that teachers have both property and liberty interests in their employment contracts and must be afforded due process protection. Property interests are legitimate claims or entitlements to continued employment under contract. Term contract teachers have property interests during the specified period of their contract. The granting of tenure or a continuing contract expands this property interest to include a right to continued employment. This means that once a teacher earns tenure or a continuing contract, the teacher may not be denied continued employment without due process.

The liberty interest for both the tenured and nontenured teacher comes to the fore when the action of the school district or principal is such that the teacher's reputation is stigmatized in a way that might interfere with the teacher's future employment opportunities. The interpretation of what may be considered a liberty interest is particularly compliant to interpretation, allowing for a wide variety of protected conduct. When liberty is challenged in areas considered to be fundamental, such as religion, speech, and press, school districts must justify restraint by demonstrating a rational purpose for any action and that such restraint was justified by a compelling legal or education interest.

Nexus

Due process requires that the dismissal of a teacher or other limitation of property or liberty be justified by demonstration of a rational "nexus" between the proscribed activity and a serious limitation of the education process. A *nexus* is commonly defined, in teacher employment issues, as a connection or link between personal conduct and unfitness to teach. In an early case (1890) involving alleged immorality, the court stated, if "it [immoral behavior] impaired the services of the teacher in properly instructing or advancing pupils, he would not then be a competent teacher. . . ."[5]

In a more recent case a court attempted to set guidelines for a nexus between unfitness or conduct, a variety of employment issues, privacy, and other constitutional rights of a teacher, stating:

> *The board may consider such matters as the likelihood that the conduct may have adversely affected students or fellow teachers, the degree of such adversity anticipated, the proximity or remoteness in time of the conduct, the type of teaching certificate held by the party involved, the extenuating or aggravating circumstances, if any, surrounding the conduct, the praiseworthiness or blameworthiness of the motives resulting in the conduct, and the extent to which disciplinary action may inflict an adverse impact or chilling effect on the constitutional rights of the teacher.*[6]

Exemplar

Scenario 4.2: Leroy and Lavern Smithers, brothers teaching in the Unarlian School District, were fired for immoral conduct after two female students testified at a grand jury hearing that they had "smoked pot" at the brothers' apartment. The jury forwarded charges against the brothers for unlawful transactions with a minor. The brothers pleaded guilty to this misdemeanor.

Points to Consider: Can the brothers be dismissed for an act committed during off-duty hours, in the summer, and in the privacy of their own apartment? Is a teacher held to a higher standard of personal conduct that does not permit the commission of alleged immoral or criminal acts? Was the brothers' action likely to leave a harmful impression on their students in the school setting? Is there a direct connection (nexus) between their conduct and the work of a teacher?[7]

Any legal obligation that suggests that a teacher serve as an exemplar or role model for students rests in the belief that students, in part, acquire their social attitudes and other important behaviors by replicating those of their teachers. As early as 1885, courts accepted this assumption as "self-evident fact."[8] If it is accepted theory that the examples set by teachers and others in the education enterprise affect students, then a determination must still be made concerning what personal conduct is permissible and what may not be permissible and warrants disciplinary or employment action. Standards of acceptable behavior significantly contrast from community to community and constantly change over time. A recent case demonstrates the fact that when teachers subscribe to personal distinctiveness that may be contrary to currently accepted norms, they can place their positions as teachers at risk.

No amount of standardization of teaching materials or lesson plans can eliminate the personal qualities a teacher brings to bear in achieving these goals. Further, a teacher serves as a role model for his students, exerting a subtle but important influence over their perceptions and values. Thus, through both the presentation of course materials and the example he sets, a teacher has the opportunity to influence the attitude of students toward government, the political process and a citizen's social responsibilities. This influence is critical to the continued good health of a democracy.[9]

Privacy

Scenario 4.3: Susan Fisher, a middle-age, divorced, high school teacher, regularly supplemented her teaching income by the short-term renting of rooms in her home. Her income supplement was dedicated entirely to the care of her son, who suffered a degenerative terminal illness and lived in her home. Since hotel/motel accommodations in the town were limited, she usually had one or two renters each week. On several occasions, at the recommendation of the school board's secretary, university-sponsored student observers stayed at Susan's house while they visited classes in the school district. Without warning, the school board informed Susan that her contract would not be renewed because (1) she was a single woman, and (2) she had permitted men to remain at her house overnight, some as long as a week.

Points to Consider: Can a teacher be dismissed because of off-campus behavior that a school board judges to be "conduct unbecoming a teacher"? Was Susan's "conduct" injurious to her ability to function in the classroom? Is the impropriety implied in the dismissal charge number 2 "idle speculation"? Is idle speculation an infringement on a teacher's private life? While the school board can inquire into the character, integrity, and personal life of its employees, must dismissal be based on supported facts that are neither arbitrary nor capricious?

If teachers have a constitutional right to privacy, then discipline or dismissal for personal conduct may encroach upon that right. Because of the uncertainty concerning the definition and amplitude of privacy rights, as well as their inexplicit constitutional basis, court decisions provide an inconsistent pattern or basis on which to use privacy rights as a defense against violations of a teacher's right to employment. Where the courts have responded, such cases tend to be those where claims of improper conduct leading to dismissal are centered around sexual matters. Courts have ruled that the conduct of a teacher's private life must be just that—private. They state that there exists not only a teacher right to privacy, but a teacher duty of privacy. It would appear that the teacher's duty to maintain privacy within the school environment is absolute. If school employees value their privacy, allowing it to become public is a choice that may bear consequences.

Vagueness

Scenario 4.4:   Board of Education Policy 1-002-91 states: "School employees shall not provide transportation for students in their own personal cars except under the following circumstances: (1) A school sponsored event and school or public transportation is not available; (2) in an emergency or otherwise to expedite the process."

Board of Education Policy 47-103-91 states: "Building personnel are responsible for the leveling of window shades in their assigned work areas at the close of each school day. Shades are to be generally uniformly configured so as to create a well-kept look. Art projects are not to be displayed in windows except when appropriate."

Points to Consider: Is the intent of or the procedure for implementation of these policies clear? Would an employee's failure to follow these policies be insubordination? Incompetency? Whose interpretation of these policies should the employee follow?

The vagueness doctrine is well defined in law, and the courts ascribe to the concept that when a rule, policy, or statute forbids or requires individuals to do something in terminology so vague that individuals of common intelligence must guess at its meaning, and often differ as to its application, then the rule violates due process of law. This doctrine has significant meaning when school districts and principals develop policies, rules, and regulations for the district or individual schools.

Notice and Rights to a Hearing

Scenario 4.5:   Glenn Costin, a full-time special education teacher, was notified on March 16 that the new program that would begin in the fall would employ two part-time teachers. The board discontinued Glenn's current position and offered him one of the part-time jobs. Glenn was advised that he was entitled to a hearing if he made the request within fourteen days. Glenn obtained an attorney and, on March 27, requested a hearing. The board stated that it received the request on March 29, and, operating under a state law that required teacher dismissals to be completed by April 1, sent Glenn and his attorney telegrams setting the hearing date for March 30, giving Glenn eighteen hours to prepare for the hearing.

Points to Consider: Can a school board dismiss a teacher without giving adequate time to prepare for a hearing? If the law in this case required "appropriate and timely" notice, was Glenn's notice timely? How is "timely" defined?

State statutes or local board policies generally establish the requirements for notice of nonrenewal or termination, including deadlines for notification, form and content of the notice, and parties designated to issue the notice.[10] A review of such requirements demonstrates that many school districts include the following requirements as a matter of policy:

- The board, after consideration of the written evaluation . . . and the reasons for the recommendation, shall, in its sole discretion, either reject the recommendation or shall give the teacher written notice of the proposed nonrenewal [or termination] on or before [date], preceding the end of the employment term fixed in the contract.
- In the event of failure to give such notice of proposed nonrenewal [or termination] within the time herein specified, the board shall thereby elect to employ such employee in the same professional capacity for the succeeding school year.[11]

Several cases illustrate the legal issues involved in notice requirements. A probationary teacher challenged a school board's nonrenewal of his contract at the end of his first year of employment. He argued that the certified letter from the superintendent did not constitute sufficient notice of nonrenewal because it only told him that his name would not be presented to the school board for action. The Arkansas Supreme Court reviewed all the evidence considered by the trial court, including letters from the principal and others noting deficiencies in the teacher's performance. Based on the evidence the court concluded that the trial court's finding that the teacher had received sufficient notice of nonrenewal of his contract was correct.[12]

In another Arkansas case the state supreme court also held that the school board had substantially complied with its dismissal policies. In this case a teacher who had been on probation for the current year, even though he had taught in the district for eleven years, received a notice of nonrenewal. Rather than sending a notice of "proposed termination," the school board sent a notice of "nonrenewal." In sustaining the action of the school board, the court found that the board had substantially complied with its policies by providing a hearing even though the notice was incorrectly drawn.[13]

The service of notice of proposed termination of a teacher's contract can create problems in terms of compliance with the statutes governing such matters. A Georgia school board sent a letter of proposed termination of a teacher's contract by certified mail to the teacher's address as listed. The mail carrier noticed that the address was no longer valid, changed the address, and forwarded the letter to the carrier for that route. After an unsuccessful attempt to deliver the letter, the carrier left notice of attempted delivery and returned the certified letter to the post office. The Supreme Court of Georgia held that there was substantial compliance with the state statute governing service of notice.[14]

In an Alabama case a teacher was found guilty of immorality by the school board and was dismissed. He appealed the dismissal on the basis that he was not adequately notified of the charges because the notice used the term "unprofessional conduct" rather than "immorality." A federal district court ruled that the use of the wrong term in the notice would not invalidate the dismissal where the teacher was presented with detailed specifications of the charges against him including exact descriptions of the improper conduct. The court concluded that the teacher was adequately warned of the charges against him.[15]

In another Alabama case the court held that oral notice to a teacher that his contract would not be renewed was insufficient since the statutes required that the notice be in writing.[16]

Hearings and Procedural Due Process

The basic elements of procedural due process are the notice of the charges and a hearing. The procedural aspects of a hearing generally are delineated in state statute or school board policy. The basic elements of due process in hearings include a notice of charges, representation by counsel, protection against self-incrimination, cross-examination of witnesses, compulsory attendance of witnesses, access to records and reports in the school district's possession, a record of the hearing, and the right to appeal.[17] Aspects that often cause legal problems are the standard of proof, burden of proof, evidence, and the impartiality of the school board as the hearing body.

A federal district court in Maine found that a school board had provided a teacher sufficient due process in a nonrenewal hearing. The teacher had received written notice of the reasons for nonrenewal and a hearing. The court noted that the teacher's lawyer had extensive discovery privileges, that the teacher was allowed to cross-examine the witnesses, that the teacher was allowed to introduce evidence, and that the teacher was provided with written facts to support the decision.[18]

The Court of Appeals of Alabama found that a teacher's right to due process had not been violated when the teacher was given written notice of the proposed grounds for termination, a full evidentiary hearing on the specified grounds, and notification in writing that the board had voted to terminate the contract after considering the evidence.[19]

A federal district court in New York found that a school board had satisfied procedural due process despite its failure to give a terminated guidance counselor a copy of the trial examiner's report prior to the public meeting of the board. The court noted that the dismissed guidance counselor had received a complete statement of the charges against her, had confronted the full case against her in hearings before the trial examiner, and was given full opportunity to present her defense with assistance of counsel; the meeting at which the board formally made its decision was open to the public; and neither the guidance counselor nor her lawyer had requested a copy of the trial examiner's report. Since the plaintiff did not request a copy of the report, failure of the board to provide it to her did not violate the counselor's due process in view of the other procedures followed by the board.[20]

Another federal court specified the procedural due process rights of a tenured teacher who was accused of being unfit to teach because of mental illness, by stating:

The teacher should be given the opportunity to rebut the findings of mental unfitness and, additionally, at the hearing he should be afforded the right to present witnesses and other evidence on his own behalf. He was entitled to representation by counsel, to cross-examine witnesses against him, to a decision based only on evidence presented at the hearing, to a written decision specifying reasons, and to have a transcript of the proceedings.[21]

Generally, the courts have ruled that if a school hearing is conducted in accordance with the dictates of procedural due process and if substantial evidence appears to support the school board's action, that ordinarily ends the matter.[22] Courts usually accede to the actions of school boards in dismissal hearings where boards have conformed to the basic elements of due process, even though they may have failed to follow the procedures precisely. The courts, however, closely scrutinize any procedural oversight that has the effect of denying a dismissed employee a substantive right.

When school boards resolve to terminate teachers for cause, a common issue that is raised is the question of which party has the burden of proof to establish cause. When confronted with this question, the Vermont Supreme Court, for example, held that the burden of proof in establishing just and sufficient cause for nonrenewal rests with the school district.[23] The court reasoned that since the teaching contract was a property right requiring a due process hearing, the school board had the burden to establish the basis for its adverse decision.

Evidence and Bias

The question of whether certain evidence used against teachers by school officials was proper has been litigated often. Concerned with hearsay evidence, an Oregon court held that hearsay evidence was admissible in proceedings and could, where appropriate, constitute substantial evidence to support a finding.[24] In a later case the same Oregon court ruled that hearsay evidence relevant to facts relied on to support a teacher's dismissal and probative of matters supported by other statements in a teacher's personnel file could be admitted and considered in a hearing.[25]

Generally, evidence presented must be substantial; relevant to establish the alleged facts; developed in a constitutionally approved way; documented, which, in its simplest form, means recording time, date, and place, with witnesses listed, if any; and limited to charges made. Rules of evidence applicable in court proceedings do not apply in a strict sense to dismissal hearings.[26]

Scenario 4.6:   The Hedgewood School Board fired teacher Billie Johnson for unprofessional conduct. Billie refused to attend faculty meetings and complete required routine paperwork. The board had granted Billie's request for a hearing, with his attorney present, in which his termination was upheld. Billie then sued the Hedgewood board claiming that his due process rights were violated because the board acted as both "fact-finder" and "judge" in the dismissal hearing.

Points to Consider: Can the board of education be considered an unbiased and impartial decision maker in matters such as this? Is a publicly elected board likely to be considered impartial by a court?[27]

Aggrieved teachers often charge that school boards serving as hearing bodies are biased and unfair in their actions. In a case involving the termination of striking teachers, the United States Supreme Court held that a school board could dismiss teachers engaged in a strike prohibited by state law.[28] The plaintiff teachers alleged that the board was not sufficiently impartial to exercise discipline over the striking teachers and that due process required an independent, unbiased decision maker. The court observed:

Mere familiarity with the facts of a case gained by an agency in the performance of its statutory role does not, however, disqualify a decision maker. Nor is a decision maker disqualified simply because he has taken a position, even in public, on a policy issue related to the dispute, in the absence of a showing that he is not capable of judging a particular controversy fairly on the basis of its own circumstances.[29]

The court concluded that there was no evidence "that board members had the kind of personal or financial stake in the decision that might create a conflict of interest, and there was nothing in the record to support charges of personal animosity."[30]

Several other courts have responded to the same issue by supporting the right of a school board to be an impartial hearing body. A federal district court held that: "To preclude a school board of its authority to conduct hearings of aggrieved teachers would require convincing proof that the board was so infected with prejudice and partiality that it was incapable of rendering a fair determination on evidence presented before it."[31]

Another federal district court noted that there are at least two component factors that must be considered in determining the impartiality of the hearing board for a teacher's dismissal. First, individual decision makers must not have exhibited bias as to factual questions to be decided at the hearing; second, the hearing must occur before dismissal except in unusual circumstances.[32]

Teacher Freedom of Speech in Evaluation and Other Teacher–Principal Matters

Scenario 4.7: In a closed-door evaluation conference with his principal, Laura Silver, teacher Fred Reed demonstrated anger at his unsatisfactory evaluation. Fred stated: "I think that the superintendent and the board are all dumb bastards, and I think that you are a prostitute to their rules. As a matter of fact", he continued, "you probably slept with all of them to get your job!"

Points to Consider: Could Fred's verbiage, under the circumstances described, be used for dismissal purposes?

In the day-to-day proceedings of school operations, and particularly during an evaluation conference between a teacher and a principal, it is likely that a variety of comments will be exchanged between the parties. Such private expressions can result in legal problems if they are used as a substantial basis for an adverse employment decision.

The United States Supreme Court has held that private expression of a teacher's views to the principal is afforded constitutional protection.[33] The Court noted, however, that a teacher's expression of disagreement with superiors may be subjected to reasonable time, place, and manner restraints in order to prevent the disruption of day-to-day school activities. The court concluded that the private context of speech does not automatically remove it from the protection of the First Amendment.

A federal district court in Delaware followed this United States Supreme Court decision when it ruled that a teacher's private comments made to a principal in response to criticisms were protected by the First Amendment.[34] In addition, the Delaware court made some applicable comments about the relationship between a principal and a teacher who has specialized teaching expertise coupled with a high degree of responsibility.

The case involved a high school band director who was terminated from his position for a number of reasons, including his vocal comments made in private to his principal in response to criticism. The court noted that a teacher's response to a principal's criticism is expected, especially when the teacher has a high degree of specialized expertise and responsibility. The court found that the additional knowledge and skills possessed by the teacher rather than the principal gave the teacher's comments additional importance. In finding that the comments were constitutionally protected, the court held that they could not be the substantial or motivating factors in the board's decision to terminate the teacher. The maintenance of "personal loyalty and confidence" was not required of a relationship between a teacher and a principal in a large, diversified high school with various teaching jobs requiring specialized expertise over which a principal could and did exercise only a limited amount of day-to-day control.[35]

Terms and Conditions of Employment—Behavior

Traditional Core Values

There are general cultural values that are commonly accepted by the majority of a society. Such values, often referred to as the *core value system,* are generally well defined, traditional, and relatively stable. Society expects school districts to support and preserve the "traditional values" inherent in the "core" of society. However, teachers, just like other members of society, may elect to adopt patterns, values, and ideals that are considered "alternatives" to the traditional or core. In this event, disputes frequently occur.

"True Values" and "Folkways"

It seems to be characteristic of our society to believe that the value an individual holds personally is the absolute or "true" value. This conviction is often the psychological rationale for attempts to force others to conform to traditional beliefs. In attempting to force coherence, those groups or individuals who hold their values as absolute often attempt to use some form of reward or punishment, commonly called *sanctions,* to encourage acceptance of their cultural values. When sanctions are evident, dispute is often inevitable among those who accept emerging values and those who reject them in favor of traditional values.

These disputes may be relatively minor, when the value at stake is a social norm that does not have a high level of personal investment. These lesser values are called *folkways*. Folkways are patterns of behavior that are accepted by the core culture, but do not carry severe punishment if broken.

Mores

The *mores* of a society are generally defined as the accepted customs of a particular social group regarded as essential to its survival and welfare. Mores often become, through general observance, part of a formalized code. The mores of a community commonly determine boundaries for teachers' attitudes and actions. When mores that are held by a core culture as "untouchable beliefs" are violated, violators place themselves at risk. When everyone accepts these mores as valid, little conflict exists. However, as our society develops and changes, evolution naturally takes place at a different cadence with individuals, groups, or generations, resulting in what some observers call a "cultural lag." It is this cultural lag that often causes disputes between communities or interest groups and the school.

Legislative bodies, including school boards, have a tendency to reflect the traditional values of the core culture. Laws or policies enacted by these bodies often reflect the protection and preservation of state and community values and principal and teacher conformity to accepted norms. Because it is generally believed that the character of the teacher is of fundamental importance in children's development, school boards feel that they can demand that teachers conform to the boards' interpretations of community values. Teachers who accept values that conflict with the mores of their communities' school boards are likely to place their teaching positions at risk.

Terms and Conditions of Employment—Dismissal

The recommendation for dismissal of a teacher is, at times, a gut-wrenching experience. At other times, when poor teaching or compromised teacher rapport is still evident after extensive counseling and remediation have been exhausted, it can be a relief. In either case, recommendations for employee dismissal are a primary professional duty for the school principal. The ability to recommend termination of an teacher, when necessary, is the mark of an effective school-site or district-level administrator. The following is an examination of some of the most common problems that can lead to teacher dismissal.

Immorality and Immoral Conduct[36]

Scenario 4.8: It was not a good year in the Greenview School District as a self-appointed committee of parents, claiming that Greenview High and

Cloverleaf Elementary were "nests of flaming liberal teachers," decided to "clean house." After an overnight senior class trip, Gwen Flippen, an English teacher at Greenview, was accused of sexual misconduct when she allegedly held hands with, hugged, and kissed a male student in the presence of other students. At the same time, Marilyn Pressman, the journalism teacher at Greenview, was criticized by the citizens' committee and the school board for "lack of good moral character." The citizens' committee alleged that Marilyn lived with her boyfriend and that this "impacted negatively on her students." Marilyn admitted that during a brief period of time, while her apartment was being renovated, she had stayed with her male friend.

The Greenview citizens' committee also alleged that Bill Jones, a counselor at Cloverleaf, had taken improper, immoral actions and indecent liberties with a 10-year-old fifth-grade girl, who was referred to him because she was failing all her subjects and her parents had failed to respond to deficiency notices. Bill allegedly met with the girl in his office on four occasions, and he is accused of showing more than professional interest in her. The committee also alleged that they had evidence that while a fourth-grade student's mother was in the hospital, he had had the girl and her sister sleep in the same bed with him.

Points to Consider: If it can be determined that there is a connection (nexus) between teachers' actions and their rapport with students in the classroom setting, could these teachers be terminated? Do teachers have a right to privacy? If the teachers have done the things of which they are accused, would you recommend termination for "immoral conduct" or "lack of judgment"?[37]

The most sensitive issue relating to the dismissal of a teacher is termination for moral cause. Traditionally, the teacher has held a very special place in American life. Perhaps in no other profession has the moral disposition of its members been monitored as closely by the public as in teaching.

Because public schools are perceived as having the moral development of the child as one of their primary goals, there is an expectation by society that teachers and others in the education enterprise exhibit moral excellence. Society's desire to ensure the highest level of moral excellence often takes statutory or contractual form. Because communities have historically thought of the teacher as a guardian of community morals, teachers are expected to conduct their personal lives accordingly.

As our culture has become more complex, the issue of what is moral or immoral has become clouded as contemporary social standards constantly change. The issue of individual freedom versus institutional responsibility is frequently in dispute.

Immorality, moral turpitude, unfitness to teach, conduct unbecoming a teacher, teacher misconduct, violation of a code of ethics, and subversive activity are common statutory grounds for the dismissal of a teacher when community values conflict with teacher values or lifestyles.[38] As previously mentioned, court definitions of immorality tend to reflect core values. The courts modify their definitions as societal values change, with a resultant modification of society's mores. What was once cause for dismissal as an immoral act may now be an acceptable behavior. The term *immorality* is a value-laden word that is defined in a subjective manner. Behavior that does not conform to the established norm is defined as deviant. Deviant behavior of school personnel inside or outside of the school may be cited as cause for dismissal.

The courts have ruled that the personal conduct of a teacher is subject to reasonable control by school officials. However, school officials cannot substitute their sense of morality for that of their teachers. The key question is not whether or not actions are immoral, but whether or not they negatively affect the educational process.

As mentioned earlier, courts have also ruled that the conduct of a teacher's private life must be just that—private. They state that there exists not only a teacher's right to privacy, but a teacher's duty of privacy. It would appear that teachers' duty to maintain privacy within the school environment is absolute. If school employees value their privacy, then allowing it to become public is a choice that may bear consequences.

In recent years there has been a significant increase in the number of court cases dealing with the dismissal of public school teachers for such causes as immodest behavior unbecoming teachers, sexual misconduct of teachers with students, sexual misconduct of teachers with adults, and homosexuality.[39] As the courts have heard such cases over time, they have slowly attempted to establish a definition of the terms *immorality* and *immoral conduct*. In 1920 the Supreme Court of Minnesota held that "immoral conduct includes such acts and practices as are inconsistent with decency, good order, and propriety of personal conduct."[40] In 1939 the Supreme Court of Pennsylvania broadened the definition of immorality to include activity "not essentially confined to deviations from sex morality; it may be such a course of conduct as offends the morals of the community and is a bad example to the youth whose ideals a teacher is supposed to foster and elevate."[41]

The attempt of school boards to enforce the core culture's standards on teachers, and the subsequent modification of such standards as a result of court action, can be seen in the following two cases. In 1915 a school district in Oregon had a policy that forbade female teachers to marry. When a teacher married, the school dismissed her. The court ruled the dismissal illegal. The court said that marriage does not in itself furnish a reasonable cause for dismissal. The school board argued that after marriage a teacher would devote her time and attention to her home rather than to teaching. The court ruled that any rule that assumes that all persons become less competent because of marriage is unreasonable because such a rule is purely arbitrary.[42] The sexism of the rule was not addressed.

By 1974 the issue changed from policies preventing married teachers from teaching to policies preventing unwed pregnant teachers from teaching. The first case involved an unwed pregnant teacher who successfully sued after being dismissed on an immorality charge. The court ignored the charge of immorality and upheld the teacher's right of privacy in sexual matters, such as deciding "to bear or beget a child." The primary grounds for supporting the teacher was that the school board offered no proof that indicated the claimed immorality had affected her competency or fitness to teach. One judge in the case offered a dissenting vote, however, stating that "she was immoral" and "rumor of immorality of a public school teacher in a small town travels fast and has a larger impact on the educational process than in a city."[43]

Fitness to teach is a subjective judgment. A Montana school board dismissed a tenured teacher for lack of fitness to teach because of immorality.[44] The reasons for the dismissal included comments the teacher made to his class concerning his living arrangement with an unmarried female, his discussion of abortion in class, and his use of human fetuses in his lecture on human reproduction. The court held that the alleged immoral conduct of the teacher must directly affect the teacher's performance of expected duties. The court noted that the abortion statement and display of fetuses, standing alone, were insufficient grounds for dismissal, but it concluded that the resulting moral protest by parents was indicative of the fact that the teacher's living arrangement with the female had an adverse effect upon his performance as a teacher.[45] The court upheld the school board, recognizing the charge of immorality was supported by evidence.

However, in a vigorously worded dissent, one judge in the case concluded that the "public knowledge within the school community was nothing but rumor." He further stated that "cohabitation out of wedlock does not render one an unfit teacher" and concluded that there was not "substantial credible evidence to show that the dismissed teacher's private life had an adverse effect upon his teaching."[46]

Shoplifting was termed immoral behavior in the dismissal of a teacher in West Virginia. In reviewing the case, the state supreme court held that the appropriate standard was that "the conduct of . . . a public employee outside the job may be examined, but disciplinary action against the employee based upon that conduct is proper only where there is a proven rational nexus between the conduct and the duties to be performed."[47] The court held that the conduct of a teacher ceases to be private in at least two circumstances: when the conduct directly affects the performance of the occupational responsibilities of the teacher, and when, without contribution on the part of the school officials, the conduct has become the subject of such notoriety as to significantly and reasonably impair the capability of the particular teacher to discharge the responsibilities of the teaching position.[48] The court found that the school board presented no evidence from which it could conclude that the teacher was unfit to teach either by affected performance or negative notoriety.

Another example of an emerging value in conflict with a traditional value is found in cases involving teachers living with someone of the opposite sex without being married. School boards often attempt to dismiss such teachers on the grounds of immorality. In a court decision involving a divorcee who taught in the high school and who was known to have young men stay in her single-bedroom apartment overnight, the courts demanded proof that such action affected her classroom performance, her relationship with students under her care, or otherwise had any bearing on her effectiveness as a teacher. The court said that, at most, the evidence may raise a question regarding the teacher's good judgment in her personal affairs.[49]

However, the cohabitation of unwed teachers with members of the opposite sex can lead to a justified dismissal. Courts have upheld the dismissal of teachers for immorality when teachers live "out of wedlock" and students of the teachers have knowledge of the relationship. Courts often rule in favor of school boards if, in such cases, the board can demonstrate that there is a direct nexus between the teacher's out-of-school behavior and the teacher's effectiveness in the classroom. The courts have approved inquiries by boards of education into the personal associations of a teacher, and school boards may legitimately scrutinize teachers about any matters that might have an adverse effect on students.

It is not only the sexual activity of unmarried teachers that has been grounds for debate or dismissal. Adultery has been cited as grounds for dismissal and for revocation of a teacher's certification in cases where such an action has adversely affected the teacher's rapport in the classroom.[50]

The courts have generally upheld a school board's right to dismiss a teacher for having sexual relations with a student. However, teachers have successfully prevented dismissal on grounds of immorality in cases where former students are involved. Courts generally rule that the private association of a teacher with a member of the opposite sex is not by itself the concern of the employing school board unless it interferes with the teacher's ability to teach. Court decisions would, in all likelihood, be different if a teacher compromised a teacher–pupil relationship.

Scenario 4.9: Parents complained to the River Run School Board about Maggie Fiero's style of dress, which they considered to be "too masculine." Maggie, a kindergarten teacher, was also subjected to, and aware of, rumors that she was involved in a homosexual relationship. Based on the complaints and rumors, the board requested a ruling from the state attorney general to determine whether Maggie could be terminated. The attorney general issued an opinion that the board could use "public reputation in the community" to establish a teacher's homosexuality and that it could dismiss a reputed homosexual teacher for "immorality."

Points to Consider: Can homosexuality be classified as immoral? Under what grounds can homosexuality be considered for termination? What is improper dress? Could Maggie be terminated if her relationship with the community and her students is connected (nexus) to ineffective teaching? Is the rumor regarding Maggie sufficient evidence to consider her homosexual?[51]

There are an increasing number of court cases that deal with the question of a teacher's sexual preference. Few school systems have written board policy governing the employment or dismissal of either heterosexual or homosexual teachers. However, most superintendents say that they would not knowingly employ a homosexual teacher.[52]

Homosexuality is an issue that demonstrates the trauma that can result when a traditional value, heterosexuality, comes into conflict with an emerging value, homosexuality. Extensive litigation concerning homosexuality has been examined by the courts. The majority of such cases result from teachers' dismissal on the grounds that a homosexual is immoral and unfit to teach. Several court decisions are worthy of attention, as they illustrate the polarization of opinion and focus attention on the rapidly changing relationship between the school and the community.

In 1967 a teacher in California was convicted of a homosexual act on a public beach. The teacher was subsequently dismissed, and the court upheld this dismissal. The court declared: "Homosexual behavior has long been contrary and abhorrent to the social mores and moral standards of the people of California, as it has been since antiquity to those of many other peoples. It certainly constitutes evident unfitness for service in the public school system."[53] The court's opinion in this case reflected the social values at that time. It implied that homosexuality, in and of itself, was grounds for dismissal.

Legal opinion had shifted by 1969, when a similar case reached the courts. In this case a state supreme court ruled that:

> Nonconventional sexual behavior *per se* does not indicate unfitness to teach, and that a clear relationship must be shown between the conduct of a teacher and the teacher's job requirements. . . . The power of the state to regulate professions or conditions of government employment must not arbitrarily impair the right of the individual to live his private life, apart from his job, as he deems fit.[54]

Although this decision clearly indicates that there must be a job-related cause for dismissal, the court failed to address the crucial issue of whether or not homosexuals should be permitted to teach. The major argument against homosexuals teaching continued to focus on the impact of homosexual teachers on the sexual identity of children.

In 1972, however, this issue reached the courts in a case brought by a newly hired teacher. When the plaintiff's school board learned of his homosexuality, they reassigned him to a nonteaching assignment. He brought suit against the board, and the court ruled that he had been unlawfully discriminated against because of his homosexuality. However, the court upheld the teacher's dismissal on the basis of his notoriety since he had appeared on state and national television shows, including "60 Minutes," defending his position. The court concluded that the knowledge base concerning whether or not a homosexual teacher would have a negative effect on the children was inconclusive.[55] The court did not seem to feel that the danger to the children was as great as school officials contended, and the court was impressed by evidence "that gender identity is established by the age of 5 or 6 in most people."[56]

In 1977 the first case regarding homosexuality was appealed to the United States Supreme Court. The Court refused to hear the case, thereby preserving the decision of the Washington Supreme Court. The Washington decision affirmed the right of a school board to dismiss a homosexual even though there was no evidence of overt homosexual acts.[57]

In a 1982 case a tenured teacher with eighteen years' experience, who had most recently been an elementary librarian, was observed by police as a participant in homosexual activities in an adult bookstore in a city some distance from his school. The teacher was not arrested; however, a description of his activities and his name were included as part of the evidence used in a suit to bar the operation of the bookstore. Later, in order to comply with a subpoena to serve as a witness, the teacher requested a leave of absence and informed his principal that he had been subpoenaed in the case. Newspaper coverage of the suit was widespread, and word of the teacher's involvement in the suit spread to the community in which he taught.

The teacher was reassigned to a position that did not involve student contact, and the school superintendent sought revocation of the teacher's certificate. The proposed revocation was dismissed for lack of probable cause. At the end of the school year, the teacher was reassigned to the elementary library where he had worked previously, but townspeople complained to the principal. The teacher again was assigned to a position with no student contact. The teacher subsequently was dismissed for immorality and appealed to the state's Fair Dismissal Appeals Board, which sustained the school board's decision. When the case went to the court on appeal, the court held that the grounds for the teacher's dismissal were rationally related to his ability to teach effectively in the school district.[58] The court noted that the teacher was not dismissed for his sexual preference, but rather because of the manner and place in which he exercised that preference, with the resultant notoriety surrounding his activities.[59] The school board, therefore, was entitled to determine if the notoriety impaired his ability to teach in the district. In making such a determination, the court held that the board could make value judgments based upon local standards.[60] Generally the courts agree that homosexuality, absent a flaunting of sexual preference, is not grounds for dismissal or for not hiring a teacher.

Although the courts appear to be exhibiting a growing sympathy and support for individual protection under the First and Fourteenth amendments, the Supreme Court has yet to rule on these freedoms in regard to the homosexual teacher. Until that happens, each state and each individual school district will probably reflect the majority opinion of the community members.

Incompetency

Scenario 4.10: Jim Lasser accidentally showed an R-rated movie, *Blue Thunder*, to his fourth- and fifth-grade classes. When Jim picked up the movie at a video rental store he did not see the "R" rating on the movie's package and assumed that it would be similar to the "Blue Thunder" TV series. Jim was grading papers while the film was running and did not notice its violence and brief nude scene.

Points to Consider: Was Jim's unintentional act sufficient ground for dismissal for incompetence or willful neglect of duty?[61]

Scenario 4.11: Terri Hamburg, a tenured seventh-grade English teacher, was fired when the school district confronted her with the following facts: (1) She prepared unsatisfactory, illegible daily lesson plans; inadequately evaluated the performance of students; and employed deficient instructional techniques. (2) In the three-year period preceding her dismissal, seven separate and independent classroom observations had been made with each observer concurring in the identification of her teaching deficiencies and in the need for corrective action. (3) The observers each issued a directive to Terri requiring improvement in her performance with advisement that her employment could be in jeopardy if she did not succeed in demonstrating improvement in identified areas.

Points to Consider: Has due process been followed? Has incompetency been established regarding Terri's teaching? Might Terri be guilty of insubordination?[62]

Incompetency is a general term used to cover a variety of problems experienced by school personnel. What constitutes incompetency is strictly decided by the courts, after considering all the particular facts of a case. The courts have given broad interpretation to the term; however, incompetency is generally defined as "want of physical, intellectual, or moral ability; insufficiency; inadequacy; specific want of legal qualifications or fitness."[63] School boards have offered a wide variety of reasons to substantiate charges of incompetency, and the courts have generally found that the following conduct is sufficient to sustain dismissals based on incompetency:

- Refusal by a teacher to respond to specific questions from a superior concerning the teacher's former lifestyle.[64]
- Excessive teacher tardiness and absence during the school year with no excuse.[65]
- Lack of classroom management, control, or discipline.[66]
- Failure to provide expected leadership as described in a job description.[67]
- Lack of knowledge necessary for competent instruction and inability to convey such knowledge effectively.[68]
- Refusal of a teacher to allow supervisory personnel to enter the teacher's classroom.[69]

The courts generally see incompetency as unfitness to teach and have included in their interpretation of unfitness such areas as lack of knowledge of subject matter, lack of discipline[70] or unreasonable discipline,[71] unprofessional conduct, and willful neglect of duty.

Some school boards have used the results of student grades or student scores on standardized achievement tests as a means to justify a charge of incompetency on the part of a teacher. The Eighth Circuit Court of Appeals reversed a federal district court in Iowa by holding that the use of student scores on standardized achievement tests was a lawful factor for a school board to consider in its decision not to renew a teacher.[72] A federal district court in Texas ruled that a teacher's procedural due process rights were not violated by the school board's introduction, as evidence, of the low achievement of the teacher's students.[73]

An Alabama teacher with fourteen years in a school system was advised of the proposed cancellation of the teacher's contract on the basis of incompetency and insubordination. Evidence at the hearing showed that the teacher willfully refused to follow reasonable rules and regulations, refused to follow grading procedures, engaged in several heated discussions with the supervisor, and blatantly refused to submit to the supervisor's authority. The court found the evidence sufficient to support the conclusion that the teacher was both incompetent and insubordinate.[74] Among the reasons used by a New York school board to dismiss a teacher for incompetency were excessive lateness, negligent conduct that resulted in a minor classroom fire, and instructional deficiencies.[75]

There are times, however, when the courts disagree with school boards on the acceptability of the charges of incompetency. In a Nebraska case the state supreme court held that there was insufficient evidence to support a school board's conclusion that a teacher should be terminated for incompetence.[76] The court noted that the teacher received above-average ratings during the entire time the teacher was employed and that the record was silent as to the performance of any other teachers in the school system. In citing an earlier case the court noted that "incompetency or neglect of duty are not measured in a vacuum nor against a standard of perfection, but, instead, must be measured against the standard required of others performing the same or similar duties."[77] In other words, the school board failed to document the charges of incompetency through comparisons with other teachers in the system.

It is essential that principals and other administrators in a school district be able to document an employee's poor performance. In addition, school officials should be able to demonstrate that they gave the employee time, opportunity, and counseling to improve or correct performance. Aside from creating a favorable impression for the defendant school district, such evidence also demonstrates that the stated rationale for the termination (incompetency) is not a pretext for a hidden, illegal reason.

Insubordination

Scenario 4.12:   Camille Conrad, concerned that she was losing her tan, wanted to take a week off in January to go to Jamaica. She was advised by her principal and the board that she could not take a one-week leave of absence. Camille went anyway, and when she returned, she found herself facing procedural due process actions that subsequently resulted in her termination.

Points to Consider: If the school board demonstrated that Camille's conduct adversely affected her relationship in the school community and with her students, would there be any possibility that Camille could, through court action, retain her position? If no adverse effects could be shown, was Camille insubordinate?[78]

Scenario 4.13:   Blaird Oglesby had been an elementary school principal in the same district for fifteen years. Two years ago, Blaird's son left on a two-year mission abroad. At that time, Blaird made a commitment to his son that at the conclusion of his mission, he would join his son in Europe and accompany him home. Blaird planned to use ten of his forty accumulated leave days for the trip. Before his scheduled departure, however, the school district changed its leave policy and limited administrators' use of earned leave to "no more than five school days per year, or two days in succession, except in cases of emergency." Blaird's request for leave was denied, but he completed the trip as planned. Upon returning, he was presented with a notice of suspension and intention of the district to initiate dismissal proceedings based on "insubordination."

Points to Consider: Was this a "willful disregard of express or implied directions?" Could Blaird's act be looked upon as a "defiant attitude" by a principal to the board? If the school district could not claim that students or the school were detrimentally affected by the principal's absence (nexus), could the school district be upheld in termination proceedings? Could this act be claimed as a simple "error in judgment, resulting in no harm to his employers"? Might a court find that Blaird's termination for "insubordination" was arbitrary and capricious?[79]

Insubordination generally refers to a failure of an employee to submit to the reasonable and lawful authority of a superior,[80] or "a willful disregard of express or implied directions of the employer and a refusal to obey reasonable orders."[81] This is the most common and simplistic rationale advanced by school officials in dismissal cases based on insubordination. However, insubordination cannot be judged in the abstract. It must be supported by specific facts before a dismissal will be upheld by the courts.

The failure of a tenured teacher to inform the board whether or not the teacher would accept employment for the next year resulted in a dismissal based on insubordination. The teacher had requested and been granted a one-year leave of absence for the school year. Prior to the next year, the teacher had applied for an extension of leave for the upcoming school year, but his application was denied. School officials set a date for the teacher to inform the district of intentions for the ensuing year. The deadline passed and the teacher failed to notify the school district whether the teacher would teach in the coming year. The board began termination proceedings and made repeated attempts to notify the teacher. When no response came from the teacher, the school board terminated his employment on the grounds of insubordination and neglect of duty. The court upheld the teacher's termination.[82]

In another case a tenured teacher, dissatisfied with his assignment for the next school year, refused to sign his contract. The teacher wrote the superintendent requesting assignment to a teaching position in the high school without additional duties as an athletic coach. The superintendent notified the teacher that if he did not execute and return the contract, it would be assumed that he did not wish to continue his employment in the district. The teacher made no timely response, but did appear before a special meeting of the school board where he repeated his position that he would not sign any contract that would require him to coach. The board voted not to rehire him for the next school year. The teacher requested and was granted a hearing, at which the board justified the termination on the basis of insubordination. By refusing to execute the employment contract offered by the board for the next school year, the federal district court reasoned, the teacher was "refusing to carry out the specific assignment of reasonable and nondiscriminatory duties by the Bristol board of education" and was, therefore, insubordinate. The teacher's dismissal was sustained by the court.[83]

In some cases a teacher can be found insubordinate for refusing to comply with an order given by someone other than the principal. One court interpreted insubordination as "the refusal to obey some order which a superior officer is entitled to give and entitled to have obeyed so long as such order is reasonably related to the duties of the employees."[84] In this case a guidance counselor had been delegated the responsibility of monitoring student behavior in the school lunchroom. The counselor directed a teacher to return to her classroom while he disciplined the children of her homeroom. She refused to obey the directive and was subsequently dismissed for insubordination.[85]

The courts have generally agreed that school employees are insubordinate when they willfully refuse to obey a reasonable and lawful order given by a superior or one who has the authority to give such orders. As with all other rationale for termination, specific evidence is necessary to substantiate a charge of insubordination. Charges of insubordination are generally not supportable in court actions if:

- The alleged conduct was not proved.
- The existence of a pertinent school rule or a supervisor's order was not proved.
- The pertinent rule or order was not violated.
- The teacher or employee tried, although unsuccessfully, to comply with the rule or order.
- The teacher's or employee's motive for violating the rule or order was admirable.
- No harm resulted from the violation.
- The rule or order was unreasonable.
- The rule or order was beyond the authority of its maker.
- The enforcement of the rule or order revealed possible bias or discrimination against the teacher or employee.
- The enforcement of the rule or order violated First Amendment or other constitutional rights.
- The rule or order was unlawful.[86]

Other Causes

Scenario 4.14:   Steve Sawyer, the high school industrial arts instructor in Spruceview, is a hobbyist gunsmith. Steve inadvertently left a revolver and some ammunition in the pocket of his jacket, which was hung in his classroom. The jacket was stolen. Although the gun and ammunition were later returned, Steve, a 12-year veteran of the school district, was concerned about rumors that the school board might dismiss him over this incident.

Points to Consider: Could Steve's error, a single isolated incident on his teaching record, brand him as "unfit to teach?"[87]

Scenario 4.15: Gary Coughlin, a nontenured but well-qualified teacher, was plagued by chronic illness. Gary was dismissed for excessive absences after missing twenty-one days during the school year. The board of education cited "good cause" for his dismissal.

Points to Consider: If "good cause" means that Bill's chronic illnesses can be demonstrated to have a reasonable relationship to his unfitness to discharge the duties assigned, or his absences are detrimental to students (nexus), would Bill be likely to retain his job if he appealed his dismissal in court?

Scenario 4.16: Mary Longview had taught in the same school district and in the same school for thirty-six years. Mary knew the board policy that teachers were to administer corporal punishment only by "blows to the child's posterior in the presence of the principal or principal's designee." Mary had worked with ten different principals during her years at the school and she always tried hard to "obey" her principal's wishes. Her principal during the year in which Mary was fired for insubordination was a young man who had been sent there to correct discipline problems that had gotten out of hand under the preceding principal. Her new principal had told teachers at the beginning of the school year that "if any of them had a discipline problem with children, to bop them in the mouth!"[88] Mary's principal had also prepared and distributed to teachers a handbook that was in conflict with the corporal punishment regulation. After the school district received complaints from parents that Mary struck students, Mary was fired. Her dismissal was based upon violation of the board's corporal punishment regulations.

Points to Consider: Which regulations should Mary have followed? If she had refused to follow the principal's regulations, would she have also placed herself in jeopardy for insubordination? Is this a common problem—board regulations versus principal practice?

A review of case law demonstrates that school officials have cited many reasons to support dismissal actions against their employees. In addition to incompetency or insubordination, case law examination reveals such rationale as negligence, failure to attend required institutes, inefficiency, disloyalty, conviction of specified crimes, drunkenness, intemperance, addiction to drugs, selling drugs, cruelty, public lewdness, alternative lifestyle choice, etcetera. No attempt is made here to provide a comprehensive review of all causes for dismissal. Selected examples of other reasons are cited for illustrative purposes.

Neglect of duty is a reason often forwarded by school officials for terminating an employee. In an Alabama case a teacher's failure to administer an individual education program (IEP) was considered to be a neglect of duty.[89]

In a North Carolina case a teacher was dismissed for insubordination, lack of mental capacity, and neglect of duty. The list of charges from the school board included the teacher's use of the words "damn" and "hell" at various times in the classroom, allowing students to play noneducational games, slapping one student and pulling the hair of another, "flogging" a male student, pulling a female student out of the girls' bathroom and kicking her, and permitting students to settle disputes by fighting. The court held that the conduct did not constitute insubordination and was not such as would indicate lack of mental capacity; however, it did amount to neglect of duty, justifying the teacher's dismissal.[90]

Examples of misconduct from a New York case included excessive lateness, neglect of duty, conduct prejudicial to the operation of the school system, and incompetent services.[91] Persistent negligence was justified by charges that a teacher slept in class, failed to comply with the lesson plan policy, inadequately prepared IEPs, and taught subjects inconsistent with IEPs the teacher had prepared.[92]

Some state statutes provide for a general category of reasons for dismissal under the cover of "just" or "good cause." This umbrella approach allows school boards to dismiss employees for a great variety of activities. Since it would be impossible for a state legislature to delineate all possible reasons to justify a dismissal, legislators in such states believe that it is necessary for school boards to have some flexibility in which to apply employment sanctions.

An Arizona court defined good cause as "a cause which bears a reasonable relationship to a teacher's unfitness to discharge the duties assigned or is in a reasonable sense detrimental to the students being taught."[93] Among the reasons given to justify the dismissal of a Nebraska principal for just cause were that the principal failed to maintain discipline, lost teacher confidence, and was ineffective in his relations with his staff and that the principal had failed to cooperate with the board in a number of instances.[94] An Alabama court found that a teacher's failure to cooperate in the solution of school problems constituted good and just cause that would justify dismissal.[95]

Mixed-Motives Dismissal

Scenario 4.17:   Sam Armstrong, a teacher/coach, was suspended because he spoke at a public meeting regarding controversy in the athletic department and because he wrote to school board members detailing his ideas for restructuring the department. On his return to work after the suspension, Superintendent Alice Noble advised Sam that he would not be given further coaching duties because of his failure to submit his suggestions through proper channels.

Points to Consider: If the athletic program had become a matter of public debate, was Sam's speech protected by the First Amendment? Might Sam challenge the application of the board's "channels" policy as a violation of his civil rights?[96]

Some dismissal cases take on constitutional dimensions when teachers allege a violation of a protected right. It is beyond question that educators have constitutional rights that they do not surrender at the schoolhouse door.[97] Conversely, the courts are not unmindful of the need of school authorities to maintain employee discipline, order, and proper supervision of public schools. The following examination of the litigation and court dicta in the cases of *Pickering, Myers,* and *Mt. Healthy* should provide an overview of dismissal for mixed motives.

Pickering v. Board of Education
The United States Supreme Court in *Pickering v. Board of Education* noted that the problem in mixed-motive cases is "to arrive at a balance between the interests of the teacher, in commenting upon matters of public concern and the interest of the State, as an employer, in promoting the efficiency of the public services it performs through its 'employees.' "[98] Pickering, a high school teacher, was dismissed from his position by the board of education for sending a letter to a local newspaper concerning a proposed tax increase. The letter was critical of the manner in which the school board and superintendent had handled past proposals to raise new revenue for the schools. In addition, the letter criticized the school district's fiscal priorities, particularly athletic expenditures. After a hearing by the board, Pickering was dismissed on the grounds that "the publication of the letter was detrimental to the efficient operation and administration of the schools of the district."[99]

Pickering took his case to court, where he claimed that his writing of the letter was protected by the First and Fourteenth amendments. This claim was rejected by a county court and, upon appeal, by the state supreme court. When the case was appealed to the United States Supreme Court, Pickering's right to freedom of speech was upheld. The Court indicated that it was neither appropriate nor feasible to prescribe a general standard for review of critical statements by teachers and other public employees thought by their superiors to justify dismissal. Instead, the Court provided some general guidelines for an analysis of the controlling interest in such cases. The Court held that Pickering's letter presented no question of maintaining either discipline by immediate supervisors or harmony among co-workers because the statements were in no way directed toward any person with whom he would normally be in contact in the course of his daily work as a teacher.[100] Since Pickering's letter was critical of the board and the superintendent, the Court noted that ". . . the employment relationships with the Board and, to a somewhat lesser extent, with the superintendent are not the kind of close working relationships for which it can persuasively be claimed that personal loyalty and confidence are necessary to their proper functioning."[101]

In addition, the Court found that ". . . it could neither be shown, nor presumed to have in any way either impeded the teacher's proper performance of his daily duties in the classroom or to have interfered with the regular operation of the schools generally."[102] The Court concluded that ". . . a teacher's exercise of his rights to speak on issues of public importance may not furnish the basis for his dismissal from public employment."[103]

Connick v. Myers

In 1983 the United States Supreme Court further defined the free speech rights of public employees. In a related nonschool case the Court upheld the discharge of an assistant district attorney for circulating a questionnaire among fellow staff members concerning internal office affairs.[104]

After Assistant District Attorney Myers was notified of a proposed transfer to another section of the criminal court, she objected and discussed the proposed transfer and other office matters with her supervisor. When her supervisor questioned whether other staff members shared Myers's concerns, Myers informed the supervisor that she would do some research on the matter. She prepared a questionnaire seeking the opinions of her colleagues about "office transfer policy, office morale, the need for a grievance committee, the level of confidence in supervisors, and whether employees felt pressured to work in political campaigns."[105] After the questionnaire was circulated among the office staff, Myers was notified that she was being terminated because of her refusal to accept the transfer and because her distribution of the questionnaire was an act of insubordination.

Myers filed suit in federal district court alleging that her termination was unlawful since she had exercised her right of free speech. The court held for Myers and ordered her reinstated. After the federal appeals court sustained the trial court's decision, the case was appealed to the United States Supreme Court. The Supreme Court reiterated the point of law "that a state cannot condition public employment on a basis that infringes the employee's constitutionally protected interest in freedom of expression."[106] The Court then evoked a balancing test, determined in the *Pickering* case, to weigh the rights of the employee to comment on matters of public concern with the rights of the employer in promoting the efficiency of the public service. After reviewing *Pickering* and other related cases, the Court concluded that the questionnaire involved matters of personal as opposed to public concern and was not constitutionally protected.[107] When the Court shifted its consideration to the government's interest under the *Pickering* balance, it found that "the limited First Amendment interest involved here does not require that [the supervisor] tolerate action which he reasonably believed would disrupt the office, undermine his authority, and destroy close working relationships."[108]

Some educators may view the Myers case as limiting teachers' rights to free speech and free expression. Others may view the case as the Supreme Court's restoring a balance to its expanded view of teachers' rights. Regardless of interpretation, the ruling must be considered, along with *Pickering,* as a point of reference when dealing with an alleged exercise of a constitutionally protected right of a teacher.

Important points to consider are whether the comments were made by a teacher as a citizen or as a public employee, and whether the comments relate to matters of public concern or relate only to internal school matters. A question emerges, however, as to whether matters of internal school concern can ever be elevated to public or community interest. In addition, it is clear that the courts will consider the manner, time, and place of a teacher's comments in examining the *Pickering* balance. Finally, the courts will weigh the close working relationship between the teacher and the supervisor to determine if the supervisor's authority was undermined or if the efficiency of the school was compromised.

Mt. Healthy City School District v. Doyle

In *Mt. Healthy City School District. v. Doyle,* the United States Supreme Court held that the reasons given by a school board for dismissal must not include a constitutionally protected right, unless it can be shown by a preponderance of the evidence that such a right was not the substantial or motivating factor in the termination decision.[109] The facts in this case are illustrative of a mixed-motive dismissal—that is, a dismissal based on legitimate school-related reasons and, possibly, constitutionally impermissible reasons.

Doyle, a nontenured classroom teacher, had been involved in a series of incidents during his employment including an argument with another teacher, which ended with the teacher slapping Doyle, and the subsequent suspension of both teachers. Doyle was also involved in an argument with employees of the school cafeteria over the amount of spaghetti that had been served to him, a reference to students as "sons of bitches," and an obscene gesture he made to students when they failed to obey his commands in his capacity as cafeteria supervisor.

However, the incident that led to Doyle's dismissal, and the subsequent claim of constitutional infringement that he presented in court, was Doyle's telephone call to a local radio station. Doyle conveyed the substance of a memorandum concerning teacher dress and appearance that the school principal had circulated to various teachers. A few weeks after his call, the superintendent made his annual recommendations to the school board concerning the rehiring of nontenured teachers. Doyle and nine other teachers were recommended for nonrenewal. When Doyle requested a statement of reasons for the nonrenewal, he received a statement citing "a notable lack of tact in handling professional matters which leaves much doubt as to your sincerity in establishing good school relationships."[110] The statement referred to his call to the radio station and to the obscene-gesture incident.

The federal district court concluded that the telephone call to the radio station was "clearly protected by the First Amendment," and that because it played a "substantial part" in the board's nonrenewal decision, Doyle was entitled to reinstatement with back pay.[111] A court of appeals affirmed this decision, but the Supreme Court took issue with the district court's reasoning in finding that the telephone call was protected by the First and Fourteenth Amendments, and that Doyle should be reinstated.[112]

The Supreme Court, in remanding the case, identified a test to be used in assessing mixed-motives dismissal:

> *Initially, in this case, the burden was properly placed upon respondent to show that his conduct was constitutionally protected, and that this conduct was a substantial factor or, . . . a motivating factor in the Board's decision not to rehire him. Respondent having carried that burden, however, the District Court should have gone on to determine whether the Board had shown by a preponderance of the evidence that it would have reached the same decision as to respondent's re-employment even in the absence of the protected conduct.*[113]

The district court, on remand from the United States Supreme Court, held that the board of education, in fact, had shown by a preponderance of the evidence that it would have reached the same decision in not renewing Doyle's contract even in absence of the protected speech, and the appeals court held that the district court's finding was not clearly erroneous, thus affirming the board's action to dismiss Doyle.[114]

Reduction in Force

Scenario 4.18: Bailey Barton, a tenured teacher who had the least amount of seniority in his department, found his position eliminated at the close of the school year. His school district, faced with substantial budget deficits and decreased enrollment, had decided to eliminate certain teaching positions. The collective bargaining agreement between the teachers' association and Barton's school district provided that teachers would be placed on unrequested leave of absence in inverse order of seniority.

Points to Consider: Absent school board actions that were arbitrary, capricious, or unreasonable, might Barton be able to regain his position if, in fact, there was a substantial decline in enrollment?[115]

Scenario 4.19: Bill Laird, a tenured business teacher in Sunny Meadows School District, was not rehired at the end of the school year because of a shuffling of the district's six business teachers for economic reasons. Five business teachers were retained.

Points to Consider: If Bill's termination was not the result of substantial decrease in enrollment or of curtailment of the district's educational program due to budget problems, would Bill be able to retain his position if he were able to demonstrate that the district was merely "juggling" teachers for economic reasons?

The number of students graduating from high school in the United States is projected to be 2 percent lower than current levels by 1995.[116] With declining enrollment as well as reduced funding, school districts are confronted with the need to reduce expenditures in order to balance their budgets. The courts have generally recognized the following rationale for school districts to implement a reduction in force (RIF): enrollment decline; fiscal, economic, or budgetary basis; reorganization or consolidation of school districts; change in the number of teaching positions; curtailment of programs, courses, or services; or other good or just cause. Because staff salaries constitute the major portion of the operating budget, eliminating faculty and administrative positions through a RIF clearly results in reduced school district expenditures. However, RIF actions have also resulted in a proliferation of court actions. Most states have enacted legislation concerning staff reduction; however, the scope and specificity of RIF provisions vary from state to state.

While school boards might prefer to eliminate positions through attrition, it is often necessary to terminate personnel for the sole reason of financial exigency. A number of legal concerns surround the decision to terminate school employees through RIF remedies. For example, the Supreme Court of South Dakota held that procedural due process was required when a tenured teacher was reduced to half-time teaching status pursuant to a staff reduction policy.[117] The court noted that the board of education's policy required the board to adhere to due process whenever a tenured teacher's contract was affected by staff reduction.

In a similar case in Pennsylvania, a tenured teacher was demoted from her position as a full-time teacher and reassigned to teach a 40-percent course load, with a commensurate decrease in pay, as the result of lack of enrollment in the courses she taught. She requested, and was granted, a hearing with the school board, at which she asserted that the demotion was arbitrary and capricious and in disregard of the express legislative intent to protect tenured teachers. The board affirmed the demotion, and she appealed to the state secretary of education, who sustained the board. The case was then taken to court, where it was held that demotions of school employees under state statutes are presumptively valid, and an employee challenging such action has the burden of proving that the action was taken arbitrarily or upon improper consideration. The court found that the board had justified its action by showing decreased enrollment in the programs for which the teacher had primary responsibility.[118]

The question of whether a school district must realign staff assignments in order to ensure continued employment of its more senior employees has frequently been litigated. In a Pennsylvania case the court held that a school district was not required to realign its staff across lines of multiple certification to ensure continued employment of more senior employees.[119] However, a New York court provided the possibility that rearranging schedules might be necessary. The court followed the principle that "though administrative convenience must fall when it collides with tenure rights, the tenure rights must fall when rescheduling is impossible." The court held that the school board had the burden of showing that schedules could not be rearranged or reshuffled so that the least senior teacher would be eliminated.[120]

An Illinois court required the rearranging of teaching schedules to protect the full-time employment of a tenured teacher. The teacher filed suit seeking a *writ of mandamus* (notification of order) compelling the school district to assign him to a full-time schedule of classes that he was qualified to teach. He had been a full-time tenured teacher for the 1979–1980 school year, but had been reduced to part-time for 1980–1981, while teachers of less seniority were assigned to teach courses he was qualified to teach. The trial court directed the writ to be issued requiring the board to assign him a full-time schedule, and the appellate court affirmed. The appeals court held that school boards, whether in good or bad faith, cannot rearrange teaching assignments in ways that defeat the rights of tenured teachers and circumvent the purpose and spirit of tenure laws.[121]

Courts have generally ruled that in making the selection of a teacher to be dismissed pursuant to a RIF, a school board may exercise its discretion and consider noneducational factors as well as educational ones. Two business teachers with the same credentials and tenure were considered for dismissal under a RIF policy. In deciding which teacher to drop from the staff, the board considered the contribution each made to the activities program. Even though the plaintiff had taught for six years, the teacher the board chose to retain had only three years experience, but was an athletic coach. This RIF was upheld.[122]

It is clear that when a school board has a RIF policy that requires procedural due process for nonrenewal or demotion, the board is legally obligated to follow procedural guidelines before taking an adverse employment action. A school district cannot avoid tenure laws by failing to provide available assignments to tenured teachers; however, the district may not be compelled to realign staff assignment across multiple lines of certification in order to ensure continued employment of its more senior employees. The school district may have to demonstrate that it was impossible to rearrange schedules so that the least senior employees are dismissed instead of more senior tenured teachers.

Remedies for Wrongful Discharge—Mitigation of Damages

When dismissed employees file suits against school boards alleging wrongful discharge, they generally seek relief in several forms, including notice and a hearing, reinstatement, back pay, compensatory damages, or attorney's fees and other costs of litigation.

Court-ordered reinstatement of a dismissed employee normally depends on whether any protected interest was involved and on the discretion of the court, unless state law provides otherwise. It is clear that school personnel dismissed for the lawful exercise of their constitutional rights will be reinstated by the courts.[123] In some cases the courts have ordered reinstatement for dismissed teachers who were denied notice and a hearing.[124]

The courts are not in agreement when it comes to whether teachers who are not properly evaluated prior to a dismissal have a cause justifying reinstatement.[125] Generally, nontenured teachers are not entitled to notice and a hearing before a decision not to renew their contracts. However, if a nontenured teacher is able to establish that a property or liberty interest has been violated, then the courts could order a due process hearing, allowing the employee an opportunity to prove the legitimacy of a claim or to clear his or her name or reputation.[126]

The doctrine of mitigation of damages imposes on the injured party the duty to exercise reasonable and ordinary care in attempting to minimize his or her damages after an injury has been inflicted. When the courts begin to determine the amount due under a back pay award, consideration is given to whether the aggrieved party took steps to mitigate or reduce the loss by seeking another job or taking appropriate employment. The source of authority for an award of back pay may be state statute, the employment contract, or a collective bargaining agreement. In addition, an employee may recover back pay where the dismissal occurred in violation of the requirements of due process, or where some other constitutional or federal statutory right has been violated.[127]

Two cases illustrate the award of back pay and the issue of mitigation of damages under state statutory provisions. In Missouri a tenured art teacher was dismissed for excessive absences. The trial court found that she had been wrongfully discharged and awarded the teacher $108,948.01 in damages. The issue, on appeal, was whether the award should be reduced for failure of the teacher to mitigate her damages.[128] Missouri law states that school boards have the burden of proving that a teacher could have mitigated damages. In examining a previous Missouri case, the appeals court found that the board must show not only that the teacher failed to mitigate, but that she had an opportunity to mitigate.[129] The court then relied on a Massachusetts case to outline the defendant's burden:

> *A former employer meets its burden of proof of "mitigation of damages" if the employer proves that (a) one or more discoverable opportunities for comparable employment were available in a location as, or more convenient than the place of former employment, (b) the improperly discharged employee unreasonably made no attempt to apply for any such job, and (c) it was reasonably likely that the former employee would obtain one of those comparable jobs.[130]*

The court concluded that the school board did not meet its burden of proof because the evidence indicated that there was no possibility that the teacher would receive a teaching position. The teacher, who was discharged for excessive absence, was 55 years old, tenured with fifteen years' experience, and held a master's degree plus 30 hours. Under these circumstances it was very unlikely that the teacher would find employment with comparable salary and benefits.[131]

The issue of mitigation of damages can also be demonstrated in a case involving the wrongful discharge of a probationary school principal. This court held that unless a wrongful discharge is malicious, the employee has a duty to mitigate damages by accepting similar employment to that contemplated by his or her contract if it is available in the local area.[132] Further, the actual wages received from the comparable employment would be deducted from any back pay award; however, the burden of raising the issue of mitigation is on the employer. Because of the social status of educators and the nature of their duties, they are not required to seek employment in any other job of significantly lower status for which they are unsuited by education or training. But there are many other jobs outside of education, which have comparable working conditions and status, for which educators are suited. The court noted that where mitigation of damages renders the final award nominal, the employee is entitled to reasonable attorneys' fees and other litigation expenses.[133] Congress enacted the Civil Rights Attorney's Fees Act in 1976.[134] This law provides that the federal court, at its discretion, may allow the prevailing party (other than the United States) in a civil rights suit reasonable attorney fees as part of the costs. The purpose of the law was to encourage individuals to take action to vindicate their civil rights.[135]

Courts have also held that a violation of an employee's due process rights can entitle the employee to back pay with interest for the entire period of his or her dismissal, if the dismissal is overturned.[136]

The Student Teacher

Scenario 4.20: Mike Ford, who had been a student teacher for seven weeks, was assigned to teacher Lilla Brown's sixth-grade class. Mike was supervising the sixth-grade area of the playground during recess while Lilla prepared some materials in the classroom. Mike decided that he would join the touch football game his class was having with another class. While he was involved in the game, another student, who had decided not to participate, was severely injured in a fall from the top of a swing set.

Points to Consider: Could Mike be held liable for improper supervision? Is Mike an agent of the school? Could Mike's cooperating teacher and principal be held liable?

Generally, states permit local school districts to enter into student teacher contracts with colleges and universities for the final training of prospective teachers. In some states the state board of education issues student teaching certificates and permits student teachers to assume certain responsibilities as fully certificated teachers. It is imperative for principals to understand that, just as with certificated teachers, a potential for liability exists with student teachers. Student teachers are the ultimate responsibility of the principal acting in concert with the college or university and the assigned supervising teacher. Legal problems affecting student teachers appear to be the same types of problems that affect certificated teachers.

Research demonstrates that the areas in which student teachers are most frequently involved in litigation are negligence that results in an injury to a student, hitting students or use of corporal punishment, and felony arrest or conviction.[137] In addition, student teachers have been involved with the courts as a result of school district and college/university decisions involving grades in student teaching, discrimination against student teachers, and withdrawal of student teachers from assignments.[138]

Student teachers are expected to comply with the rules, regulations, policies, and procedures of local school districts, and, in most jurisdictions, student teachers may be assigned any duties or responsibilities granted to certificated teachers. This includes the responsibility for student management, curricular goals, etcetera.

One area of continuous concern for principals is determining whether or not student teachers can be used as substitutes for their supervising teachers or, on occasion, other teachers in the school building. Local school district policies are often silent on this issue, and principals should not use student teachers in this manner without consulting superiors and the student teacher's college or university supervisor.

Generally, depending upon individual state statutes, a student teacher may substitute under the following circumstances:

- A substitute teacher is not immediately available.
- The student teacher has been in that student teaching assignment for a minimum number of school days.
- The supervising teacher, the principal of the school, and the university supervisor agree that the student teacher is capable of successfully handling the teaching responsibilities.
- A certificated classroom teacher in an adjacent room or a member of the same teaching team as the student teacher is aware of the absence and agrees to assist the student teacher if needed.
- The principal of the school or the principal's representative is readily available in the building.
- The student teacher is not paid for any substitute service.

Principals are advised to approach the use of student teachers as substitutes with caution and in accordance with local school district policies.

Summary

Although much of the foregoing discussion about the legal aspects of teachers' employment focuses on issues of concern to the school board, it is crucial that principals understand the broad range of legal issues surrounding school employment. This chapter examined the rights of teachers in employment matters. It is clear that laws, policies, practices, or procedures that are arbitrary, capricious, unreasonable, unlawful, or vague violate the due process clause of the Fourteenth Amendment. In working with teachers and other staff, the essential factor for principals is fairness. The fact that the principal is on the front line of most employment issues is sufficient reason to be well informed about the legal dimensions of employment law. It is through a competent teaching force and the principal's leadership that effective schools are created.

The profile of employment relations has been clearly developed in the legal environment. A number of legal principles emerge from the cases examined in this chapter. Perhaps the most important—certainly the areas of dispute that appear most often in litigation—center around situations in which school administrators have forgotten or ignored the following major tenets of law:

- Teachers have constitutionally protected rights that are not surrendered in public employment.
- A constitutionally protected right cannot be the substantial or motivating factor in a school board's decision to dismiss a teacher.
- The exercise of a teacher's constitutional rights to free speech or expression can be balanced against the interests of the school district in the operation of an efficient system.
- Most courts recognize that teachers should not be penalized for their private behavior unless it has a clear impact on their effectiveness as educators.
- Comments made by a teacher, as a citizen, on matters of public concern generally are constitutionally protected. A teacher's comments about the internal concerns of the school that undermine supervisors' authority are not protected.
- Private comments made by a teacher to a superior are given constitutional protection, but may be subject to reasonable time, place, and manner.
- In mixed-motives dismissals, plaintiffs have the initial burden of demonstrating that their conduct was constitutionally protected and was a substantial or motivating factor in the decisions to dismiss. If plaintiffs meet this burden, courts will generally enter a judgment in their favor, unless the defendant school board proves by a preponderance of the evidence that the same decision to dismiss would have been reached in the absence of the protected conduct.

Endnotes

1. Tinker v. Des Moines Independent Community School District, 393 U.S. 503 (1969).
2. See for example, Mann v. Board of Education, 402 N.E. 2d 345 (Ill. App. 5th Dist. 1980).
3. Hanna v. Larche, 363 U.S. (1960).
4. Meyer v. Nebraska, 262 U.S. 390, 399 (1923).
5. School District of Fort Smith v. Maury, 14 S.W. 669 (Ark. 1890).
6. 461 P.2d 375 (Cal. 1969).
7. Board of Education v. Wood, 717 S.W. 2d 837 (Ky. 1986).
8. McClellan v. Board of St. Louis Public Schools, 15 Mo. App. 362, 365 (1885).
9. 99 S.Ct. 1589 (1979).
10. M. McCarthy & N. Cambron-McCabe, Public School Law: Teachers' and Students' Rights (Boston: Allyn and Bacon, 1987), 390.
11. Texas Educational Code Ann. § 21.204 (Vernon Supp. 1982).
12. Allred v. Little Rock School District, 625 S.W. 2d 487 (Ark. 1981).
13. Chapman v. Hamburg Public Schools, 625 S.W. 477 (Ark. 1981).
14. Andrews v. Howard, 291 S.E. 2d 542 (Ga. 1982).

15. Kilpatrick v. Wright, 437 F. Supp. 397 (M.D. Ala. 1977).

16. Johnson v. Selma Board of Education, 356 So. 2d 649 (Ala. 1978).

17. L. French, Teacher Employment, Evaluation and Dismissal, THE SCHOOL PRINCIPAL AND THE LAW (Topeka, Kansas: National Organization on Legal Problems in Education, 1978), 39–40.

18. Perkins v. Board of Directors, 528 F. Supp. 11313 (D. Maine 1981), aff'd 686 F.2d 49 (1st Cir. 1982).

19 Gee v. Alabama State Tenure Commission, 419 So. 2d 227 (Ala. Civ. App. 1982).

20. Buck v. Board of Education, 553 F.2d 3135 2d. Cir. (N.Y. 1977).

21. Doe v. Anker, 451 F. Supp. 241 (S.D.N.Y. 1978).

22. Jordan v. Cagle, 474 F. Supp. 1198 (N.D. Miss. 1979), aff'd 620 F.2d 298 (5th Cir. 1980).

23. Burroughs v. West Windsor Board of School Directors, 446 A. 2d 377 (Vt. 1982).

24. Matthew v. Juras, 519 P.2d 402 (Ore. App. 1980).

25. Vorn v. David Douglas School District No. 40, 608 P.2d 193 (Ore. App. 1980).

26. McCARTHY & CAMBRON-McCABE, supra note 10 (1 ed.), at 113–114.

27. Rouse v. Scottsdale Unified School District, 752 P.2d 22 (Ariz. App. 1987).

28. 426 U.S. 482 (1876).

29. Id. at 493.

30. Id. at 491–92.

31. Supra, note 22.

32. Bogart v. U.S.D. 298, 432 F. Supp. 8895 (D. Kan. 1977).

33. Given v. Western Line Consolidated School District, 439 U.S. 410 (1979).

34. Eckerd v. Indian River School District, 475 F. Supp. 13500 (D. Del. 1979).

35. Id.

36. Note: Some of the case law review for this chapter was conducted by Sparkman and Shoop during research for their book cited in chapter 1 at 7.

37. See for example, Holmes v. Turlington, 480 So. 2d 150 (Fla. App. 1st Dist. 1985); Shelburne v. School Board of Suwannee County, 455 S. 2d 1957 (Fla. App. 1st Dist. 1984); Board of Education v. Sickley, 479 N.E. 2d 1142 (Ill. App. 3rd Dist. 1984); Lile v. Hancock Place School District, 701 S.W. 2d 500 (Mo. App. 1985).

38. F. DELON, LEGAL CONTROLS ON TEACHER CONDUCT: TEACHER DISCIPLINE (Topeka, Kansas National Organization on Legal Problems of Education, 1986), 12.

39. S. Francis and C. Stacey, Law and the Sensual Teacher, PHI DELTA KAPPAN, October 1977, 98.

40. Paust v. Georgian, 179 N.W. (1920).

41. Horosko v. Mt. Pleasant Township School District, 335 Pa. 369, 6 A. 2d 866 (Pa. 1939).

42. Richards v. District School Board, 78d Ore. 621, 153 P. 482 (Ore. 1915).

43. Drake v. Covington County Board of Education, 371 F. Supp. 974 (D.C. Ala. 1974).

44. Yanzick v. School District No. 23, 631 P.2d 431 (Mont. 1982).

45. Id. at 435.

46. Id. at 447.

47. Golden v. Board of Education, 285 S.E. 665 (W. Va. 1982).

48. Id.

49. Fisher v. Snyder, 346 F. Supp. (D.C. Neb. 1972).

50. K. Ostrander, The Teacher's Duty to Privacy: Court Rulings in Sexual Deviancy Cases, PHI DELTA KAPPAN, September 1975, 22.

51. Conway v. Hampshire County Board of Education, 352 S.E. 2d 739 (W. Va. 1986).

52. S. Elam, *Homosexual Teachers: The Hidden Minority,* Phi Delta Kappan, September 1975, 22.

53. Sarac v. State Board of Education, 57 Cal. Rptr. 69 (Cal. Ct. App. 1967).

54. "Morrison v. State Board of Education, 461 P.2d 375 (Cal. 1969).

55. *Supra,* note 53 at 20–21.

56. *Id.*

57. Gaylord v. Tacoma School District, 535 P.2d 804 (Wash. 1975).

58. Ross v. Springfield School District, 6411 P.2d 600 (Ore. App. 1982).

59. *Id.* at 608.

60. *Id.*

61. Terry v. Houston County Board of Education, 342 S.E. 2d 774 (Ga. App. 1986).

62. Parmeter v. Feinburg, 482 N.Y.S 2d 80 (A.D. 3d Dept. 1984).

63. Beilan v. Board of Education, 357 U.S. 399 (1958).

64. *Id.*

65. Granderson v. Orleans Parish School Board, 216 So. 2d 643 (La. Ct. App. 1968).

66. Hatta v. Board of Education Union Endicott Central School District, 394 N.Y.S. 2d 301 (N.Y. App. Div. 1977).

67. Pratt v. Alabama State Tenure Commission, 394 So. 2d 18 (Ala. Civ. App. 1980).

68. Wright v. Superintending School Commission, 331 A. 2d 640 (Me. 1976).

69. Tichenor v. Orleans Parish School Board, 144 So. 2d 603 (La. Ct. App. 1962).

70. Board of Directors of Sioux City v. Moroz, 295 N.W. 2d 447 (Iowa 1980).

71. Gwathmey v. Atkinson, 447 F. Supp. 1113 (D. Va. 1976). *See also,* Kinsella v. Board of Education, 64 A.D. 2d 738, 407 N.Y.S. 2d 78 (1978).

72. Scheelhasse v. Woodbury Central School District, 488 F.2d 237 (8th Cir. 1973).

73. Karstetter v. Evans, 3500 F. Supp. 209 (D. Tex. 1971).

74. Aaron v. Alabama State Tenure Commission, 407 So. 2d 136 (Ala. Ct. App. 1981).

75. Levyn v. Amback, 445 N.Y.S. 2d 303 (N.Y. App. Div. 1981).

76. Schulz v. Board of Education of School District of Freemont, 315 N.W. 2d 633 (Neb. 1982).

77. Sanders v. Board of Education, 263 N.W. 2d 461 (Neb. 1978).

78. *See for example,* Board of Education v. Lammle, 596 P.2d 48 (Ariz. App. 1979); Fernald v. City of Ellsworth Superintending School Committee, 342 A. 2d 704 (Me. 1975).

79. Rust v. Clark County School District, 683 P.2d 23 (Nev. 1984).

80. *See for example,* Stat *ex rel.* Steele v. Board of Education, 40 So. 2d 689 (Ala. 1949); State Tenure Commission v. Madison Cty. Board of Education, 213 So. 2d 823 Ala. 1968); Board of Trustees v. Colwell, 611 P.2d 427 (Wyo. 1980).

81. School District No. 8, Pinal County v. Superior Court, 102 Ariz. 478, 433 P.2d 28 (1967).

82. Keene v. Creswell School District No. 40, 643 P.2d 407 (Ore. Ct. App. 1982).

83. Booher v. Hogans, 468 F. Supp. 28, 32 (E.D. Tenn., 1978).

84. Heath v. Alabama State Tenure Commission, 401 So. 2d 68, 709 (Ala. Civ. App. 1981).

85. *Id.*

86. 70 A.L.R. 3d 83, 87.

87. Wright v. Superintending School Commission, 331 A. 2d. 640 (Me. 1976).

88. Shepard v. South Harrison R-II School District, 718 S.W. 2d 195 (Mo. App. 1986).

89. *Id.*

90. Thompson v. Wake County Board of Education, 230 S.E. 2d 164 (N.C. Ct. App. 1976).

91. Levyn v. Amback, 445 N.Y.S. 2d 303 (N.Y. App. Div. 1981).

92. Board of School District v. Fasnacht, 441 A. 2d 481 (Pa. Commw. Ct. 1982).

93. Board of Education v. Lammle, 596 P.2d 48 (Ariz. Ct. App. 1979).

94. Kennedy v. Board of Education, 314 N.W. 2d 14 (Neb. 1981).

95. *Supra* note 93.

96. Anderson v. Central Point School District No. 6, 746 F.2d 505 (9th Cir. 1984).

97. *See for example,* Pickering v. Board of Education, 391 U.S. 563 (1968); Tinker v. Des Moines Independent Community School District, 393 U.S. 503 (1969); Given v. Western Line Consolidated School District, 439 U.S. 410 (1979).

98. Pickering v. Board of Education, 391 U.S. 563, 568 (1968).

99. *Id.* at 564.

100. *Id.* at 569–70.

101. *Id.* at 570.

102. *Id.* at 572–73.

103. *Id.* at 574.

104. Connick v. Myers, 51 L.W. 4436 (April 19, 1983).

105. *Id.*

106. *Id.* at 4437.

107. *Id.* at 4438.

108. *Id.*

109. 429 U.S. 274 (1977).

110. *Id.* at 282.

111. *Id.* at 283.

112. *Id.* at 285.

113. *Id.* at 287.

114. Doyle v. Mt. Healthy City Board of Education, 670 F.2d 59 (6th Cir. 1982).

115. *See for example,* Laird v. Independent School District No. 317, 346 N.W. 2d 153 (Minn. 1984); Theros v. Warwich Board of School Directors, 401 A. 2d 575 (Pa. Commw. 1979).

116. EDUCATIONAL RESEARCH SERVICE, INDICATORS OF FUTURE SCHOOL ENROLL-MENTS: A REFERENCE MANUAL FOR PLANNERS (Arlington, Vir.: ERS, 1980).

117. Ward v. Viborg School District No. 605, 319 N.W. 2d 502 (S.D. 1982).

118. Green v. Jenkintown School District, 441 A. 2d 816 (Pa. Commw. Ct. 1982).

119. Godfrey v. Penn Valley Area School District, 449 A 765d (Pa. Commw. Ct. 1982).

120. Rappold v. Board of Education, Cleveland Hills Union Free School District, 447 N.Y.S. 2d 126 (N.Y. App. Div. 1982).

121. Hayes v. Board of Education of Auburn, 431 N.E. 2d 690 (Ill. App. Ct. 1982).

122. Dykeman v. Board of Education of the School District of Coleridge, 316 N.W. 2d 69 (Neb. 1982).

123. *See for example,* Greminger v. Seaborne, 584 F. 385 A. 2d 275 (8th Cir. 1978); Eckerd v. Indian River School District, 475 F. Supp. 1350 (D. Del. 1979).

124. *See for example,* McKelvey v. Colonial School District, 35 Pa. Commw. 264 (1978).

125. *See for example,* Dore v. Board of Education, 499 A. 2d 547 (N.J. Super. Ct. App. Div. 1982); Lipan v. Board of Education, 295 S.E. 2d 44 (W. Va. 1982).

126. *See for example,* Bomhuff v. White, 526 F. Supp. 488 (D. Ariz. 1981); Perry v. Sindermann, 408 U.S. 593 (1972); Dicello v. Board of Directors, 380 A. 2d 944 (Pa. Commw. 1977).

127. Brooks v. School Board of Brevard County, 419 So. 2d 659 (Fla. App. 1982).

128. Steward v. Board of Education, 630 S.W. 2d 130 (Mo. App. 1982).

129. Curlee v. Donaldson, 233 S.W. 2d 746 (Mo. App. 1950).

130. Ryan v. Superintendent of Schools, 373 N.E. 2d 1178 (Mass. 1978).

131. *Supra,* note 129.

132. Mason County Board of Education v. State Superintendent, 295 S.E. 2d 719 (W. Va. 1982).

133. *Id.*

134. 42 U.S.C. § 1988 (1976).

135. Johnson v. George Highway Express, Inc., 488 F. 2d 714, 717–719 (5th Cir. 1974).

136. *Supra,* note 128.

137. J. Yates and J. Johnson, *A National Survey of Student Teaching Programs,* (Unpublished manuscript, Northern Illinois University, 1982) as quoted in Morris et al., (Eds.), *Legal Issues Related to Field-Based Excellence in Teacher Education,* JOURNAL OF TEACHER EDUCATION, M-A11983 xxxiv, no. 2, 3.

138. *Id.*

SECTION THREE

The Legal Relationship of the Principal to the Student

Introduction

Section III focuses on the relationship of the principal to the student. It provides principals with a framework in which to help students grow into responsible adults. In order to understand the relationship between the school and the student, it is necessary to understand how this relationship has emerged in response to the changing associations between the family, the school, the larger society, and the law.

Early in the history of this country, education was primarily the responsibility of the family. As society gradually accepted the need for general education for its children, public, tax-supported schools developed. As the schools took over the responsibility of education, a tradition of administrative authority developed. With this development there arose a need for educators to supervise and stand in loco parentis (in the place of the parent.) Gradually the principal and teacher became responsible to the student in a "parental" relationship.

The concept of in loco parentis developed as the community gave school authorities almost complete control over students. Educators were thought to be experts in what was best for the student, and the responsibility for disciplining and directing the work and the development of the student was regulated by the general concept of reasonableness. The courts traditionally found that various forms of punishment were necessary and even essential to ensure the orderly operation of a school. Courts have upheld such punishments as withholding privileges, removal from classroom, suspension or expulsion, detention after school if no hazard is incurred, and reasonable corporal punishment.[1]

In the past when parents and the school were in conflict, the courts usually made an assumption in favor of the school. They tended to believe that "education should be left to the educators" and were reluctant to overrule what they believed to be the in loco parentis responsibility of the school. An example of this early judicial attitude is seen in the case of a young boy who was expelled from school for what the school called "conduct that tended to cause confusion and distraction of other scholars from their studies and recitation." The court accepted the decision of the educational experts and did not intervene in this case. This decision reinforced the concept that schools have the right to discipline as well as educate students and strengthened the concept of in loco parentis. [2]

Courts stated that they had other and more important functions to perform than that of hearing complaints of disaffected students against school rules. They argued that "respect for constituted authority and obedience thereto was an essential lesson to qualify for the duties of citizenship, and the school was an appropriate place to teach that lesson." [3]

Although contemporary courts maintained the right of the school to regulate its own activities, an increasing number of citizens challenged this right. When courts were first asked to decide whether the authority of the school was superior to the authority of the parent, they reaffirmed the authority of the school. Education continued to be seen as a privilege, not a right, as courts ruled that school board decisions were final insofar as they related to the rights of a student to enjoy school privileges. [4]

In the early 1940s the courts began to take a more critical look at the process of education decision making. In the 1943 case of West Virginia Board of Education v. Barnette, [5] the court ruled that students had a constitutional right to refuse to follow the school requirement to salute the American flag in the school room. The court stated, ". . . local authorities, in compelling the flag salute and pledge, transcend constitutional limitations on their power and invade the sphere of intellect and spirit which it is the purpose of the First Amendment to our Constitution to reserve from all official control."

The attitude of courts shifted from one of "hands off" to one of critical examination. The concept that students retain their constitutional protection and that the need to protect individual liberty transcends the right of the school to control its students began to gain acceptance.

By 1954 it was clear that the courts were no longer going to leave education to the educators. Although Brown v. Board of Education of Topeka, Kansas is primarily remembered because it ruled that racial segregation of students in public schools denied minority students equal protection under law and was unconstitutional, [6] it is also significant because it called into question the judgment of school officials. The Brown decisions marked a point of departure. In 1955 the court ruled that all cases arising under the Brown decision should come under the jurisdiction of the federal district court.[7] From these cases forward, the professional expertise of the educator was open to review by the courts.

A series of cases in the mid-1960s reinforced the fact that the protections provided by the United States Constitution and the Bill of Rights were not for adults alone and called into question the concept of in loco parentis. The case of Kent v. United States[8] laid the groundwork for the "student rights" cases that followed. The court held that the school's responsibility to act in the place of the parent did not give it the right to deny the student the essentials of due process and fair treatment. This decision reaffirmed the right of the student to procedural due process.

Due process is not a technical concept with specific step-by-step requirements. It is, rather, the guarantee that life, liberty, or property will not be taken without fair treatment.[9] Courts have ruled that the right to an education is a liberty interest that must be protected.

The relationship of the student to the school was further refined in 1964, as a result of a case involving a minor, Gerald Gault. In responding to this case, where due process was not afforded Gault, the United States Supreme Court reaffirmed that the basic requirements of due process must be followed in all cases and that juveniles as well as adults deserve due process and a fair trial. The court was clear in its statement that neither the protection of the United States Bill of Rights nor the fairness demanded by the United States Constitution is for adults alone. Accordingly, educators across the United States received a warning that the traditional role of the school, standing in the place of the parent, had changed. The principal now had the dual responsibility of protecting the rights of the total student body while at the same time protecting the rights of individual students.[10]

This new role of the school principal was made even more obvious by a series of events that began in December of 1965. In Des Moines, Iowa a group of students and adults decided to publicize their objections to the hostilities in Vietnam and their support for a truce by wearing black arm bands. Some principals learned of this plan, met, and adopted a policy stating that any student who wore such an arm band to school and who refused to remove it when asked would be suspended until the arm band was removed. When several students wore the arm bands and refused to remove them, they were suspended.

The constitutional issue at stake in Tinker v. Des Moines Independent Community School District was the right of students to express opinions versus the right of local school authorities to regulate the operation of the schools.[11] The United States Supreme Court held that the wearing of arm bands by students was protected under the Constitution, as arm bands are considered "symbolic speech," which is related to "pure speech." In so ruling, the Court stated that, in the absence of any evidence that the wearing of the arm bands created a disturbance, the students had a right to wear them. The Court asserted that First Amendment rights, applied in light of the special characteristics of the school environment, are available to teachers and students. "It can hardly be argued that either students or teachers shed their constitutional rights to freedom of speech at the schoolhouse gate. This has been the unmistakable holding of this Court for almost 50 years."[12]

School administrators traditionally have argued that it is necessary to regulate students' behavior because of the potential for disruption. In order to justify the prohibition of a particular expression of opinion, school officials must be able to show that their action was motivated by something more than the mere desire to avoid discomfort and unpleasantness that may accompany an unpopular view.[13] According to the Tinker court, ". . . in our system, state-operated schools may not be enclaves of totalitarianism."[14] This decision marked the beginning of an entirely new era, in which some of the power to control students was transferred from school officials to the courts.

One important consequence of the Tinker decision was increased interest in the area of students' rights and responsibilities. In the early 1970s many statewide efforts were begun with the goal of defining the legal relationship between the student and the school. Few areas of education were the subject of so much controversy. During this period, numerous and seemingly contradictory regulations and court decisions emerged. Many school systems and state departments of education began to assess the adequacy of their existing policies and regulations. The concept of "due process" replaced in loco parentis. Due process legitimized the concept that every student accused of an offense must be guaranteed his or her "day in court." The word due is derived from duty. It means that the state (in this case the school) has the duty to see that all citizens, (in this case the students) are treated equally and fairly. The exact elements of due process have been debated in the courts and in the schools since the Gault and Tinker decisions.

Endnotes

1. K. Alexander, R. Corns & W. McCann, Public School Law (St. Paul, Minn.: West, 1969), 622.
2. Hodgkins v. Rockerport, 105 Mass. 475 (1870).
3. Pugsley v. Sellmeyer, 250 S.W. 538 (Ark. 1923).
4. Stromberg v. French, 236 N.W. 477 (N.D. 1931).
5. West Virginia Board of Education v. Barnette, 319 U.S. 624 (1943).
6. Brown v. Bd. of Educ. of Topeka, 347 U.S. 453 (1954).
7. Brown v. Bd. of Educ. of Topeka, 349 U.S. 294 (1955).
8. Kent v. United States, 383 U.S. 541 (1966).

9. U.S. Const. amend. XIV, § 1.
10. *In re* Gault, 387 U.S. 541 (1966).
11. Tinker v. Des Moines Independent Community School District, 393 U.S. 503 (1969).
12. *Id.*
13. ALEXANDER, *supra,* at 506.
14. *Id.* at 511.

CHAPTER FIVE

Academic Issues

Grade Assignment

Scenario 5.1: Ronnie Silver, a high school English teacher, had a class rule that stated, "A student must earn a 70 percent average in order to pass the course." She included attendance and class participation in her grading requirements. Sandy Grogan often came to Silver's class late, seldom handed in her assignments on time, and was surly and belligerent in class. Although Sandy earned above average grades on her tests, her grade was reduced to below 70 percent because of her behavior.

Scenario 5.2: Robert Buck passed all of his courses, but failed to pass a district-administered competency test. He was prevented from graduating with his class.

Scenario 5.3: Ralph Edwards was identified as being moderately mentally disabled. Although he attended classes with nondisabled students, he did not do the same level of academic work. At graduation he was given a "special education" diploma.

Points to Consider: How much discretionary power do teachers have in assigning grades? Can a student's grade be reduced because of behavior or absences? Can a school prevent students from graduating if they fail a minimum competency test? Can a regular high school diploma be denied to a disabled student?

Schools use a variety of criteria to determine whether a student may be promoted or receive a diploma; such as, "teacher assigned grades, student performance on standardized tests, pupil performance on basic competency tests, student attendance records, and student conduct records."[1] As school boards throughout the country have adopted more stringent promotion standards for students, policies regarding grading, promotion, and retention have increasingly been challenged in court.

Courts have traditionally been reluctant to substitute their judgment for the expertise of educators. They recognize the classification of students as being rationally related to the permissible governmental end of furthering the education of students, and therefore they have supported the authority of teachers to assign grades.[2] Policies authorizing retention for students who do not perform satisfactory work have been found to be both acceptable and desirable.[3] It is unlikely that a teacher's grade assignment will be successfully challenged in court, unless the teacher has discriminated against an identifiable or protected class of students or has been arbitrary.

Minimum Competency Tests

The majority of states have enacted some type of minimum competency testing. In a number of these states, students must pass a test as a prerequisite to receive a high school diploma. These tests have been challenged as denying procedural due process or denying equal protection. The most well-known challenge to the use of competency tests to determine whether students should receive a diploma is the *Debra P.* case.[4] In this case the State of Florida required all students to pass a functional literacy examination in order to receive a high school diploma. A suit was filed, under the due process and equal protection clauses of the Fourteenth Amendment, that challenged the use of the test because students were not given adequate notice of the test requirement for graduation and, it was alleged, the test was discriminatory against black students. The district court held that diploma sanctions in Florida could not be enforced until the effects of prior school desegregation had been eliminated. The federal court of appeals affirmed the district court's findings and held that after the students that were not educated in a unitary system had graduated, Florida could deny diplomas to students who did not pass the Florida test.[5]

Whether state mandated or locally developed, courts have upheld requirements for students to pass certain tests to qualify for a high school diploma. However, courts have ruled that students must have adequate notice of the requirements, be provided with remedial classes if they need them, be tested with tests that are reliable and valid, be tested with nondiscriminatory tests, and be tested on what they were actually taught.[6]

Minimum Competency Tests and Disabled Students

The minimum competency test adopted by the school board of Peoria, Illinois required that students pass the test before being eligible for a regular high school diploma. Those who failed the test were eligible to receive only a certificate of program completion. This practice was challenged in a federal district court in 1982, when several disabled students who failed the minimal competency test were denied a regular diploma and were given, instead, the certificate of program completion. The state superintendent of public instruction, on administrative appeal, ruled in favor of the students and ordered the school board to grant the students a regular diploma. A federal court, however, determined that the minimal competency test used in Peoria was a reasonable means to determine the effectiveness of the educational program and held that the test did not have to be modified to take into account a student's lack of mental ability or capacity. The court held that regular high school diplomas could be denied disabled students who failed to pass the competency test.[7]

Based on such court rulings, testing programs must not perpetuate segregation, "track" or in any way promote segregation of students, be punitive in nature, or deny equal protection guaranteed for students who had attended segregated schools for some portion of their education.[8]

Grade Reduction

Student Attendance

Some school districts have policies that authorize the reduction of a student's grade or the denial of credit in a course as punishment for truancy. Sometimes this is a district policy, and other times it is the result of the unilateral decision of a teacher or principal. Although the courts are reluctant to interfere with the academic decisions of local school officials, they have intervened in cases where the penalty was out of proportion to the conduct being punished[9] or in violation of the state's attendance statute, and in cases where the punishment did not bear a reasonable relationship to some legitimate educational purpose. Thus, punishment will not be allowed if there is a sufficient disparity between the punishment and the offense.[10]

Courts have held that students are entitled to proper notification of the process available to contest any penalty before a grade reduction can be made. Such penalties must be administered free from teacher subjectivity.[11] Courts will be more willing to require a student to receive a hearing in cases where there was no school board policy authorizing the use of grade reduction for truancy.

If a school board desires to reduce grades as a punishment for truancy, it should adopt a policy that contains a prohibition against unauthorized absenteeism and truancy, gives notice that such absenteeism will result in the reduction of the student's grades in the classes missed, establishes a clear relationship between the absenteeism and the grade reduction, and provides that the final determination of the grade to be given under the policy would be left to the subjective analysis of the classroom teacher(s) involved.[12]

Student Misconduct

Courts have generally not been supportive of school policies that allow students to be both suspended and penalized academically for their absences. In a Pennsylvania case a student drank a glass of wine in a restaurant while on a field trip with her class. In addition to being expelled from the cheerleading squad and National Honor Society, she was suspended from school for five days and had each of her grades reduced two percentage points for each day of absence. The court was not sympathetic toward a rule that would penalize a student academically for a disciplinary offense. It clearly stated that academic grades should not be enhanced or reduced based on activities unrelated to academic performance.[13]

Academic and State Standards for Athletes

Scenario 5.4:   Kenny Striker was a three-year letterman on the football team. His school district had a policy that required all students who participate in any extracurricular activity to maintain a "C" average in all academic courses. Kenny's average fell below this standard, and he was removed from the football team. His parents argued that this action would deny Kenny an opportunity to receive a college football scholarship and was, therefore, an unconstitutional denial of his liberty interest.

Scenario 5.5:   The state high school activities association approved a rule that prevented a student from participating in any extracurricular activity in the semester following the student's 19th birthday. David Allen's 19th birthday was December 29. However, his school allowed David to play on the basketball team in the second semester.

Points to Consider: Can an individual school approve a state policy, or create a local policy, that connects participation in school-sponsored activities with student grades? Are school districts required to conform to all rules and regulations of their state activities associations?

No Pass/No Play Rules

There is a trend for states to adopt uniform guidelines governing academic eligibility standards for athletic and nonathletic extracurricular activities. The Texas legislature was the first to enact a "no pass/no play" statute. This legislation grew out of a concern that participation in extracurricular activities necessarily meant time away from studies, and that the school day should be preserved for academic pursuits. The Texas statute was intended to encourage students to improve their grades by rewarding them with the right to participate in outside activities for achieving satisfactory grades.

In 1984 this statute was challenged as unconstitutional because it classified students by achievement levels. The Texas Supreme Court ruled in *Spring Branch v. Stamos*[14] that there is no "fundamental right" to participate in extracurricular activities. In so ruling, it reasoned that providing quality education to students in Texas public schools was a legitimate state purpose, and it was reasonable for legislators to use academic classifications to further that interest. The court further indicated that even though there may be a "disproportionate impact on minority and learning disabled students, that alone will not support a finding that the statute [violated the constitution]."[15]

In 1984 the West Virginia State Board of Education established a similar policy, but one that differentiated between regular and disabled students.[16] Under this policy the Secondary School Activities Commission was empowered to adopt a statewide regulation setting standards for all nonacademic activities in grades 7–12, such as interscholastic athletics, cheerleading, student government, class offices, and clubs that are not closely related to the program of study. Disabled students were protected by the policy. If grades were given to disabled students, all grades received from placements in both regular classrooms and special education classrooms were to be included when computing the GPA. Students placed in ungraded programs would be eligible for participation in extracurricular activities if their records indicated that they were making satisfactory progress in meeting the objectives of their individualized education plan.[17]

A Montana school district adopted a higher standard for extracurricular participation than was required by the state for either extracurricular participation or graduation. When this policy was challenged, the Montana Supreme Court ruled that although extracurricular participation is clearly subject to constitutional protection because of the "extreme importance attached to the various elements of education by the people of Montana," the district's policy was substantially related to an important governmental objective, and the school district's standard was upheld.[18]

A number of states have delegated the enactment of appropriate standards to individual school districts or state athletic associations. In 1990 the Kentucky Court of Appeals ruled that a school district may deny athletic participation to students who fail to maintain a satisfactory grade average. The case involved a student who was barred from participating in interscholastic wrestling competition because his grade point average was below the required 2.0. The student sued the school district, claiming that his exclusion was an unconstitutional violation of his civil and property rights. The court dismissed the charges and declared that the policy was reasonable and legitimate. The court ruled that "a student has neither a property interest nor any fundamental right to participate in extracurricular activities in Kentucky."[19]

Extracurricular Activities

Students who participate in extracurricular activities are usually subject to the rules and regulations of state high school activities associations or other voluntary associations of member schools. These associations have rules governing eligibility, transfer, and discipline. Legal questions often emerge when school authorities deny student participation in certain extracurricular activities under rules promulgated by state associations.

Generally, the courts will not interfere with the rules and procedures of state associations unless there is fraud, denial of a student's substantive rights or procedural due process, lack of jurisdiction, or the organization has exceeded its general powers.[20] However, these rules must be based on legal and rational reasons and must be applied uniformly.[21] Schools may not arbitrarily allow a privilege to some students and not to others. If a school or association can show a rational basis for excluding some students, then such decisions will withstand court scrutiny unless the basis for exclusion is illegal; for example, racial classifications.[22]

The courts have held that participation in extracurricular activities is a privilege and not a property right. A privilege may be withdrawn by a school or a voluntary association if a student fails to qualify for it.[23] Since participation in such activities is not a property right, due process is not required in order to withdraw that privilege. However, a federal court has suggested that total exclusion from extracurricular activities for a lengthy period of time, depending on the circumstances, could be sufficient deprivation to implicate due process.[24]

Historically, residency requirements and transfer rules that require a definite period of residence in a school district before a student may participate in athletics or that prohibit for a fixed time the right of transfer students to play have been upheld by the courts as a reasonable exercise of state power.[25] In addition, such transfer rules have been found not to violate the United States Constitution.[26]

However, there is a trend for courts to strip away some of the authority of state high school athletic associations. In 1988 a student transferred from a Tennessee private school to a public school in Nashville. Under a Tennessee Secondary School Athletic Association's (TSSAA) rule, the student was barred from interscholastic athletic participation for a year after transfer. The TSSAA received numerous appeals from the student's parents and the high school, requesting an exception to the transfer rule. The TSSAA found no hardship and denied each appeal.

It was then determined that the student had a learning disability and was certified as handicapped under the federal Education of the Handicapped Act (EHA). The parents sued the TSSAA, claiming that its refusal to allow their son to participate in interscholastic sports deprived him of his rights under the EHA. The United States District Court ruled that although the EHA does not require local and state education agencies to provide extracurricular activities for handicapped students, it does prohibit discrimination against those students.[27] Therefore, the student was allowed to participate in athletics. Other challenges to state athletic associations regulatory powers have occurred in Michigan, Louisiana, California, New York, and West Virginia.[28]

Since courts have held that extracurricular activities are a privilege and not a right, school authorities can discipline students by withholding the privilege to participate in these activities. School authorities should make sure that their rules demonstrate a recognized, legitimate educational purpose or that they can be reasonably judged to deter the targeted misconduct. These rules should be definite and provide sufficient notice of their requirements.

Married Students

School rules that exclude the participation of married students in extracurricular activities have been found illegal by the courts.[29] In the past it was not uncommon for the courts to find such rules forbidding the participation of married students in school activities to be within the discretion of local school boards.[30] The courts now have guaranteed married students the same rights as any other student.

Endnotes

1. J. Walden and L. Gamble, *Student Promotion and Retention Policies: Legal Considerations,* JOURNAL OF LAW & EDUCATION, October 1985, 610.
2. Sandlin v. Johnson, 643 F.2d 1027 (4th Cir. 1981).
3. Board of Curators, Univ. Of Missouri v. Horowitz, 435 U.S. 78, 88–90 (1978).
4. Debra P. v. Turlington, 644 F.2d 397 (5th Cir. 1981)
5. Debra P. v. Ralph D. Turlington, 730 F.2d 1405 (11th Cir, 1984)
6. *Id.*
7. Brookhart v. Illinois State Bd. of Educ., 534 F. Supp. 725 (C.D. Ill. 1982).
8. Pell, *Functional Literacy Testing,* 3 ED. LAW REP. 469, 472 (1982).
9. Knight v. Bd. of Educ., 348 N.E. 2d 299 (Ill. App. Ct. 1976).
10. Jacobs v. Benedict, 301 N.E. 2d 723 (Ct. Common Pleas 1973).
11. Hamer v. Bd. of Educ., 383 N.E. 2d 231 (Ill. App. Ct. 1978).
12. L. Liggett, *Discipline by Grade Reduction and Grade Denial Based on Attendance,* in SCHOOL LAW IN CHANGING TIMES (Topeka, Kansas: National Organization on Legal Problems of Education, 1982), 41.
13. Katzman v. Cumberland Valley School Dist., 479 A.2d 671 (Pa. Commw. 1984).
14. 695 S.W. 2d 556 (Tex., 1984) at 559.
15. Stamos v. Spring Branch ISD, No. 85, 25201 at 1 (334th D.Tex. Sept. 30, 1986).

16. West Virginia Code 18-2-5 (1984 replacement vol.).

17. Id., § (1) g.

18. State *ex rel* Bartness v. Board of Trustees of School District No. 1, 726 2d 801 (Montana, 1986).

19. Thompson v. Tates Creek H.S. Lexington, 786 S.W. 2d 879.

20. J. Abbott, *The Developing Case Law of Public School Extra-Curriculum Activities*, in School Law In Contemporary Society, (Topeka, Kansas: National Organization on Legal Problems of Education, 1980), 231, 236.

21. *Id.*

22. *Id.*

23. Menke v. Ohio High Sch. Athletic Ass'n, 441 N.E. 2d 620 (Ohio Ct. App. 1981).

24. Pegram v. Nelson, 469 F. Supp. 1134, 1140 (M.D.N.C. 1979).

25. Kulouitz v. Illinois High Sch. Ass'n, 462 F. Supp. 875 (N.D. Ill, 1978); Kriss v. Brown, 390 N.E. 2d 193 (Ind. App. 1979).

26. *In re* U.S. *ex rel.* Missouri State High Sch. Activities Ass'n, 682 F.2d 147 (8th Cir. 1982).

27. Crocker v. Tennessee Secondary School Athletic Association (735 F. Supp. 753).

28. Athletic Director and Coach, vol. VII, no. 9, September 1990, 2.

29. Holt v. Shelton, 341 F. Supp. 821 (M.D.Tenn. 1972). *See also,* Davis v. Meek, 344 F. Supp. 298 (N.D. Ohio 1972); Bell v. Lone Oak Independent Sch. Dist., 507 S.W. 2d 636 (Tex. Civ. App. 1974).

30. State *ex rel.* Baker v. Stevenson, 189 N.E. 2d 181 (Ohio C.P. 1962).

CHAPTER SIX

Students' First Amendment Rights

Introduction

The rights of students to exercise freedom of speech have undergone several major transformations. Court decisions upholding schools' rights to set certain limits on student speech reflect a changing interpretation of the First Amendment's ban on making laws ". . . prohibiting the free exercise thereof; or abridging the freedom of speech, or of the press; or the right of the people peaceably to assemble. . . ."[1]

Historically, there has been disagreement over the way this amendment should be applied. Some believe that the First Amendment was written primarily to protect citizens from being punished for political dissent.[2] Others take the broader view that the First Amendment extends protection to all expression, leaving only overt, anti-social, physical behavior outside its shelter. Oliver Wendell Holmes proposed, in his famous "clear and present danger" doctrine, that speech loses its First Amendment protection when it conflicts with other important social interests.[3]

Even proponents of a "full protection" theory of freedom of speech set limits on speech. For example, obscene telephone calls, threatening gestures, disruptive heckling, and sit-ins have been classified as "actions" rather than protected expression. Recent court interpretations support the argument that each generation should be free to interpret the provisions of the Constitution in light of present-day circumstances.

Symbolic Expression

Symbolic expression is nonverbal expression that conveys the personal ideas, feelings, attitudes, or opinions of an individual. Symbolic expression can be exhibited in a variety of forms; that is, physical gesture, clothing, hair, buttons, badges, arm bands, etcetera. Symbolic expression contains an element of subjectivity, and in determining whether or not a form of expression is, in fact, symbolic, some consideration must be given to the intention of the persons who are expressing themselves in an ostensibly symbolic manner.

In 1943 the United States Supreme Court heard its first freedom of expression case that involved the public schools. The case was brought against a West Virginia public school system by the parents of children who refused to participate in the daily ritual of saluting the American flag because they were Jehovah's Witnesses. Although the parents objected to this requirement as a violation of their religious beliefs, the Supreme Court decided this case on free speech grounds. The Court ruled that ". . . the flag salute is a form of utterance. Symbolism is a primitive but effective way of communicating ideas . . . a short-cut from mind to mind."[4] Therefore, the students could not be required to salute the American flag.

During most of this century, students were regularly disciplined for engaging in expression that displeased school authorities. A major turning point in the courts' interpretation of the First Amendment occurred in the 1969 landmark case of *Tinker v. Des Moines*.[5] In this case, discussed in detail earlier in this section, the United States Supreme Court declared that students are "persons" under the Constitution, who must be accorded all of its rights and protections, especially the right to freedom of expression, and that the school board's subjective fear of some disruption was not enough to override the students' rights to express their political beliefs.[6]

The Supreme Court noted that schools cannot be "enclaves of totalitarianism" and in this case clearly affirmed that students possess fundamental rights that schools must respect. However, a controlling principle of *Tinker* was that ". . . conduct by the student, in class or out of it, which for any reason disrupts class work or involves substantial disorder or invasion of the rights of others is, of course, not immunized by the constitutional guarantee of freedom of speech."[7]

Symbolic Expression Through Buttons, Badges, Arm Bands

Scenario 6.1:   The community had recently become multicultural. In the process there had been some racial conflict between white and Hispanic students. A group of students started a "white power" club, the members of which wore "White Power" buttons to school.

Points to Consider: Is there a protected right for students to express themselves through badges, buttons, and the like? May schools ban the wearing of symbols that school officials find offensive?

Students' rights to wear insignia, buttons, badges, arm bands, and other symbols of political or controversial significance are firmly protected by the Constitution and the courts. Like other student rights, this right may be forfeited when the wearing of such symbols causes a material disruption of the educational process. A federal appeals court held that school authorities may establish policies regulating these activities when the rule is not arbitrary and is applied, without exception, to all insignia and not just one type of insignia.[8]

This decision addressed a situation in which a rule had been a long-standing policy of a school where a good deal of prior disruption of the educational process had resulted from the wearing of insignia. This case dealt specifically with racial tensions and an explosive school environment that made severe disruption imminent. In situations where the wearing of insignia has not caused, and probably will not cause, material disruption of the educational process, courts have generally ruled that students cannot be deprived of their basic rights to express themselves by wearing insignia.[9]

Symbolic Expression Through Dress and Hair Style

Scenario 6.2: Because of its concern about the increase in drug use by high school students, the school board approved a dress code that prohibited students from wearing T-shirts that promoted drugs, alcohol, sex, or violence. A group of sixty students came to school dressed in T-shirts that mocked the dress code. Written on the front of the shirts was, "This shirt does not pertain to sex, drugs, alcohol, or violence." And on the back was, "Where are our rights?" The principal ordered the students to turn their shirts inside out. A number of students refused and were sent home for the rest of the day.

Scenario 6.3: Pam Stroop got a phone call from the principal of her son Scott's school informing her that Scott would be suspended if he did not get his hair cut above his collar and ears. Scott was a member of a rock band, and his hair style was part of the band's "image."

Points to Consider: May a school regulate student dress or hair style? May a school overrule parents' decisions about appropriate dress?

Some schools have implemented grooming policies in an attempt to improve school discipline and bring order to the classroom environment. Among the items prohibited by various school dress codes have been articles of clothing associated with gang activities, shorts, tight or immodest clothing, earrings for boys, undergarments worn outside of clothes, sweatpants and jogging suits, torn clothing, visible gold or jewelry with semi-precious stones, night clothes, muscle shirts, halter tops, and fur coats. While some of these items of dress have been banned as a matter of taste, others have been outlawed to protect the students from becoming the victims of theft or violence. Some school districts have become so concerned about the expense of the clothing students consider to be "in" that they have even proposed the adoption of uniforms for all students.

When dress codes and grooming standards have been challenged, the courts have not always agreed regarding the authority schools have to control students' appearance. In 1970 a federal court of appeals concluded that compelled conformity to conventional standards of appearance does not seem a justifiable part of the educational process.[10] However, in a 1971 case in which students claimed that personal grooming was a liberty right, the court rejected the claim and upheld the right of elementary and secondary schools to promulgate dress codes.[11] In another case, in the same year, the same court ruled that students at a public community college did have a liberty right to personal grooming.[12] However, the majority of these decisions have recognized a constitutional protection for students to regulate their own appearance within the bounds and standards of common decency and modesty.[13]

The courts have tended to distinguish hair from clothing, and have indicated that restrictions on hair style are more serious invasions of individual freedom than are clothing regulations.[14] However, courts do give schools wide discretion to regulate appearance in the interests of health, safety, order, or discipline. In 1984 a federal court of appeals upheld a high school's right to set policy prohibiting certain types of facial hair for athletes on the school's football and basketball teams.[15]

Symbolic Expression Through Physical Gestures

Scenario 6.4: Ralph Darnell had a history of conflict with various teachers at the high school. During one such conflict he "gave the finger" to a substitute teacher. Upon hearing of this behavior, the principal suspended Ralph.

Points to Consider: Do students have the right to use obscene gestures? Is there a difference between banning an obscene gesture and a less offensive gesture such as the "peace sign" or "power to the people" sign?

Most people are familiar with a variety of physical gestures used by groups or individuals to express an idea, concept, or opinion. Though most would agree that obscene, disrespectful, or obviously annoying gestures should be banned from schools, from a policy context they should be viewed on the basis of the degree to which such gestures impinge on the rights of others and their likelihood of creating substantial disruption.

Gang Regalia and Behaviors

Scenario 6.5: Rachel Moore, a member of the school board, was asked by a parent what she thought about the gang situation at the high school. When Moore asked what he had heard, the parent said, "Well, I've heard that there have been several fights recently between members of rival gangs. In fact, my daughter won't wear red or blue hair ribbons because she's afraid she'll be hassled. I gather that one gang wears red neck scarves while the other wears blue. Wearing the wrong color may be enough to invite violence." Moore called Connie Fischer, the high school principal, and suggested that Fischer should act quickly to put a stop to the gang activity in the school.

Scenario 6.6:   Because of gang-related violence, the high school revised its student handbook to include the following statement: "No student may advertise membership in any gang by (1) word or gesture, and (2) clothing or jewelry."

Points to Consider: Do the problems specifically associated with gang activity provide schools with more authority to regulate student dress and grooming standards?

Many communities have seen an increase in gang activity that has caused substantial interference with school programs and activities. Since students announce their membership in a gang by wearing certain colors or emblems, students in some communities where gang activity has increased have responded by wearing only "neutral" colors. Many school administrators have revised their student dress code policies to prohibit the wearing of gang colors or emblems. In doing so, these administrators have again raised the legal questions regarding whether students have the right to choose their own dress styles and whether schools can limit that right.

As previously discussed, students have a constitutional right to wear clothing of their own choice, absent a showing of material disruption. The majority of courts have ruled that as long as clothing is neat and clean, the school does not have sufficient reason for interfering with student freedom. In order to be constitutional, a dress code must be reasonably related to the school's responsibility or its curriculum. Those school districts that have adopted rules prohibiting the wearing of gang symbols and jewelry believe that the presence of gangs and gang activities threaten a substantial disruption of the schools' programs.

In 1987 a federal district court was asked to determine the constitutionality of the Midlothian, Illinois school district's anti-gang dress code. The Midlothian school board had discovered that, beginning in 1981, gang activity had severely disrupted their educational program. Students had been intimidated by gang members, both in and around the schools; gang members had attempted to recruit new members in the school buildings; many acts of gang-related violence had occurred on school grounds; and many students had been reluctant to come to school for fear of the violence. The board had concluded that it needed a comprehensive policy to prevent the gangs from operating in its schools and had developed one that banned the wearing or display of any gang symbol, any act or speech showing gang affiliation, and any conduct designed to further gang activity.[16]

In a suit challenging the constitutionality of the policy, a student at Midlothian High School claimed that the policy violated his right of free speech under the First Amendment and his right to equal protection under the Fourteenth Amendment.[17] The court affirmed the district's right to enforce the dress code, saying that school boards have the responsibility to teach not only academic subjects, but also the role of young men and women in a democratic society. It went on to say that students are expected to learn that, in our society, individual rights must be balanced with the rights of others. The court's decision indicated that the First Amendment does not necessarily protect an individual's appearance from all regulation. When gang activities endanger the educational process and the safety of students, schools have the right to regulate students' dress and actions during school hours and on school grounds. Those who challenge such regulation must show the absence of a rational connection (nexus) between the policy and the accomplishment of a public purpose.

The following policy was developed by the Midlothian, Illinois school board:

> *No student on or about school property or at any school activity shall:*
>
> 1. *Wear, possess, distribute, display or sell any clothing, jewelry, emblem, badge, symbol, sign or other thing that is evidence of membership or affiliation in a gang;*
> 2. *Commit any act or omission or use any speech either verbal or nonverbal (gestures, handshakes, etc.) showing membership or affiliation in a gang;*
> 3. *Use any speech or commit any act or omission in furtherance of the interests of any gang or gang activity, including but not limited to:*
>
>   a. *soliciting others for membership in a gang;*
>   b. *requesting any person to pay protection or otherwise intimidating or threatening any person;*
>   c. *committing any other illegal act or other violation of school district policies;*
>   d. *inciting other students to act with physical violence upon any other person.[18]*

School Mascots as Symbols

Scenario 6.7: Since the high school was founded sixty years ago, the school mascot has been the "red raider." Before each athletic event a student dresses up like an American Indian, paints his face with "war paint," and performs a characterization of an "Indian war dance." For the past two years, American Indian students have protested this characterization. This year the Indian students have been joined by the American Civil Liberties Union. A poll of the community indicates that 80 percent of the citizens want to keep the red raider mascot.

Points to Consider: Does the school have the responsibility to change or retain a mascot in the face of community protest? Do students have the right to demand the removal of a historic mascot?

With the changing awareness of the importance of symbols in communicating values, a number of school districts have found their mascots the targets of community attacks. For example, in 1988 the principal of a Virginia high school decided to discontinue the use of a cartoon figure named "Johnny Reb" as the school's mascot because of complaints that it offended black students. A group of students protested the principal's decision as a violation of their First Amendment rights. Though the lower court ruled in favor of the students who wished to retain "Johnny Reb" as their mascot, a federal appeals court ruled in favor of the principal.[19] The appeals court recognized that school officials need not sponsor or promote all student speech, and that because a school mascot may be interpreted as bearing the school's stamp of approval, the principal was justified in banning a symbol that offended a segment of the student population.

Guidelines Regarding Students' Symbolic Expression

1. Rules and regulations regarding symbolic expression should be developed and maintained as official policy by boards of education.
2. In order to be reasonable, rules and regulations should be specific. A board policy allowing individual schools to set their own standards generally will be upheld as long as the rules are specific.
3. The key questions to be answered are: Does the expression cause a health, safety, or disruptive hazard; are the rules based on objective needs; and will the rules constitute an arbitrary infringement of constitutionally protected rights?[20]

Students' Oral Communication

Scenario 6.8: Two weeks before the homecoming dance, Fred Elliott, a high school senior, informed the principal that he wanted to bring a date of the same gender to the dance. When the principal told Fred that this would not be allowed, Fred decided to ask his fellow students and teachers to support his cause. During study periods and between classes, Fred lobbied his cause. When the principal told Fred to stop "trying to cause trouble," Fred called him a "Nazi." Fred was suspended from school.

Points to Consider: Could Fred's behavior cause a material disruption of the school? Does a school have the right to restrict student speech? Do students have individual rights to freedom of speech, even when their viewpoints are unpleasant or unpopular?

The Supreme Court has relied primarily on two tests to determine whether the school may control freedom of speech or expression: The first is the "clear and present danger" doctrine; the second is the "material and substantial disruption" doctrine. The second of these rationales is the standard derived from the *Tinker* decision.[21]

More recently, in *Bethel v. Fraser,*[22] the courts have had occasion to expand the rationale for schools to limit students' freedom of speech when obscenity is involved. The *Fraser* case grew out of the events leading to the suspension of a student for delivering a speech nominating another student for elective office. The speech, which was delivered during a required student assembly, made use of a "graphic sexual metaphor." The student had been warned by two teachers not to deliver the speech, but he proceeded to do so anyway. The student was subsequently suspended from school for three days, and his name was removed from a list of graduation speakers.

The student brought suit on First and Fourteenth amendment grounds. While the lower courts affirmed the student's claim, the United States Supreme Court ruled that no constitutional rights had been abridged. In its decision the Court drew a distinction between the silent political speech involved in *Tinker* and the "lewd and obscene speech" of *Fraser.* The Court also stressed the value of the schools in teaching socially appropriate behavior and held that ". . . the determination of what manner of speech in the classroom or in a school assembly is appropriate properly rests with the school board." The Court went on to say that while students have the right to advocate unpopular and controversial rules in school, ". . . that right must be balanced against the school's interest in teaching socially appropriate behavior. The Court observed that such standards would be difficult to enforce in a school that tolerated the 'lewd, indecent and offensive' speech and conduct which the student in this case exhibited."[23]

The Court further ruled that the disturbance test enunciated in *Tinker* applied, since some younger students had been confused and upset, and that there had been outbursts at the assembly. The *Tinker* distinction between the rights of students and school officials was more clearly defined in *Fraser.*[24]

Guidelines Regarding Students' Oral Expression

1. It is recommended that schools encourage the free expression and exchange of ideas and thoughts among students and teachers and promote respect for differences of opinion.

2. Teachers should not require students to accept an arbitrary opinion or idea, but should instead provide appropriate forums for the exchange of ideas and guidance in the fundamental rules of fairness in dialogue.
3. Students who abuse their freedom of expression or impinge on the freedom of others may be disciplined appropriately.[25]

Students' Written Expression

Scenario 6.9: A group of male journalism students published a satirical magazine parodying the school in the manner of a popular magazine, and the principal ordered it banned. The principal's decision was based on his belief that the articles that mocked the school were apt to undermine school discipline.

Scenario 6.10: Debbie Winter was the student editor of the high school newspaper. When she was informed that the athletic department would provide all news of all future athletic events, Debbie refused to comply with what she labeled "prior restraint." As a result, Debbie was removed as editor of the paper.

Scenario 6.11: Mary Marks, the journalism teacher who advised the high school newspaper, was very proud of the school paper. In her small town it was read in every home. In fact, parents and other citizens frequently wrote articles for the paper, and many bought advertising space. One day Mary was stopped in the hall by the principal, who said, "Mary, we've got to get our committee going to write our censorship policy, now that we have this *Hazelwood* thing to deal with." Mary was stunned that he had said "censorship policy," rather than "our policy dealing with censorship." The principal went on to say that it was his understanding that each school had to have such a policy.

Points to Consider: Are student newspapers public forums? Can principals control the content of student newspapers? What determines whether a paper is curriculum-related? If an article in a school-sponsored publication is found to be libelous, can the principal be held liable?

Just as the right of students to express themselves orally has undergone recent modification, their right to freedom of written expression has also been modified. In 1988 the United States Supreme Court heard the case of *Hazelwood v. Kuhlmeier*,[26] involving a Missouri high school student paper. In this case the principal had deleted two full pages from the student newspaper produced in the journalism class. In his view the deleted pages contained two "objectionable" articles, which he characterized as "inappropriate, personal, sensitive and unsuitable." One article documented three Hazelwood East students' experiences with pregnancy; the other discussed the impact of divorce on Hazelwood East students.

In its decision the Court held that the First Amendment does not prevent educators from exercising editorial control over the style and content of school-sponsored student newspapers. The Court reasoned that high school papers published by journalism classes do not qualify as "a public forum," open to indiscriminate use, but one "reserved . . . for its intended purpose as a supervised learning experience for journalism students."[27] School officials, therefore, retain the right to impose reasonable restrictions of student speech in those papers, and the principal, in this case, did not violate students' speech rights.[28]

The "public forum doctrine" was designed to balance the right of an individual to speak in public places with the government's right to preserve those places for their intended purposes.[29] Although there is considerable doctrinal conflict in recent public forum cases, the *Hazelwood* court placed school-sponsored activities in the middle ground of a "limited public forum." While speech may not be regulated in a public forum, it may be regulated in a nonpublic forum, and school-sponsored speech may be regulated if there is a compelling reason.

The Court also drew a "two-tiered scheme of protection of student expression; one for personal speech, and the other for education-related speech. . . ."[30] According to the *Hazelwood* decision, personal speech, of the type discussed in *Tinker,* is still protected by a strict scrutiny under the material and substantial disruption standard. However, speech that is curriculum-related, whether in a class, an assembly, a newspaper, or a play, may be regulated. Such speech is protected only by a much less stringent standard of reasonableness.

The *Hazelwood* decision rekindled heated debate about the practice of censoring school newspapers.[31] Many school officials who have the duty to formulate and implement curricular policy applauded the decision. For them it was a long-awaited affirmation of their right to edit school newspapers. Administrators welcomed its direction regarding what restrictions can be placed on content and on the time, place, and manner of distribution of student newspapers. On the other hand, the decision was deplored by every major national organization of journalism educators. These groups considered this decision a mistake,[32] and one that ignored the value of a vibrant student press and encouraged a repressive school environment."[33]

The *Hazelwood* decision has moved the argument about students' rights to freedom of expression from the courthouse to the state house. A significant number of state legislatures have debated whether or not *Hazelwood* has unduly infringed upon the rights enunciated by *Tinker.* The high level of state legislative activity since the Court's 1988 decision reflects the fear that school administrators will censor legitimate student freedom of expression if *Hazelwood* is not challenged. By 1990 two states, Iowa and Colorado, had passed laws that reject the *Hazelwood* decision for students in their states. The California and Massachusetts legislatures had "also declined to embrace *Hazelwood,*" based on earlier state precedents.[34]

The legislative debates have focused on the appropriate balance between the rights of students and the schools. Specifically, they have attempted to define the circumstances that would allow school authorities to limit students' free speech. Proponents of state legislation rejecting *Hazelwood* generally contend that *Tinker* set all the necessary standards for limiting student speech. Opponents of such legislation approve of the latitude given to principals by *Hazelwood* and contend that *Hazelwood* "simply confirms the broad discretion that educators have always had over curriculum."[35] They argue further that student journalists must be subject to the same level of editorial responsibility as professional journalists, whose work is subject to the editing of the publisher.[36]

The Colorado law states: "There will be no prior restraint on the student press—except for expression that is obscene, libelous, would substantially disrupt the operation of the school, violates the privacy rights of others, or incites students to commit unlawful acts."[37] It would seem that whether principals are operating under *Hazelwood* or a state statute like Colorado's, they have the ultimate responsibility for what is published in the student press, and the *Hazelwood* decision has clearly complicated the principal's job.

Advertisements in Student Newspapers

Scenario 6.12:   The editor of the school newspaper received a request to publish a paid advertisement announcing the formation of a support group for gay and lesbian students. The editor accepted the ad, but the faculty advisor refused to permit the ad to appear in the paper.

Points to Consider: What restrictions may be placed on advertisements in school papers? Is commercial speech accorded the same degree of protection as other speech? Are there valid grounds for restricting the advertisements placed in student newspapers?

Some schools permit students to solicit advertisements to be placed in school-sponsored publications. Problems can arise when school authorities determine that the content of an advertisement is inappropriate for a school paper. In 1980 a federal court found that a secondary school's interest in protecting students from unhealthful activities was a valid reason to justify the restriction of paid advertisements in student papers. The case of *Williams v. Spencer*[38] involved an advertisement for drug paraphernalia in a student newspaper distributed at school. The court affirmed the right of the school to prevent any conduct on school grounds that endangers the health and safety of students and upheld the prior restraint of material that encouraged actions that might endanger students' health or safety.[39] Based on this decision, schools may restrict advertisements that promote unhealthy or dangerous products or activities.

Schools have also been concerned about advertisements that promote controversial points of view. In 1986 a court ruled that a school board cannot, absent a compelling interest, exclude speech simply because the board disagrees with the content. Specifically, the school board cannot allow the presentation of one side of an issue but prohibit the presentation of another viewpoint.[40]

If the school newspaper is clearly identified as part of the curriculum, rather than a public forum, the school has a greater latitude in regulating advertisements. For example, a federal court ruled in 1989 that a school had the right to reject advertisements from Planned Parenthood that promoted such services as gynecological examinations, birth control counseling, pregnancy testing and verification, and pregnancy counseling and referral.[41]

Non–School-Sponsored Publications

Scenario 6.13:   Although an underground newspaper called "The Student Voice" was printed and distributed off school grounds, a number of copies were seized by teachers in the school. The main themes of the paper were that the food in the school cafeteria was overpriced and of poor quality and that a number of named teachers were incompetent.

Points to Consider: What rights do students have regarding the publication of newspapers off of the school grounds? How should principals deal with underground newspapers or handbills?

Courts that have supported schools' rights to regulate student newspapers have made a distinction between off-campus and on-campus publications. Courts have generally held that the arm of school authority usually does not reach beyond the school grounds, and school officials do not have the power to discipline students for distributing underground newspapers off campus.[42] In a case in which students were suspended from school for publishing and distributing an underground newspaper, the court ruled that the suspensions were unconstitutional.[43]

However, some of the rules that apply to sponsored publications also apply to unofficial student publications. Unofficial publications must not interfere with the normal operation of the school and must not be obscene or libelous. Although students have the right to express themselves, schools retain the right to regulate the distribution of materials to protect the welfare of other students.[44]

Prior Restraint

Prior restraint is official government obstruction of speech prior to its utterance.[45] As agents of the state, the school boards or their agents may not exercise prior restraint, unless the content of the publication would result in substantial disruption of the educational process, is judged to be obscene or pornographic, libels school officials or others, or invades the privacy of others. Courts have ruled that a school board is not required to wait until the distribution of a publication takes place to determine whether any of these criteria has been met. Schools have the right to establish rules on prior review procedures, as well as standards regulating the times, places, and manner of distribution of student publications. If a school chooses to establish rules that govern the distribution of student publications, these rules must be reasonable and relate directly to the prevention of disruption or disorder.

Guidelines Regarding Students' Written Expression

1. Boards of education should formulate and disseminate a clear and definite policy regarding the writing, editing, publication, and distribution of literature by students.
2. The publication of official school newspapers should be supervised by qualified professional personnel, and the faculty advisor should be responsible for ensuring that the publication reflects the ideas, tastes, feelings, and opinions of the students, within the bounds of responsible journalism.
3. Any rules or regulations concerning the publication of unofficial student publications should address only writing, editing, or distribution that occurs on school grounds.
4. Reasonable and clearly stated rules and regulations should be promulgated concerning the distribution of any student publication on school grounds and prohibiting material that is obscene, libelous, or inflammatory.
5. Literature in the possession of students that is alleged to be obscene, libelous, or inflammatory should be considered in light of the possibility of substantial disruption of the educational process. Open display or distribution by the student is a key factor. When a student is in possession of such materials, and such possession does not adversely affect the operations of the school, no formal action, with the exception of individual counseling, is appropriate.
6. A decision against the distribution of a publication should be distinguished from a decision to deprive students of possession of a publication. The latter does not necessarily follow the former.[46]

7. The process of writing the rules and regulations that govern student publications should be accomplished by a committee composed of faculty, students, and parents to ensure that the interests of each group are expressed and incorporated into the final policy.

Summary of Written Expression Rights

In 1969 the *Tinker* decision put school officials on notice that they do not possess absolute authority over their students and challenged them to have a greater faith in the democratic process. In 1988 the *Hazelwood* decision made it clear that the Supreme Court has more faith that school officials will protect students' rights than it has in students' ability to act responsibly. By ruling that "school newspapers are non-public forums" and are thus subject to reasonableness-based censorship by school officials, the Court seems to have placed the interests of school authorities over students' First Amendment rights. The Court further curtailed students' rights by severing *Tinker* protection from student speech in curriculum-related activities.[47]

Student journalists should have the same rights and responsibilities as any other journalists, and it will be up to the individual states to ensure that these rights are maintained. Adult journalists have limits placed on what they can write. There are prescribed consequences for copyright infringement and plagiarism, false advertising and the advertising of illegal products, inflammatory literature, obscenity, libel, invasion of privacy, fraud, and threats, for example.[48] Any additional restrictions on student expression "inhibit understanding of the Bill of Rights among America's youth, and add to the general disregard for free speech guarantees in our democracy."[49]

Students' Rights of Freedom of Assembly

Scenario 6.14: Because of budget restraints, the school board voted to cut five teaching positions at the high school and to eliminate portions of the vocational education program. In response to this announcement, 80 percent of the school's 550 students participated in a peaceful sit-in that halted classes at the school for three hours. The students demanded that the president of the school board meet with them to discuss the situation and answer their questions.

Points to Consider: Should students be allowed to assemble peacefully to discuss common concerns or make a political statement? How should a principal respond should the assembly become disruptive?

Students' freedom of assembly rights are protected by the First Amendment; however, the *Tinker* decision made it clear that students' First Amendment rights are protected only so long as they do not substantially disrupt the educational process. Therefore, schools are well within the scope of their authority to adopt rules that restrict student gatherings to nondisruptive times, places, and behaviors.

A school that allows students to gather, even peacefully, whenever they wish obviously cannot function effectively. On the other hand, a school that does not allow adequate time for students to meet and discuss relevant issues, or that denies use of school facilities for such assemblies outside regular school hours, clearly discourages one of the most fundamental perquisites and options of good citizenship.

The key to distinguishing between the use and abuse of the students' right to assemble peacefully, then, lies in balancing the fundamental nature, necessity, and usefulness of the freedom itself with the duty to carry out the educational process effectively. Although students' rights to freedom of assembly have not generated many court cases, school principals need to be sensitive to potential lawsuits in this area.

Guidelines Regarding Students' Freedom of Assembly

1. Impromptu or spontaneous assembly of large groups of students called for the specific purpose of disrupting the school day should be prohibited.
2. If the assembly is peaceful in nature, school staff members should be patient in disbursing the gathering without incident, and any required disciplinary action should be taken after the students have returned to their classrooms.
3. If the assembly is riotous or violent in nature, proper authorities should be notified at once, and all necessary steps should be taken to disburse the gathering as quickly as possible.
4. Each principal should have a written, board-approved plan for dealing with both peaceful and disruptive unauthorized assemblies of students, which the entire staff is prepared to implement.[50]

Related Issue—Cults and Satanism

Scenario 6.15:   As Greg Willow, a teacher at the high school, drove to school, he noticed the graffiti on the bridges and culverts he passed. Traditional messages such as "Jesus loves you," "Elvis lives," and "Mary loves John" had been replaced by drawings of pentagrams, upside-down crosses, swastikas, hexagrams, and various configurations of the numbers

"666" and the letters "fff". It occurred to Greg that he had recently seen similar drawings on students' notebooks and backpacks.

Points to Consider: Since such symbols are historically associated with satanic cults and clash with traditional core values, should schools ban such symbols in the school setting?

Teachers and parents have become concerned about children wearing T-shirts to school that advertise "heavy metal" music and about their listening to music groups that some believe espouse satanic activity. Many people are concerned that some of this music condones murder, rape, sacrifice to Satan, and suicide, and have expressed a fear that teenagers may turn these lyrics into a belief system. Others see these activities as simply another fad, in the tradition of beatniks, surf bums, flower children, urban cowboys, break dancers, and rappers.

In its least objectionable form, teen preoccupation with the occult amounts to little more than a fondness for ripped black T-shirts and heavy metal recordings. At the extreme, however, satanism practiced by teenagers may take on all the trappings of an ancient religion. Some students have become deeply involved in a variety of rituals and perceive themselves as religiously committed to a cult. Still others seem to be passively allowing the influence of their peers to dictate their behavior.

Principals have a dual duty: to protect the rights of the entire student body and to protect individual students' rights. These sometimes contradictory roles are sure to become increasingly polarized as principals attempt to cope with the current satanic cult movement.

Summary

Schools, by their very nature, must encourage free inquiry and free expression of ideas. Such expression should include the personal opinions of students relevant to the subject matter being taught, school activities and policies, school administrators, and matters of broad social concern and interest. In expressing themselves on such issues, students have a responsibility to refrain from using defamatory, obscene, or inflammatory language and to comport themselves in such a way as to allow others to exercise their First Amendment rights as well. The courts have affirmed that students' free speech rights are protected by the Constitution only so long as they do not present a clear and present danger or threaten a material disruption of the educational process. In the event that students' activities do threaten the effective operation of the school, principals are given clear authority to ban the students' activities and silence the students' words.

Endnotes

1. U.S. Const., amend. I.
2. Zachariah Cafee, *Free Speech in the United States,* New York, Atheneum, 1969. FREE SPEECH IN THE UNITED STATES, at 21
3. Gitlow v. New York, 268 U.S. 652 (1925).
4. West Virginia Board of Education v. Barnette, 319 U.S. 624 (1943).
5. Tinker v. Des Moines Independent Community School District, 393 U.S. 503 (1969).
6. *Id.* at 506.
7. *Id.*
8. Gusick v. Drebus, 431 F.2d 594 (6th Cir. 1970).
9. *See* Burnside v. Byars, 363 F.2d 744 (5th Cir. 1966); Tinker v. Des Moines Independent Community School District, 393 U.S. 503 (1969); Augustus v. School Board of Escambia City, 361 F. Supp. 383 (N.D. Fla. 1973); Banks v. Muncie Community Schools, 433 F.2d 292 (7th Cir. 1970).
10. Richards v. Thurston, 424 F.2d. 1281 (1st Cir. 1970).
11. Smith v. Tammany Parish School Board, 448 F.2d 414 (5th Cir. 1971).
12. Lansdale v. Tyler Jr. College, 470 F.2d 659 (5th Cir. 1972).
13. Karr v. Schmidt, 460 F.2d 609 (5th Cir. 1972).
14. Dunham v. Pulsifer, 312 F. Supp. 41 419 (D. Vt. 1970).
15. L. Jennings, *Stricter Rules on Student Dress, Decorum Revive Familiar Civil-Liberties Questions,* EDUCATION WEEK, October 1989, 14.
16. Board of Education of School District 228, Cook County, Illinois, *Prohibiting Gangs and Gang Activities,* Policy adopted April 24, 1984.
17. Olson v. Board of Education of School District No. 228. 676 F. Supp. 829 (N.S. Ill. 1987).
18. *Supra,* note 16.
19. Crosby v. Holsinger, 852 F.2d 801 (4th Cir. 1988).
20. R. SHOOP & W. SPARKMAN, KANSAS SCHOOL LAW (Des Moines, Iowa: Bowers, 1983), 161.
21. *Supra,* note 5.
22. Bethel School District No. 403 v. Fraser, 755 F.2d 1356 (9th Cir. 1985), *rev'd,* 106 S.Ct. 3159 (1986).
23. 1989 DESKBOOK ENCYCLOPEDIA OF AMERICAN SCHOOL LAW (Rosemount, Minn.: Data Research, 1989), 78.
24. *Supra,* note 22 at 3165.
25. *Supra,* note 20 at 108–09
26. Hazelwood School District v. Kuhlmeier, 484 U.S. 260, 108 S.Ct. 562, 98 L.Ed. 2d 592 (43 E.d Law 515) (1988). *See also,* Kuhlmeier v. Hazelwood School District, 607 F. Supp. 1450 (E.D. Mo. 1985).
27. *Id.* at 570.
28. *Id.*
29. G. Sorenson, *Public Forum Doctrine: Use and Abuse in Schools and Colleges,* NOLPE NOTES. vol. 25, no. 2, February 1990, 1.
30. W. Valente, *Student Freedom of Speech in Public Schools—Another Turn,* ED. LAW REP. 889, July 21, 1988, 46.
31. Kay Beth Avery & Robert J. Simpson, *The Constitution and Student Publications: A Comprehensive Approach,* JOURNAL OF LAW AND EDUCATION, vol. 16, no. 1, Winter 1987, 1–16.
32. Mark Goodman, "Iowa Legislature Rejects Supreme Court Decision, Upholds

Free Expression Rights of Students," undated press release issued by the Student Press Law Center.

33. Statement in Response to the Supreme Court's Decision in *Hazelwood v. Kuhlmeier*," issued by the Association for Education Journalism and Mass Communication, Secondary Education Division, January 16, 1988.

34. Nat Hentoff, *Students Have Rights, Too,* THE WASHINGTON POST, November 17, 1990, A21.

35. David Schimmel, *Censorship of School-Sponsored Publications: An Analysis of Hazelwood v. Kuhlmeier,* 45 ED. LAW REP., June 9, 1988, 941.

36. *Supra,* note 34.

37. *Id.*

38. Williams v. Spencer, 622 F.2d 1200 (4th Cir. 1980).

39. *Supra* note 31 at 35.

40. San Diego Comm. Against Registration and the Draft v. Governing Board of Grossmont Union High School District., 790 F.2d 1471 (9th Cir. 1986).

41. Planned Parenthood v. Clark County School District, 887 F.2d 935 (9th Cir. 1989).

42. Thomas v. Board of Education, 607 F.2d 1043 (2d Cir. 1979).

43. Shanely v. Northeast Independent School District, 462 F.2d 960 (5th Cir. 1972).

44. F.C.C. v. Pacifica, 438 U.S. 1726 (1979).

45. *Supra,* note 31 at 3, *citing* Southeastern Promotional Ltd. v Conrad, 420 U.S. 546, 559 (1975).

46. *Supra,* note 20 at 111–12.

47. Elaine M. Russo, *Prior Restraint and the High School 'Free Press': The Implications of* Hazelwood *School District v. Kuhlmeier,* JOURNAL OF LAW AND EDUCATION, vol 18. no. 1, Winter 1989, 15.

48. *Supra,* note 2 at 4–5.

49. Statement adopted at the 1988 National Convention, Society of Professional Journalists.

50. *Supra,* note 20 at 115–116.

CHAPTER SEVEN

Student Records

Introduction

Scenario 7.1: Jill Jones, a high school journalism teacher, was preparing to leave on summer vacation when she received a phone call from Jackson Pruitt, the president of a community service organization. Jackson told Jill that David Hoopen, one of Jill's former students, was being considered for a college scholarship. Jackson told Jill that they had a record of David's grades, but "we want you to tell us what kind of student he was." Jill thought for a minute and said, "Well, David got a 'B' in my class, but I gave him a gift. He gets a lot of breaks like that because he is such a nice boy. I hope you give him the scholarship."

Scenario 7.2: Sally Summer, a third-grade teacher, posts the test papers of her better students on the class bulletin board. She feels that this practice recognizes the effort of her better students and serves as a motivator for her weaker students. She also has her students grade each other's tests.

Scenario 7.3: Marion Miles, a parent of a disabled student, requested that Brian Miller, the high school principal, give her copies of all of her child's test scores. In fact, she demanded that she be given the official file immediately. Brian told her to call for an appointment, and he would give her the files he thinks she should have.

Scenario 7.4: Mary Kate Murray, a special education teacher, was frustrated that the school did not have enough money to allow her to take her students on two field trips. She decided to raise the money by asking local business owners to make contributions. Before speaking with the business people, she brought her camera to school and took "candid" photographs of all her students. She then labeled a photo album with the caption, "Don't you want these special children to have the best education possible?" and showed it to the business people.

Scenario 7.5:   Julia Kasper, a member of the state department of education staff, requested that Randy Brown, the high school principal, send her all the records concerning disabled students in his school. Brown refused to release the records on the grounds that they are confidential.

Scenario 7.6:   Jimmy Smith lives with Mrs. Jordan, his grandmother. Mrs. Jordan attends all the parent-teacher conferences and receives Jimmy's report cards.

Points to Consider: What constitutes a record? What is directory information? What are parental rights to access to student records? What notification is required before records are released? What are the rights of noncustodial parents with regard to access to student records? What are a parent's rights if he or she disagrees with information contained in a child's record? May teachers display photos of students without parental permission?

The Family Educational Rights and Privacy Act

As a result of growing concern about the potential invasion of privacy associated with the amount and type of personally identifiable data that were being collected by various agencies, the Family Educational Rights and Privacy Act (FERPA) was passed in 1974. This act, also known as the Buckley Amendment, guarantees parental access to the education records of children as well as limiting the disclosure of those records.[1]

Prior to the passage of FERPA, educators maintained student records and shared the contents of those records at their own discretion, including the posting of student grades. As a result, it was possible for incorrect, misleading, embarrassing, or damaging information to be maintained and disclosed without the knowledge or consent of the parent or student. Furthermore, parents had no access to the records or any right to correct inaccurate information.

FERPA was enacted to correct some of the real or potential abuses in the access to and disclosure of education records. FERPA established a student's right to privacy in his or her educational records. For purposes of this legislation, the term *education records* means" . . . those records, files, documents, and other materials which (1) contain information directly related to a student; and (2) are maintained by an educational agency or institution or by a person acting for such agency or institution."[2] Education records do not include notes, memory aids, and other similar information that is maintained in the personal files kept by school officials and is not accessible or revealed to authorized school personnel or any third party. Such information may be shared with the student or parent, but if it is released to authorized school personnel or any third party, it becomes part of the student record subject to all the provisions of FERPA.

FERPA requires that schools formulate policy and procedures related to parental access to the educational records of their children. The policy should provide parents with the right to:

1. Inspect and review the education records
2. Amend the education record
3. Limit the disclosures of personally identifiable information from education records[3]

One major limitation imposed by FERPA is that educational records may not be destroyed when there is a current request by a parent or student to see them.

In 1978, FERPA was amended to restrict the purpose for which psychiatric examinations, testing, or treatment may be used. The new section specifies that no student shall be required to submit to any psychiatric examination, testing, or treatment for which the primary purpose is to reveal information concerning political affiliations; mental and psychological problems potentially embarrassing to the student or the family; sex behavior and attitudes; illegal, anti-social, self-incriminating, and demeaning behavior; critical appraisals of other individuals with whom respondents have close family relationships; legally recognized privileged and analogous relationships, such as those of lawyers, physicians, and ministers; or income, under certain circumstances.[4]

Directory information refers to information that is generally available through various sources and is often reported by the schools in student directories, athletic programs, and news releases. The law requires that public notice be given by any school regarding the categories of directory information that it intends to make public. A reasonable period of time must be given after the notice so that a parent can inform the school of any material that cannot be released without the parent's prior consent. Directory information includes:

- Name, address and telephone number
- Date and place of birth
- Major field of study
- Participation in officially recognized activities and sports
- Weight and height of members of athletic teams
- Dates of attendance
- Degrees and awards received
- Most recent previous school attended
- Other similar information[5]

FERPA gives parents the right to review the education records of their children; to have access to the education records of their children within 45 days of the initial request; to have a hearing by the school to challenge the content of the student's education record; to correct or delete any inaccurate, misleading, or inappropriate data contained in the education record; to insert into the records their written explanation respecting the content of such record; and to give or withhold consent for the records to be released. The right of consent shifts to the student at age 18, or when the student enters an institution of postsecondary education.[6]

Courts have ruled that both parents have the right to inspect their child's records unless there is a separation agreement in which the noncustodial parent waives such a right.[7]

FERPA provides that a school can release a student's educational records without the written consent of the parents to:

1. Other school officials determined by the school to have a legitimate educational interest in the information.

2. Officials of other schools or school systems in which the student seeks or intends to enroll, provided that the student's parents are notified of the transfer, receive a copy of the records if desired, and have an opportunity for a hearing to challenge the content of the records.

3. Certain authorized representatives of the federal government and state educational authorities, in connection with the audit and evaluation of federally sponsored education programs, or with the enforcement of the related federal legal requirements. Any and all personally identifiable information must remain confidential and must be destroyed when no longer needed.

4. Local and state officials to whom information, in connection with a student's application for or receipt of financial aid, is specifically required to be reported or disclosed pursuant to state statutes.

5. Organizations conducting studies with certain specific limitations.

6. Accrediting organizations when performing their responsibilities.

7. Parents of a dependent student.

8. Authorized persons in connection with an emergency as specified.[8]

Enforcement

If the U.S. Department of Education finds that there has been a violation of FERPA, the parties must be notified, and the Secretary of Education must attempt to effect compliance through voluntary actions. If the school system fails or refuses to comply, the school district may have its federal education funds terminated. The act does not create any independent cause of action.[9] If it is found that the school district's actions deny students' civil rights, damages and attorney's fees may be awarded.[10]

Guidelines for Student Records

1. Clear and detailed procedures for handling student records should be kept as official board policy.
2. Student files should be divided into two categories: nonclassified and classified.
3. Professional staff members should have access to the nonclassified and classified files and all persons should follow the procedures for gaining access to the classified files.
4. A log should be kept of each student's record. If parts of the student record are separately located, a separate log should be kept with each part. The log should indicate all persons who have obtained access to the student record, stating the name, position, and signature of the person releasing the information and the name, position and, if a third party, the affiliation, if any, of the person who is to receive the information.
5. The consent of the student and one parent or guardian is required each time (and for each item) the student's record is divulged to persons other than the certified professional personnel.
6. All records on a student, except personal evaluations submitted in confidentiality before the enactment of FERPA, should be open to the student, with the consent of one of his or her guardians.
7. The school should provide assistance, when necessary, to enable students and their parents or guardians to understand the material in their records.
8. The student and parents or guardians should be allowed to submit any materials to the record—e.g., results of outside testing and evaluation, medical or psychological reports, and explanations of unfavorable evaluations.
9. In the event that a decision of a principal or other official regarding any of the provisions of FERPA is not satisfactory to students or parents, they have the right to appeal to the superintendent of schools.[11]

Endnotes

1. 20 U.S.C., §1232(g)–1232(i) (1976).
2. 20 U.S.C. §1232(g) (a)(4)(A)(1982).
3. *Id.*
4. Pub. L. 95-561, 92 Stat. 2413 (1978).

5. *Supra,* note 1.

6. *Id.*

7. Page v. Rotterdam-Monohauser Central School Dist., 441 N.Y.S. 2d 323 (N.Y. Sup. Ct. 1981).

8. *Id.*

9. Girardier v. Webster College, 563 F.2d 1267 (9th Cir., 1977).

10. Fay v. South Colonie Central School District, 802 F.2d 21 (2nd Cir., 1986).

11. R. Shoop & W. Sparkman, Kansas School Law (Dubuque, Iowa: Bowers, 1983) 163.

CHAPTER EIGHT

Search and Seizure

Introduction

Scenario 8.1: Responding to rising violence, the school board employed security personnel using hand-held metal detectors to check high school students, their belongings, and their lockers for weapons.

Scenario 8.2: Connie Watts, a teacher, reported to Principal Tom Jones that she smelled marijuana smoke coming from a large gathering of students. Jones ordered ten students into the building, where the boys and girls were taken into separate rooms. The male students contended that the principal ordered them to remove their shoes and socks, drop their pants and underwear and spread their legs. Jones contended that the students were not ordered to strip. He said they were told to take off their shoes and socks and to loosen their trousers and shake them to see if anything fell out.

Scenario 8.3: A student informed Katie Gibbs, the principal, that Roger Black was selling drugs. Gibbs took Roger to her office and asked him to empty his pockets. Roger was found to be carrying cash, a telephone pager, and a book containing names with dollar amounts written next to the names. Roger refused Gibbs's request that he open his car. Gibbs pried the trunk open and found twelve marijuana cigarettes.

Scenario 8.4: Security guards periodically walked "sniff dogs" through the high school and parking lot. As one of the dogs passed Mindy Miles in the hall, the dog went on "alert." The dog had a very good record for reliability, which led the security guard to detain Mindy on suspicion of possession of marijuana. Police were called. They conducted an investigation and arrested Mindy.

Scenario 8.5: Dan Allen, an elementary teacher, was told to enforce the policy against students using tobacco products. When Joe Green came into his classroom, Allen saw the outline of what he believed to be a can of snuff in Joe's pocket. Joe denied having snuff. Allen then reached into Joe's pocket and extracted the can. He then patted Joe down to determine if he had any other contraband on him.

Scenario 8.6:   Kindra Johnson, a middle school principal, was informed that someone had stolen a baseball card worth over $100. Repeated efforts had failed to identify the culprit. Johnson had all students report to the gym, where they were detained by several teachers. Meanwhile, she and several other teachers searched every locker in the school. In addition to finding the missing baseball card, Johnson found missing jewelry, pornographic magazines, two knives, a pistol, some beer, and several small packets of marijuana. Johnson turned the material over to the police and informed them of which students' lockers contained which items.

Points to Consider: When and under what circumstances is a search of a student legal? Do students have privacy rights in connection with their lockers, desks, or other storage areas that the school provides? Do standards regulating student searches change if the police are involved? Is a general suspicion adequate reason to conduct a search? What are the legal issues involved in searching a student's car? Is it legal to use "sniff dogs" to conduct searches? Under what circumstances, if any, is a strip search permitted in public schools?

With the increase in the number of students using drugs and carrying dangerous weapons into schools, many principals have been confronted with situations requiring them to search students and their lockers or automobiles. Sometimes the principal must make an immediate judgment because of the gravity of a situation that could result in serious injury to the student or to other students (e.g., bomb threats, dangerous weapons, or illegal drugs.)[1] Searches for drugs and weapons have ranged from routine inspections of lockers, cars, pockets, and purses to very intimate strip searches. Trained dogs have been enlisted to aid searchers.[2] The Fourth Amendment to the Constitution guarantees the right of people to be secure in their persons, houses, papers, and effects, against unreasonable searches and seizures without probable cause.[3] In 1961, in *Mapp v. Ohio*, the United States Supreme Court ruled that the Fourth Amendment protects citizens from the actions of state as well as federal governments.[4]

In determining exactly how this constitutional protection should be applied in a school setting, courts have balanced the school's legitimate need to obtain information and the students' right to privacy. In balancing these two rights, courts have weighed several variables: (1) the purpose of the search, (2) the person doing the searching, (3) the place being searched, (4) the background of the person being searched, (5) the severity of the penalties resulting from the search, and (6) the degree to which the person's privacy was invaded by the search.[5] (See Figure 8-1.)

Although police officers generally must convince a magistrate that probable cause exists before a warrant is issued for a search, courts have been mixed in their opinions on how the Fourth Amendment applies in cases of school personnel searching students on school grounds. Some have argued that because school personnel are private persons and not agents of the state, the Fourth Amendment does not apply to them. Court decisions that reinforce this argument are based on the *in loco parentis* theory that the school is acting in place of the parent and not as an agent of the state. When students have pled that warrantless searches conducted by school officials infringe upon their Constitutional rights guaranteed by the Fourth Amendment, school officials have claimed that such searches are compelled by their affirmative duty to protect people and place.[6]

In 1985 the Supreme Court ruled, in the case of *New Jersey v. T.L.O.* (a student), that the Fourth Amendment applies to school searches and seizures.[7] Although this decision left some questions unanswered, it did give educators some guidance. T.L.O. was found smoking a cigarette in the high school rest room, and a teacher took her to the principal's office. The principal asked to see her purse, and upon opening it, found a pack of cigarettes and what appeared to be drug paraphernalia and evidence of drug dealing. T.L.O. was arrested and found guilty of delinquency charges. On appeal, T.L.O. asserted that the exclusionary rule should operate to bar consideration in admission of the evidence found in her purse as well as her confession. (The *exclusionary rule* simply means that evidence found through an illegal search may not be used in court. This rule is presumed to deter illegal searches.) T.L.O. argued that the evidence was obtained in violation of the Fourth Amendment and that the confession was unlawfully tainted by the illegal search.

The juvenile court ruled that a school official may properly conduct a search of a student's person if the official has a reasonable suspicion that a crime has been or is in the process of being committed, or reasonable cause to believe that the search is necessary to maintain school discipline or enforce school policies. The appellate court agreed with the standard used by the juvenile court but disagreed that the search had been reasonable. The New Jersey Supreme Court reversed the juvenile court's ruling. The State of New Jersey appealed to the United States Supreme Court.

The United States Supreme Court found that the search resulting in the discovery of the evidence of marijuana was reasonable and reversed the judgment of the Supreme Court of New Jersey. In deciding the case the Supreme Court had to decide whether the Fourth Amendment's prohibition on unreasonable searches and seizures applies to searches conducted by public school officials. The Court rejected the *in loco parentis* argument as being out of touch with contemporary reality. It affirmed that schools act as representatives of the state, not as surrogates for the parents. The court then decided that "reasonable-

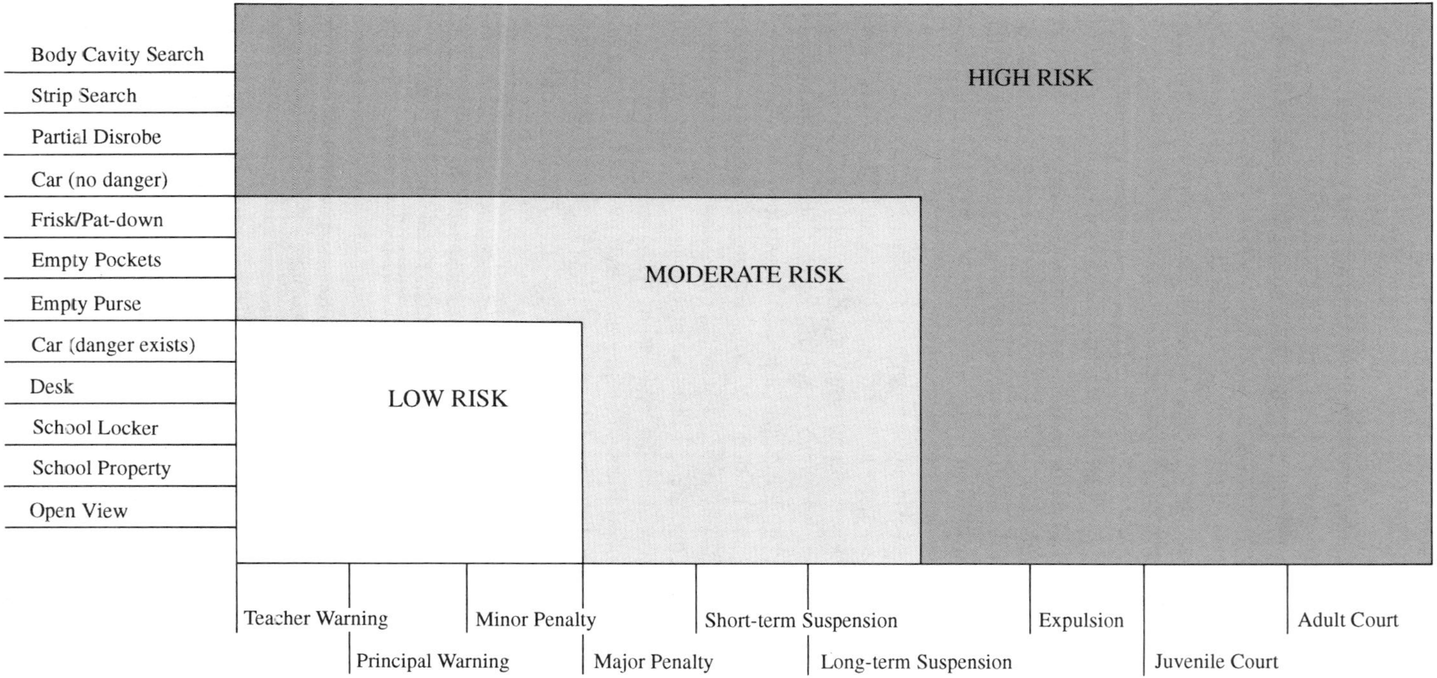

Figure 8-1 • *Risk Continua for Conducting Student Searches*

ness" in the context of the school setting is determined by balancing the need to search against the invasion that the search entails. The two-dimensional "reasonableness test" requires that a search must be justified at its inception and reasonable in scope.

The T.L.O. Reasonableness Test

Before conducting a search of a student's person or property, including school lockers, a school official must have a reasonable suspicion that a student has violated a law or school policy, and, in conducting the search, the school official must use methods that are reasonable in scope. In other words, the search must be reasonably related to the objectives of the search and not excessively intrusive in light of the age and sex of the student and the nature of the infraction. Considerations of student age, sex, and emotional condition are directly applicable as inhibitions to searches that must be justified by reason and common sense.

A school official's reasonable suspicion that a search will reveal evidence that a student has violated or is violating a law or school policy is a less rigorous test than the probable cause required for a police officer to obtain a search warrant. In an education setting a school official may rely on his or her good judgment and common sense to determine whether there is sufficient probability of an infraction to justify a search.[8] Further, the level of suspicion may vary depending on the circumstances of the particular situation. In emergency situations where there is a potential danger, or when there is a critical element of time, less suspicion is necessary to justify a search; for example, the suspected presence of a weapon or explosive device, or of drugs that might be quickly disposed of.

The school official's good judgment also applies to the determination of whether the information recommending the need for a search came from a reliable source. The courts have generally agreed that school officials may reasonably rely on information by school personnel or by a number of students, but information from a single student or from an anonymous source should be weighed more carefully before any action is taken.[9]

Reasonable suspicion in the latter situation would be based on the details of the information and whether those details are credible in the current overall situation. Reasonable suspicion may be based on the school official's knowledge of the student's prior history or on the official's past experience.[10]

Once the school official has met the standards of reasonable suspicion, reasonable scope is considered. The place or person identified through reasonable suspicion has a direct bearing on the scope of the search. The closer the searcher comes to the person, the higher the intrusiveness and, as a result, the higher the scope of the search. The highest degree of intrusiveness would be the strip search of a person.[11] The lowest degree of intrusiveness would be the search of an inanimate object such as a locker.[12]

While school officials may find comfort in the relaxed "reason and common sense" standard articulated by the Court, they have not been provided with unlimited discretion or license in conducting student searches. Nothing in *T.L.O.*, for example, suggests that the limitations of schools' search authority announced in *Doe v. Renfrow* or *Horton v. Goose Creek School District*[13] regarding strip searches or dragnet searching have been overturned. However, *T.L.O.* does suggest that justifications for such actions would be judged by more relaxed standards than in past cases. The significantly reduced exemption for obtaining search warrants granted to school officials by *T.L.O.* provides additional strength to the search process.

The *T.L.O.* Court conceded that school searches may involve other areas where students may keep personal belongings; however, it declined to decide how the reasonable suspicion standard would apply to these types of searches.[14] Administrators who wish direction in making decisions regarding other types of searches must look to lower court decisions that were left in place.

Locker Searches

There is some question whether a search of a student's locker falls within the protection of the Fourth Amendment. The Fourth Amendment only protects a person's reasonable expectation of privacy. Therefore, some courts have ruled that because students know when they are issued a locker that the school administrator keeps a duplicate key or a copy of the combination, their expectation of privacy in the locker is so diminished that it is virtually nonexistent.[15] Courts have noted that students have use of the lockers, but the lockers remain the exclusive property of the school. School authorities, therefore, have both the right and duty to inspect a locker when they believe that something of an illegal nature may be stored in it or, simply, to remove school property at the end of the school year.[16] Therefore, locker searches may be conducted with a fairly low degree of suspicion.

Before police or other law enforcement officials may search students' lockers, they must have a search warrant. They must demonstrate "probable cause" as the basis to justify the issuance of a search warrant. This also holds true when a law enforcement official requests that school personnel do the actual searching. By acting with the police the school official becomes an "arm of the state" and subject to due process requirements and illegal search and seizure sections of the United States Constitution; therefore, a search warrant is necessary.[17] Evidence seized without a warrant will not be admissible in court.

Cars

The search of a student's car, even when the car is on school grounds, is highly controversial. Because a car is privately owned, the search of a car is a greater invasion of privacy than the search of a locker. However, because the car is parked on school property, in public view, there is not a very high expectation of privacy. Even in the search of a car, courts have identified degrees of privacy. For example, objects in open view are less protected than objects in the trunk or glovebox.[18] Generally principals will want to avoid searching a student's car, unless there is clear reason to believe that there is imminent danger, either to the student or to others, should the student come into possession of the items. The student should be detained until either parents or authorities arrive.

Bookbags and Purses

A search of a student's personal effects requires a higher standard of protection than a car search, because such a search involves personal belongings in which the student has a higher expectation of privacy. While lockers are the property of the schools, personal effects are the property of the individual. School personnel are not forbidden to search student possessions, but they must exercise greater care in doing so. The Court in *T.L.O.* affirmed that students do not waive all rights to privacy in such items by bringing them onto school grounds.[19]

Metal Detectors

In an effort to reduce the number of guns, knives, and metal weapons carried into schools, some school districts have begun using metal detectors. The districts that use these devices argue that they are one of the less intrusive search techniques for searching for dangerous items. Opponents of this method argue that such searches are violations of students' privacy rights.

Pockets, Pat-down, and Strip Searches

When a school employee actually touches a student's clothing while engaged in a search, the search becomes more invasive. The risks of this type of search increase if it is conducted by a person of the opposite gender. Courts have warned that because this type of search may inflict great indignity and arouse strong resentment, it should not be undertaken lightly.[20]

The most controversial search of students is the strip search. There have been situations where school officials have ordered students to remove their clothes down to the undergarments in a search for stolen money or illegal drugs. Even though in most cases the boys and girls were placed in separate rooms and searched by school personnel of the same sex, the courts have generally condemned strip searches in the public schools as impermissible and, in some cases, have awarded money damages to the students who were illegally searched in such a manner.[21] A body cavity search is the most intrusive type of search and should not be conducted by school employees.

Surreptitious Observation

In an effort to deal with the drug problem, one school installed a one-way mirror in the boys' rest room to be used for observation. A student was found to have marijuana on his person, and after he informed on the other student involved, both students were turned over to the local police. The students went to court challenging the use of the one-way mirror in the rest room as a violation of their right to privacy.[22] In this case the court found that the limited visual surveillance was done by school officials and not police authorities, only school disciplinary action and not criminal action was taken as result of the surveillance, and there existed a significant community interest with respect to the drug problem. Therefore, the school's search was upheld as valid and not an infringement of the privacy rights of the students.

"Sniff Dog" Searches

The courts are split on the legality of using dogs in a dragnet search of students. In the case of *Horton v. Goose Creek,* the court held that because the canine actually touched the students while sniffing, the students' Fourth Amendment right to be free from unreasonable searches was violated. The court also found that the school district failed to establish an individualized suspicion of the students searched.[23]

In the case of *Doe v. Renfrow,* the court held that the use of dogs to sniff out drugs was not a search within the meaning of the Fourth Amendment and therefore not a violation of the Fourth Amendment.[24] This court's opinion seems to suggest that if a school district clearly establishes an individualized suspicion of certain students, then a use of dogs might be appropriate.[25] Whether or not a search warrant would be necessary in such a situation was left unclear. When school authorities find the use of sniff dogs necessary to combat a drug problem, it is suggested that they coordinate the proposed search with law enforcement officials who have search warrants. In addition, the use of dogs should be subject-specific rather than a dragnet of all students and should be done in private.

Informed Consent, Emergency and Administrative Searches

A student may willingly waive his or her rights of privacy under the Fourth Amendment. However, this waiver must be given free of even the slightest coercion.[26] In an emergency situation, when the school authorities are faced with a situation that demands immediate action to prevent injury or substantial property damage, the requirements of the Fourth Amendment are relaxed. Searches conducted to ensure standards of safety or cleanliness or locating and recapturing school property, such as an expensive library reference book, are permitted.[27]

Guidelines for Search and Seizure

1. Both individual principals and school districts can be held liable if a student can show that the principal acted with malice in conducting a search of the student and/or the student's property in a manner that denied the student's constitutional rights. Liability may also be incurred when a principal acts in ignorance or disregard of the law. Absent these conditions, the principal has general immunity.
   a. Each board of education should maintain, as official policy, a clear set of rules and regulations regarding search and seizure activities by school administrators.
   b. All in-school searches should be authorized by the principal.
   c. Law enforcement officials must have a search warrant in order to conduct any searches in public schools. Search warrants are also necessary when a school official is acting at the behest of a law enforcement agent in conducting a search on school premises.
   d. If school officials have reason to believe that there is imminent danger or harm, they may take any reasonable steps necessary to prevent such harm.
2. The legal basis for student searches is provided by the Supreme Court's decision in *New Jersey v. T.L.O.;* however, individual states or school districts may set more restrictive standards for conducting such searches, and principals should always follow the more restrictive standards.
3. Prior to undertaking a search of a student or a student's property (an exception to the student's general Fourth Amendment right to privacy), the principal must have a reasonable suspicion that the student is in possession of contraband that violates school policy or law.
4. To the extent that the alleged contraband poses an immediate physical danger to students, teachers, or the searcher, or that the probability

exists that the contraband will be used, distributed, or destroyed if a search is not undertaken immediately, an emergency exception to the student's right to privacy may exist, and the search may be conducted on the basis of less certain information; that is, less reasonable suspicion.

5. Under current legal precedents, reasonable suspicion is generally deemed to exist when:

   a. The source of information is credible. The most credible sources are: (1) school personnel, (2) more than one student, (3) a single, highly reliable student, (4) an outside or anonymous informant who provides a significant level of detail concerning the name of the student and the specific nature and location of the contraband.

   b. The search involves a student who has a prior history of suspicious activity or infractions of school policy or law relevant to the current situation.

   c. The school official who has provided the information prompting the search has had prior experience in correctly identifying similar illegal activity.

6. When conducted, the search must be reasonable in its scope; that is, limited to the student or students most likely to be involved in an infraction of school policy or law and no more intrusive than necessary. As a general rule, the more intrusive the search methodology, the more individualized the suspicion and the stronger the rationale for the search must be. Further, every search procedure must take into account, and be appropriate to, the student's age, sex, and emotional maturity.

   a. An example of the least intrusive search would be a search of an inanimate object; that is, locker, desk, or automobile that the student does not have access to during the normal school day.

      1) School authorities, on their own, may inspect students' lockers for illegal or dangerous materials or substances. When possible, locker searches should be conducted in the presence of another staff member. Unless there is clear reason to believe that upon opening the locker the student will attempt to seize and use the dangerous item, the student should also be present when the locker is searched.

      2) If a student who is believed to have an illegal or dangerous substance on his person or in his locker refuses to acknowledge or discuss the presence of such an item, school officials should consider notifying proper authorities, who in turn may obtain a search warrant.

      3) Systematic, secretive searches of student lockers or other closed areas where students keep personal items are not recommended.

b. An example of a moderately intrusive search would be a search of a student's personal property; that is, purse, school bag, pockets of a jacket not being worn by the student, an automobile to which the student has free access, or a request that the student make available for scrutiny the contents of his or her pockets, purse, school bag, etcetera.

1) School authorities may search students' clothing or personal effects only with reasonable suspicion that contraband is present. Such a search, however, must be subject-specific rather than a random "fishing expedition."

2) Objects discovered in a student search remain the property of the student and should be returned. Illegal objects should be turned over to the police. Dangerous objects should be turned over to the student's parents.

3) These suggestions should apply to the search of a purse, bookbag, satchel, briefcase, or any other container used by the student for carrying personal items.

c. An example of a highly intrusive search would be the physical search of a student—a "pat down" search or a strip search.

d. The younger the students, the less intrusive the search procedure should be. Further, the more intrusive the search, the more appropriate it becomes that searcher and student be of the same sex.

e. It is important to note that the courts have not, in most cases, been willing to accept the rationale for a strip search of any student, unless the evidence substantiates strong probable cause or emergency. In general, strip searches by school personal should be avoided.

f. Generalized (dragnet) searches, as opposed to individualized searches, should be limited to searches of inanimate objects such as lockers. Even these generalized searches should be conducted under circumstances and according to procedures formalized in a school policy about which the students and their parents have been fully informed at the beginning of each school year. For example, a school policy that student desks and lockers will be routinely inspected by school personnel for general housekeeping purposes is reasonable.

7. Whenever police or other law enforcement personnel are involved, the higher standard of probable cause (as opposed to reasonable suspicion) must be applied, and, except in emergency situations, a warrant must also be obtained.[28] School security personnel, whether uniformed or plain clothed, are generally considered by the courts to be law enforcement officers.

8. The use of canines to sniff out contraband in inanimate objects, such as lockers or empty classrooms, is generally not viewed by the courts as a student search. However, the courts may view the use of canines to sniff students as a highly intrusive search procedure requiring a high level of reasonable and individualized suspicion of a student or students. Trained sniff dogs may be used to search students' lockers and automobiles even without a warrant. (The dog's nose, in sniffing the air, has been compared to the light of a flashlight shining on an object in plain view.)

9. Drug testing through urinalysis comes under the scrutiny of the Fourth Amendment. Such testing is considered a highly intrusive search and requires strong reasonable and individualized suspicion that a student is a drug user.[29]

10. A principal is not protected from liability because students have given their permission for any kind of search to be conducted of their persons or property. The courts have determined that, because students are expected to be cooperative in the school setting, they cannot be deemed to have freely given their consent to a search.

Endnotes

1. For a detailed discussion of drug testing as a search, see Chapter 14.

2. For background material concerning the Fourth Amendment, see L. Goering, *Constitutional Law: Privacy Penumbra Encompasses Students in School Searches,* 25 WASHBURN L.J. 135 (1985); C. Avery & R. Simpson, *Search and Seizure: A Risk Assessment Model for Public School Officials,* JOURNAL OF LAW & EDUCATION, vol. 16, no. 4, Fall 1987; A. Quick, *The School Administrator's Guide to Search and Seizure,* JOURNAL OF LAW & EDUCATION, vol. 14, no. 3, July 1985; B. Walts, *New Jersey v. T.L.O.: The Questions the Court Did Not Answer About School Searches,* JOURNAL OF LAW & EDUCATION, vol. 14, no. 3, July 1985.

3. U.S. Const., amend. IV.

4. Mapp v. Ohio, 367 U.S. 643 (1961).

5. Goering, *supra,* note 2.

6. *Constitutional Law: Juvenile Rights and Public School Searches [Kuehn v. Renton School District, 694 P.2d. 1078 (Wash. 1985)],* 21 GONZ. L. REV. 285 (1985–86).

7. New Jersey v. T.L.O., 105 S. Ct. 733 (1985).

8. Martens v. District No. 220, 620 F. Supp. 29 (N.D. Ill. 1985).

9. Illinois v. Gates, 462 U.S. 213 (1983).

10. Nelson v. State, 319 So. 2d 154 (Fla. Dist. Ct. App. 1975).

11. Doe v. Renfrow, 475 F. Supp. 1012 (N.D. Ind. 1979). *See also,* Picha v. Weilgos, 410 F. Supp. 1214 (N.D. Ill. 1970); Tartar v. Raybuck, 742 F.2d 977 (6th Cir. 1984).

12. State v. Stein, 459 P.2d 1 (Kan. 1969).

13. Horton v. Goose Creek, 690 F.2d. 470 (5th Cir. 1982).

14. Walts, *supra,* note 2.

15. People v. Overton, 24 N.Y.2d 522, 249 N.E.2d 366, 301 N.Y.S.2d 479 (1969).

16. *Supra,* note 12.

17. Stern v. New Haven Community Schools, 529 F. Supp. 32 (D. Mich. 1981).

18. State v. D.T.W., 425 So.2d 1383 (Fla. Dist. Ct. App. 1983).

19. *Supra,* note 7.

20. Terry v. Ohio, 392 U.S. 1, 17 (1968).

21. Doe v. Renfrow, 631 F.2d 91 (7th Cir. 1980).

22. Stern v. New Haven, *supra.*

23. *Supra,* note 13.

24. *Supra,* note 21.

25. Jones v. Latexo Independent School District, 499 F. Supp. 223

26. Schneckloth v. Bustamonte, 412 U.S. 218, 222 (1973).

27. Avery & Simpson, *supra,* at 421-22.

28. *Supra,* note 15.

29. *Compulsory Urinalysis of Public School Students: An Unconstitutional Search and Seizure,* 18 Colum. Hum. Rts. L. Rev. 111 (1986–87).

CHAPTER NINE

Student Discipline

Introduction

One of the most difficult issues facing principals is the question of how to deal with unacceptable student conduct. Principals must be able to balance the need for a safe and orderly school against the rights of individual students to be free from "unreasonable discipline." Although the doctrine of *in loco parentis* has been eroded by the courts, it is still invoked to sanction reasonable disciplinary control by school officials. The courts typically will not interfere with the discretion of school personnel in matters of student discipline, unless a student's liberty or property rights are threatened, or in cases where the punishment is unreasonable or arbitrary under the circumstances.

School officials have a long-established right to make and enforce reasonable rules of student conduct, as long as the rules are necessary to carry out the school's educational mission. In addition, rules must be specific enough so that students, as well as parents, know what actions are not allowed in the school or at school-related activities. Rules must be applied uniformly to all students, and any punishment should be appropriate to the offense with due consideration given to the circumstances.

Due Process

The right to due process of law is the cornerstone of our civil liberty. It is the essence of the guarantee of fairness to all citizens, a protection for the powerless from the oppression of the strong. The primary source of this guarantee is the Fifth Amendment, which protects individuals against double jeopardy and self-incrimination and guarantees that no person shall be deprived of life, liberty, or property without "due process of the law." This protection was also incorporated into the equal protection clause of the Fourteenth Amendment. In addition, each state has incorporated some form of "due process" language into its constitution.

It must be remembered that states have plenary, or total, power for education. Therefore, schools act under state law and are required to provide students and teachers with due process before they can be deprived of any right. Courts view due process in two ways: substantive due process and procedural due process. Substantive due process requires that the rules or policies be fair in and of themselves. Procedural due process requires that the policies, rules, and regulations be carried out in a fair manner.

Rather than defining an inflexible due process procedure universally applicable to every situation, courts have preferred to decide the required elements of due process on a case-by-case basis. The most commonly accepted elements of due process are proper notice of the charges and a fair and impartial hearing. However, courts generally do follow "precedent." This means that when a court rules a certain way, the same court or a lower court is obliged to rule the same way in similar cases. A court is not bound by precedent if it can "distinguish" the case; that is, if it can show that the case before it is significantly different, despite its apparent similarity.

Corporal Punishment

Scenario 9.1: Richard Ford entered a class a few minutes late and walked in front of Betty Smith, who was giving an oral report. The teacher told Richard to apologize and be seated. When Richard mumbled something disrespectful, the teacher twisted his arm behind his back and pushed him out into the hall. The teacher then shoved Richard down the hall to the principal's office.

Scenario 9.2: Two elementary school students who were fighting on the playground were warned that if they fought again they would be paddled. Several minutes later they got into another fight. The teacher who was supervising the playground gave each student three swats on the buttocks with a paddle. One of the students developed severe bruises requiring medical attention. The child's father filed a complaint against the teacher, in which he stated that he was not notified of the paddling prior to or after the punishment was administered. He also reported that he had specifically told the school not to paddle his child.

Scenario 9.3: Larry Costello, a middle school student, was sent to the principal's office because he had shown his classmates a lewd photograph. The principal informed Larry that his punishment was five swats with a paddle. After two swats Larry refused to be hit again. The principal called in a teacher to make Larry bend over a chair to receive three additional blows. During the ensuing struggle, Larry hit his head on the corner of the desk. Larry's injury required medical treatment.

Points to Consider: Is due process required prior to the administration of corporal punishment? Is the school required to notify parents prior to or following the administration of corporal punishment? What distinguishes corporal punishment from battery? Does a student have the right to bodily security? How much force may a school official reasonably use in disciplining a student?

Corporal punishment is physical punishment applied to modify behavior. The use of corporal punishment by teachers and administrators in the public schools is based on the concept of *in loco parentis.*

Because of the decision in the case of *Baker v. Owen,* some confusion exists over the requirement of procedural due process for corporal punishment. In this case a sixth-grade student and his mother sued a school principal and others, alleging that the student's constitutional rights were violated when the student was paddled by his teacher, over his mother's objections (parental rights), without procedural due process.[1] The student was paddled for throwing a kickball during a nonplay period. The student's mother had previously requested of the principal and certain teachers that her son not be corporally punished because she opposed it on principle. The mother alleged in her lawsuit that (1) the administration of corporal punishment over the mother's objections violated the parental right to determine disciplinary methods for her child, (2) the use of corporal punishment violated the student's right to procedural due process, and (3) the corporal punishment amounted to cruel and unusual punishment.

In response to the first issue, the federal district court held that parents generally have the right to discipline their children. However, in school matters the state has a countervailing interest in the maintenance of order in the schools, sufficient to sustain the right of teachers and school officials to administer reasonable corporal punishment for disciplinary purposes.[2]

On the second issue the court held that students must be afforded minimal procedural due process before corporal punishment is used. The court dispensed with the final issue by holding that the paddling the student received did not amount to cruel and unusual punishment.[3]

Confusion over the due process requirements began to occur after *Baker* was appealed to the United States Supreme Court. When the Supreme Court summarily affirmed without opinion the judgment of the district court in the *Baker* case, some people interpreted this to mean that it had approved the procedural due process requirements. However, a year later, as the case of *Ingraham v. Wright* was making its way through the federal court system, the court of appeals concluded that it was not bound by *Baker* and held that procedural due process was not required before using corporal punishment.[4] The appellate court noted that the *Baker* appeal did not place the procedural requirements before the Supreme Court, only the matter of whether school officials can paddle a child over the objections of the parent.[5]

Whether students have the right to due process in relation to corporal punishment was clarified when the United States Supreme Court ruled, in *Ingraham v. Wright,*[6] that corporal punishment is not constrained by either the Eighth or Fourteenth amendments. Regarding the issue of procedural due process, the court held that the requirement of even an informal hearing before any paddling could occur would impose an unjustifiable burden on the administration of the school. The Court also ruled that corporal punishment does not constitute cruel and unusual punishment as prohibited by the Eighth Amendment. The Court noted that although the potential for abuse of corporal punishment exists, there also exists traditional common law remedies such as civil suits in tort to protect against any excesses. Although procedural due process before the use of corporal punishment is not required by the Fourteenth Amendment, it may be mandated by state statute or local school board policy.

Even though the use of reasonable corporal punishment has been sustained by the courts, school personnel do not have an unfettered right to administer it. Excessive punishment resulting in injury to a student has resulted in cases of assault and battery against teachers or principals who inflicted such punishment.

A noteworthy corporal punishment case was decided in 1980 in *Hall v. Tawney,* where a federal court of appeals ruled that a child has a constitutional right to "bodily security" against corporal punishment.[7] This court concluded that there may be circumstances, independent of an allegation of cruel and unusual punishment, whereby the use of corporal punishment may raise a substantive rights issue.

The *Ingraham* case indicated that the availability of civil or criminal penalties for the excessive use of corporal punishment should serve as a sufficient deterrent to abuses by teachers and administrators.[8] Since the law does provide remedies for abuses in disciplining students, educators should be on notice that unreasonable or excessive punishment will not be sanctioned.

The common law rule on the subject of corporal punishment allows one standing *in loco parentis* to use reasonable force as he or she reasonably believes necessary for the child's proper control, training, or education.[9] In determining if the force is reasonable for those purposes, the following factors are to be considered:

1. The age, sex, and condition of the child.
2. The nature of the offense or conduct and the student's motives.
3. The influence of his or her example upon other students.
4. Whether the force was reasonably necessary to compel obedience to a proper command.
5. Whether the force was disproportionate to the offense, was unnecessarily degrading, or was likely to cause serious injury. Force applied for any purpose other than the proper training or education of the child or for the preservation of discipline, as judged by the above standards, is not allowed.[10]

In a Texas case a football coach yelled at a player, struck him in the helmet, and grabbed his face mask. As a result of the coach's actions, the student was hospitalized; he charged the coach with assault. At the trial the coach claimed that he had struck the boy, not for discipline, but for the purpose of "firing him up" or "instilling spirit in him." The trial court found the coach innocent of the charge and concluded that "the contact with the student was done for instruction and encouragement without any intent to injure him."[11]

The appeals court overturned the trial court on procedural issues and reiterated the legal basis for the support of corporal punishment in schools, but stated some limitations for corporal punishment. The appeals court said that a teacher or coach may not use physical violence against a student merely because the student is unable or fails to perform, either academically or athletically, at a desired level of ability. Privileged force must be reasonably necessary to enforce compliance with a proper command issued for the purpose of controlling, training, or educating the student or to punish the individual for prohibited conduct; and such force or physical contact must not be disproportionate to the activity or the offense.[12]

Some states specifically allow the use of reasonable physical force by school authorities to discipline students. For example, the Texas Penal Code provides that nondeadly force against a person is justified if the actor is entrusted with the care, supervision, or administration of the person for a special purpose; and when and to the degree the actor reasonably believes the force is necessary to further the special purpose or to maintain discipline in a group.[13]

However, as of 1990, twenty states had banned the use of corporal punishment in public schools. In states where corporal punishment is banned, each school district and each individual school must have a clear policy banning corporal punishment.

In those jurisdictions that retain the right to discipline by using corporal punishment, the following policy is offered as a model.

Principals, designated representatives and teachers are authorized to impose corporal punishment on students for disciplinary reasons whenever, in their judgment, the act or acts of a student warrant such punishment. Such punishment shall be administered in private either by the principal, designated representative or teacher, but in the presence of another adult witness."[14]

Corporal punishment policies may also include some or all of the following points.

1. The student should be informed beforehand of the specific misbehavior that would result in the use of corporal punishment, and corporal

punishment should not be used as first line of discipline for mis-behavior.

2. Corporal punishment should be used only in relation to behavior arising in the student–school relationship, and corporal punishment should not be cruel, unusual, or excessive, or be administered in anger or with malicious intent.

3. The principal or superintendent should receive a written report from the person administering any such punishment within 24 hours of the administration of the punishment.

Criminal Liability

Scenario 9.4: While a teacher was reprimanding a student for violating a school rule, the student turned and began walking away. The teacher grabbed the student, slammed him into the wall, and attempted to shake him by the shoulders. The student broke free, punched the teacher in the face, and ran away. A few minutes later the teacher entered the boy's classroom, pulled him from the room, and punched him several times.

Points to Consider: What is the difference between corporal punishment and assault and battery? How much force may a teacher use in disciplining a student?

If teachers use unreasonable force when administering corporal punish-ment, they may be subject to criminal liability for criminal assault or battery. Assault is the intentional threat of harmful or offensive contact.[15] It is not necessary that the teacher bear malice to the student or intend to do harm, only that it appear to the student that the harm being threatened is imminent and that the teacher has the present ability to commit the threatened contact. However, words alone are not sufficient to constitute an assault. The words must be accompanied by some overt act, no matter how slight, that adds to the threaten-ing character of the words.

Battery, on the other hand, is the actual intentional infliction of harmful or offensive bodily contact.[16] It is the intent to make contact, not the intent to do injury, that is the essential intent element in an action for battery. Even if a teacher has intended only to frighten a student by grabbing the student's arm and accidentally injures the student, the teacher has technically committed battery. It is not necessary that the contact actually cause pain or bodily damage. Battery also occurs when the contact damages the student's reasonable sense of dignity. When a court is asked to determine if the action was an offensive contact, the standard is not whether the particular student was offended, but whether "an ordinary person not unduly sensitive as to his or her dignity" would have been offended.

Once a court determines that a teacher intended to commit a harmful or offensive touching and such a contact occurs, the teacher is liable for any consequences that ensue, even though the teacher did not intend them, and in fact might not have foreseen them.

Liability for Violation of Student Rights

Civil Rights Act of 1871

Although many corporal punishment cases are based on charges of assault or battery, an increased amount of litigation is based on the allegation of a civil rights violation. Section 1983 of the Civil Rights Act of 1871[17] provides that a person who deprives another of rights, privileges, or immunities secured by the Constitution is liable to the injured party. In order to recover damages, it is essential that it be established that there was an invasion of federally protected constitutional right.

Because federal law prevents school districts from claiming immunity for the civil rights violations committed by an employee, many individuals choose to seek damages in federal court under section 1983.[18] In addition, under federal law the actions of public officials are not legally presumed to have been committed in good faith; consequently, the school district must prove that it acted in a reasonable manner. And, finally, federal law permits plaintiffs who have proved that their civil rights have been violated to collect "reasonable attorney's fees" under the Civil Rights Attorney's Fees Awards Act of 1976.[19]

Section 1983 of Title 42 of the United States Code authorizes a civil action for a deprivation of federally protected civil rights against a person acting under state law, custom, or usage. While this statute was enacted after the Civil War to protect the rights of freedmen, it has been extended to a variety of other situations including school authorities.[20] In 1975 this statute was construed by the United States Supreme Court to include school officials who knowingly, willingly, or maliciously intend to deprive a student of constitutional rights.[21] Additional court rulings have expanded this coverage.

In establishing that school officials are covered under the law, the Supreme Court held that a compensatory award in the form of monetary damages would be appropriate if school officials maliciously disregarded a student's clearly established constitutional rights. This would be true whether the school official knew, or reasonably should have known, the results of his or her actions against the student. Later, the Court clarified its ruling by limiting damages to those situations when an actual injury resulted from an unconstitutional deprivation.

An actual injury must be proved by the student before any substantial compensatory monetary award could be allowed by federal courts.[22]

Not only may school officials, as individuals, be sued under section 1983, but the Supreme Court has held that school boards, as a whole, can be sued for civil rights violations.[23] This has been construed to cover school boards even when a constitutional violation has been committed in good faith.[24] In other words, a good faith defense is no longer satisfactory. In addition, the Supreme Court has held that the protection includes not only constitutional claims, but also claims under federal statutes.[25] In one of the few times the Supreme Court has narrowed its construction of section 1983, it held that local governments, including school boards, cannot be subjected to punitive damages in civil rights suits.[26]

School principals and teachers must know their district's policy regarding the use of corporal punishment. In the absence of local policy, educators are advised to follow a common sense approach to physical punishment. The following guidelines should serve as a useful reminder.

Guidelines for the Administration of Corporal Punishment

1. Know the local school board policies governing the use of corporal punishment and follow them carefully.
2. Corporal punishment does not constitute "cruel and unusual punishment" under the Eighth Amendment to the United States Constitution.
3. Due process (notice and hearing) is not required prior to the imposition of corporal punishment under the Fourteenth Amendment to the United States Constitution; however, it may be required by local policy.
4. School personnel may corporally punish a child over the objections of the parents unless otherwise restricted.
5. School personnel can be held liable for monetary damages to a student in a civil or criminal action, if the corporal punishment caused injury to the student.
6. If a local school board does not have a policy covering the use of corporal punishment, consider the following:

    a. Make sure the student has been informed as to what conduct might lead to corporal punishment.
    b. Try other methods of punishment first; use corporal punishment as the last resort.
    c. Administer the punishment in the presence of another school person who has been informed beforehand of the reasons for the punishment.
    d. Be prepared to provide a written explanation of the reasons corporal punishment was administered and the name of the person who was present to the child's parent, if requested.

7. The child's age, stature, physical condition, mental capacity, and health should be considered, and corporal punishment should be appropriate.

8. School personnel who are visibly angry or emotionally upset during a confrontation with a student should not be allowed to administer corporal punishment until they have regained their composure.

9. Corporal punishment should not be administered in such a way as to cause undue humiliation of the student.[27]

These guidelines can serve school personnel well when considering school rules and forms of punishment for student violators, but state laws including state board of education regulations and local school board policy must be consulted for the legal specifics applicable to a situation. Even the most common forms of student discipline, such as verbal chastisement, denial of a privilege, after-school detention, and corporal punishment, should be scrutinized under the guidelines. The key for school personnel should be whether the rule is reasonably connected to a valid educational purpose and is reasonable in terms of deterring improper conduct. Reasonableness, consistency, and moderation are sound principles for disciplinary decisions.

Suspension and Expulsion of Students

Scenario 9.5:   Three weeks prior to the end of the semester, Connie Williams and Katie Stevenson were caught drinking beer at a football game. The principal told them that they were suspended for the rest of the semester, "starting right now." The students' appeal to the school board was denied.

Points to Consider: Must students be provided with a hearing before they are suspended? Are the due process requirements the same for short- and long-term suspensions and expulsions?

Short-term Suspensions

Students have certain constitutional rights that cannot be denied by school authorities without due process. Disciplinary proceedings involving the exclusion of students from public schools have been the focus of much litigation.

Case law regarding short-term suspensions is derived primarily from *Goss v. Lopez.*[28] During a period of widespread student unrest in the schools of Columbus, Ohio, several students were suspended from school. The students alleged that they had been suspended for up to ten days without a hearing. The students filed suit against the Columbus Board of Education and several administrators. The students claimed that the suspension was unconstitutional in that it permitted school administrators to deprive students of their rights to an education without a hearing, in violation of the procedural due process component of the Fourteenth Amendment. In hearing this case the district court declared that there were minimum requirements of notice and hearing that must take place prior to suspension.

On appeal, the school district contended that, because there is no constitutional right to an education at public expense, the due process clause does not protect against expulsions from the public school system. The Supreme Court refuted this contention and affirmed that the due process clause forbids arbitrary deprivations of liberty. The Court argued, "When a person's good name, reputation, honor or integrity is at stake because of what the government is doing to him, the minimal requirements of the due process clause must be satisfied."[29]

The *Goss* decision affirmed that education is perhaps the most important function of state and local governments. The Court recognized that because of the complexity of public schools, some modicum of discipline and order is essential if the educational function is to be performed. However, the Court required schools to set up hearing procedures that must be available to students before they are suspended. These due process procedures must include an oral or written notice of the charges against the student and an explanation of the evidence that the authorities have to support their charges. The student also must have the opportunity to present his or her side of the problem.[30] The Court noted that if the continued presence of the student in the school posed a danger to persons or property, he or she may immediately be removed from school. In this case, notice and hearing should follow as soon as possible. The Court stopped short of requiring that the student must be afforded the opportunity to secure counsel, cross-examine the witnesses, or call his or her own witness.

The Supreme Court held in *Wood v. Strickland* that in the context of school discipline, school board members are not immune from liability for damages, if they knew, or reasonably should have known, that the action would violate the constitutional rights of the students affected.[31] This decision clearly indicated how far the pendulum has moved, from the earlier "hands off" policy that left education to the educators to a position of strict legal accountability. The tradition had been that educators and school board members had a good faith immunity from liability for damages and that if educators acted with no intent to commit a wrongful act, they were protected from being held liable for their errors of judgment.

Between 1975 and 1990, more than twenty cases citing *Goss* dealt directly with short-term suspensions.[32] Courts continue to be reluctant to become involved in the day-to-day operation of schools, and in the majority of these cases, schools were successful if the *Goss* requirements were followed.[33] However, it is clear from dicta of many of these decisions that the educator's absolute control over the maintenance of student discipline has been limited. The intent of the

Goss and *Wood* decisions seems to be to respect both the discretionary powers of the educator and the constitutional protection of students. These decisions have formalized the requirement of fairness in the relationship between students and educators.

Guidelines for Short-term Suspensions

1. Oral notice is generally sufficient even when the local district requires written notice.
2. Rules do not have to be in writing to be enforced.
3. If school administrators afford *Goss* procedural requirements, substantial compliance with local policies that extend greater due process will be allowed.
4. Adversary type hearings are not required for short-term suspensions.
5. Admission of guilt by students precludes the necessity of a fact-finding hearing.
6. Parents do not have due process rights to notice and a hearing when their children are excluded from school.
7. When students' own actions cause the suspension to be longer than imposed, courts generally refuse to require more than *Goss* minimum due process.
8. *Miranda* warnings are not required in school disciplinary cases.
9. The exception language in *Goss* may apply when school administrators suspend without prior notice and a hearing even if the facts in the case do not indicate.[34]

Long-term Suspension and Expulsion

In general, the more severe the punishment the more formal the due process requirements. The *Goss* court prescribed a ten-day limit to separate short-term suspensions from long-term suspensions and expulsions. Courts require the same due process protection in cases involving long-term suspensions and expulsions. Expulsion hearings are not judicial trials, and common law rules of evidence do not apply.[35] However, students facing a long-term suspension or an expulsion should have the right to: (1) written notice,[36] (2) an impartial hearing,[37] (3) inspection of evidence,[38] and (4) cross-examination of witnesses.[39] Courts are not in agreement as to whether students have a right to representation by counsel.[40]

The purpose of these requirements is to ensure that when students are faced with severe penalties, they are treated fairly. Students have the right to know the type of conduct that if engaged in will subject them to long-term suspension or expulsion. They also have the right to be informed if they are being accused of violating a school rule. This notice gives students a fair opportunity to prepare their defense. Although this notice may be given orally, it is recommended that students and their parents be notified of the charges and of the time and place of the hearing in writing.

The student has a right to expect a fair hearing before any action is taken. At the hearing the student must be told of the evidence against him or her. Unless it can be shown that the principal cannot be impartial and fair, the school principal may be the trier of fact in such hearings. Students should be given the right to cross-examine adverse witnesses.

Discipline of Children with Disabilities

Scenario 9.6: Billy O'Brien, a learning-disabled student, was found to be in possession of three marijuana cigarettes. The school had a policy requiring that any student caught possessing marijuana be suspended for fifteen days.

Points to Consider: Must students with disabilities be treated differently than nondisabled students? Are schools ever allowed to suspend disabled students?

Perhaps the most controversial aspect of student discipline involves children with disabilities. Both federal and state laws have specified the rights of disabled children to a "free, appropriate public education" and have provided procedural protection in the placement and treatment of these special children.[41] In addition, the law provides that children with disabilities shall be educated in the "least restrictive environment." This mandate is the basis for the mainstreaming concept. Discipline of students with disabilities has been one of the controversial aspects of judicial activity in the interpretation of the law and regulations. What has emerged is a dual standard of discipline for disabled and nondisabled students.

Courts have generally held that students with disabilities cannot be suspended or expelled if the misconduct is a function of the disability.[42] This does not mean that the student must be continued in the current placement. However, if a change in placement is needed, it can only be made according to the procedures governing placement decisions. This involves the team or committee of professionals designated for such purposes and a hearing, if the change is challenged by the parents.

The determination of the origin of the student's misbehavior can only be made by an individual or individuals trained for such diagnostic purposes. If the professional diagnosis is that the misconduct was not a result of the disability, then the proper disciplinary hearing must be conducted, including the range of procedural protection available under school board policy. If the decision is to expel the student from school, the school board must provide educational services under the terms of the law. During the time of the diagnostic evaluation, school board hearing, and all appeals, the student must be continued in the same placement until such time as a final decision is made.[43]

In 1982 a federal court held that a five-day suspension of an eleventh-grade student with learning disabilities for verbal abuse of a teacher was appropriate. The court found that the suspension was not an expulsion from, or termination of, special education services. The court determined that the suspension was a disciplinary interruption that was reasonably calculated to teach the student a lesson in an effort to deter future misconduct.[44]

Because there are a number of procedural steps in the hearing and appeals process involving placement decisions of children with disabilities, the courts have held that these children must exhaust their administrative remedies before bringing a court action under federal law.[45] Therefore, school officials must know all the procedural steps in the hearing and appeal process and diligently carry them out as a deterrent to immediate court action.

The discipline of children with disabilities will continue to pose difficult problems for school personnel. The key factor in any decision should be what is best for the well-being of the student. (For a more detailed discussion of suspension of disabled students and the laws that protect such students, see Chapter 12.)

Institutional Authority Off School Grounds

Scenario 9.7: John Gaylor intercepted Steve Michaels several blocks away from school. He knocked Steve to the ground and stole his $100-dollar basketball shoes. When Steve's mother informed the principal of the robbery, the principal said that he was sorry, but he had no control of students once they left the school property. He suggested that Steve should not wear such expensive shoes to school.

Scenario 9.8: The wrestling coach had a rule forbidding members of the team from drinking alcohol. Rickie Bair, the star of the team, was seen drinking a beer at a local restaurant. The coach suspended Rickie from the team. Rickie's father asked the court for a restraining order requiring that Rickie be reinstated on the team.

Points to Consider: Is it legal for a school to have rules that govern student activity off school grounds? Can a school have more restrictive discipline policies for students who participate in extracurricular activities?

The authority of school officials to control the conduct of students off school grounds, to take responsibility for conduct, and to punish misconduct having a negative impact on the schools is very broad in terms of school-related activities. This authority has developed over time through court cases and is implied in state statute. The courts have upheld school authorities for disciplining students for misconduct off the school grounds.[46] The common law basis for the control of student activities or conduct off school grounds is based on the assumption that the authority of the teacher extends to any acts of students that are detrimental to the good order and best interests of the school, whether such acts are committed during school hours, while the student is going to or from school, or after the student has returned home.[47]

School boards may make rules and regulations governing extracurricular activities of students in athletic competition, musical organizations, dramatic organizations and productions, social activities, class and school trips, cheerleading, school and class elective offices, literary activities, service clubs, scholastic activities, and honor groups. When these activities take place off school grounds as officially sanctioned school activities, or where it can be shown that the off-campus activities have a detrimental effect on the schools, school boards may make reasonable rules and regulations for the control of conduct on the part of participating students.

Summary

Courts recognize that school authorities may adopt reasonable regulations for maintaining necessary order in schools. Rules and regulations for student conduct should be adopted as official board policy. It must be remembered, however, that only the board of education, and not individual school administrators, is authorized to make such policies. Positive means for teaching students the fundamentals of good citizenship, including their responsibilities toward others, should be developed and implemented. For the purpose of teaching such principles, schools should look toward the development of a curriculum that appropriately involves students in practical and relevant exercises in citizenship.

The discipline of students in public schools has increasingly come under court review. While it might appear that the courts are willing to second-guess the actions of school officials in matters of school discipline, the truth is that courts continue to give great weight to the discretion of school authorities. In fact, courts increasingly defer to school boards on the assumption that the school boards reflect the values of the communities. However, the fact remains that students and their parents will continue to seek court review when they feel that a right has been violated, the school failed to follow proper procedures in disciplinary actions, or the punishment was unreasonable and arbitrary under the circumstances.

Endnotes

1. Baker v. Owen, 395 F. Supp. 294 (M.D.N.C. 1975).
2. *Id.* at 296.
3. *Id.* at 302–03.
4. Ingraham v. Wright, 525 F. 2d 909 (5th Cir. 1976).
5. *Id.* at 918.
6. Ingraham v. Wright, 430 U.S. 651 (1977).
7. Hall v. Tawney, 621 F.2d 607 (4th Cir. 1980).
8. *Supra*, note 6.
9. THE RESTATEMENT OF TORTS, 2d ed. § 21. American Law Institute, St. Paul, Minn. 1965.
10. *Cited in* Hogenson v. Williams, 542 S.W. 2d 456, 459 (Tex. Civ. App.—Texarkana 1976).
11. *Id.* at 457.
12. *Id.* at 460.
13. Tex. Penal Code Ann. § 9.62 (Vernon Supp. 1982)
14. *Policy on Paddling,* KANSAS SCHOOL BOARD JOURNAL, November 1990, vol 29, no. 4.
15. *Supra*, Note 9, 21.
16. *Id.* at §§ 13, 18.
17. 42 U.S.C. § 1983, The Civil Rights Act of 1871.
18. Owen v. City of Independence, Mo., 445 U.S. 622 (1980).
19. State of Maine v. Thiboutot, 448 U.S. 1 (1980).
20. *Supra*, note 17.
21. Wood v. Strickland, 420 U. D. 308 (1975).
22. Carey v. Piphus, 435 U.S. 247 (1978.
23. Monnell v. Dept. of Social Services, 436 U.S. 65 (1978).
24. Owen v. City of Independence, Missouri, 589 F.2d 335 (8th Cir. 1978), *rev'd* 100 S. Ct. 1398 (1980).
25. Maine v. Thiboutot, 100 S. Ct. 2502 (1980).
26. City of Newport v. Fact Concerts, Inc., 49 LW 4860 (1981).
27. W. SPARKMAN & R. SHOOP, TEXAS SCHOOL LAW (Dubuque, Iowa: Bowers, 1984), 135.
28. Goss v. Lopez, 419 U.S. 565 (1975).
29. *Id.*
30. *Id.* at 511.
31. 420 U.S. 308 (1975).
32. D. Cooper & John Strope, *Short-Term Suspensions Fourteen Years Later,* 58 ED. LAW REP. 871 (April 12, 1990).
33. *Id.* at 881.
34. *Id.* at 882.
35. Betts v. Board of Educ. of Chicago, 466 F.2d 629, 633 (7th Cir. 1972).
36. Strickland v. Inlow, 519 F.2d 744 (8th Cir. 1975).
37. Dixon v. Alabama State Board of Education, 294 F.2d 150,158–59 (5th Cir.), *cert. denied,* 365 U.S. 930 (1961). *Also see,* Sullivan v. Houston Indep. School Dist., 475 F2d. 1071 (5th Cir.), *cert. denied,* 414 U.S. 1032, 1077, (1973).
38. Graham v. Knutzen, 362 F. Supp. 881 (D. Neb. 1973).
39. Morrison v. City of Lawrence, 186 Mass. 456, 460, 72 N.E. 91, 92 (1904).
40. Cases upholding a student's right to counsel include: Black Coalition v. Portland School Dist. No. 1, 484 F.2d 1040, 1045 (9th Cir. 1973); Givens v. Poe, 346 F.

Supp. 202, 209 (W.D.N.C. 1972); and Mills v. District of Columbia Bd. of Educ., 348 F. Supp. 866, 881 (D.D.C. 1972). Cases upholding the school's right to prohibit a student from being represented by legal counsel include: Linwood v. Board of Educ., 463 F.2d 263, 770 (7th Cir. 1972), *cert. denied,* 409 U.S. 1027 (1972); Haynes v. Dallas City. Junior College Dist., 386 F. Supp. 208 (N.D.Tex. 1974); and "R.R." v. Board of Educ., 109 N.J.Super. 337, 263 A.2d 1880 (1970).

41. The Education for All Handicapped Children Act of 1975, Publ. L. 94-142, 20 U.S.C. §§ 1401 (1976).

42. Stuart v. Nappi, 443 F. Supp. 1235 (D. Conn. 1978). *See also,* Doe v. Koger, 480 F. Supp. 225 (N.D. Ind., 1979).

43. S-l v. Turlington, 635 F.2d 342 (5th Cir. 1981). *See also,* Honig v. Doe, 108 S.Ct. 592 (1988).

44. Bd. of Educ. Sch. Dist. 150 v. Illinois State Bd. of Educ., 531 F. Supp. 148 (C.D. Ill. 1982).

45. H. R. v. Hornbeck, 524 F. Supp. 215 (D. Md. 1981).

46. *See, for example,* O'Rourke v. Walker, 128 Conn. 25 (Conn. 1925); Hutton v. State S.W. 122 (Tex. Civ. 1887); Fenton v. Stear, 423 F. Supp. 767 (W.D.Pa. 1976).

47. K. ALEXANDER & D. ALEXANDER, THE LAW OF SCHOOLS, STUDENTS, AND TEACHERS IN A NUTSHELL, (St. Paul, Minn: West, 1984), 157.

SECTION FOUR

Program Management

With the advent of site-based management, principals are increasingly held accountable for the effectiveness of their schools. While the courts typically have shown a great deal of deference for the principal's right to make programmatic decisions, there is a growing trend of judicial intervention when such decisions are arbitrary and capricious, violate an individual's rights, or impose different standards based on an unlawful classification. When the courts do become involved in the program decisions of school administrators, they are concerned about the legality of the decision, and not the wisdom of it.

Principals are on the firing line every day. By being well informed about legal issues relating to program management, principals will function effectively with less fear of judicial intervention. This section focuses on selected issues that have the greatest potential for legal problems. These issues are: compulsory attendance, religion in the public schools, special education, bilingual and special language programs, health and safety issues, copyright law, textbook selection and censorship, parental rights, and community–school interaction.

CHAPTER TEN

Compulsory School Attendance

Introduction

By the end of the eighteenth century, most states had enacted compulsory attendance laws. However, it was not until the beginning of this century that these laws began to be enforced. These laws have withstood legal challenges with the courts sustaining the right of the state to enforce reasonable regulations to compel school attendance as a duty for the public good. The United States Supreme Court held in *Pierce v. Society of Sisters*[1] that the state's right to require school attendance did not give it the right to limit attendance only in public schools. The court found that such a law violated parents' rights to control the education and upbringing of their children and was an unreasonable exercise of state power. Thus, compulsory attendance can be satisfied in either public or private schools, including parochial schools.

In 1944 the United States Supreme Court reaffirmed the right of the state to regulate school attendance. The court declared that "the family itself is not beyond regulation in the public interest . . . neither rights of religion nor rights of parenthood are beyond limitations."[2] Exceptions to compulsory school attendance laws have been granted for such limited reasons as suspension or expulsion, quarantine, marriage, attendance at private schools, or approved programs of home instruction.[3]

> *Scenario 10.1:* When informed that a new family in the attendance area did not plan to enroll its children in school, the principal informed the parents that "the state requires all children to either attend school or meet specific requirements for home school instruction." The parents kept their children home, saying, "Our religion requires that children be kept from the evils of society."

> *Points to Consider:* Does a home school have to be approved by the state in order to qualify as a school? If parents keep their children home from school, what form of education must they provide?

Scenario 10.2:   A man entered the principal's office and requested that his children be enrolled in school. Upon questioning, it was learned that the father was unemployed and the family had no home. The principal informed the man that, without an address in the attendance area, the children could not be enrolled.

Points to Consider: Do children have to have a permanent address in the district before they are owed a free public education?

Home Instruction

Some parents, seeking greater control of their children's education, remove them from the public schools and enroll them in established private or parochial schools. In some cases, parents have organized their own private schools that provide an educational program consistent with their own philosophical or religious beliefs. Still others have sought the right to educate their own children at home.

Home instruction, regardless of the motivation, challenges the concept that the state has a compelling interest in ensuring that children are provided a minimum level of formal education. By 1987, every state permitted home instruction in some form. Local school superintendents are charged with the responsibility of ensuring that the quality of home instruction attains at least the minimum legal requirements prescribed by state law. This requires public officials to become involved in alternative educational programs provided in the home.

It is estimated that there are in excess of 100,000 families educating their children at home in violation of compulsory attendance laws. In the 1972 case of *Wisconsin v. Yoder*,[4] the United States Supreme Court modified the state's power to impose regulations on parents. The Court held that Wisconsin was prevented from requiring members of the Old Order Amish religious sect to send their children to formal schools beyond the eighth grade. The Court said that even though the state had the power to impose reasonable regulations governing school attendance, the exercise of the power must not inhibit the deeply held religious beliefs of parents. In this case the parents' right to the free exercise of religion was sufficient to override the state's power to compel formal school attendance to age 16. The general application of the Court's ruling is limited because the Amish objected only to post-eighth grade compulsory attendance of 14- and 15-year-olds, based on well-established Amish custom.[5] Important to the Court's decision was the fact that the Amish beliefs were long-standing and were an important part of their total religious tradition.

Efforts to extend the *Yoder* decision have not been successful. The West Virginia Supreme Court refused to extend the dictum of *Yoder* to "Biblical

Christian" parents who chose to educate their children at home. In this case, when a family refused to comply with the state's compulsory attendance laws, they were arrested by a local truancy officer. The court found that even though the family was apparently doing a good job of educating their children and were sincere in their beliefs, the state had the right to require compliance with its attendance laws.[6]

Private Schools

Legal problems can also occur when parents decide to enroll their children in a private school. In *State v. Popanz*,[7] the Wisconsin Supreme Court was confronted with the issues of whether the term "private school," as used in the state's compulsory attendance law, was "impermissibly vague," and whether prosecutions involving private schools were, therefore, a violation of the due process clause of the Fourteenth Amendment. Popanz requested that local public school administrators inform him of what was necessary in order for a private school to be in compliance with the state law. He was told, among other things, that a district administrator would have to visit the school, personally, to ensure that the school complied with certain standards "of which someone at the Department of Public Instruction had advised him orally. . . ."[8] The county district attorney was requested by local school officials to institute proceedings against Popanz under the law. Popanz was found guilty by the trial court because he failed to establish that he had caused his children to attend a private school that met state standards.

The state supreme court concluded that ". . . due process requires that the law set forth fair notice of the conduct prohibited or required and proper standards for enforcement of the law and adjudication."[9] The court elaborated on the principle by noting that a criminal statute must be sufficiently definite to give a person of ordinary intelligence, who seeks to avoid its penalties, fair notice of required or prohibited conduct, and to allow law enforcement officers, judges, and juries to apply the terms of the law objectively and determine innocence or guilt, without having to create or apply their own standards.[10]

After reviewing state statutes, administrative rules and regulations, and official writings of the state department of education for a definition of *private school*, the court concluded that no such definition existed. The absence of an adequate definition meant that the decision about what constituted a private school was within the sole discretion of the local public school administrator. The court concluded that the statute was, therefore, unconstitutionally vague in that it failed "to provide fair notice to those who would seek to obey it and also lacks sufficient standards for proper enforcement."[11] Therefore, Popanz's conviction was reversed.

Even though the ruling has application only in Wisconsin, the legal basis could have profound effects in other states where violations of the compulsory attendance laws are punishable by criminal sanctions. Statutes involving criminal penalties must be definite and fair.

Although administrators should be careful in prosecuting a person who claims to be sending his or her child to a private school, the majority of courts have rejected parental claims of a constitutional nonreligious right to educate their children at home.

Homeless Children

The National Academy of Sciences reports that the phenomenon of homeless children "is nothing short of a national disgrace that must be treated with the urgency such a situation demands."[12] It is estimated that between 2 and 3 million people are without homes in the United States.[13] Families with children are now the fastest-growing segment of the homeless population.[14] Many children of these homeless families are denied access to schooling because they have difficulty complying with bureaucratic requirements. Residency requirements, lost records, the time lines for special education placement, lack of transportation, and problems with substantiating legal guardianship are common examples.[15]

Although students have a property right to attend school, most states and school districts require that the student satisfy some type of residency requirement. Because public schools are financed primarily by local property taxes, some local boards of education argue that they are responsible only for educating children who are residents of their school district. Although this may have an economic justification, it presents serious problems for children who live in hotels, boarding houses, motels, shelters, tents, over heating grates, or in doorways.

Homeless children and their parents win some challenges to their exclusion from public education. For example, when four children who were living with their parents in a tent in a Massachusetts state park were denied enrollment in the local school, they appealed to the state commissioner of education. The Commissioner ruled that children from homeless families have a right to be educated in the town in which they live. He concluded that Massachusetts state law required that local communities be responsible for educating the children within their boundaries, "irrespective of their living situation."[16]

The McKinney Homeless Assistance Act of 1987 was the first federal legislation to address the concerns of emergency shelter and long-term housing; the provision of food, health care, training, and community services; and the educational needs of the homeless.[17] This legislation requires that each state review school attendance residency requirements to assure that homeless children have access to free appropriate public education that is comparable to the services provided to other students in the school being attended. Homeless children may either continue to be enrolled in the school district of origin for the remainder of the year or enroll in the school district in which he or she is living, whichever is in the child's best interests. In addition, the educational records of each child must be maintained so that the records are available in a timely fashion.

Endnotes

1. Pierce v. Society of Sisters of the Holy Names of Jesus and Mary, 268 U.S. 510 (1925).
2. Prince v. Massachusetts, 321 U.S. 158 (1944).
3. J. A. Avner, *Home Schoolers: A Forgotten Clientele?* SCHOOL LIBRARY JOURNAL, 1990, pp. 29–33.
4. 406 U.S. 205 (1972)
5. K. ALEXANDER, PUBLIC SCHOOL LAW, (St. Paul, Minn.: West, 1980), p. 266.
6. State v. Riddle, 282 S.E. 2d 359 (1981).
7. 332 N.W. 2d 750 (Wis. 1983).
8. *Id.* at 752.
9. *Id.* at 754.
10. *Id.*
11. *Id.* at 756.
12. NATIONAL ACADEMY OF SCIENCES, HOMELESSNESS, BROKEN LIVES (Washington, D.C.: 1987).
13. J. KOZOL, RACHEL AND HER CHILDREN: HOMELESS FAMILIES IN AMERICA, (NEW YORK: CROWN, 1988).
14. NATIONAL COALITION OF THE HOMELESS, BROKEN LIVES (WASHINGTON, D.C., 1987).
15. P. First & G. Cooper, *Access to Education by Homeless Children,* 53 ED. LAW REP. (July 20, 1989), p. 757.
16. *Id.* at 759.
17. P.L. No. 100-77.

CHAPTER ELEVEN

Religion in the Public Schools

Introduction

Among the most emotional and controversial aspects of school program management are the questions of the propriety of religious activities. The religion clause of the First Amendment stipulates that "Congress shall make no law respecting an establishment of religion or prohibiting the free exercise thereof." Because the Fourteenth Amendment protects individual freedom from state action, the Supreme Court has applied the "establishment" and "free exercise" clauses to state government action. The United States Supreme Court has articulated a three-part test, known as the "Lemon Test," to be used to evaluate state statutes and local school board policies. To satisfy the prohibitions of the establishment clause of the Constitution, governmental action must pass all three prongs of this test: It must have a "secular legislative purpose" and "a primary effect that neither advances nor inhibits religion," and it must not foster "excessive entanglement between government and religion."[1] Courts attempt to balance the right of free exercise of religion against the right not to have a religion established. Problems arise when these two rights are perceived as being in conflict.

Prayers and Bible Reading

Scenario 11.1: In an elementary school situated in a conservative rural community, the principal began each school day by reading a brief inspirational message over the public address system. Because the majority of the community supported this practice, the school board had given its blessing.

Points to Consider: If no one complains, are Bible readings or individual prayers permitted in public schools? Would such prayers be allowed if students who do not wish to participate are permitted to excuse themselves?

The United States Supreme Court has made it clear that prayers and Bible reading in public school classrooms are a violation of the First Amendment's establishment clause. In 1962 the Supreme Court ruled in *Engel v. Vitale*[2] that the New York State–adopted nonsectarian prayer for all public schools constituted state-sponsored religious activity prohibited by the First and Fourteenth amendments.

In 1963, in *Abington Township v. Schempp*,[3] the United States Supreme Court struck down a Pennsylvania law requiring the reading of Bible verses at the opening of public schools each day. The law required that "at least ten verses of the *Holy Bible* shall be read, without comment, at the opening of each public school on each school day. Any child shall be excused from such Bible reading upon the written request of his parent or guardian." The morning religious exercises were conducted by students under teacher supervision and were broadcast into each classroom. The Bible reading was followed by the recitation of the Lord's Prayer by all students. The Court held that the required Bible reading violated the establishment clause because the primary effect was the advancement of religion. Neither the voluntary participation of the students nor the nondenominational nature of the religious observances reduced the constitutional violation.

School prayers have continued to be among the most persistent religious issues confronting public schools. A variety of practices relating to school prayer have been challenged as violating the establishment clause of the First Amendment. In addition, state statutes and state constitutional amendments have attempted to permit school prayer. Federal courts have ruled the following religious activities unconstitutional: voluntary spoken prayer, student-led prayers in school assemblies, teacher-initiated devotional activities in public schools, and the posting of copies of the Ten Commandments in public school classrooms.[4] Courts have also prohibited school prayers by pupils before eating a mid-morning snack, voluntary prayer on school premises before the beginning of the school day with parent approval, and voluntary religious exercises before the school day involving the reading by a student volunteer from the Congressional Record the "remarks" of the chaplain of that body.[5]

Silent Meditation or Prayer

Several state constitutional amendments and state laws calling for silent meditation or prayers in public schools have been struck down under the establishment clause. For example, in Alabama a parent challenged the action of several elementary school teachers who conducted prayers in their classrooms, including group recitations of the Lord's Prayer. The original complaint was amended to include a challenge to two Alabama statutes, enacted in 1982, authorizing a period of silence for meditation or prayer in the public schools and permitting instructors in public education institutions in the state to lead willing students in prayer. The 11th Circuit Court of Appeals held that the nonstatutory school prayers recited in public school classrooms under the direction of teachers, as well as the two state statutes allowing silent meditation and permitting prayer, were unconstitutional under the establishment clause.[6]

The governor of Alabama sought review of the appeals court's decision by the United States Supreme Court. The Court affirmed the decision of the federal court of appeals,[7] concluding that the statute was intended to convey a clear preference for students to engage in devotional activities during the moment of silence. In a concurring opinion, one justice noted that the Supreme Court's order was a holding that the state statute permitting teachers and professors in public education institutions to lead willing students in a prescribed prayer was unconstitutional and a violation of the establishment clause of the First Amendment, applicable to the states under the Fourteenth Amendment. This Supreme Court decision left intact the established precedent prohibiting prayer in public schools.

A unique prayer case in 1982 involved the recitation and singing of a school prayer to music played by the band. In this case a suit was filed alleging that the practice violated the establishment clause.[8] The words of the prayer were:

Dear God, please bless our school and all it stands for. Help keep us free from sin, honest and true, [sic] courage and faith to make our school the victor. In Jesus' name we pray, Amen.[9]

The words of the prayer were posted in raised block letters on the wall above the entrance to the high school gymnasium and were recited or sung by students to music played by the band at various school activities. The school principal or other school employees often initiated the prayer at the events. Student attendance at any event during which the prayer was recited or sung was voluntary, and no one was required to participate in the prayer, nor obligated to stand when the words were spoken or sung.

The federal district court reviewed the facts and subjected the prayer to the three-part test used to evaluate statutes or policies under the establishment clause. The court concluded that the practice violated the establishment clause according to the purpose, effect, and entanglement analysis. In addition, the court held that the prohibition of the recitation or singing of school prayer would not be an infringement on the students' free exercise rights as had been alleged by the school district.[10]

Team Prayers

Scenario 11.2: Upon being criticized by the media, the head football coach said, "Tonight's game, like every game for the past 43 years, will begin with a public invocation and a team prayer. I'm a God-fearing person and it's definitely needed; it's needed in our society."

Points to Consider: Is it constitutional for coaches or other persons to deliver public prayers prior to school-sponsored functions?

In many communities a minister gives an invocation over the public address system prior to the start of athletic contests. A circuit court of appeals ruled that this practice violates the First Amendment.[11] The court ruled that a religious invocation given over a school's sound system at a school-sponsored event conveys the inescapable message that the school endorses the religious activity.[12] In 1989 the United States Supreme Court declined to review this decision, thus letting it stand. Efforts to avoid compliance with this decision include: ministers using bullhorns to lead prayers; ministers seated at various locations in the stands, cuing the fans to chant the Lord's Prayer; and ministers encouraging fans to take radios to the game and turn up the volume as the station broadcasts a prayer.

It is also commonplace for coaches, sponsors, or students to lead teams in prayer before, during, or after competition. In a case involving a band director who led band members in prayer at rehearsals and performances, a federal district court ruled that the school district, in permitting the prayer, violated the First Amendment rights of the plaintiffs.[13] The court issued a permanent injunction against the use of prayers in the district and awarded the plaintiff $15,103.97 in fees and costs.

Religious Expression in Ceremonial Programs

Because of their ceremonial and minimal nature, courts have traditionally upheld prayers in graduation exercises.[14] However, a United States district court rejected a unique attempt to advocate the right to religious expression at a valedictory address.[15] Angela Guidry earned a perfect 4.0 grade point average and was scheduled to give an address at her graduation exercises. When Guidry refused to omit references to her personal religious beliefs, she was excluded from the program.

Her proposed remarks included the following:

I would first like to thank my Lord Jesus who has allowed me to be in this position tonight. . . . To me the most important thing in your life today is not whether you have a good education or a good job, but whether or not you have the Lord in your life. . . . Some of you don't realize that when you die either you go to Heaven or you go to hell to stay forever. God only looks at one thing to determine that, & [sic] that's whether or not you have Jesus in your heart. . . . I challenge you tonight to seek the Lord Jesus,

believe in Him & [sic] give your heart & [sic] your life to Him so you can
live forever in Heaven with Him.[16]

Guidry argued that this "censorship" was a violation of her freedom of expression, that it was unconstitutional prior restraint, and that her speech was allowed under the Lemon Test because it had a secular purpose.[17] She also sued the principal and the counselor seeking monetary damages.

The court ruled that the crucial question was not whether or not the speech had a secular purpose, but whether the "primary effect" of the speech was to communicate a governmental endorsement of religion. The court affirmed the principal's actions as a reasonable attempt to "avoid the appearance that the school was fostering, or even foisting, religion."[18] The United States court of appeals dismissed the case and pointed out that both the principal and the counselor were acting in their official capacities when they censored her speech and thus were protected from liability damage obligations.[19]

Christmas Observance

Scenario 11.3:   As a strategy to build student pride in their school, every month one class is assigned the responsibility of putting up a display in the lobby and the main hall. Sometimes the display represents student projects from a recent unit they have studied; other times the students choose to create a display that expresses their feeling about a season or an important historical event that occurred in that month. December was the month assigned to Sue Jones's third-grade class, and the students decided to decorate the building with Christmas decorations. They put a traditional Christmas tree in the lobby and filled the walls of the hall with "Christmas Decorations from Around the World" that they had made.

Points to Consider: May schools display religious symbols? Can schools have Christmas trees in their classrooms or halls?

Although Christmas is essentially a Christian holiday, it permeates Western civilization in both sacred and secular traditions and has an impact on Christian church services, on social life, and on the business community. The intertwining historical, religious, and commercial strains are not easily separated. Many public schools display Christian symbols during the winter holiday season, and these displays have been the source of much public debate.

Some believe that to prohibit such displays would be a violation of the free exercise clause of the First Amendment. Others criticize the displays as being in violation of the establishment clause of the First Amendment. In the case of

Allegheny County v. American Civil Liberties Union Greater Pittsburgh Chapter,[20] the Supreme Court examined the constitutionality of Allegheny County placing a creche in front of its courthouse and a Christmas tree, a Chanukah menorah, and a statement about liberty in front of its county building. The Court ruled that the creche conveyed government support of Christianity and was a violation of the First Amendment prohibition on establishment of religion. However, the Court upheld the constitutionality of the other displays, noting that a Christmas tree is primarily a secular symbol and the other displays simply acknowledged Christmas and Chanukah as parts of the same winter holiday season without endorsing either the Christian or Jewish faiths.[21]

Public schools cannot ignore Christmas nor its reflections in the art, music, drama, literature, commerce, and folkways of this country. Nor can a public school as an agency of the state impose upon students a set of religious beliefs. Thus, for public schools, the recognition of Christmas should be neither doctrinal nor devotional in nature. Such cultural expressions as Christmas parties, wreaths and candles, Christmas trees, the rendition of the Christmas theme in art and music—when carried out with no religious implication—are permitted. However, consideration should be given to the impact of these activities on the entire school community. It would appear that if a school district chooses to have such displays, the emphasis must be on the secular aspect of the holidays and on religious pluralism.

Student Distribution of Religious Materials

In an effort to reduce student disruption and remain neutral as an educational institution, some schools have adopted policies that limit the distribution of noncurricular materials on school property. These policies cover a broad range of subject matter, from so-called "hate" literature to commercial advertising. When a Colorado school district policy included a ban on "materials that proselytize a particular religious or political belief," a group of students sued the school, claiming such a ban violated their First Amendment free speech rights. The United States district court ruled that the district's ban on religious publications was unconstitutional. The court said that such a policy creates an impermissible risk of suppression of ideas.[22]

Instruction about Religion

Scenario 11.4: As part of a course in comparative religion, all students in the eighth grade were required to read sections from various religious documents, including the Bible. A group of non-Christian parents asked that this course be abandoned.

Points to Consider: Are all religious works banned from use in public schools?

Although the Supreme Court prohibited prayers and Bible reading in the public schools, it did not foreclose the study of the Bible or of religion as part of the secular education program. The Bible and other religious documents can be presented in public schools from a literary, cultural, or historical perspective. The United States Supreme Court ruled that: "The Bible is worthy of study for its literary and historic qualities. Nothing we have said here indicates that such study of the Bible or of religion, when presented objectively as a part of a secular program of education, may not be effected consistent with the First Amendment."[23]

For example, a course or unit on comparative religion, the study of the Psalms during a literature course, or sacred music in a choir program would seem to be appropriate ways to approach religion in the classroom. It is, however, important that any such study or presentation be done in an objective manner, without any efforts on the part of the teachers or students to proselytize others in the school setting.

Teacher Proselytizing

Teachers have been dismissed for refusing to refrain from religious practices or discussions in the classroom. In Pennsylvania a teacher was dismissed for refusing to comply with the superintendent's directives to cease the religious exercises he conducted in the classroom. These activities included, among other things, the recitation of the Lord's Prayer and the reading of a Bible story, with an explanation if the students did not understand. After the school board objected to these practices, the teacher began using an extemporaneous prayer and read only one Bible story without comment. When the teacher refused to stop the religious activities, he was dismissed.

In court the teacher testified that he believed he had a constitutional right to do what he was doing, and that he felt a need to ask God for his guidance at the beginning of each school day. The court held that the practices violated the establishment clause. Furthermore, the teacher's right to free exercise of religion did not give him the right to conduct religious activities in his classroom. The court upheld the teacher's dismissal for refusing to comply with the superintendent's directives.[24]

Teaching about Creationism

In South Dakota the contract of a science teacher was not renewed because he devoted excessive time to creationism and religion in his biology class, and he failed to cover basic scientific principles, in accordance with the policies and guidelines set and explained to the teacher by the board. The state supreme court sustained the action of the board by concluding that the nonrenewal was neither arbitrary, capricious, nor an abuse of discretion.[25]

Values in the Curriculum

Scenario 11.5: A group of parents contacted the principal of an elementary school and demanded that she discontinue the school's tradition of celebrating Halloween with parties and costume parades. They felt that such activities celebrated the feast day of ghouls and goblins, which were manifestations of witchcraft. These parents also wanted the school to stop teaching about values, sex education, and other religions.

Points to Consider: Do parents have the right to make choices about the school's curriculum? Do parents have the right to remove their child from classes that discuss topics of which they do not approve? Do community groups have the right to remove materials from the curriculum?

A growing number of national and local groups attempt to exclude certain educational activities from the curriculum on religious or other grounds. They not only want their children excluded from certain activities; they want the school to accommodate their religious beliefs by removing specific courses, activities, and instructional materials. Frequently they charge that the school curriculum promotes "secular humanism," which they allege is a belief that disavows God and places reason above divine guidance.

Courts have, so far, rejected such claims. The case of *Mozert v. Hawkins County Board of Educators*[26] illustrates the court's attempt to balance the rights of parents to make choices about their child's education and the public school's right to make educational decisions. In this case, parents challenged the requirement that all students participate in a reading program that contained stories and poems with ideas contrary to the parents' religious beliefs. The district court ruled that the parents' religious beliefs were burdened, awarded damages, and would have permitted home instruction under the state compulsory attendance statute.[27] The federal court of appeals reversed this decision, recognizing the broad discretion of school boards to establish curriculum, even in the face of parental disagreements.

The Hatch Act

Conservative groups that want to control the content of public school instruction are not a new phenomenon.[28] However, these groups now believe that they have a law that supports their cause. In 1984 the federal rules for a minor piece of legislation were published. These rules, written by the Department of Education, define the implementation of the 1978 legislation commonly known as the Hatch Amendment. Although not directed specifically at elements in the curriculum that deal with religion, the Hatch Act has been used by parents to support their efforts to remove their children from classroom activities dealing with subjects or ideas that the parents find offensive.

Simply stated, these regulations require parental consent before students take part in federally funded psychiatric or psychological experimentation, testing, or treatment. These rules say that schools must obtain parental permission before administering psychiatric or psychological tests or treatment to students, in which the primary purpose is to reveal one or more of the following: political affiliation; mental and psychological problems; sexual behavior and attitudes; illegal, anti-social, self-incriminating and demeaning behavior; critical appraisals of family members; legal relationships such as those of lawyers, physicians, and ministers; and income.

An intense debate continues over the interpretation of these rules. Competing groups have mounted active campaigns to expand or restrict their application. Conservative groups want to give parents total control over the content of the curriculum. In some communities this campaign has resulted in the banning or restricting of controversial topics, including religion, communism, abortion, witchcraft, and homosexuality.[29] Although only a few complaints against school districts have reached the federal level, many opponents of the rules believe that the regulations permit virtually indiscriminate federal probing of curricula that should be the exclusive domain of local school boards.

Senator Hatch has criticized parent groups that "have interpreted both the statute and the regulations so broadly that they would have them apply to all curriculum materials, library books, teacher guides, etc., paid for with state or local money." He has also criticized education groups that he believes have "over-reacted to the regulations."[30] According to Hatch, the purpose of the amendment was to "guarantee the right of parents to have their children excused from federally funded activities under carefully specified circumstances."[31] He emphasized that the amendment was not intended to apply to any curriculum or other school activities not directly supported by federal funds.

Use of School Facilities for Religious Activities

Scenario 11.6:   A group of students requested that they be allowed to use a classroom after school for the purpose of conducting Bible study classes. The principal refused permission on the grounds that this would be a violation of the separation of church and state.

Points to Consider: Is it permissible to prevent religious activities in a public school building?

Scenario 11.7: As part of the school's outreach/community education program, the school offered adult reading programs at locations throughout the city. One of these classes was located in the Church of the Living Word School.

Points to Consider: May public school monies be spent to offer classes or activities in religious schools?

The Equal Access Act

In response to community demands, many school districts have expanded their programs of community and adult education. These programs have resulted in a wide range of enrichment, academic, recreational, and social courses and activities being offered in the schools. In 1984 a law was enacted that, at first glance, appeared to help in this effort. Upon closer examination, however, the Equal Access Act may prove to have exactly the opposite effect.[32]

The act made it unlawful for any public school to deny equal access to school facilities to students wishing to conduct a religious, political, or philosophical meeting. It specifically gave students the right to conduct these meetings, if the school received federal financial aid and had a limited open forum. The financial aid clause is clear and presents little problem. But the "open forum" clause would seem to force a choice between two contradictory directives. The First Amendment, which guarantees freedom of religion but prohibits the establishment of religion, has historically prohibited religious activities in public school facilities. The Equal Access Act, however, prohibits public schools from discriminating against any student group on the basis of religious, political, or philosophical beliefs.

It is the open forum clause of the Equal Access Act that presents a possible threat to the process of opening school facilities for community and student use. The Equal Access Act defines an open forum as a school district's action that "grants an offering to, or an opportunity for, one or more non–curriculum-related student groups to meet on school premises during non-instructional time." "Non-instructional time" is defined as that time set aside by the school before actual classroom instruction begins or after actual classroom instruction ends.

The law specifically states that school districts have the option of not coming under the act. To exercise that option, they must keep their facilities closed to all noncurriculum-related student meetings and activities, including religious meetings, thereby not creating a limited open forum. In other words, to avoid the risk of prosecution for an unconstitutional establishment of religion or for violating the Equal Access Act, a school district might decide to disallow all noncurricular activities in the school.

Historically, school administrators who sought guidelines for deciding whether or not to allow students to participate in religious-oriented activities on school property could look to the three-pronged Lemon Test established by the Supreme Court. Following the guidelines the test provides, public schools could not allow students to conduct religious activities on school property.

In 1989 the United States Supreme Court ruled for the first time on the constitutionality of the Equal Access Act. In *Mergens v. Board of Education of West Side Community Schools,*[33] the Court had the opportunity to rule on the relationship of the Equal Access Act to the First Amendment.

This case began in 1985 when several students at an Omaha high school were denied permission to form a Christian group devoted to fellowship and Bible study. The students filed suit, arguing that their rights under the Equal Access Act had been violated. They contended that their school had sanctioned several extracurricular clubs on topics ranging from chess to scuba diving. School officials countered that all their clubs were related in some way to the broad goals of the school curriculum. They also argued that the Equal Access Act violated the First Amendment.

In 1989 the United States Supreme Court ruled that the 1984 Equal Access Act does not violate the First Amendment's prohibition against government establishment of religion. In its decision the Court said that if a school sanctions even one student group that is not directly tied to coursework, the act requires that the school cannot discriminate against other student organizations based on the religious, philosophical, or political views of their members. The decision further stated: "There is a crucial difference between government speech endorsing religion, and private speech endorsing religion, which the free speech and free exercise clauses protect."[34]

According to the Court:

> *A student group directly relates to a school's curriculum if the subject matter of the group is actually taught, or will soon be taught, in a regularly offered course; if the subject matter of the group concerns the body of courses as a whole; if participation in the group is required for a particular course; or if participation in the group results in academic credit.*

The Court gave the example of a French club, which would be considered curriculum-related if the school offered a French course. Chess, stamp collecting, or community service, however, would most likely be considered noncurriculum-related, and thus their existence would create a limited open forum at the school requiring the accommodation of religious groups.

Conservative groups hailed this decision as going a long way toward eliminating bigoted attitudes toward Christian student groups in public schools.[35]

Some education groups and advocates of strict separation of church and state worry that this decision will create a host of new problems for the schools. As a result of this decision, school districts may become more cautious about their willingness to allow groups to meet in school.[36] Some districts will undoubtedly try to figure out what they need to do to maintain a closed forum.

School districts have three options: (1) drop all extracurricular programs to ensure a closed forum, (2) only permit those groups that directly relate to the curriculum, or (3) open their doors to all student groups.[37]

Excessive Entanglement

In 1985 the United States Supreme Court handed down two decisions dealing with the First Amendment's establishment of religion clause. The decisions in *Grand Rapids School District v. Ball*[38] and *Aguilar v. Felton*[39] have received a great deal of attention in active public debate regarding the appropriate relationship between religion and public education. Both cases involved the use of public funds to provide services to non–public school students in non–public school settings. The *Grand Rapids* case involved community education programs, and the *Aguilar* case involved the use of federal funds received under Title I of the Elementary and Secondary Education Act. Although the specifics of the cases differ, the Court used the same arguments in both decisions and ruled both programs unconstitutional.

The Court held that offering services for private-school children at public expense, in classrooms located in parochial schools, was unconstitutional. The activities in question were administered by an employee of the public district but taught by non–public school teachers employed on a part-time basis and paid by the public schools.

The Court did not believe that the non–public employees would deliberately try to subvert their task to the service of religion, but it felt that the pressures of the environment might alter their behavior. Although the record revealed no evidence whatever of specific incidents of indoctrination, the Court stressed that, by having the classes in the non–public schools and taught by non–public school employees, there was a strong chance that teachers might knowingly or unwittingly tailor the content of the courses to fit the school's announced religious goals. It was the belief of the majority of the justices that if this ideological influence did occur, it would probably not be reported by students, their parents, or the school system itself.

The Court reaffirmed that ". . . the First Amendment rests upon the premise that both religion and government can best work to achieve their lofty aims if each is left free from the other within its respective sphere." The concern that the state should not become too closely entangled with the church is based on the belief that when the state becomes enmeshed in a given religion, the freedom of religious beliefs of others suffers. In addition, the freedom of those who belong to the specific denomination is limited by governmental intrusion into sacred matters.

The major point of contention between those justices who found the activities of the two school districts unconstitutional and those who disagreed is the historical interpretation of the meaning of the First Amendment establishment clause. The majority of justices followed the Court's traditional Lemon Test. Even though the majority of the justices acknowledged the benefits of both programs, they found that the critical elements of entanglement were present in this case. They further believed that the aid was being provided in a "pervasively sectarian environment," and that the comprehensive program of supervision that would be necessary to ensure that one specific religion would not be advanced would lead inevitably to an unconstitutional administrative entanglement between church and state.

It is tempting to come to the defense of the two school districts on the grounds that some interaction between church and state is unavoidable; that an attempt to eliminate all contact between the two would be both futile and undesirable; and that these particular programs did much good and little, if any, detectable harm. To ensure freedom of religion for all, it is essential that the state not single out one religion for special treatment or appear to endorse the practice of one religion.

Summary

1. The courts will scrutinize state laws or local policies involving religion and the public schools according to the three-part test of secular purpose, primary effect, and excessive entanglement. If the activity violates any one of the three criteria, then the courts will probably declare it unconstitutional under the establishment clause.
2. Bible reading as part of a school's religious exercise in the classroom is prohibited.
3. Prayers, whether voluntary or required as part of religious exercises in the classroom, are prohibited.
4. The Bible may be studied for its literary and historical qualities when presented objectively as part of the secular program of education.
5. Religion may be studied in the public schools as part of the secular education program.
6. School districts may not deny the use of school facilities to a religious organization solely because of the group's purpose if the facilities are available and open to other noncurriculum-related groups.
7. School districts may not adopt policies permitting student groups to meet voluntarily either before or after school with teacher supervision for religious purposes.

8. There is a question as to whether moments of silence for meditation or prayer are permissible in public schools.

9. Teachers who refuse to comply with board policy concerning personal religious practices in the classroom may be dismissed for insubordination.

10. If prayers are conducted at ceremonial gatherings, it is suggested that sensitivity, awareness, and respect be given to persons of various faith groups. Such prayers should be nonsectarian so as to represent the entire assembly. The language of such prayers should include all present—Jewish, Christian, Islamic, Buddhist, etcetera.

Endnotes

1. Lemon v. Kurtzman, 403 U.S. 602 (1971).
2. 370 U.S. 421 (1962).
3. 374 U.S. 203 (1963).
4. M. McCarthy, *Church-State Relations*, in CRITICAL ISSUES IN EDUCATION LAW: THE ROLE OF THE FEDERAL JUDICIARY IN SHAPING PUBLIC EDUCATION (Topeka, Kansas: National Organization on Legal Problems of Education, 1989).
5. E. REUTER & R. HAMILTON, THE LAW OF PUBLIC EDUCATION (Mineola, N.Y.: Foundation Press, 1976) pp. 26–7.
6. Jaffree v. Wallace, 705 F.2d 1526 (11th Cir. 1983).
7. Wallace v. Jaffree, 104 S.Ct. 1704 (1984).
8. 563 F. Supp. 883 (S.D. Tex. 1982).
9. *Id.* at 884.
10. "Unconstitutional Song Still Sung," The University Daily, Nov. 10, 1982.
11. E. Bjorklun, *School District Liability for Team Prayers*, 59 ED. LAW REP. 7 (May 10, 1990).
12. Jager v. Douglas County School District, 862 F.2d 824, 831 (50 ED. LAW REP. 694) (11th Cir. 1989).
13. Steele v. Van Buren Public School District, 845 F.2d 1492 (46 ED. LAW REP. 572) (8th Cir. 1988).
14. *Id.*
15. Guidry v. Calcasieu Parish School Board, et al., Civil Action No. 87-2122-LC (W.D.La. Feb. 22, 1989).
16. J. Vile, *Religious Expression in High School Valedictory Addresses:* Guidry v. Calcasieu Parish School Board, 53 ED. LAW REP. 1051 (Aug. 3, 1989), 1057.
17. *Id.* at 1060–1.
18. *Id.* at 1064.
19. Guidry v. Calcasieu Parish School Board, 897 F.2d 181 (1990).
20. 109 S.Ct. 3086 (1989).
21. D. Tatel & E. Mincberg, *The 1988–89 Term of the U.S. Supreme Court and Its Impact on the Public Schools*, 55 ED. LAW REP. 827 (Nov. 9, 1989).
22. Rivera v. East Otero School District R-1, 721 F. Supp. 1189 (D. Col. 1989).
23. Sch. Dist. of Abington Tp. v. Schempp, 374 U.S. 203 (1963).
24. Fink v. Bd. of Educ., 442 F. 2d 283 (Pa. Commw. Ct. 1982).
25. Dale v. Bd. of Educ., 316 N.W. 2d 108 (S.D. 1982).
26. 827 F.2d 1058 (6th Cir. 1987).

27. R. Mawdsley, *Parental Rights and Public Education,* 59 ED. LAW REP. 271 (May 24, 1990).

28. *Id.* at 97.

29. *Id.* at 65.

30. *In Senate, Hatch Asks for "Common Sense" on Parents' Rights,* EDUCATION WEEK, Feb. 27, 1985, p. 1.

31. *Id.*

32. 20 U.S.C. §4071.

33. 867 F.2d 1076 (8th Cir. 1989).

34. M. Walsh, *School Religion Club Is Constitutional, Court Rules,* EDUCATION WEEK, vol IX, no. 38, June 13, 1990, A 1.

35. *Id.* at A 10.

36. M. Walsh, *Effects of Decision on Extracurricular Raise Thorny Issues,* EDUCATION WEEK, vol IX, no. 38, June 13, 1990.

37. *Id.* at A 12.

38. 105 S.Ct. 3216 (1985).

39. *Id.* at 3232.

CHAPTER TWELVE

Special Education

Introduction

Historically, children with physical or mental disabilities were denied the right to a public education either by being totally excluded from schools or by not being provided appropriate instruction or other special services. In recent years, these children have won the right to a free appropriate public education. Through much litigation and legislation, states have been required to provide needed educational services to children with disabilities in order to guarantee them the right to an education.

A series of federal court cases during the early 1970s addressed the rights of disabled children to an appropriate education. In Pennsylvania a federal district court in a consent decree held that all children, regardless of disability, have a basic right to an education under the Fourteenth Amendment. The court held that the state could not apply any law that would postpone, terminate, or deny mentally retarded children access to a publicly supported education, including a public school program, tuition or tuition maintenance, and homebound instruction.[1] In the District of Columbia a federal court affirmed that education is a fundamental interest for all excluded children and stated that a claimed lack of funds was no excuse for not providing special education services.[2] Another federal court ruled that whenever possible a child with a disability should be included in the mainstream.[3]

Section 504 of the Rehabilitation Act of 1973

The first major legislation protecting the rights of disabled persons was Section 504 of the Rehabilitation Act of 1973, which stated: "No otherwise qualified handicapped individual in the United States . . . shall, solely by reason of his handicap, be excluded from the participation in, be denied the benefits of, or be subject to discrimination under any program or activity receiving Federal assistance."[4] Failure to comply with the regulations could result in the withdrawal of federal funding.

The term *handicap* or *disability* includes, for example, such diseases or conditions as speech, hearing, visual and orthopedic impairments; cerebral palsy; epilepsy; muscular dystrophy; multiple sclerosis; cancer; diabetes; heart disease; mental retardation; emotional illness; and specific learning disabilities such as perceptual handicaps, dyslexia, minimal brain dysfunction, and developmental aphasia.

Section 504 requires that programs must be made accessible to students with disabilities. In school buildings this means that ramps, elevators, and other devices designed to overcome physical barriers must be provided, and buildings constructed after June 3, 1977 must be barrier free.[5] Principals should inventory their school building to make sure that physical barriers are removed.

The first Supreme Court case interpreting Section 504 was *Southeastern Community College v. Davis*,[6] in which a practical nurse with a serious hearing disability was denied admission to the college's registered nurse program. The admission denial was based solely on her hearing disability. In a unanimous decision the Court held that there was no violation of Section 504 because Ms. Davis was not an "otherwise qualified handicapped individual." The Court noted that:

> *Section 504 by its terms does not compel educational institutions to disregard the disabilities of handicapped individuals or to make substantial modifications in their program to allow disabled persons to participate. Instead, it requires only that an "otherwise qualified handicapped individual" not be excluded from participation in a federally funded program "solely by reason of his handicap," indicating only that mere possession of a handicap is not a permissible ground for assuming an inability to function in a particular context.*[7]

"An otherwise qualified handicapped individual" was defined by the court as one who is able to meet all of a program's requirements in spite of the handicap.

In 1982 a court was asked to decide what "an otherwise qualified individual" meant in the public school setting. The case involved a high school student who was handicapped by a congenital limb deficiency.[8] She was enrolled in a Spanish class and desired to take part in a trip to Spain as part of the class activities. When she was notified that she would not be allowed to participate in the trip without being accompanied by an aide, provided at her family's expense, she sued the school district.

The federal court sustained the decision of the school board in not allowing the student to participate in the trip. Although the court noted that she was a handicapped individual within the meaning of Section 504, it ruled that it could "consider whether the program required applicants to possess certain physical qualifications necessary for participation . . ., and . . . may also consider the state's *parens patriae* interest in protecting the disabled against physical harm when the state has shown a risk to safety in a particular activity."[9] The court concluded that the student was not otherwise qualified since she was "unable to fulfill the physical requirements of the trip, and since a substantial degree of physical risk to her safety had been demonstrated were she to participate in the program."[10]

Since Section 504 provides broad civil rights protections to handicapped individuals, there will be continued litigation impacting on the schools. School officials must be cognizant of the law and regulations and take appropriate action to provide program accessibility. Schools may deny access where the individual lacks certain physical qualifications necessary for participation, and where the school has an interest in protecting the person against physical harm where a substantial risk is involved in the program's activities.

The Americans with Disabilities Act (ADA) of 1990 extends many of the requirements of Section 504 of the Rehabilitation Act of 1973 to all employers. Under this act, schools must make every reasonable accommodation to ensure access to all students and employees.

The Education for Handicapped Children Act and The Individuals with Disabilities Education Act

The Education for All Handicapped Children Act of 1975 (P.L. 94-142) committed the federal government to a substantial financial contribution toward the education of students with disabilities.[11] The law refined and strengthened the education rights of disabled children and their parents by providing procedural safeguards in placement and program decisions. Most important, it ensured a free appropriate public education, emphasizing special education and related services, for children ages 3 to 21.

Under P.L. 94-142, disabled children are those who are "mentally retarded, hard of hearing, deaf, speech impaired, visually disabled, seriously emotionally disturbed, orthopedically impaired, or other health impaired . . . or with specific learning disabilities, who by reason of the handicap require special education services."[12] The Individuals with Disabilities Education Act (P.L. 101-476) adds two new categories of disability, "autism" and "traumatic brain injury." In addition, the act changes all references to "handicapped children" to "children with disabilities."[13]

State Plans for Special Education

Each state and school district is required to have a plan to implement the federal statutory requirements under P.L. 94-142. While principals are not directly involved in the delivery of programs and services to children with disabilities, they play a key role when a child is referred to special education. The principal, as the responsible administrator of an attendance center, must follow all steps in the procedures involved in special education referral and placement. If any one of the required steps is overlooked, then everything after the error is nullified, and the law has been violated.

Comprehensive Individual Testing

Each student referred to special education must be provided a comprehensive individual assessment. The purpose of the assessment is to determine whether the student has a disability that qualifies the student for special education. Parents have the right to obtain an independent assessment of the student's educational needs and abilities from qualified professionals, at the parents' own expense. The school has the responsibility to provide information about where the parent can obtain such an assessment, to tell the parent about the specified criteria required for the assessment, and to consider the information obtained from the independent assessment in any decision made about the student's school program.

The Student's Individual Education Program (IEP)

The student's individual education program (IEP) states in writing the specific services the student needs and how these services will be provided. The IEP is a detailed document developed by a multidisciplinary team that includes statements of the specific educational services to be provided the student through regular and special education and related services. It specifies the amount of time in each setting for each of the services, the type of personnel responsible for providing each related service, and the modifications necessary for the student to be successful in the various programs. Statements of the projected dates for beginning and ending special education instruction and related services must be included, as well as statements of objective criteria to be used to evaluate the student's progress. The IEP must be reviewed at least once a year to assess the student's progress and decide if any changes need to be made. The parent must be notified within a reasonable time before the school makes plans to, or refuses to change, the educational placement of the student or makes major changes in the student's IEP.

The IEP should make reference to the appropriate discipline of the challenged child and should specify disciplinary options, which may include summary suspension, short-term suspension, and long-term suspension. Even if a special education student is suspended from school, the school cannot deny educational services under the law. By specifying disciplinary options in the student's IEP, the IEP committee can review the program or the problem behavior to determine if a change in placement is necessary.

P.L. 101-476 made two additions to IEP requirements. The IEP must include a statement of the needed transition services for students beginning no later than age 16 and annually thereafter, including, when appropriate, a statement of the interagency responsibilities or linkages, before the student leaves the school setting. The IEP team must reconvene to identify alternative strategies to meet the transition objectives if a participating agency fails to provide agreed-upon service.[14]

Least Restrictive Environment

Least restrictive environment (LRE) refers to the appropriate placement on a continuum from the least to the most restrictive environment. Any educational placement of a disabled student must be in a setting that will allow for the development of the student's abilities in accordance with the needs stated in the IEP. The placement must allow the student to be educated, as much as possible, with students who are not disabled. In addition, the placement must be as close to the student's home as appropriate, in the school the student would attend if not disabled, unless the IEP requires a different placement, or a program is not available in the student's home district. Regardless of the educational placement, the student has the right to the same opportunity to participate in extracurricular activities, meals, and recess as nondisabled students.

A federal court developed a two-part test to aid in determining whether a particular child should be mainstreamed. First, it must be determined whether education in a regular classroom, with supplementary aids and services, can be achieved satisfactorily. Second, if the regular classroom is not appropriate and special education must be provided, then a determination of whether the school has mainstreamed the child to the maximum extent possible must be made.[15]

Free Appropriate Education

In 1982 the United States Supreme Court reviewed P.L. 94-142 for the first time in *Board of Education v. Rowley.*[16] The primary issue before the court was the meaning of the term "free appropriate public education." A deaf student (Amy) had sought a qualified sign language interpreter in all of her academic classes, in addition to the other special education services provided by the school district. School officials denied the request after consulting with various school personnel. A hearing was provided before an independent examiner who agreed with the school official's assessment that an interpreter was not necessary, since the student was making good progress without the service.

The Supreme Court concluded that the requirement for a "free appropriate public education" is satisfied when a state provides "personalized instruction with sufficient support services to permit the child to benefit from that instruction."[17] The Court concluded that the statute did not specify the level of education to be afforded challenged children. The Court specifically rejected the position of the district court that "states maximize the potential of handicapped children."[18] The Court held that as long as the state adhered to the basic requirements of P.L. 94-142 and that if the IEP was formulated properly and reasonably designed to enable the child to receive some educational benefits, it had satisfied its legal obligation to the student. The Supreme Court rejected the lower court's requirement of a sign language interpreter because ". . . of the fact that Amy was receiving personalized instruction and related services calculated by the . . . school administrators to meet her educational needs. . . ."[19] The school district was doing all that was required under the law.

Related Services

The Supreme Court decided a case in 1984 that involved a controversy about what constituted a related service. In *Irving Independent School District v. Tatro*,[20] a female child with spina bifida was assessed by the school district for special education, placed in early childhood development classes, and provided services including physical and occupational therapy. The parents, however, had requested that the district provide clear intermittent catheterization (CIC) to empty the child's bladder, which she was incapable of doing because of conditions related to spina bifida. The district refused to provide CIC, maintaining that it was not legally obligated to do so, since it was not a related service under P.L. 94-142.

After exhausting the administrative appeals provided under the law, the parents filed suit in federal court. They contended that the district was required to provide CIC as a related service, and that its refusal to do so was a violation of Section 504.

The federal appeals court ruled that "CIC falls within the literal terms of the statutory definition of 'related services,' which includes 'supportive services' . . . as may be required to assist a handicapped child to benefit from special education."[21] The court noted that the child would be unable to attend classes without catheterization during the day, and concluded that CIC was essential if she was to benefit from special education. Therefore, the court found that CIC was a related service in the child's case and must be provided by the school district.

The court noted three conditions that must exist in order for a service to be required: A child must be handicapped so as to require special education; the life support service must be necessary to aid a handicapped child to benefit from the special education to be provided, and the life support service must be one that a nurse or other qualified person can perform.[22]

In addition to ordering that the child receive the catherization services, the court ruled both the local school district and the state board of education liable for attorneys' fees under Section 505 of The Rehabilitation Act of 1973.[23] In 1984 the United States Supreme Court affirmed the court of appeal's holding that CIC is a "related service" under P.L. 94-142.[24]

Exclusion of Special Education Students

Scenario 12.1: Denny Russell was in a class for behaviorally disordered students. He had a hard time controlling his temper, got into fights with other students, and was frequently suspended from school. Denny punched Richard as they passed each other in the hall. The school had a policy requiring an "automatic" three-day suspension for fighting. If Denny were suspended it would mean that his semester total for suspension would be twelve days.

Points to Consider: Is a disciplinary removal a change of placement? May a violent or dangerous student be removed to ensure a safe school? How long a removal is permitted? What services must be provided during a disciplinary removal?

The so-called "stay-put" provision of P.L. 94-142 requires that while administrative and judicial proceedings are pending, the child is to remain in the present educational placement, unless the parent or guardian agrees to the change.[25] This provision has resulted in a significant amount of litigation, primarily related to disciplinary removals.

In *Honig v. Doe*,[26] the Supreme Court focused on the interpretation of the "stay put" provision, addressed the issue of disciplinary removals, and provided a significant degree of guidance as to these issues. The litigation grew out of efforts of school officials of the San Francisco Unified School District to expel indefinitely two emotionally disturbed children for violent and disruptive conduct related to their disabilities. The state argued that when handicapped students pose a continuing danger, they can be suspended or expelled like other students. They reasoned that Congress could not have intended that educators be forced to keep unquestionably dangerous students in the classroom, even if the student has a handicap.[27]

The Supreme Court reaffirmed its desire to observe the separation of powers that distinguishes Congress's role from the Court's. The Court ruled that the language of P.L. 94-142 is unequivocal "(and) means what it says."[28] Administrators cannot expel or suspend a handicapped student for more than ten days where the student's misbehavior is related to the handicapping condition.

Such a removal would constitute a change in placement and would trigger due process procedures. This decision does allow a school district to go immediately to court when faced with a dangerous handicapped student, where a judge will have the option of removing the student.

Zero Reject

Scenario 12.2: Rickie Rogers was profoundly mentally and developmentally retarded. His doctors had stated that he had no potential for the development of self-care functions and no educational potential. In response to a districtwide directive to cut costs for the special education program, the principal informed Rickie's mother that he would no longer receive educational services.

Points to Consider: Are the schools responsible for the education of children who show no sign of benefiting from education? Are budgetary constraints valid grounds for terminating or reducing special education services?

The term *zero reject* means that no child with a disability can be excluded under the so-called "mandatory" legislation requiring education of all disabled children. The case of *Timothy W. v. Rochester School District*[29] involved a student with the most severe disability of any student to have reached the courts. Timothy was born two months premature and suffered from severe respiratory problems accompanied by brain disorders. He was profoundly mentally and developmentally retarded. He had received services since he was one year of age. His doctors stated that he had no potential for development of self-care functions and therefore had no educational potential. In addition, they reported that he was capable only of reflex responses. His mother's request for special education services for her son was denied on the grounds that Timothy was incapable of benefiting from educational services.

The school district persuaded the district court that the statute supported their refusal of services because: (1) Timothy was a "handicapped child" if he required special education; (2) he could not be said to require something if it would not do him any good; (3) education would not do Timothy any good; therefore, (4) Timothy was not a "handicapped child" and had no P.L. 94-142 entitlement. The district court concluded that "Congress could not possibly have meant to 'legislate futility,' i.e. to educate children who could not benefit from it."[30]

The court of appeals rejected the district's argument and ruled that the plain meaning of the act was that "All" means "all," "every," and "each." Therefore, "All" included Timothy. This decision made it clear that the protections of P.L. 94-142 are not dependent on a showing of expected benefit.[31] The Supreme Court denied the school district's petition to review the case.

Reimbursement for the Costs of Unilateral Parental Placement

P.L. 94-142 and P.L. 101-476 provide detailed procedures to protect the interests of disabled children. Although these procedures were created to ensure the best placement for the child, they can be very time consuming. The requirement that the children remain in their current placement pending the final decision presents problems when parents disagree with the current placement. Many parents respond to this dilemma by unilaterally placing their children in alternative settings and paying for the expense themselves. When they request reimbursement from the school district, they are often refused on the grounds that such a placement violates the "stay put" requirement. In *Burlington School Committee v. Massachusetts Department of Education*,[32] the Supreme Court ruled that a unilateral placement does not constitute a waiver of reimbursement. However, parents who unilaterally change their children's placement while review proceedings are pending, without the consent of state or local school officials, do so at their own financial risk. If the courts ultimately determine that the IEP proposed by the school officials was appropriate, the parents would be barred from obtaining reimbursement for any interim period in which their child's placement violated P.L. 101-476. A subsequent federal district court decision held that "because the parents did not take advantage of ample opportunities to participate in the IEP, they could not be reimbursed for a unilateral placement."[33]

Attorneys' Fees

The passage of the Handicapped Children's Protection Act (HCPA) in 1986 amended P.L 94-142[34] to allow courts to award attorney's fees and costs to parents who succeed on a significant issue that achieved some of the benefit sought.[35]

Section 1983 of the Civil Rights Act[36] allows individuals deprived of the rights, privileges, or immunities of the Constitution or federal law to recover damages. Therefore, it is clear that damages in the form of attorneys' fees are available if the action is for a violation of Section 504. However, the Supreme Court ruled in *Smith v. Robinson*[37] that except in cases where P. L. 94-142 does not provide substantive protection, Section 504 and constitutional actions could not be used to redress special education disputes.

A federal circuit court ruled in *Moore v. District of Columbia*[38] that the attorneys' fees provision of HCPA applies only to court actions. Therefore, in cases where the family succeeds at the administrative due process level and the school district does not appeal, the family would be unlikely to be awarded attorneys' fees.

Aversive Therapy for Students With Disabilities

Scenario 12.3: Kathy Greenburg, a student in a personal and social adjustment special education class, continued to use vulgar language and gestures after several methods of behavior modification were initiated. She was told that if she continued to use inappropriate language, alum would be placed in her mouth. After several such warnings, alum was administered. Kathy suffered an allergic reaction and was taken to the hospital. Her parents filed a complaint with the Office of Civil Rights.

Points to Consider: What type of physical punishment is allowed? Does the type of punishment have to be indicated in the child's IEP?

Because the behavior problems of some children with disabilities can be quite severe, some special education staff employ aversive reinforcement techniques. *Aversive therapy* is the use of stimuli that an individual finds unpleasant or painful in order to discourage undesirable behaviors.[39] This form of systematic behavior modification ranges in severity from the commonly used "time-out" and physical restraint, to more controversial forms such as slapping and the use of noxious liquids.

The courts have been mixed in their rulings on the use of aversive therapy. They have generally allowed the use of time-out unless it was shown to be excessive or unjustified.[40] Decisions have been more mixed on physical restraint, usually depending upon whether the treatment is in accordance with the IEP and individually justified.[41] Slapping and other forms of corporal contact have been allowed if clearly therapeutic, not excessive, and individually determined.[42] (See Chapter 9 for a general discussion of discipline of children with disabilities.) The use of noxious substances such as hot pepper sauce, lemon juice, vinegar, and shaving cream has been supported when administered with appropriate safeguards and as part of an IEP.[43]

Parental Rights in Special Education

Children with disabilities and their parents or guardians have certain rights in regard to special education services. These rights pertain to records, independent evaluation, notice, consent, hearings, evaluation procedures, and placement in the least restrictive environment.

P.L. 101-476 clarifies congressional intent that states are not immune, under the Eleventh Amendment of the Constitution, from suit in federal court for a violation of the act. This provision reverses the 1989 Supreme Court decision that held that children with disabilities who are denied access to free appropriate education are not entitled to be reimbursed by the state for any tuition paid by parents for appropriate placement.[44]

It is the school's responsibility to inform parents of their rights in the areas discussed below.

Records

Parents have the right to: (1) be informed of the type and location of all records pertaining to their child, (2) inspect and review all records, (3) receive a response to reasonable requests for an explanation of the records, (4) ask for an amendment of any record, (5) receive a hearing if the agency refuses to make an amendment, (6) enter their comments or reasons for disagreeing with a decision, (7) withhold consent to disclose records, (8) be informed before the records are destroyed, and (9) be told to whom information has been disclosed.

Evaluation Procedures

Parents have the right to: (1) receive a full and individual evaluation of their child's educational needs, (2) be given the opportunity for a personal conference concerning the reason(s) for the recommendation for a comprehensive evaluation, (3) have more than one criterion used in determining an appropriate educational program, (4) have the evaluation performed by a multidisciplinary team, (5) have their child assessed in all areas pertaining to the suspected disability, and (6) have a reevaluation every three years or more frequently if conditions warrant.

Independent Evaluation

Parents have the right to: (1) seek an independent evaluation, (2) have the independent evaluation considered when placement and program decisions are made, (3) be told where an independent evaluation may be obtained at no expense or low expense, and (4) be told the procedures for obtaining an independent evaluation at public expense and the conditions under which such an evaluation may be obtained.

Least Restrictive Environment

Parents have the right to: (1) have their child educated with children without disabilities to the maximum extent appropriate; (2) have their child removed from the regular educational environment only after supplementary aids and services are tried and found unsatisfactory; (3) have a continuum of alternative placements so that removal from the regular educational environment can be the least necessary deviation; (4) have supplementary services such as a resource room to make it possible for their child to remain in a regular class placement; (5) have placement in the school their child would attend if nondisabled unless the individual education plan requires some other arrangement; and (6) have their child participate with nondisabled children in nonacademic and extracurricular services and activities such as meals, recess, counseling, clubs, athletics, and special interest groups to the extent appropriate.

Notice

Parents have the right to: (1) receive notice before a change of placement takes place, (2) receive written notice in their native language, (3) receive an explanation of reasons for proposed action including the options considered and why those other options were rejected, (4) receive notice of each valuative procedure to be used, (5) be notified of the estimated duration of the evaluation procedure, (6) be advised regarding procedural due process, and (7) consent or object to any proposed action.

Due Process Hearings

Parents have the right to: (1) request an impartial due process hearing provided for by the educational agency, (2) be told of low-cost or free legal counsel or other relevant services, (3) have the hearing chaired by a nonschool employee, (4) see a statement of the hearing officer's qualifications, (5) be accompanied at the hearing by counsel, (6) have their child present, (7) have the hearing open to the public, (8) present and refute evidence, (9) obtain written findings of fact and a written decision within ten days after the hearing is completed, (10) appeal the hearing officer's decision, (11) have their child remain in the present placement during the process of the hearings, and (12) be informed that courts may award attorney fees to the parent if the parent is the prevailing party. Civil actions are allowed after the final decision of the administrative agency. Except in unusual circumstance, parents must exhaust their administrative remedies before they can appeal to the federal court system.[45]

Summary

Based on the courts' consistent interpretations of federal legislation protecting the rights of children with disabilities, principals are advised to:

1. Be familiar with the federal statutes and administrative regulations, state statutes and state board of education rules, local school district policies and administrative guidelines, and an emerging body of case law.
2. Know all policies and procedures specified in state and local policy documents that relate to the principal's role in the appropriate aspects of the special education process, especially referral and assessment.
3. Follow precisely all steps in the specified procedures including all time lines.
4. Make sure that the individual education plan for each disabled student provides the student the opportunity to make satisfactory progress in the essential elements identified in the state plan.[46]

Endnotes

1. Penn. Ass'n for Retarded Children v. Commonwealth, 334 F. Supp. 1257 (E.D. Pa. 1971), 343 F. Supp. 297 (E.D. Pa. 1972).
2. Mills v. Bd. of Educ., 348 F. Supp. 816 (D.D.C 1972).
3. LeBanks v. Spear, 60 F.R.D. 135 (1973).
4. 29 U.S.C. § 794(a) (1976), Pub. L. 93-112, Title V, 87 Stat. 394 (1973).
5. C.F.R. 84. 22a (1982), 454 C.F.R. § 84.23a (1982).
6. 442 U.S. 397 (1979).
7. *Id.*
8. Wolff v. Colonie Central Sch. Dist., 534 F. Supp. 758, 760 (N.D.N.Y. 1982).
9. *Id.* at 761–2.
10. *Id.* at 762.
11. 20 U.S.C. §§ 1401, 1411–1420 (1978) (Pub. L. 94-142).
12. *Id.*
13. Pub. L. 101-476, §§ 602 (a)–676(b)(8).
14. Pub. L. 101-476, § 602(a)(20).
15. Daniel R. v. State Board of Education and El Paso Independent School District, 874 F.2d 1036 5th Cir., 1989.
16. 102 S. C. 3034 (1984).
17. *Id.* at 3049.
18. *Id.* at 3042.
19. *Id.* at 3053.
20. 468 U.S. 883 (1984).
21. *Id.*
22. *Id.* at 827.
23. *Id.* at 830.
24. *Id.*
25. 20 U.S.C. § 1415(e)(b).
26. 484 U.S. 305, 108 S.Ct.529.
27. J. Champagne, *Special Education Law—Sometimes It's Simple: An Examination* of Honig v. Doe, Timothy W. v. Rochester, New Hampshire, School District; Dellmuth v. Muth, *and* Moore v. District of Columbia, 59 ED. LAW REP. 587 (June 7, 1990).

28. 484 U.S. 305, 108 S.Ct. 605.
29. 875 F.2d 954 (1st Cir. 1989).
30. *Id.* at 972.
31. *Id.* at 960.
32. 471 U.S. 359 (1985).
33. Scituate School Committee v. Robert B., 620 F. Supp. 1224 (D.R.I. 1985).
34. 20 U.S.C. § 415(e)(4).
35. Rollison v. Biggs, 660 F. Supp. 875 (D.Del. 1987).
36. 42 U.S.C. § 1983.
37. 468 U.S. 992 (1984).
38. 886 F.2d 335 (D.C.Cir., 1989).
39. S. Seiden & P. Zirkel, *Aversive Therapy for Handicapped Students,* 48 ED. LAW REP. 1029.
40. *Id.* at 1040–4.
41. *Id.* at 1039–41.
42. *Id.* at 1037–9.
43. *Id.* at 1036–7.
44. Pub. L. 101-476, § 604(a).
45. *Id.*
46. W. SPARKMAN & R. SHOOP, TEXAS SCHOOL LAW (Dubuque, Iowa; Bowers, 1984), p. 207.

CHAPTER THIRTEEN

Bilingual and Special Language Programs

Introduction

With each passing year the student population becomes more diverse, with a growing percentage of limited English-proficient (LEP) students. Many of these students need special language programs in order to overcome the language barriers to an equal education.

Title VI of the Civil Rights Act of 1964 required programs receiving federal financial assistance to be operated without discrimination in terms of race, color, or national origin. It required federal agencies providing the financial assistance to issue regulations to achieve the objective. The law provided that recipient programs could have their aid terminated if they persistently denied program benefits on discriminatory grounds.

The Bilingual Education Act

The first federal bilingual education legislation was Title VII of the Elementary and Secondary Education Act, also known as the Bilingual Educational Act, enacted in 1968.[1] This act created a discretionary grant program providing federal financial assistance, primarily to local school districts, to develop and implement "new and imaginative . . . school programs." These grants were to meet the special needs of children between the ages of 3 and 18 who had limited English-speaking ability and came from low-income families.[2] Subsequent amendments to the law extended the fiscal authorizations, made some minor changes, and expanded the purpose and scope of the act through increased authorizations for new and existing programs.[3]

The act was later broadened to serve those students who could not "read, write, or understand English at the level appropriate for their age and grade."[4] Local projects were required to set goals for children involved in bilingual programs and provide necessary follow-up services for children who were exited from the programs. More stringent requirements for parental involvement in the bilingual programs were included.

One of the most important aspects of the 1978 amendments was the clarification of bilingual education program goals. The amendments emphasized that the goal of the Bilingual Education Act was to help develop the English language skills of students who were deficient in these skills, while simultaneously providing instruction in the native language so students could progress effectively through the educational system. Instruction given in the native language was to serve only as a temporary bridge until the necessary English skills were acquired. The number of English-proficient participants in bilingual programs was limited to a maximum of 40 percent of the total number of participants. Finally, the amendments required improved methods of identifying students who were eligible for the programs, specified program entry and exit criteria, and improved progress evaluation. The Bilingual Education Act and its amendments did not require school districts to provide bilingual programs; the law provided financial assistance for those districts that desired to implement such programs.

In 1970 the Department of Health, Education and Welfare (HEW) developed and issued guidelines, known as the May 25th Memorandum, that addressed the rights of non–English speakers protected by the Civil Rights Act of 1964.[5] The memorandum included a number of provisions designed to give direction to school districts when confronted with children with special language needs. Local school districts were required to implement programs to help overcome the language deficiencies of national origin minority students, but the regulations did not specify the types of programs or methods to be used in the effort.

In 1974 the United States Supreme Court in *Lau v. Nicholas,*[6] ruled that the San Francisco Unified School District had violated the rights of Chinese-speaking students by failing to provide them an education commensurate with their special language needs.[7] The school district denied any obligation to respond specifically to the communication difficulties of the non–English-speaking students, arguing that since the Chinese-speaking students were being taught in the same facilities, by the same teachers, at the same time as everyone else, they had equal opportunities and there was no discrimination.

The Supreme Court rejected the argument that equal access to school facilities and teachers provided equal treatment and equal educational opportunity. The Court said:

> *Basic skills are at the very core of what these public schools teach. Imposition of a requirement that before a child can effectively participate in the educational program he must already have acquired these basic*

skills is to make a mockery of public education. We know that those who do not understand English are certain to find their classroom experiences wholly incomprehensible and in no way meaningful.[8]

The Court ruled against the school district and required that action be taken to address the special language needs of the non–English-speaking children. The Court's rationale was based on Section 504 of the Civil Rights Act of 1964 that prohibits discrimination on the basis of race, color, or national origin. Since the school district was receiving federal funds it could not discriminate against non–English-speaking students by refusing to provide them the benefits of public education through meaningful programs. The Court also affirmed the validity of HEW's May 25th Memorandum.

On remand to the federal district court, a consent decree was entered into by the school district providing for bilingual-bicultural programs for Chinese, Filipino, and Spanish-language groups within the district.[9] The decree also required the implementation of English as a second language (ESL) and other special programs, including bilingual education where feasible, for students from other language groups. Although a consent decree is not precedent-setting, it is enforced by the court that accepted it.

One important result of the *Lau* decision was an intensive evaluation of school districts by HEW and the Office of Civil Rights (OCR) to determine the extent of violations identified by the court's decision in *Lau*. This investigation gave rise to administrative guidelines known as the Lau Remedies, or Lau Guidelines, issued jointly by HEW and OCR in the summer of 1975. Although never enacted by Congress nor officially adopted as federal policy, the Lau Remedies eventually became publicly recognized, even by many courts, as the minimal standards for designing or evaluating an educationally effective program to overcome discriminatory practices against limited English-speaking students.[10] School districts were required to identify all students who might be limited English speakers and to develop programs depending upon the language category in which the students were placed. Once students were involved in special language programs, they were not to be exited from them until it could be shown that they could compete on an equal basis with their English-proficient peers.

A school district challenge of the legal force of the Lau Remedies resulted in a consent decree in 1978 under which the federal government agreed that the remedies were unenforceable and that it would promulgate official rules for the enforcement of Title VI of the Civil Rights Act of 1964.[11]

The Proposed Title VI Language Discrimination Guidelines were published in 1980.[12] The proposed regulations contained the basic components of the Lau Remedies, including identification, assessment, program assignment, and exit criteria, but differed in the specific requirements in each area. In addition, the proposed regulations specified that no minimum number of students was required before the mandated programs were to be implemented. Other organizational methods could be used, however, when student populations from a particular language background were too small to combine conveniently into a single class with a single teacher.

Summary

There have been a number of federal court cases that have defined the parameters of bilingual or special language programs in local school districts and established a legal basis for challenges to school districts failing to provide bilingual or special language programs or providing inadequate programs.[13] The primary legal guideline that has emerged from these cases is the tripartite test set forth in *Castaneda:*[14] (1) Is the challenged program educationally sound? (2) Are the practices and programs of the school reasonably calculated to implement effectively the educational theory adopted by the school? (3) Are the practices accomplishing the desired objectives?

Under the Bilingual Education Act, its amendments, and various court cases, school districts must take appropriate action to overcome language barriers. Both federal and state funds are available to accomplish this goal.

Endnotes

1. Pub. L. 90-247, 81 Stat. 816 (1968).
2. Bilingual Education Act, Pub. L. 95-561 (1978).
3. Pub. L. 95-230 (1978), Pub. L. 93-380 (1974).
4. Pub. L. 95-561 (1978).
5. H.E.W. Memorandum, 35 FED. REG. 11.595 (1) (1970).
6. 414 U.S. 563 (1974).
7. *Id.*
8. *Id.* at 566.
9. H. Teitelbaum & R. Hiller, *Bilingual Education: The Legal Mandate,* IN-EQUALITY IN EDUCATION No. 19, 144 (1975).
10. H. TEITELBAUM & R. HILLER, A HANDBOOK OF THE ENFORCEMENT OF LAU V. NICHOLAS, B 97-98 (Washington, D.C.: Office of Civil Rights, 1979).
11. *New Bilingual Policy Emerging: Strategy Debated,* EDUCATION WEEK 17 (April 28, 1982).
12. *Title VI Language Discrimination Guidelines,* 45 FED. REG. 152.52056 (1980).
13. *See,* Serna v. Portales, 499 F.2d 1147 (10th Cir. 1974); Aspira v. New York, 58 F.R.D. 64 (S.D.N.D. 1975); Clintron v. Brentwood Union Free Sch. Dist., 455 F. Supp. 547 (E.D.N.Y. 1978); Keys v. Sc. Dist. No. 11, Denver, 413 U.S. 189 (1973); Morgan v. Kerrigan, 401 F. Supp. 4341 (E.D.Tex. 1981).
14. Castaneda v. Pickard, 648 F.2d 989 (5th Cir. 1981).

CHAPTER FOURTEEN

Health and Safety Issues

Child Abduction

Scenario 14.1: Cliff Brown, a fifth-grade teacher, was standing at the front of his class when there was a knock at the door. He opened the door to find a person he vaguely recognized. She said her name was Mrs. Koskie and she needed to take her son Brian to the dentist. Brian got his books, left, and was never seen again.

Points to Consider: Who has the right to take a child out of school? Is the teacher liable if the child leaves the school with someone other than his or her guardian?

Because of the amount of publicity about child abduction, principals should be concerned about releasing a child to an adult. Not only must the principal be alert to the possibility of a stranger taking a child without permission, but also to the possibility of a child being taken by a parent contrary to a custody decree. The first national study of missing children revealed that a surprisingly high number of children are abducted each year by members of their own families. For example, in 1990 there were about 350,000 abductions of children by family members. By contrast, only between 200 and 300 children were abducted by strangers.[1] In 1980 Congress responded to the increase in child abduction by family members by passing the Parental Kidnapping Prevention Act, which created the crime of flight to avoid prosecution or giving testimony.[2]

When deciding whether or not to release a child from school, the first issue that must be resolved is the question of who has parental rights. The legal parent is that person whom the legal system recognizes as having the legal rights of parenthood. Usually both parents' rights are recognized. Therefore, either parent, acting alone, has the legal right to make decisions on behalf of the child. In the event of the death of a parent, the surviving parent has sole custody. Because the law has traditionally respected the privacy of the family, the law presumes that when a man and woman present themselves to be married and live together as husband and wife, they are married.[3]

In states that have not adopted uniform parentage acts,[4] if a child is born to biological parents who are not married, the mother alone enjoys parental rights. The biological father would gain parental rights by marriage or by a court finding of paternity. The United States Supreme Court has ruled that states must recognize parental rights of a biological father who has married the mother or been adjudicated as the legal father.[5]

In the case of divorce, the court may grant custody to one parent or it may grant joint custody to both parents together. In the case of sole custody, the custodial parent alone has the power to make parental decisions.

Modern adoption laws have created a new and exclusive parent–child relationship and establish parental rights and duties where they would not otherwise exist. When a court issues a decree of adoption, the natural parents no longer have a legal relationship to the child. The status of the legal rights of various parties in cases of artificial insemination, *in vitro* fertilization, or surrogate parents remains ambiguous.[6]

School personnel should be very cautious about the physical custody of children. If the school has no information to the contrary, it can assume that both parents have parental rights. However, if the school is informed that there has been some modification of parental rights, then the noncustodial parent does not have the right to remove the child from school without permission of the custodial parent.

Although it may cause some embarrassment or inconvenience, it is better to err on the side of protecting the child. When a nonparent seeks possession of a child, school personnel should ask for some authorization and should notify the parent before the child is released into the other person's custody. In the case of a person who cares for a child on a regular basis, such as a neighbor, child-care giver, or grandparent, the school should request that the parent give written permission prior to the release of the child. School personnel should request to see a court order before releasing a child to a public employee such as a police officer, social worker, or probation officer.

Child Abuse

Scenario 14.2:   A third-grade student told her teacher that she was forced to participate in an organized prize fight. She said she had been taken someplace by her uncle during the weekend and had been forced into a $100 fist fight. She said she lost the fight, and her mother used a belt and large wooden spoon to hit her when she came home without the $100 prize.

Scenario 14.3:   At an inquest into the death of an elementary school child, the principal of the boy's school testified that he had suspected that the boy was being abused ever since "the boy came to school with injuries so obvious that he was left out of the class picture. He had two black eyes and the whites of his eyes were blood red. We knew that something was wrong."

Scenario 14.4: Judy Tucker was a very shy elementary school student. She cried often and was wary of physical contact, especially when it was initiated by an adult. She became apprehensive when an adult approached another child, particularly one who was crying. She often arrived at school too early and remained after class rather than return home.

Points to Consider: Are teachers responsible for reporting suspected child abuse? Can teachers be held liable if they report suspected child abuse and it turns out that no abuse has occurred? How much proof is needed before one reports suspected child abuse? What are the categories of child abuse?

Child abuse is legally defined as the physical or mental injury, sexual abuse or exploitation, negligent treatment, or maltreatment of a child under the age of 18 (or the age specified by the child protection law of the state in question) by a person immediately responsible for the child's welfare. Many believe that child abuse is the largest killer of children in the United States. More than 2.4 million incidents of child abuse or neglect were reported to child protective service agencies in 1989. More than 1,200 of these children died from their injuries. Many researchers contend that abuse-related fatality reports are low because many suspicious deaths among children are labeled as accidents.

Nearly 2 million cases of child abuse a year are reported, of which 45.3 percent are substantiated on investigation.[7] National data collected in 1988 by the American Humane Association indicated an increase of 121 percent in the number of reported cases of child abuse and neglect during the previous ten years.[8] In addition, many states reported increasingly more serious and complex cases.[9] In its most extreme form, child abuse results in an estimated 2,000 to 5,000 children killed each year by their parents.[10] More children under the age of five years die from parent-inflicted injuries than from all childhood diseases.[11]

Because attendance in school is compulsory, there are few youngsters who do not come into contact with teachers and principals. Therefore, teachers and principals have a special obligation to be aware of child abuse warning signs and to report suspected cases to the proper authorities.[12] Educators are not only morally responsible to report suspected cases of child abuse, but are also legally liable if they fail to do so. Every state has enacted reporting laws requiring certain professionals, including teachers and administrators, to report suspected cases of child abuse. Each of these state laws has a clause providing some kind of immunity from prosecution for those who, without malice, report cases of suspected abuse. Each state statute also specifies the penalties for mandatory reporters who fail to report cases of suspected child abuse.

The U.S. Department of Health, Education and Welfare has published the following list of observable signs that may identify abused or neglected children. Of course, these are only indicators and are not absolute. They should be signs, however, that arouse concern, especially when several of these characteristics are present. The abused child:

- Seems unduly afraid of parents.
- Often bears welts, bruises, untreated sores, or other skin injuries.
- Shows overall evidence of poor care.
- Has injuries that seem inadequately treated.
- Exhibits behavioral extremes, such as crying often, being excessively fearful, or unusually aggressive and destructive, or being extremely passive and withdrawn.
- Becomes apprehensive when an adult approaches or when another child is crying.
- Is overly hungry for affection.
- Exhibits sudden changes in behavior or displays regressive behavior, such as excessive thumb sucking, pants wetting, disruptiveness, or uncommon shyness or passivity.
- Is habitually truant or late to school; has frequent or prolonged absences.
- Arrives at school too early and remains after classes rather than returning home.
- Is inappropriately dressed for the weather; for example, has no coat in winter or regularly wears long pants or long sleeves in summer.[13]

Child abuse is a phenomenon that any principal or teacher may encounter. It is not a problem of a particular social class or income level. Evidence indicates that abused children tend to become abusive parents. By doing nothing about suspected child abuse, principals not only neglect their responsibility to the child and parent, but also contribute to the perpetuation of the problem and violate the law.

With these responsibilities in mind, it is recommended that:

1. Schools have a clearly defined school board policy on child abuse.
2. Formal policies be established for reporting suspected child abuse, and widely publicized to all personnel.
3. Each school provide inservice training concerning family violence, child abuse, and teachers' legal requirements in reporting suspected child abuse.
4. Formal communication be established between schools and local and state agencies responsible for investigating suspected child abuse.

5. Schools ensure that they receive feedback about action taken after reports of suspected child abuse. Such information is important to maintain the involvement of teachers as mandatory reporters.

School Violence

Scenario 14.5: James Johnson, a ninth-grader, got into an argument with one of his classmates in the hall. As the argument escalated, James pulled a hunting knife from his belt and slashed his classmate's arm. A teacher was able to grab the knife from James's hand, and take him to the principal's office. The principal put James on immediate five-day suspension. The injury was not serious, but the boy's parents demanded that James not only be expelled from school but arrested for assault with a deadly weapon.

Points to Consider: Does the school have any special responsibilities in cases of student violence that involve the use of weapons?

Parents are responsible for sending their children to school, and schools have a corresponding responsibility to provide a safe environment. While the school's tort liability for providing a safe environment is discussed in detail in Section V of this book, one element of ensuring a safe school deserves attention here—the growing incidence of violent behavior in schools.

The problem of school-related crime has reached a crisis. A 1986 national survey on crime reports that nearly three million incidents of assault, rape, robbery, and theft took place in schools or on school property.[14] In *New Jersey v. T.L.O,* Justice Powell noted that in recent years, "school disorder has taken particularly ugly forms; drug use and violent crime in the schools have become major social problems."[15]

A number of states have responded to school violence by enacting some form of "safe school act." Illinois, for example, revised its Juvenile Court Act and sections of its criminal code with the intent of getting tough on school-related crime.[16] This legislation upgraded assault to aggravated assault and upgraded battery to aggravated battery, if the perpetrator knew that the victim was a teacher or other school employee, or if the assault or battery occurred in a school or on school grounds.[17] The legislation also provided an exception to the insulation of juveniles under age 17 from criminal prosecution. If a minor above the age of 14 is found in possession of a weapon in school or on school grounds, the case would automatically be transferred from juvenile court to criminal court.[18]

In 1988 the Illinois Juvenile Court Act was challenged in *People of Illinois v. M.A..*[19] The challenge was based on the argument that the provision for transferring the case to criminal court was an unconstitutional violation of the due process clause of the Fourteenth Amendment. In deciding this case the Illinois Supreme Court reasoned that, although juveniles charged with unlawful use of a weapon commit intrinsically the same crime whether on or off school property, it was rational for the legislature to conclude that deterring juveniles from carrying weapons on school grounds is more important than doing so elsewhere, given its responsibility for maintaining safe schools and compulsory attendance at them. The court reversed the lower court decision, rejecting the Fourteenth Amendment challenges to the statute and holding the automatic transfer provision to be valid.

The judicial trend is clearly to give greater weight to rights of students to have a safe school, and less weight to the constitutional rights of those accused of school violence.

Students with AIDS

Scenario 14.6: Barbara Baker recently returned to school following another extended absence. Concerned about the effect on her grades, her counselor asked Barbara's parents in for a conference. During the conference the parents confided that Barbara had AIDS. Barbara wanted to stay in school, but did not want teachers or other students to know of her illness.

Points to Consider: What are the legal rights of the infected student? What are the rights of other children in this school? Do the rights of the AIDS victim or the nonvictim take precedence? Do the teachers have a right to know when one of their students has AIDS?

Scenario 14.7: The state legislature recently passed legislation requiring that all school children receive instruction concerning the transmission and prevention of AIDS. John Hanna, middle school principal, received a written request to exclude children who were members of a devoutly religious group from the AIDS education program. The parents of these children protested that their religion of spiritual separatism required that their children be excluded from such instruction.

Points to Consider: Does the state or school district have the right to require that all children receive AIDS prevention education?

Most Americans became aware of the tragedy of children with AIDS through the dramatic and heroic struggle of Ryan White.[20] Ryan acquired the HTLV-III/LAV virus from a tainted blood transfusion. By the time a test became available to screen for the AIDS antibody, it was too late for Ryan.

Just as Ryan's community was not prepared for the news that one of its children had AIDS, many other communities have no policies to guide them. In the event of a student's contracting the AIDS virus, school administrators are required to deal with the seemingly conflicting needs of the infected student and a community concerned about the safety of its children. Some school boards allow children with AIDS to attend school; others refuse permission. Although many students, parents, and teachers are supportive of the decision to allow an AIDS patient to attend school, others react with fear and panic.

AIDS is an incurable disorder characterized by a severe depression of cellular immunity. The scientific community has devised a three-tiered classification of people who have been infected by the HTLV-III/LAV virus. The largest group of these individuals test positive for the presence of the antibody yet remain virtually symptomless. However, they are considered viral carriers and can transmit the virus through their blood. The second group is classified as having AIDS-related complex (ARC). It appears that between 6 and 20 percent of ARC cases eventually develop the full-blown syndrome. The final category of infected individuals have the disease, AIDS. They are the most severely ill and exhibit extreme symptoms caused by opportunistic infections. Statistics indicate that over 85 percent of them will die within two years of diagnosis.

The Centers for Disease Control (CDC) and most other medical groups have stated repeatedly that AIDS cannot be transmitted through casual or airborne contact and that AIDS victims normally need not be excluded from school. The type of contact that occurs in a school setting does not result in a significant degree of risk for infection.

Public policy is made within a given political ideology and is drawn from particular moral principles. At the heart of the debate about the rights of students with AIDS is the perplexing dilemma of how to reconcile the rights of the individual with the collective interests of society. State legislatures have ensured that a public education is the legal right of every child in this country. Therefore, children with AIDS have the legal right to a free public education with their peers.

Conflicts arise because all states also have communicable disease laws that compel school officials to provide a safe, healthy learning environment. Some argue that, in the face of an incurable, inevitably fatal, infectious disease, the schools are legally and morally obligated to exclude a child with AIDS to protect the health of other students. Proponents of this argument believe that children with AIDS should be provided an alternative means of education, usually through tutoring or private home instruction.

As the number of pediatric AIDS cases has increased, school officials have begun to develop policies for the education of students afflicted by the disease, and courts have begun to rule on the validity of these plans. Parents seeking to have their AIDS-afflicted children admitted to public schools look to the protection provided by Section 504 of the Rehabilitation Act of 1973,[21] the equal protection clause of the Fourteenth Amendment, and the Education for All Handicapped Children's Act of 1975 (P.L. 94-142); the Supreme Court has ruled that a contagious disease can be considered a handicapping condition.[22]

In a 1989 case a 6-year-old mentally retarded student with ARC was refused admission to a public school classroom and was assigned to homebound instruction. The court determined that the medical evidence indicated that the possibility of transmission to others was "not a significant risk." Thus the child was otherwise qualified and the school was ordered to readmit her.[23]

In order to remove students from the regular classroom, the schools must prove that the infected pupils are health hazards to the other children. Under Section 504, before a district may exclude a child with AIDS from school, it must first show that the presence of AIDS-infected students constitutes a significant health risk that outweighs the detrimental effects isolation would inflict on the excluded children. Since there are no known cases of the infection being transmitted in the school setting or through other casual person-to-person contact, exclusion from school constitutes a violation of Section 504. If the medical evidence changes, it is probable that more weight will be placed on the welfare of the other children. At present, it seems that many AIDS-infected children may face a greater risk that they will acquire any of various debilitating infections while in school with other students.

Because the HTLV-III/LAV virus destroys lymphocytes, a child with AIDS clearly has a "physical impairment" and thus is considered handicapped within the meaning of the Rehabilitation Act. The U.S. Department of Justice believes that the disabling consequences of AIDS infection qualify as handicaps, but the mere presence of HTLV-III/LAV in the body does not. In other words, individuals experiencing the opportunistic infections of full-blown AIDS are protected as handicapped under the act, but those who are asymptomatic are not handicapped simply by virtue of their communicability. This interpretation presents obvious problems, because the vast majority of students who need protection under Section 504 will be viral carriers and those with nondebilitating ARC. The student with full-blown AIDS rarely, if ever, will be physically able to attend classes.

A second cause for action for children with AIDS who are excluded from school is the equal protection clause of the Fourteenth Amendment. When the New York City Board of Education adopted a policy that children with AIDS could not be automatically excluded from regular school attendance, it was challenged in a state court. The court found that denying a child admission was a violation of the equal protection clause.[24] The court reasoned that because there probably are many undetected HTLV-III/LAV carriers within the school, exclusion of those students identified as having the disease would be denying them equal protection of the law.

Finally, a school district's policy to bar infected children from the classroom may be challenged as a violation of P.L. 94-142.[25] This act authorizes the denial of all federal aid to districts who fail to educate handicapped children with nonhandicapped children and make sure they are integrated to the maximum extent appropriate. Courts have ruled that the term "handicapped" is more restrictive in P.L. 94-142 than in Section 504. Under P.L. 94-142 a child suffering from AIDS must have a deterioration of his or her health. If a student is asymptomatic or an HTLV-III/LAV carrier, he or she will be unprotected under this statute.

In determining whether or not to exclude a child from school, some courts have ruled that the district must evaluate each case individually. This appraisal must consider such factors as the characteristic of the disease, the behavior of the child, and the particular options available to the school in reducing the likelihood of transmission. If the risk is low, the school is obligated to enroll the student in a regular classroom. The question then centers around whether the unconfirmed possibility of transmitting the disease is sufficient to bar such pupils from the classrooms.

In *Ray v. School District of DeSoto*,[26] the court ruled that three brothers, all hemophiliacs and carriers of the AIDS virus, were entitled to access to a regular classroom setting, "unless and until it could be established these children posed a real and valid threat to the school population of DeSoto County." In this case the court stated that students who are carrying the virus also will be considered handicapped.[27] The three were granted the right to attend school unless it could be established that they posed a threat to the school population. However, the court required that the children assume adult responsibility for protecting themselves from substantial risk at school and protecting the school population from exposure to the virus. The court also required that the infected children avoid contact sports in the school environment; the afflicted students and the entire school system of the county be provided with education pertaining to the potential transmission of AIDS through sexual contact; educational programs concerning AIDS be offered to parents; the afflicted children's parents submit reports from any physician or health care provider who had examined their children, outlining the nature of the visit; the children be retested for AIDS every six months; and the parents undergo testing every year.

Medical research indicates that AIDS cannot be transmitted through casual physical contact. The school-age child infected with the disease presents a negligible risk for transmission to his or her classmates or to other adult school personnel and thus does not affect their health and safety. Therefore, children with AIDS, in most instances, should continue to attend school and participate fully in programs and activities offered by the school district. Although removal of a student infected with AIDS from the school setting normally is not justified, guidelines need to be established for a case-by-case review process.[28]

Confidentiality Rights of Students with AIDS

In some states only the teacher knows the identity of a child with AIDS; however, in other states it is illegal to notify a teacher that a child has AIDS without parental consent.[29] The Family Educational Rights and Privacy Act (FERPA) requires that student records be kept confidential. Therefore, if a parent voluntarily discloses to school officials a student's medical condition, such record is entitled to all of the protections of FERPA. School districts will need compelling reasons to justify any disclosure. In 1987 a group of nationally recognized superintendents reported that access to students' HIV test results should be limited to the superintendent, the personnel officer, and the health officer.[30] They placed principals and teachers low on the list of those who should be given access to the test results. School boards will be under increasing pressure to disclose the identity of afflicted children, but FERPA protects all such medical records.

School District Policy on AIDS

Based on current case law, school district counsels suggest that districts adopt policies and procedures for dealing with all contagious diseases. When school officials are notified that a student is infected, they would then have a procedure in place to ensure the safety of persons in the school setting and to provide support for the person with the illness.

The recommended policy includes the designation of the individual person responsible for ensuring compliance with the policy and the appointment of a team to implement it. This team should consist of a school staff person, the coordinator of nursing services, the infected person's physician, the infected person, the student's parents or guardians, and a public health official. In determining whether a person who is infected constitutes a recognized risk in the school setting, the team should consider the behavior, neurological development, and physical condition of the student; the expected type of interaction with others in the school setting; and the impact on both the infected student and others in that setting.

The team should also consider ways in which the school district can anticipate and meet the needs of the infected student. If there is a secondary infection that constitutes a medically recognized risk of transmission in the school setting, it may be necessary to develop an individually tailored plan for the student. Mandatory screening for communicable diseases that are not spread by casual everyday contact, such as HIV infection, should not be a condition for school entry or attendance. If an infected student with a secondary infection is not able to attend classes or participate in school activities, the district should offer the student appropriate alternative education.

The board policy should specifically state that the identity of an infected individual shall be known only by the designated staff for decision making, unless the infected child or the child's parent chooses to inform other people. Although this policy is aimed at protecting the infected person's confidentiality rights, the possibility is great that this confidentiality could be breached through a variety of sources.

The unfortunate public disclosure of such a situation could create additional problems at the building level for an infected person. Therefore, a contingency plan should be developed for reentering students with AIDS when public attention has become an issue. A case manager should be appointed to coordinate monitoring and consultation with representatives of the medical community. The community relations department should assist the principal. The special education department should be consulted regarding possible homebound instruction or assignment to an alternative placement. The case manager should coordinate staff information meetings and parent information meetings. Regular review meetings should be held by the case manager.[31]

Required AIDS Education

Because of the perception that the AIDS crisis has reached epidemic proportions, numerous states and school districts have established AIDS education programs. In some instances, parents have argued that such instruction violates their privacy rights or their constitutionally protected religious freedom. In 1990 a New York appellate court ruled that compulsory AIDS instruction does not violate the constitutional rights of students.[32] Because the purpose of the educational requirement, in this case, is the protection of the public health, the court ruled that the state has a compelling interest in this controversy.

Drug Testing of Students

Scenario 14.8: As a result of an increase in drug abuse by students, one school board began a drug testing program. According to the policy, any student suspected of being under the influence of an illegal drug must either submit to a drug test or withdraw from school. Sandy Smith, a tenth-grade student, was brought into the principal's office by a teacher. The teacher believed that Sandy had been smoking marijuana in the rest room.

Points to Consider: Is it constitutional to require drug tests of students? What procedural safeguards must exist if testing is allowed? Does it matter whether the test given is a urine, blood, or breath test?

Scenario 14.9:   Because of reports of drug use by members of the high school's football team, a district instituted a random urine testing program for interscholastic athletes and cheerleaders. Three students objected to undergoing urinalysis and were denied permission to participate.

Points to Consider: Are the rights of student athletes different than those of nonathletes? What rationale is necessary prior to beginning a drug testing program?

The Debate over Drug Testing

Proponents of drug testing cite dramatic evidence that testing has been effective in reducing drug abuse. They argue that drug testing results in a safe and orderly environment.

Arguments against drug screening center on both technological and constitutional considerations. Some opponents argue that mandatory testing should be avoided at all costs. They cite charges of inaccuracy and outright fraud, medical unreliability of detection technology,[33] uncertainties in qualifications for medical technicians,[34] and security problems in handling specimens.[35] As evidence that drug testing causes greater harm than benefit, they cite documented widespread false positive results caused by common substances including herbal teas, poppy seeds, medication, and passive inhalation.[36] Urinalysis, the most common detection method, is only 95 percent accurate.[37]

Opponents argue further that forced random or uniform drug testing severely endangers constitutional democracy. The Fourth Amendment issue of reasonable suspicion provides the fundamental objection to mandatory and comprehensive drug screening. While opponents do not claim that the Fourth Amendment precludes all search and seizure, they argue that individuals are protected from unreasonable invasion of privacy and that there must be a particularized relationship between individuals and a search. It is unreasonable, therefore, to require students not individually suspected of drug abuse to submit to any screening method.[38]

The Fourth Amendment protection against causeless search leads opponents to conclude that mandatory testing is an unlawful search of an individual without cause and that forcible acquisition of blood or urine is an unlawful seizure.[39]

There is a distinction between drug testing for students and for teachers.[40] Testing of teachers is concerned with determining an individual's fitness to teach, and the effect of causeless search may result in loss of employment, contractual rights, and possible criminal charges. On the other hand, the primary object of student testing is to preserve safety in schools.

The Carlstadt-East Rutherford, New Jersey School District was the first in the United States to adopt a policy under which all of the students at a high school would be required to submit to a chemical test for the identification of illicit drugs. The test was part of a more comprehensive physical examination required of all students. A state superior court judge ruled the proposed program to be unconstitutional.[41] The court ruled that drug testing was an unreasonable search, and the school's interest in discovering student drug use did not justify interference with student privacy. The court also held that the school district's program violated the students' rights to due process because of the possibility that the results of testing could lead to suspension or expulsion from school without following the usual rules for such actions.

A case in Arkansas dealt not only with urinalysis, but also with the use of breathalyzer testing for the detection of alcohol.[42] This case did not deal with a mass testing program, but with a policy that required individual students suspected of using drugs to submit to urinalysis. The federal district court found that students have privacy interests that are protected by the Fourth Amendment, but the interests of a school district necessitate a balancing of the interests in any given situation. The court found the test to be useless in determining whether a student had used marijuana in school or somewhere else outside the scope of the school's disciplinary authority. It found the district's use of the test to be "irrational, arbitrary, and capricious."

In 1990 a United States district court ruled that urinalysis drug testing of public school students who are not suspected of drug use is a violation of the Fourth Amendment. The drug testing program in question was instituted in a Wyoming high school after a group of parents and students demanded more stringent measures to combat student drug and alcohol abuse. The test was a prerequisite for participating in extracurricular activities. The penalty for refusing to submit to the test was exclusion from extracurricular activities until the student agreed to be tested. The school district defended the testing on the grounds of discouraging drug use and preventing impaired students from participating in extracurricular activities. The court found no evidence that those goals were legitimate. The court said that students wishing to continue drug use could merely forgo extracurricular activities, urine tests do not measure present impairment, and a urine test so remote in time does not give any information about recent drug use that might affect performance.[43]

Student Athletes and Drug Testing

Because some people expect student athletes to be role models for other students, many school districts consider implementing a drug testing program for athletes only. A federal appeals court in Indiana was asked to rule on such a program in 1988.[44] The Tippecanoe County School District approved a policy that required students wishing to participate in athletics or cheerleading and their parents or guardians to sign a consent form agreeing to have the student submit to random urinalysis.

Each student selected for a team was assigned a number to be placed in a box for random drawing. When a student's number was drawn, the student would enter a lavatory stall and close the door in order to produce a sample. A monitor would stand outside the stall, listen for the normal sounds of urination, and check the temperature of the sample to ensure its genuineness. If testing by a simple technique produced a positive result, a second portion of the sample would be tested by a further method. If this test was also positive, the parents were given the opportunity to have the remaining portion of the sample tested at a laboratory of their choice. If no satisfactory explanation was produced for a student who tested positive, the student would be suspended from participation for a portion of the season.

The court decided that, although random urine testing was a search, athletes and cheerleaders did not have a strong expectation of privacy. Therefore, the school district's drug testing program was a reasonable and limited response to the serious problem of drug abuse in the schools. Because some courts have held that participation in extracurricular activities is a privilege, not a right, a separate set of rules for athletes has been allowed.

School Policies on Drug Testing

The Fourth Amendment will be applied to all student drug tests. If a district chooses to have a drug testing policy, it must demonstrate a sufficient interest in public health and welfare to outweigh the students' privacy interests. School districts should establish clear, concise, and reasonable policies that have wide input and expert counsel. These policies should:

1. Leave no room for misinterpretation, and should be widely disseminated and explained.
2. Be clear in intent, and the consequences for violating them should be specific to prevent claims of failure to notify under due process considerations.
3. Be more concerned with prevention than detection.
4. Provide notice and a due process hearing that conforms with constitutional, statute, and local due process requirements, when sanctions may result.[45]

Medication Administration

Scenario 14.10: Katie Marlborough was a fifth-grade student who had allergies and had to take several medicines each day. She carried the medicine in her back pack and took it three times a day.

Scenario 14.11: Roger Dawson, a senior in high school, injured his knee playing tennis. His doctor prescribed a pain killer and told him to take it three times a day. At noon he went to his locker and took two small white pills.

Scenario 14.12: Ben Bradley occasionally had headaches, and today he had a bad one. He went to the school secretary, who gave him two aspirin.

Scenario 14.13: Molly Bunker, a diabetic, required intramuscular injections of insulin once a day. Because she was only in the first grade, Molly's parents asked that her teacher help Molly with her injections.

Points to Consider: Is the administration of medication a medical procedure? Is it proper procedure to allow students to carry their own medication and self-medicate? Who should administer intravenous or intramuscular injections?

Because many schools do not have full-time nursing services, it has been the traditional practice for students to either carry their own medication or leave it in the office. When students needed medication they would either take it themselves or ask the school secretary to give it to them. As a result of the proliferation of illegal substances in schools and the increase of liability suits against schools for negligence, there is a need to establish guidelines for medication administration.

Diagnosis and treatment of illness and prescription of medication, including over-the-counter drugs, are not the responsibility of the school and should not be practiced by any school employee, including school nurses, without proper authorization. Proper authorization means a written prescription, from a person licensed to practice medicine, for the administration of all medication, including over-the-counter drugs.

In order to ensure the safety of school children and minimize the administration of medications to children during the school day, each school district should develop guidelines for the administration of medications. Recommended guidelines are:

1. A written request from the physician or dentist should accompany any medication to be administered, including over-the-counter drugs such as aspirin and cough medicine. Any changes in type of drugs, dosage, and/or time of administration should be accompanied by new physician and parent permission signatures and a newly labeled pharmacy container.

2. The physician request form should be dated and identify the medication, dosage, time of day to be given, and anticipated number of days to be provided. The official prescription container should accompany all medication.

Two containers, one for home and one for school, should be requested from the pharmacist. All medication maintained in the school setting should be kept in a locked container. Medications should be inventoried at least every semester by a licensed health professional (registered nurse, licensed practical nurse, physician, pharmacist). Out-of-date stock should be picked up by parent or destroyed. Needles and syringes should be sealed in a puncture-proof container and properly disposed of.

   3. A written request from the parent or guardian should accompany any medication. (See sample form in Figure 14-1.)

   4. Only oral or topical (for the skin) medications should be administered, except in emergency situations. Exceptions might include the administration of eye drops, ear drops, and rectal suppositories. After medication is administered, students should be observed for possible reactions to the medication for approximately twenty minutes. This observation may occur at the site of administration

---

**REQUEST FOR MEDICATION TO BE ADMINISTERED
DURING THE SCHOOL DAY**

Name of Student: _____

Grade: _____   (Homeroom) Teacher: _____

Medication: _____   Dosage: _____
Date Medication Started: _____   Diagnosis: _____
Date Medication To Be Stopped: _____

ALL MEDICATIONS WILL BE GIVEN OVER THE NOON HOUR,
UNLESS PHYSICIAN ORDERS OTHERWISE.

Signature of Physician _____   Date _____

I hereby give my permission for _____ to take the above prescription
                              (Name of Student)
at school, as ordered. I understand that it is my responsibility to furnish this medication. I further understand that any school employee who administers this drug to my child shall not be liable for damages due to adverse drug reaction, improper dosage, or failure to administer at the prescribed time.

Signature of Parent (Guardian) _____   Date _____

Note: The medication is to be brought to school in the original container, appropriately labeled by the pharmacy or physician, stating the name of the medication, the dosage, and the number of days to be administered at school.

Figure 14-1 • *Sample Form for Medication Administration*

or in the classroom as a part of the normal routine. The classroom teacher is responsible for observing the student if he or she is returned to the classroom. Otherwise, the person who administers the medication assumes this responsibility.

5. Registered nurses, physicians, or dentists should be responsible for the overall administration of all medication in schools. Administration may be delegated to a licensed practical nurse or an unlicensed staff member after receipt of the medication, the signed parent and physician forms, and an initial assessment of the student by the school nurse.

6. An individual and comprehensive record should be kept of any medication administered to students.

7. Over-the-counter medications should not be maintained on any school premises, including athletic areas, unless a prescription is provided along with written parent permission to administer.

8. The school board–approved policy should be shared with all local physicians and dentists. Forms should be made available to the health care providers in the community.[46]

Vaccinations

> *Scenario 14.14:* The first week of school had been going surprisingly well until the principal of Prairie Dog Elementary School got a call from the minister of a local church. The minister informed the principal that six children who had been attending the church's preschool program would be starting public school this week, and that these children may not receive any vaccinations. This presented a problem for the principal because the school district had a policy that required that all students be vaccinated for diphtheria, measles, rubella, and polio prior to admission to kindergarten.
>
> *Points to Consider:* Can a district require all students to be vaccinated prior to enrollment? What are the options if a parent refuses to comply with this regulation?

There is a mounting battle over parental rights as an increasing number of parents refuse to allow their children to be immunized. This opposition to vaccination is based both on philosophical or religious grounds and on parental fears that the risks associated with vaccinations are greater than the dangers of being infected. Parents are especially concerned about the pertussis (whooping cough) component of the DPT series. While some parents have campaigned to relax state vaccination requirements, the American Medical Association (AMA) has called on states to revoke any rights parents may now have to object on philosophical or religious grounds.[47] This stand by the AMA was prompted by evidence that a growing number of parents have not had their children vaccinated. For example, in 1989, 60 percent of people with measles were un-vaccinated or inadequately vaccinated.[48]

Vaccines have significantly reduced the occurrence of many contagious diseases. Although there is some public resistance and legal challenge to manda-tory vaccination, all states require some immunization for most children prior to the admission to public school, in order to protect them from infectious diseases. Medical exemptions are permitted if a physician states that a specific child would be endangered by immunization. Twenty-two states provide exemptions for philosophical reasons, and religious exemptions are permitted in every state except Mississippi and West Virginia. All states have statutes requiring vaccina-tion for diphtheria, measles, rubella, and polio. There are state-by-state varia-tions in the requirements for vaccines for tetanus, whooping cough (pertussis), and mumps. Parents who refuse permission for their child to be vaccinated and who do not qualify for some exemption may be fined or even imprisoned.[49]

When groups have challenged legislation requiring all school children to be immunized, the courts have held that a person's religious freedom ceases when it overlaps and transgresses the rights of others. The courts reasoned that other school children have a right to be free from mandatory association with persons not immunized against contagious diseases.[50]

Smoking Policies

Scenario 14.15: The school board approved a policy that prohibited students from using tobacco products on school grounds at all times. Several students were suspended for violating this policy. The suspended students and their parents argued that the policy denied the students due process because school employees were permitted to use tobacco products in the teachers' lounge.

Points to Consider: May schools enact policies that forbid students to use tobacco products on school property? Must such policies treat students and teachers equally?

By 1990, thirty-eight states and the District of Columbia had enacted legislation restricting smoking in school buildings or on school grounds. These statutes range from restricting student and staff smoking to specified areas, to total bans on all smoking on school property. Although some state statutes mandate school smoking policies, many others allow the local school boards to decide who, if anyone, will be allowed to smoke in the schools.[51]

In cases where school policies prohibiting students from smoking on school property have been challenged, courts have upheld the school district's authority to adopt such policies.[52] In the 1975 case of *Randol v. Newberg Public School Board,*[53] the court ruled that decisions regarding restricting or prohibiting students from smoking in school were administrative rather than judicial.[54] In a 1986 case the court recognized the difference between students and adults when it upheld a school rule that banned student smoking while allowing adult school personnel to smoke in the teachers' lounge.[55]

Endnotes

1. EDUCATION WEEK, May 16, 1990, 5.

2. 28 U.S.C.A. 1738(a) 1980.

3. R. Stenger, *The School Counselor and the Law,* JOURNAL OF LAW & EDUCATION, vol. 15, no. 1, Winter 1986.

4. Uniform Parentage Act, 9A U.L.A. 579 (1983).

5. Lalli v. Lalli, 439 U.S. 259 (1978).

6. *Supra*, note 3, at 108–9.

7. House Select Committee on Children, Youth and Families, *Abused Children in America: Victim of Official Neglect,* 100th Cong., 2d Sess. 10-18 (March 1987).

8. 134 CONG. REC. S3468 (daily ed. Mar. 30, 1988) (statement of Sen. Kennedy, speaking in favor of the Child Abuse Prevention, Adoption, and Family Services Act).

9. *Id.* at xii.

10. R. Gelles, *Child Abuse and Family Violence: Implications for Medical Professionals,* in E. NEWBERGER (Ed.), CHILD ABUSE, (Boston: Little, Brown, 1982), p. 27.

11. U.S. Bureau of Census; National Committee for Prevention of Child Abuse, 1985.

12. R. Shoop & L. Firestone, *Mandatory Reporting of Suspected Child Abuse: Do Teachers Obey the Law?,* 46 ED. LAW REP. 1115 (Aug. 4, 1988), pp. 1117–18.

13. CHILD ABUSE AND NEGLECT: THE PROBLEM AND ITS MANAGEMENT, vol. 1 (OHD 75-30073), Department of Health, Education and Welfare.

14. NATIONAL INSTITUTE OF JUSTICE NIJ REPORTS, No. 212, November/December, 1988. p. 9.

15. 469 U.S. 325 (1985).

16. J. Menacker, *Getting Tough on School-Connected Crime in Illinois,* 51 ED. LAW REP. (March 30, 1989), p. 347.

17. *Id.*

18. *Id.*

19. 124 Ill.2d 135 (1988).

20. Ryan White died in April of 1990 of complications from AIDS.

21. 29 U.S.C §§ 701–796 (1982).

22. School Board of Nassau County v. Arline, 107 S.Ct. 1123 (1987).

23. Martinez v. School Board of Hillsborough County, Florida, 711 F. Supp. 1066 (M.D. Fla. 1989).

24. District 27 Community School Board v. Board of Education, 502 N.Y.S. 2d 325 (32 ED. LAW REP. 740) (Sup. Ct. 1986).

25. 20 U.S.C. §§ 1401–1461 (1975 ed. & Supp. III 1979).

26. 666 F. Supp. 1524 (ED. LAW REP. 632) (M.D. Fla. 1987).

27. *Id.*

28. R. Shoop, *AIDS, Infected Children Have the Right to Attend School,* USA TODAY, vol. 117, no. 2528, May 1989, pp. 68–70.

29. S. Reed, *Children with AIDS: How Schools Are Handling the Crisis,* PHI DELTA KAPPAN, vol. 69, no. 5 (1988).

30. K. Keogh & G. Seaton, *Superintendents' Views of AIDS: A National Survey,* PHI DELTA KAPPAN, vol. 69, no. 5 (1988).

31. Topeka Public Schools Board of Education, Board Policy No. 4230-4235, 2-14-90.

32. Ware v. Valley Stream High School District, 545 N.Y.S. 2d 316 (A.D. 2 Dept. 1989).

33. Wall St. J., Apr. 14, 1986; National Law J., Apr. 8, 1986.

34. H. Grossman & M. Lopez, *Testing and Screening Employees and Students: Drugs and Alcohol,* paper presented at the ABA-NOLPE Symposium, Nov. 3, 1986.

35. *Id.*

36. E. Miller & A. Shultz, *Testing and Screening Employees and Students: Drugs and Alcohol,* paper presented at the ABA-NOLPE Symposium, November 1986.

37. R. James, R. Papkin, & M. Fortney, *Substance Abuse in the Workplace* (1986), in P. ZIRKEL & K. KILCOYNE, DRUG TESTING OF PUBLIC SCHOOL EMPLOYEES OR STUDENTS, 37 ED. LAW REP. 1029, p. 1029.

38. *See generally,* ACLU Briefing Paper, *Drug Testing in the Workplace;* I. GLASSER, *Why Indiscriminate Urine Testing Is a Bad Idea,* Seminar in Occupational Medicine, Dec. 1986, p. 254; T. Cohen, *Drug Use Testing: Costly and Corruptible,* N.Y. Times, Aug. 20, 1986, p. A23; Anable v. Ford, 653 F. Supp. 22 (37 ED. LAW REP. 1114) (W. D. Ark., 1985).

39. Terry v. Ohio, 392, U.S. 1, 20-21 S.Ct. 1868, 1873, 20 L.Ed.2d 889 (1968). *See also* New Jersey v. TLO, 469 U.S. 325, 105 S.Ct. 733, 83 L.Ed.2d 720 (21 ED. LAW REP. 1122) (1985).

40. People v. Scott D., 34 N.Y.2d 483, 358 N.Y.S.2d 403, 315 N.E.2d 466 (1974).

41. Odenheim v. Carlstadt-East Rutherford School Dist., N.J. Super. Ct., 1985.

42. Anable v. Ford, 84-6033 (W.D. Ark., 1985).

43. Brooks v. East Chambers Consolidated Independent School District, 730 F. Supp. 759 (S.D. Tex. 1989).

44. Schaill v. Tippecanoe County School Corp., 864 F.2d 1309 (7th Cir. 1988).

45. D. Thompson & R. Shoop, *Drug Testing of Public Employees: Anatomy of a Statute,* 52 ED. LAW REP. 869.

46. *Guidelines for Medication Administration in Kansas Schools,* Kansas Department of Health and Environment, revised and approved March, 1989.

47. S. Nazario, *"A Parental-Rights Battle Is Heating Up over Fears of Whooping-Cough Vaccine,"* Wall St. J., June 20, 1990, p. B1.

48. EDUCATION WEEK, June 13, 1990, p. D3.

49. S. THOMAS, HEALTH RELATED LEGAL ISSUES IN EDUCATION, (National Organization on Legal Problems of Education, 1987), pp. 7–13.

50. Brown v. Stone, 378 So.2d 218 (Miss. 1979).

51. F. Hartmeister, *Smoking Policies: An Analysis of School District Obligation and Liability,* 61 ED. LAW REP. (Sept. 27, 1990), p. 794.

52. *Id.* at 797.

53. Randol v. Newberg Public School Board, 23 Ore. App. 425, 542 P.2d 938 (1975).

54. *Id.* at 939.

55. Craig v. Buncombe County Board of Education, 80 N.C. App. 638, 343 S.E. 2d 222 (1986).

CHAPTER FIFTEEN

Copyright Law

The Copyright Law of 1976

Scenario 15.1: A national education association sponsored a teleconference on school discipline. Eisenhower High School was one of over forty sites across the country that paid a fee and participated. The program was broadcast by satellite and shown on television monitors at each location. The Eisenhower media center made a videotape of the broadcast and made it available to teachers who were unable to attend the presentation.

Points to Consider: When you pay to receive a teleconference, do you have the right to make copies of the presentation?

Scenario 15.2: Two years ago, when Superior Middle School's eleven-station computer room was set up, the software was purchased under a "one package to one work station" license agreement. Many of the software programs have had several updates. Because there was not enough money to buy eleven updates of each software package, the computer teacher bought one copy of each program and made eleven "back-up" copies.

Points to Consider: Because the original software was purchased, there was no profit motive, and the copying was done for the benefit of students, was there any violation of the copyright law? When you purchase a software package, do you have the right to use it any way you choose?

Scenario 15.3: As a treat for her students, who had been particularly well-behaved, a fifth-grade teacher rented a popular film to show to her class. To make the afternoon especially enjoyable, she allowed them to invite their preschool brothers or sisters to come and watch the film.

Scenario 15.4: A pay television channel showed a series of children's classic films. A public school teacher videotaped several of these films for future use in her classroom.

Points to Consider: May a teacher rent a videotape for use in a class? Are there any restrictions on how such a tape can be shown? May people from outside the school view a videotape rented for use in a classroom? May a teacher legally tape a television program to show later in class? Is there any limit to how long such a tape may be retained?

Scenario 15.5:   Because of a budget cut, no new textbooks had been purchased for several years. The high school principal told her teachers to use some creativity and generate some "teacher-made" materials. The advanced placement history teacher responded by spending his summer reviewing and compiling journal articles. Just before school started, he gave the packet of 30 articles to the copy room staff and asked them to make 100 copies of each.

Points to Consider: May a teacher photocopy material from journals and distribute them to students? Should copy center staff copy whatever a teacher requests?

As the world has become more complex and our technological capabilities more sophisticated, the laws that regulate our society have increased in intricacy. The copyright law is one example. A copyrighted work is the property of the author, who may assign it in exchange for some remuneration, usually in the form of royalty on copies sold. The behavior of many educators toward the copyright law is very interesting. People who would not dream of stealing money or goods make photocopies of books, duplicate records and video and audio cassettes, copy televised programs, and make copies of computer software with no sense of guilt.

The copyright law has expanded from denying only the copying of excerpts from books, periodicals, other print materials, and printed music to include audio recordings, off-air videotape recording and, more recently, computer software. The Copyright Act of 1976 (the first general revision of the Copyright Law of 1909), amendments, and issued guidelines form the basis for most of the litigation involving alleged infringement of copyright.[1]

The current law contains many additions and changes from the previous legislation. Intellectual property subject to copyright has been broadened and made more flexible by the use of the phrase "original works of authorship" instead of "all the writings of the author" as used in the earlier law. The judicial doctrine of "fair use" is given statutory recognition for the first time, and the law establishes a single system of federal statutory copyright protection from the time of the actual creation of intellectual property. The duration of copyright protection is the life of the author plus fifty years.

The four sections of the law having the most significance for educators are: Section 107, Fair Use; Section 108, Reproduction by Libraries and Archives;

Section 110, Exemption for Educators; and Section 117, Scope of Exclusive Rights: Use in Conjunction with Computers and Similar Information Systems.

Section 107—Fair Use

Section 107 specifies the judicial doctrine of fair use and is used to determine whether the reproduction of a copyrighted work violates the rights of the copyright owner. Fair use allows copying of a limited amount of material without permission from, or payment to, the copyright owner, where the use is reasonable and not harmful to the rights of the owner, especially the owner's income.[2] Copying for purposes such as criticism, comment, news reporting, teaching (including multiple copies for classroom use), scholarship, or research is not an infringement of copyright.[3]

Congress established the following statutory criteria to be used to evaluate fair use of a copyrighted work:

1. The purpose and character of the use, including whether such use is of a commercial nature or for nonprofit educational purposes
2. The nature of the copyrighted work
3. The amount and substantiality of the portion used in relation to the copyrighted work as a whole
4. The effect of the use upon the potential market for, or value of, the copyrighted work.[4]

Guidelines for Classroom Copying

The copyright law does not contain specific guidelines; however, a report accompanying the legislation provides an indication of the legislative intent, and is intended for use by individuals and the courts in deliberations concerning copyright use and abuse. Although these guidelines do not have the force of law, the courts may consider them in litigation involving copyright violations.

Single Copying for Teachers

Teachers may make a single copy of the following for their scholarly research or use in preparation for or teaching of a class:

1. A chapter from a book
2. An article from a periodical or newspaper
3. A short story, essay, or poem, whether or not from a collective work

4. A chart, graph, diagram, cartoon, or picture from a book, periodical, or newspaper

Multiple Copies for Classroom Use

Teachers may make multiple copies (not more than one copy per student in a course) for classroom use or discussion, provided that the copying meets the tests of *brevity, spontaneity,* and *cumulative effect* as defined below.

Brevity

A teacher may copy a complete poem if it contains fewer than 250 words and if it is printed on no more than two pages, and may copy an excerpt of no more than 250 words from a larger poem. A copy may be made of a complete article, story, or essay of fewer than 2,500 words or an excerpt from any prose work of not more than 1,000 words or 10 percent of the work, whichever is less. A teacher may use one chart, graph, diagram, drawing, cartoon, or picture per book or periodical issue.

"Special" works—those that combine language and illustrations but fall short of 2,500 words—may not be reproduced in their entirety. A teacher may copy one or two of the published pages of a special work, so long as those pages do not contain more than 10 percent of the words found in the work.

Spontaneity

All copying must be at the instance and inspiration of the individual teacher. The use of a copyrighted work is considered spontaneous if the inspiration and decision to use the work and the moment of its use for maximum teaching effectiveness are so close in time that it would be unreasonable to expect a timely reply to a request for permission.

Cumulative Effect

A teacher is limited to copying material for only one course in the school in which the copy is made. The teacher is also limited to copying not more than one poem, article, story, or essay or two excerpts from the same author, and not more than three excerpts from the same collective work or periodical volume during one class term. This limitation does not apply to current news periodicals, current news sections of other periodicals, or newspapers.

Additional Prohibitions

Copied materials may not be used to create, replace or substitute for anthologies, compilations, or collective works. This limitation applies whether the replacement or substitute copies are accumulated or reproduced and used separately. Copied materials may not be used as "consumables" (i.e., work-books, exercises, standardized test booklets, or answer sheets) in the course of study or teaching. In addition, copying may not:

1. Substitute for the purchase of books, publisher's reprints, or periodicals
2. Be directed by higher authorities
3. Be repeated with respect to the same item by the same teacher from term to term.

Finally, a teacher may not charge students for copied materials, beyond the actual cost of the photocopying.[5]

Guidelines for Educational Use of Music

Permissible Uses

School music departments may make copies of music in emergencies when purchased music is not available, for any reason, for an imminent performance, provided purchased replacement copies will be substituted in due course. For academic purposes other than performance, multiple copies of excerpts of works may be made, provided that the excerpts do not comprise a "performable unit" (i.e., section, movement, aria) of a work or more than 10 percent of the whole work. The permissible number of copies is limited to one per student. In addition, a single copy of an entire performable unit that is out of print or unavailable except in a larger work may be made by a teacher solely for the purpose of scholarly research or preparation to teach a class. Printed copies of purchased music may be edited or simplified, provided that the fundamental character of the work is not distorted, or the lyrics (if any) altered, or lyrics added if none exist.

Single copies of recordings of performances by students may be made for evaluation or rehearsal purposes and may be retained by the school or teacher. A single copy of a sound recording (tape, disc, or cassette) of copyrighted music may be made and retained by the school or teacher for the purpose of construct-ing aural exercises or examinations. (This pertains only to the copyright on the music itself, and not to any copyright that may exist in the sound recording.)

Prohibited Use

A teacher may not copy to create, replace, or substitute for anthologies, compilations, or collective works or to create consumables (i.e., workbooks, exercises, tests, and answer sheets) for a class. A teacher may not use copied material as a substitute for the purchase of music, and any copy made must include the copyright notice that appears on the printed copy.[6]

The Copyright Law and the Library

Section 108

It is not an infringement of copyright for a library or archives, or any of its employees acting within the scope of their employment, to reproduce one copy or phono record, or to distribute the copy under the following conditions:

1. The reproduction or distribution is made without any purpose of direct or indirect commercial advantage.
2. The collections of the library are open to the public or available to researchers from outside as well as inside the institution.
3. The reproduction or distribution of the work includes the copyright notice.[7]

Libraries are permitted to make:

1. A single archival reproduction of an entire unpublished work for the purpose of preservation, security, or for deposit for research in another library, if the copy is currently in the collection of the first library
2. A replacement copy of an entire work that is damaged, deteriorating, lost, or stolen, if the library has, after a reasonable effort, determined that an unused replacement cannot be obtained at a fair price
3. A single copy of an entire work from the library's own collections for another library, if it has been established, after reasonable investigation, that a copy cannot be obtained at a fair price. The required scope and nature of the reasonable investigation depends on the particular circumstances.

Guidelines for Library Copying

The Library's Own Collections

A single copy of a single article or a copy of a small part of a copyrighted work from the library's own collections may be made, provided that the copy becomes the property of the user and the library has no notice that the copy would be used for any purpose other than private study, scholarship, or research. The library must display prominently at the place where copying requests are accepted, and include on its order form, a warning of copyright in accordance with regulations from the Register of Copyrights.

Interlibrary Loan Copying

A single copy of a single article or small part of a copyrighted work for the purpose of interlibrary loan may be made, provided that all of the above conditions are met, and further provided that the requests for interlibrary loan photocopies are not in such aggregate quantities as to substitute for purchases or subscriptions. The responsibility for compliance is on the library requesting the photocopy, not on the library fulfilling the request.

Coin-Operated Copying Machines

Neither libraries or library employees are liable for the unsupervised use of reproducing equipment located on library premises, provided that the machine displays a notice that the making of a copy may be subject to the copyright law. Library patrons making the copies are not excused from liability for copyright violation if their copying exceeds fair use.[8]

Libraries involved with copying on request must post a warning concerning copyright restrictions. The federal regulation requires that the display warning be printed on heavy paper or other durable material, in type at least 18 points in size, and displayed prominently so as to be clearly visible, legible, and comprehensible to a casual observer in the immediate vicinity of the place where orders are accepted. An Order Warning of Copyright must be printed in a box located prominently on the order form itself, either on the front side of the form or immediately adjacent to the space calling for the name or signature of the person using the form. This notice must be printed in a type size no smaller than that used predominantly on the form (eight points or larger) and be clearly legible, comprehensible, and readily apparent to a casual reader of the form.[9]

It is recommended that a warning also be placed on any coin-operated copying machine in the school building. The intent of the warning is to notify users of their potential liability for any copyright violation.[10]

Guidelines for Off-Air Recording

Although not enacted into law, the following guidelines, which apply only to off-air recording by nonprofit educational institutions, were issued by a negotiating committee of Congress.[11]

1. A broadcast program may be recorded off-air simultaneously with the broadcast transmission (including a simultaneous cable retransmission) and retained by a nonprofit educational institution for up to forty-five calendar days from the date of recording. After forty-five days have elapsed, the off-air

recordings must be erased or destroyed. Broadcast programs are television programs transmitted by television stations for general reception without charge.

2. Off-air recordings may be used once by individual teachers in the course of relevant teaching activities and repeated only once, when instructional reinforcement is necessary, during the first ten consecutive school days of the forty-five calendar days. The relevant teaching activities may take place in a single classroom, a single building, on a single campus, or in the homes of students receiving formalized home instruction. School days do not include days when school is not in session (e.g., weekends, holidays, vacation periods, examination periods, or other scheduled interruptions).

3. Off-air recordings may be made only at the request of, and used by, individual teachers; they may not be regularly recorded in anticipation of requests. No broadcast program may be recorded off-air more than once at the request of the same teacher, regardless of the number of times the program may be rebroadcast.

4. A limited number of copies may be reproduced from each off-air recording to meet the legitimate needs of teachers under these guidelines. Each additional copy is subject to all of the provisions governing the original recording.

5. After the first ten consecutive school days, the recordings may be used up to the end of the forty-five calendar day retention period for teacher evaluation purposes only; that is, to determine whether or not to include the broadcast program in the teaching curriculum. The recordings may not be used for student exhibition or any other nonevaluation purpose without authorization.

6. Off-air recordings need not be used in their entirety, but the recorded programs may not be altered from their original content. The recordings may not be physically or electronically combined or merged to constitute teaching anthologies or compilations.

7. All copies of off-air recordings must include the copyright notice on the broadcast program as recorded.

8. Educational institutions are expected to establish appropriate control procedures to maintain the integrity of these guidelines.

While the guidelines are useful in establishing some parameters for the fair use of copyrighted materials, a federal court of appeals has noted that "the line which must be drawn between fair use and copyright infringement depends on an examination of the facts of each case. It cannot be determined by resort to any arbitrary or fixed criteria."[12]

A federal district court in New York held that the Board of Educational Services in Erie County, New York was guilty of copyright violations by videotaping television programs, maintaining a library of the tapes, and circulating the tapes to member school districts for classroom use.[13] The service center had videotaped entire programs including the copyright notices from broadcasts of the local public television station. In addition, the service center made videotapes of films it had purchased for the film library. The tapes were maintained in a regional library for circulation on a request basis to teachers in the member school districts for classroom use. Service center personnel admitted that there was no prior permission secured from the copyright owners or any fees paid for the copying. The service center had no contractual relationship with the copyright owners or the television station for the purchase or licensing of the off-air videotapes derived from the television broadcasts.

The court found that the "videotaping practices interfere with . . . the marketability of plaintiffs' copyrighted works; these practices tend to diminish and prejudice the potential sale of plaintiffs' works in videotape format."[14] When evaluating the service center's practices under the concept of fair use, the court noted that:

> *Fair use is a concept based upon reasonableness and although the purpose and character of the use here is clearly educational and non-commercial, the massive scope of the videotape copying and the highly sophisticated methods used by the defendants in producing and distributing these copies cannot be deemed reasonable, even under the most favorable light of fair use of non-profit educational purposes.*[15]

The court granted an injunction prohibiting the service center from videotaping and distributing off-air copies of the television programs and films for classroom use. The court also allowed damages to the copyright owners.

The fair use doctrine does not allow a school district or school to engage in a systematic plan of videotaping television programs or films for repeated classroom use. Before principals develop such an arrangement for their schools, they must obtain permission from the copyright owners or be willing to pay a licensing fee. In no circumstance may principals or other administrators direct the teachers or personnel under their authority to videotape television programs for classroom use. Copying under the fair use doctrine may not be directed by higher authority, but may be done only at the request of an individual teacher. Principals who become aware that a classroom teacher is abusing the fair use doctrine have a responsibility to take actions to prevent a violation.

Section 110—Exemption for Educators

Section 110 of the Copyright Law provides an exemption for educators under certain circumstances.[16] A school is permitted to display a copyrighted work if it is shown:

1. As part of the instructional program
2. By students or instructors
3. In the classroom or other school location
4. In a face-to-face setting
5. Only to students and educators
6. If it has been legally produced, including the copyright notice

Schools are prohibited from displaying a copyrighted work if it is:

1. Used for recreation or entertainment
2. Transmitted by closed or open circuit radio or television
3. Shown to an audience that is not confined to teachers and students
4. Illegally acquired or duplicated[17]

Section 117—Computer Software

The Copyright Act speaks directly to the issue of making a back-up copy of computer software. For computers with hard disks (not networked to other computers), section 117 clearly allows the copying of the entire program from the original disk to the hard disk for use with that computer. In such cases the original disk may be thought of as the archival copy, and the copy on the hard disk as the working copy. A person may not, however, copy the program onto the hard disk of more than one computer, unless that person destroys other such copies before doing so.

Two other computer software issues are "booting" a program into the memory of more than one computer for simultaneous use by several users, and the use of a software program on a computer network with a file server that has the ability to "serve" software and data files to multiple computers for possible simultaneous use.

The booting of a program requires that the program in question be "memory resident"—that is, totally loadable into the random access memory (RAM) of the computer. The disk containing the program can then be removed from the disk drive of the booted computer and transferred to another computer. The booting process can then be endlessly repeated. Typical software documentation will include a statement such as: "It is against the law to copy any of the software in the XYZ package on cassette tape, magnetic disk or any other medium for any purpose other than personal convenience." Assuming that the RAM is a medium as used in the copyright notice, each time a program is booted into a second computer, the copyright law has been violated. Unless specific permission is given or purchased, or the program is labeled as a "Multi-load Program," it is illegal to boot to RAM.

Networking a program—that is, storing a copy of the program on a network file server and serving that program to any computer on the network that requests it, although not yet tested in court, would appear to be a violation of copyright. As more public schools connect their computers into networks, the issue of networkable software will receive more public debate.

Request for Permission

An educator wishing to use a copyrighted work outside the copyright limitations may write for permission. Such a request should be mailed with adequate time for the copyright holder to respond. This letter should include complete information about how the material is proposed to be used.

Remedies for Copyright Infringement

The law provides substantial remedies for the infringement of copyright. For example, the courts are authorized to order temporary and/or final injunctions, as well as ordering the impoundment and/or destruction of all illegal copies. The copyright owner may sue for actual damages and any additional profits of the infringer. The courts are authorized to award statutory damages ranging from as little as $100, where the infringer was unaware of the violation, to as much as $50,000, where the infringement was willful. Along with actual monetary damages, court costs and attorneys' fees can also be awarded in a copyright infringement suit.

Congress has extended the protection of teachers, librarians, archivists, public broadcasters, and the nonprofit institutions they represent by providing a general "innocent infringer" clause.[18] If these individuals are acting within the scope of their employment, or the institution infringed copyrighted material in the honest belief that what they were doing constituted fair use, the court will not require them to pay damages.[19]

Endnotes

1. 17 U.S.C. § 101 (Pub. L. 94-553).
2. AMERICAN LIBRARY ASSOCIATION, LIBRARIAN'S GUIDE TO THE NEW COPYRIGHT LAW, (Chicago: 1977), p. 1.
3. 17 U.S.C. § 101 (Supp. 1978).
4. *Id.*
5. Copyright Law Revision, H. R. REP. NO. 1476, 94th Cong., 2d Sess. § 68, reprinted in 1976 U.S. CONG. & AD. NEWS at 5684.

6. *Id.* at 70.

7. 17 U.S.C. § 108(a) (Supp. II 1978).

8. *Supra,* note 2.

9. 17 U.S.C. § 108 (1978).

10. *Id.*

11. 127 Cong. Rec. E4750-52 (daily ed., Oct. 14, 1981).

12. Meeropol v. Nizer, 560 F.2d 1061, 1068 (2d Cir. 1977).

13. Encyclopedia Britannica Educational Corporation v. Crooks, 542 F. Supp. 1156 (W.D.N.Y. 1982).

14. *Id.* at 1169.

15. *Id.* at 1175.

16. 17 U.S.C. § 110 (Supp. II 1978).

17. Public Broadcasting Service, Copyright: Staying Within The Law, A Resource Guide for Educators, (PBS, Washington, D.C.: 1988), p. 6.

18. 17 U.S.C. § 504(c) (Supp. II 1978).

19. R. Shoop and W. Sparkman, Kansas School Law (Dubuque, Iowa; Bowers, 1983), p. 174.

CHAPTER SIXTEEN

Textbook Selection and Censorship in the Schools

Introduction

Censors have been at work at least since the time of Sparta, and the word *censorship* dates from the Roman Empire. The word *censor* is derived from the office of censor, the Roman officials who were expected to use their authority to sustain public morals and restrict and criticize certain forms of public misconduct. Today's censors may be state-appointed or self-appointed. They may be school employees or members of citizens groups, and they may be found on both the right and the left ends of the political spectrum.

Although the most ironic example of school censorship might be a Virginia school district's attempt to ban *The Adventures of Huckleberry Finn* from the curriculum of the Mark Twain Intermediate School, school censorship is not an isolated occurrence. It is a growing phenomenon in public education, in spite of such ludicrous examples as the demand that the *American Heritage Dictionary* be removed because its seventh definition of "to bed" is "to have sexual intercourse with," or a school's banning of *Making It with Mademoiselle* until it learned that the book, published by *Mademoiselle* magazine, was a how-to dressmaking book for teen-agers.

Members of the "Moral Majority" claim they are engaged in a battle to determine who will use the schools to indoctrinate young people. Feminists claim that they have a right to remove educational material that fosters sexual stereotypes. Civil liberty advocates say that they have a right to remove books that are racist and replace them with books that present positive role models for racial and ethnic minorities. National groups such as The Liberty Federation, Mel and Norma Gabler's Educational Research Analysts, Phyllis Schlafly's The Eagle Forum, People For the American Way, the National Organization for Women, the Council on Interracial Books for Children, and the National Council of Teachers of English are all are active in attempting to control the content of public school curricula.

An example of a force on the political right are the Gablers, who want books that are pro-life, pro-family, anti-homosexual, pro-creationist, and pro-back-to-basics. They warn parents about books that they believe should be banned from public schools and lobby for statewide adoption of the text books that meet their conservative criteria.

A force on the political left, the Council of Interracial Books for Children, monitors children's books for signs of "racism, sexism, ageism, materialism, elitism, and individualism." Members believe that individualism should be discouraged as a highly negative force and that children should be taught the value of working for the collective good.

Although the increase in citizen pressure to censor books is the result of many causes, a spokesperson for the American Library Association (ALA), has suggested that citizen pressure results from very deep-seated feelings of political and economic helplessness. The ALA's representative suggests that many people are frustrated by societal changes. They are angry and afraid and feel that they cannot control their own lives. They find that by protesting they can control part of their children's lives. It is easier to censor school books than it is to deal with the larger problems that are bothering them. They seem to believe that if they take books that deal with controversial subjects out of schools, these issues will no longer exist for their children.[1] During the past decade, would-be censors have attacked the textbooks adopted by school districts, books selected for school libraries, and visuals used in classrooms as supplemental learning materials.

Textbook Selection

Although about half of the states delegate the responsibility for textbook selection to local boards of education, the other half exercise this authority directly. In adoption states a single text is selected for each subject, and publishers supply the textbooks statewide at a fixed price over a fixed period, called an adoption period. Typically, local school districts in adoption states may not use state funds to buy books that are not on the state list.

Whether adopted at the state or the local level, the selection of textbooks often becomes an issue of public debate. Because the question of whether the parent or the school has the final word regarding the education of children is often difficult to answer, the selection of textbooks can bring parents and educators into conflict. Controversies over textbooks seem to cluster around several broad issues: sex, politics, traditional values, war and peace, religion, sociology, race and language, drugs, and adolescent behavior.[2]

Although the courts have ruled that citizens of the community cannot use court action to require a board of education to use a certain textbook, school boards are very responsive to vocal pressure.[3] In some cases, textbooks have been removed from schools as the result of pressure from less than a dozen citizens.

One case involved a Florida high school humanities course for eleventh- and twelfth-grade students, in which students read portions of *Lysistrata* aloud in class. Following a parent's complaint, the board created a policy regarding the use of challenged textbooks. The board initially decided to retain the disputed book; however, they later removed it. A citizen's group challenged the board's action, complaining that removal of the textbook violated the First Amendment. A federal district court ruled in favor of the school board, noting that educators have a great deal of discretion over curriculum-related speech and expression relating to educational goals. The court concluded that exclusion of the textbook was a reasonable and legitimate educational decision.[4]

In another case, *Mozert v. Hawkins County Board of Educators,*[5] a parent challenged the requirement that all students participate in a particular reading program, which contained stories and poems with ideas contrary to the parent's religious beliefs. The federal court of appeals held in favor of the school board and recognized the broad discretion of school boards to establish curriculum even in the face of parental disagreements.

Censorship of Educational Materials in Classrooms and Libraries

Scenario 16.1: The librarian at the middle school found the photos in the swimsuit issue of a popular magazine to be "in bad taste." She sent the magazine back to the publisher and posted the following note on the shelf where the magazine was usually displayed: "This issue of this magazine is banned from this library because of obscene photographs."

Scenario 16.2: A group of teachers gathered in the parking lot outside of the high school to burn forty books that they believed did not belong in their school. All of the books had previously been used in courses in black literature, gothic literature, mythology, and creative writing.

Scenario 16.3: A local minister called for a community review board to screen all books used in the school. He especially wanted all novels of Judy Blume banned. He considered Blume's books to be "sexual how-to lessons for young students."

Scenario 16.4: A parent asked the teacher of his fourth-grader to stop using *The Gnats of Knotty Pine* by Bill Peet. The parent believed the story wrongly depicted hunters as "macho-types" who harm little animals.

Scenario 16.5: A local civil rights group notified the principal it was initiating a court action to stop the school from using educational materials it considered sexist, racist, ageist, and elitist.

Scenario 16.6: An elementary school teacher confiscated all of the school's copies of the *American Heritage Dictionary* on the grounds that it defines vulgar and scatological phrases.

Points to Consider: Do students have a First Amendment right to access to ideas? Do parents who wish to shield their children from works they believe are "immoral" or "unpatriotic" have the right to do so? Do parents who want schools to expose their children to a broad range of materials have a right to demand books be retained in the school? Do democratically elected school boards have the power to decide what ought not to be in schools?

In addition to attacking textbook adoptions, school patrons and individual board members sometimes demand that certain materials they consider objectionable be removed from classrooms or libraries. School boards faced with such complaints have often been willing to order school administrators to remove the materials from the schools. In some cases, school officials have not only ordered materials removed from schools, but have also ordered that its content not be discussed in classrooms. School boards have justified their actions by asserting that they have absolute discretion in all curriculum matters in the school and that they must be permitted to establish and apply the curriculum in such a way as to transmit community values. Those who oppose the removal of school curriculum materials or library books from schools argue that the practice is a violation of the First Amendment's guarantee of free speech.

A few of the books that have been taken out of schools are: *American Heritage Dictionary, The Koran, The Talmud, Little Black Sambo, The Wizard of Oz, The Living Bible, The Good Earth, Alice in Wonderland, Don Quixote, Green Pastures, The Divine Comedy, The Adventures of Sherlock Holmes, Ann Frank, The Adventures of Robinson Crusoe, Black Like Me, Ordinary People, Jude the Obscure, Brave New World, To Kill a Mockingbird, The Voyages of Dr. Dolittle, The Call of The Wild, Mary Poppins,* and *Charlotte's Web.*

A number of federal courts have heard cases involving efforts to censor various reading materials in the schools. In *Presidents Council, Dist. 25 v. Community School Board No. 25,*[6] a federal appeals court upheld the right of a school board to remove Piri Thomas's *Down These Mean Streets* from junior high school libraries because some of the language and scenes in the book were "ugly and violent." This court found no violation of any basic constitutional right and concluded that any intrusion on any First Amendment right was only "minuscule."[7]

On the other hand, in *Minarcini v. Strongville City School District,*[8] another federal appeals court overruled a lower court and denied a school board's right to remove Joseph Heller's *Catch-22* and Kurt Vonnegut, Jr.'s *Cat's Cradle* from a high school library. This court ruled that if a school board sets up a library, that library becomes a forum of silent speech protected by the First Amendment. Therefore, it is unconstitutional to place conditions on its use based solely on the social or political tastes of school board members.

In 1982 the United States Supreme Court heard its first school library book banning case. This case of censorship involved the removal of nine books from the school library shelves of the Island Trees Union School District.[9] The board defended its decision by claiming the books contained "material which is offensive to Christians, Jews, Blacks, and Americans in general," as well as "obscenities, blasphemies, brutality and perversion beyond description." The board's action prompted Steven Pico and four other high school students to sue the school district. They charged that the board ignored the advice of literary experts, libraries, and teachers, as well as publications that rate books for secondary students, and based its decision solely on a list of objectionable books put out by a conservative parents group.

In hearing the *Pico* case the Supreme Court affirmed the appellate court's decision that school officials can be taken to federal court if they are challenged about removing books from school libraries; however, it did not clarify just how far a school board may legally go in removing books from a school library. In writing for the majority, Justice Brennan focused his opinion on very narrow terms—whether the First Amendment limits the discretion of a local school board to remove library books from junior and senior high schools. The intent of the school board was a decisive factor in the decision. Because the Court believed that the school board was attempting to deny the students access to ideas with which the school board disagreed, their action was ruled unconstitutional. The Court relied on the concept that the "right to receive ideas is a necessary predicate to the exercise of speech, press and political freedom." The Court believed that the school library is an especially important factor in the preparation of students for active and effective participation in the pluralistic, often contentious society in which they will soon be adult members.

The *Pico* decision sends several messages to school officials: Board members can rightfully claim absolute discretion in curriculum matters by reliance on the duty to inculcate community values in the schools, but that duty is misplaced when a board attempts to extend its claim of absolute discretion beyond the compulsory environment of the classroom into the library, where voluntary inquiry is paramount. In addition, although school boards have significant discretion to determine the library's content, such discretion cannot be exercised in a narrowly partisan or political manner. The Court ruled that "our Constitution does not permit the official suppression of ideas."

The courts have clearly ruled that books cannot be removed simply because school officials disagree with the ideas, or because they wish to impose an intellectual straitjacket on the students.[10] It has been suggested that removal decisions should be based on a book's or other curriculum material's educational suitability, considering such "politically neutral" factors as relevance, quality, pervasive vulgarity, and appropriateness to age and grade level. Such decisions should consider the views and opinions of a variety of professional educators, as well as parents and students, and no decision should be based on objections of narrow interest outside the school.

CITIZEN'S REQUEST FOR RECONSIDERATION OF A BOOK OR OTHER INSTRUCTIONAL MATERIAL

Title: _____

Author: _____   Publisher/Copyright _____

The instructional material in question is a: (Please circle)

Book   Periodical   Slide Presentation   Film   Video Tape

Other (Specify): _____

Request Initiated By: _____   Date: _____
                      Name of Citizen

       Address: _____

               _____

       Telephone Number: _____   _____
                           (Day)   (Evening)

This request is being made on behalf of:

_____ Myself

_____ An Organization (please specify) _____

---

1. How is this book or material used in the instructional program?

   _____ Required reading/viewing as part of course work:

   _____ Available in classroom as supplemental material:

   _____ Available in media center for assigned reading/viewing:

   _____ Available in media center for recreational reading/viewing:

   _____ Other: _____

2. What is your understanding of the teacher's purpose in assigning or suggesting this material to students? _____

3. For what age group is this material intended? _____

4. Have you read/viewed the entire work?   Yes   No

5. If this work is part of a set or series or materials, have you read/viewed the entire series?   Yes   No

6. Please identify what you find objectionable in this instructional material.
   (Please be specific and cite pages, pictures, etc.) _____
   _____
   _____
   _____
   _____
   _____

7. What action(s) are you requesting the school take regarding this book/material?
   _____ Do not assign it to my child.
   _____ Have the material re-evaluated by the appropriate district personnel.
   _____ Withdraw the material from the classroom and/or media center.

8. In its place, what book (film, tape, periodical, etc.) of equal literary quality
   would you recommend that would convey as valuable a picture or perspective of a
   society or set of values?

   Title: _____

   Author: _____ Publisher/Producer _____

   _____   _____   _____
   Signature of Citizen   Received by   Date

FIGURE 16-1 • *Sample Form for Challenge Procedure*

Summary

In the face of increasing numbers of challenges to materials used in classrooms and school libraries, educators need to establish policies for dealing with issues such as textbook selection or removal of materials.

Guidelines for Including and Excluding Educational Materials

1. Procedures should be developed that ensure that the selection of educational material is based on an evaluation of how the material will assist the student to reach previously agreed-upon goals.
2. The procedures should encourage teachers to consider the age and maturity of the student when assigning any material.
3. All material should be examined for problems of style, language, and content.
4. Provisions should be made for alternative materials for those students whose parents object to specific material.

5. Each school district should have a board policy for handling complaints.

6. The policy should include a specific procedure to follow in the cases of material being challenged.

7. The procedure should be based on a standardized form (See Figure 16-1, pages 250–251).

8. All principals, librarians, and teachers should receive inservice instruction on the implementation of this policy.[11]

Endnotes

1. Judith Krug, *Survey Reports Rise in School Library Censorship,* NEWSLETTER ON INTELLECTUAL FREEDOM, Jan. 1983.

2. K. Donelson & F. Dean, *Facing School Censorship,* in H. Ehlers, CRITICAL ISSUES IN EDUCATION (New York: Holt, Rinehart and Winston, 1977), pp. 215–217.

3. Wright v. Houston Independent School District, 486 F.2d 137 (5 Cir 1973); Mercer v. Michigan State Board of Education, 279 F. Supp. (E.D. Mich. 1974).

4. Virgil v. School Board of Columbia County, Florida, 677 F. Supp. 1547 (M.D.Fla. 1988).

5. 827 F.2d 1058 (6th Cir. 1987).

6. 457 F.2d 289 (2d Cir. 1972), *cert. denied,* 409 U.S. 998 (1972).

7. *Id.* at 292.

8. 541 F.2d 577 (6th Cir. 1976).

9. Island Trees Union School District v. Pico, 102 S. Ct. 2799 (1982).

10. D. Schimmel, *The Limits on School Board Discretion:* Board of Education v. Pico, 5 ED. LAW REP. 285, 301.

11. ROBERT SHOOP & WILLIAM SPARKMAN, KANSAS SCHOOL LAW, (Dubuque, Iowa; Bowers, 1983), p. 185.

CHAPTER SEVENTEEN

Community Education

Scenario 17.1:   A school had long had a comprehensive program of adult and community education. The principal received an angry phone call from the head of a local business group, who accused the school of "infringing on their businesses." The business leader said that many of the school's adult and community education programs were in unfair competition with some of their members. The businesspeople who were especially affected were the proprietors of dance, martial arts and crafts studios, and day care centers.

Points to Consider: Is it legal for a state-funded school to compete with private businesses?

Scenario 17.2:   A local club leased a school's auditorium and multipurpose room for a meeting and social event. While at the event, one of the attendees slipped on some spilled food, fell, and was injured.

Points to Consider: "Someone" may be legally liable for damages—who? Is there a way to protect the school district?

Community education is a process designed to promote quality education for the total community by developing a closer working relationship between the school and the community. Community education programs are increasing in number and scope as school districts have recognized their potential for solving a number of problems. Some districts see such programs as a means to reduce the growing alienation between schools and communities. Other schools, faced with declining enrollments, increasing percentages of citizens with no children in school, and escalating teachers' salaries and other operating costs, open their buildings to the community for economic reasons.

Community education programs significantly increase the usefulness of the school building. Although the public school building is frequently the largest and most expensive building in a community, a school year is only two-thirds of the calendar, a school day is only one-third of the clock, and students are only one-fifth of the population. When a school becomes a community school, many things about its program change. Community members begin to feel welcome to come to the school. Each school is a community of patrons, parents, teachers, administrators, and students who join together to solve common problems and who can gain a significant return on their common involvement in public education.

Legal Basis for Community Education

Although some states have enacted state community education legislation that specifically permits the development of programs of community education, the majority of schools must look to statutory designations regarding the use of school property. Some states have "civic center" legislation that provides for broad nonschool use of school buildings, so long as the activities do not interfere with school activities. Other states have legislation that simply places the schools under the direction of the board, specifying nothing about community use.[1]

Early court decisions took a restrictive view of community use of school property, ruling that money raised through taxation for the schools could be used only for a very narrowly defined educational instructional purpose.[2] Gradually the courts began to allow use for nonschool purposes, but only when the use was clearly temporary, casual, or incidental and thus would not mean a total diversion of the property from instructional purposes.[3]

The current judicial position seems content to allow local school boards to make decisions about authorizing school property to be used for nonschool purposes. Their main concerns are proper maintenance, noninterference with the regular school program, and equal access.

Competition with the Private Sector

Many activities and services offered by public school programs of community education appear to compete with similar services offered by the private sector. It is not uncommon for community education programs to offer classes in art, music, dance, crafts, and martial arts. Other after-school programs offer academic training programs, counseling services, and child care.

Small businesses are finding it hard to survive, and some blame the schools' after-hours programs for their economic troubles. Some have turned to the courts to challenge the legality of using tax dollars and public facilities to support activities that they believe compete with their personal and property rights. Most of the objections center on the following two arguments: Statutes restrict the use of school facilities to very specific educational purposes, and monies raised by taxation may be used only for specific purposes.

The use of school funds and school property has been the basis for a number of lawsuits. Because constitutions and statutes cannot specifically cover all possible uses, the courts are asked to decide the issue. Most suits have been aimed at preventing anything but the most traditional educational activities.

In the case of *Kiddie Korner v. Charlotte-Mecklenburg* (North Carolina)[4] the owners and operators a of private child care center asked the court to stop the Charlotte-Mecklenburg Board of Education from conducting its extended-day program at an elementary school. The superior court ruled against the day care center owners, who then appealed the decision.

Although the case is complex, it presents a vivid picture of the legal issues involved. The controversy in this case revolves around the school board's involvement in the initiation and operation of an enrichment program designed to alleviate the problem of children who are unsupervised from the time that school closes and the time that their parents come home from work. The school board agreed to initiate the program after community residents, educational consultants, staff members, parents, and the ministerial association studied the community need and recommended the program. The program was administered by a community committee, operated at an elementary school, and was open to all students.

Instead of leaving the building at the end of the regular school day, the students enrolled in the program remained at school, where, under the direction of the school staff, they did homework, studied, and engaged in athletic or artistic activities. The program operated from 2:00 p.m. until 5:30 p.m. Operating costs were covered by a $15.00 a month charged each participant. The school board provided the use of the school and fuel and lighting costs.

The owners of the day care centers argued that the program violated the constitutional mandate for a central and uniform system of free public schools, that it violated the personal and property rights of the plaintiffs, that school funds were being used to establish and maintain the program, and that the legislature could not delegate to the school board the power to maintain the program.

The court described the program as an educational service offered by the school-sponsored committee. The court ruled that each school in the state did not have to be identical in all aspects, that the school board was not required to provide identical opportunities to every student, that the state constitution did not require that education be completely free, that supplemental fees were constitutional as long as the school board offered free basic education, and that school boards were allowed some degree of latitude in allocating state funds distributed for educational purposes.

The court reaffirmed that, generally, school facilities are the responsibility of the school board and are to be used for educational purposes. The court cited the Community School Act as encouraging greater community input to the operation of the public schools, including input to the curriculum and greater use of school facilities by community groups. The court affirmed its conviction that school boards should make available extended educational opportunities for their students and that school boards are required to consider the needs of the community in shaping their programs.

The court denied the plaintiffs' claims that expenditures of school funds for the extended-day program do not serve a public purpose and summarily rejected the plaintiffs' argument that the school board is in unauthorized competition with them and that the child care program violated their personal and property rights.

The importance of this unanimous decision for public schools is that it reaffirms that there is both constitutional and statutory authority for school boards to be involved with enrichment programs outside of the regular school day. Although only a few states (California, Arizona, New York, and Utah) have statutes that specifically require expanded use of school facilities, many others have provisions similar to North Carolina's that allow the public schools to be used for all activities that serve an educational purpose.

It is an accepted precept of community education that new programs should not duplicate existing programs. But it is a precept against needless duplication. Such factors as cost, location, time, and population served must also be examined in deciding whether or not to offer a program or service. If, after a needs and resources assessment, the community educator and community council believe that a program is justified, they must first answer the following questions: Does the program further the educational achievement of the students, and does it have a public purpose? If the answer to both of these questions is yes, it appears that the courts will support the development of a wide variety of community education programs even in the face of the charge of unfair competition.

Access to Facilities by School and Public Groups

Public schools have always been used by nonschool groups. Some allow church groups to hold religious services on Sunday mornings; some rent their cafeterias to service groups for community get togethers; some allow local groups to use their athletic facilities when they are not being used by students. Courts have generally given school boards great discretion in determining the management, control, protection, and use of school property.[5] As long as the district does not selectively discriminate against particular groups regarding the use of school facilities and does not violate federal law, school boards have broad discretion.

Courts have traditionally ruled that any incidental use of school grounds that does not interfere with the conduct of the school and serves a legitimate public purpose is permissible.[6] In *Perry Education Association v. Perry Local Educators Association,*[7] the United States Supreme Court ruled that the right of access to school property depends on the type of forum that has been created. The *Perry* Court offered a three-level categorization of forums: (1) public forums, areas that by long tradition or by governmental fiat have been devoted to assembly and debate; (2) limited public forums, areas that a state has voluntarily opened for use by the public as a place for expressive activity, and (3) nonpublic forums, property that is not by tradition or designation an area for public communication.[8] Using this categorization the *Perry* court ruled that schools are not considered traditional public forums in which outside visitors may freely espouse their views.[9] Since the school is not an open forum, the school has broad discretion in allowing nonschool groups access to the school.

Hold-Harmless Agreements

When school districts allow individuals or groups to use district facilities, it is recommended that a lease contract be signed that includes a clause called a *hold-harmless agreement*. Such an agreement protects the parties to a contract by establishing liability. Elements of the hold-harmless clause can usually be found under the hold-harmless, indemnification, insurance, or similar section of the lease contract. Here are three of the most common types of hold-harmless agreements:

1. The lessee is asked to hold the school district (lessor) harmless for liability caused by the lessee's negligence.
2. The lessee is asked to hold the district harmless for liability due to lessee negligence as well as district negligence, unless the district is deemed to be grossly negligent.
3. The lessee is asked to hold the district harmless for any lessee or district negligence, even if the district is grossly negligent. Many courts, however, have ruled that this clause confers an unfair advantage on the lessor in precontract negotiations.

School districts should require lessors to provide proof of insurance that covers losses caused by their negligence. Potential lessor-caused exposures may be covered under the terms of your district insurance contract. As policies vary, it is in a school district's best interests to review district-held insurance.

The following are examples of questions that should be raised by the school district when district property is requested for private or public use:

- Who is responsible if an accident occurs?
- Has the board protected itself by reserving the right to revoke a permit if the strong possibility of an accident exists?
- Has the board required the outside user group to offer evidence of insurance by providing the appropriate certificates of insurance with an endorsement showing the district as one of the insured parties?
- What amounts of coverage apply to claims arising from community use? The school district's legal counsel should be involved to negotiate the

best terms possible and recommend ways to minimize district risk through hold-harmless agreements or other transfer mechanisms.

Endnotes

1. E. Wood, *An Identification and Analysis of the Legal Environment for Community Education,* JOURNAL OF LAW AND EDUCATION, vol. 3, no. 1, Jan. 1974, p. 7.

2. Bender v. Streabich, 182 Pa. 251, 37 A 853 (1896).

3. *Supra,* note 1 at 7–8.

4. NC App. 285 S.E. 2d 110 (1981).

5. J. Horner, *Access to Educational Facilities for School and Public Groups,* 54 ED. LAW REP. (Aug. 17, 1989), p. 7.

6. Royse Independent School District v. Reinhardt, 159 S.W. 1010 (Tex. Civ. App. Dallas 1919).

7. 460 U.S. 37 (1983).

8. *Supra,* note 5 at 2.

9. *Id.*

Principal's Tort Liability for Negligence and Risk Management

The obligation of the school to provide a safe place can hardly be overemphasized. It is a legal principle with strong and widely spread roots in the ethics of our society. Adults are responsible for the care and protection of children; teachers and administrators are responsible for the care and protection of students. A high standard of performance in the area of student welfare by educators is demanded by our courts of law. In addition, the courts expect a high standard of rational or reasonable person traits to be inherent in educators. When accepted for a position in a school system, educators are expected by citizens, the state and the courts to have the knowledge, preparation, and skills necessary to function in the teaching/learning or administrative processes. [1]

Tort liability laws are the primary source for the definition of the educator's basic responsibilities for duty and standard of care. Without an adequate knowledge of liability, educators cannot have a clear understanding of their status under the law.

CHAPTER EIGHTEEN

Tort Liability for Negligence

Introduction and Foundations of Tort Liability for Negligence

It would be premature to discuss the specific concepts of tort liability without first reviewing current trends in our society and how society and the courts view real or perceived wrongful acts on the part of educators. Educators have entered into a period of time in which long accepted societal norms and standards are being tested and challenged in the courts. When education policy or practice interferes with society's new norms, conflict exists between the home and the school, and litigation is possible, if not probable. The increasing specter of litigation and the potential for legal liability have important implications for educators. The threat of litigation, combined with rising insurance costs, has forced many schools to review and, in some cases, to eliminate programs.

Changes in certain legal doctrines have modified the special status accorded to schools. For example, the doctrine of governmental immunity, protecting the public school from legal liability, has been judicially or legislatively abrogated in some states. Education personnel duty has been reduced by statutes that provide qualified immunity for employees or denote liability only for injuries resulting from willful or wanton misconduct; however, the school is still frequently given the same status and held by the courts to the same duty as any individual or corporation providing goods or services. The problem facing school districts, and ultimately teachers and principals, is not whether they are immune from lawsuits but whether they can develop solutions to minimize their legal liability. Current and continuously updated knowledge of the law of tort liability for negligence can provide the educational practitioner with the framework for accident prevention. Lack of such prevention can and does cost school districts valuable resources each year.

The Law of Torts

The law of torts is difficult to define and difficult to understand. Since tort law is essentially the result of judicial decisions—case or common law rather than statutory or legislative law—the study of torts can be inconclusive in answering specific inquiries. Court decisions are primarily of two sorts: (1) interpretations of constitutional and statutory law, and (2) the application of common law principles. The latter are applied when a particular set of circumstances has not been legislated upon and the rights of the parties must be decided by the court on general principles handed down over the years.

A *tort* is defined as an actionable wrong against the person, property, or reputation of another, exclusive of a breach of contract, that the law will recognize and set right. Torts are historically classified into three categories:

1. The direct invasion of some legal right of the individual (e.g., invasion of privacy)
2. The infraction of some public duty by which special damage accrues to the individual (e.g., denial of constitutional rights)
3. The violation of some private obligation by which like damage accrues to the individual (e.g., negligence).

The underlying concept of torts involves the relationship between individuals. Under our system of law, individuals have the right to be free from bodily injury whether intentionally or carelessly caused by others. However, societal changes have caused the courts to define new legal responsibilities between individuals with each litigated verdict.

This chapter confines itself to the tort liability of educators for *negligence*—that is, the personal liability for injury to students or others for which school personnel may be held accountable under the law. Negligence is the main cause of tort liability suits filed against educators, and due to their more direct contact with students, teachers and principals are the class of school employees most likely to have suit brought against them. Judgments in negligence suits can be financially and emotionally crippling; for that reason, teachers and principals have a very real need to know what constitutes the basis for a charge of negligence.

Tortious actions speak directly to the professional educator through the principle of *in loco parentis*. While the *in loco parentis* doctrine is continuously challenged, the current interpretation assigns definite responsibility to the school for the welfare of each student it serves in the absence of the student's parent or guardian. With this assignment, society legally assumes that, during the time the student is away from home, the student's interests, welfare, and safety are directed by responsible adults trained as teachers and administrators. Since all elementary and most secondary students are compelled by law to attend school, courts usually review very carefully any alleged breach of normally expected duty and standard of care by educators. Failure to meet such duty and standard of care is negligent, and the courts may find the educator guilty of a tort.

Within the framework of the tort of negligence, this chapter emphasizes the specific areas of duty and standard of care, proper instruction, proper supervision, proper maintenance, post-injury treatment, and field trips. In addition, the chapter examines the standards and relationships inherent in these areas.

The Concept of Negligence

Scenario 18.1:   Richie Ford, an eight-year-old student, was burned when his costume for a school play caught on fire from a lighted candle on his teacher's desk.

Points to Consider: Was this danger foreseeable? Was the teacher negligent?

Scenario 18.2:   Kelly Pomeroy, a sixth-grade student, was struck in the eye by a pencil eraser just prior to the start of class. The mishap was caused by a fellow student who was tapping his pencil against his desk, causing the eraser to separate and fly through the air. The teacher, following school regulations, was standing outside the classroom monitoring passing students at the time of the incident.

Points to Consider: Was the incident foreseeable? Is the teacher liable for negligent supervision?

Scenario 18.3:   Twelve cheerleaders riding in a van owned and driven by one of the cheerleaders were injured in a collision. The accident occurred while they were "bannering" the homes of the school's football team in anticipation of the season's first game. The incident took place during the summer when school was not in session.

Points to Consider: What is the relationship between the school and the cheerleaders in this activity since this action was known to the school as a "tradition"? Would the school be solely responsible if liability is found in this case? Was there a duty by the school to supervise this activity even though it took place during summer recess?

Scenario 18.4:   Bart Stinson, a third-grade student known for his propensity to "horse-around", was given a pass to go to the rest room down the hall. The eight-inch plywood pass, made by his teacher, had a 20-inch nylon cord attached, and students often wore the pass around their necks as they went to the rest room. Bart was discovered hanging from a stall brace with the pass around his neck. Earlier, Bart had been joking and pretending to do this with other students in the bathroom. Bart suffered irreversible brain damage from his actions.

Points to Consider: Was Bart too young to be trusted to go to the rest room by himself? Was the pass a potentially dangerous instrument for a third-grader? If Bart was known to his teacher as a "problem child," might such an incident have been foreseeable?

Scenario 18.5:   A junior high school football coach stated that "yelling at players on the football field for failure to perform adequately was a form of instruction." In one situation the coach yelled at player Billy Miller, banged Billy's helmet with his fist, grabbed the face mask, and threw Billy to the ground (Billy had missed a blocking assignment). Billy was injured to such an extent that he spent the next eight days in the hospital.

Points to Consider: Is the coach liable for assault? Is the coach liable for battery? Did Billy assume this risk when he joined the football squad?

Negligence Defined

Prior to a review of the important areas of duty and standard of care, proper instruction, proper supervision, proper maintenance, field trips, and post-injury treatment, the concept of negligence must be examined to provide the foundation for a basic understanding of the elements inherent in the specific areas of tort law discussed later. *Negligence* is the failure to exercise the degree of care for the safety and well-being of others that a reasonable and prudent person would exercise under similar circumstances. Negligence may occur in one of three ways:

1. *Nonfeasance*—failing to act when there is a duty to act
2. *Misfeasance*—acting, but in an improper manner
3. *Malfeasance*—acting, but guided by a bad motive

Nonfeasance is an act of *omission,* such as passive inaction, by which an injury occurs due to the lack of protection the law expects of a reasonable individual. In order for nonfeasance to result in liability for negligence, a duty to take positive action or to perform a specific act must be established. This duty may be established by a legal statute or by the relationship (e.g. principal/ teacher/student) between the parties involved.

An example of nonfeasance may be found in a case involving an eighth-grade girl who complained to the school guidance counselor regarding her fear of being physically harmed, based on verbal threats by another student. The other student was summoned to the counselor's office, where she was told that fighting would not be tolerated and would result in suspension. Later, in the school yard, the other student struck the complaining girl in the eye with her fist, causing a serious injury. The injured student claimed that the school's response to a given and known threat of violence on school premises was inadequate. The court ruled in favor of the injured girl.[2]

Misfeasance is the taking of an improper action when there is a duty to act. It may be either an act of commission or an act of omission. An act of *omission* may be illustrated by a case involving a student who fell into a ditch while attempting to catch a pass in a game of football played during the school's lunch period. The principal was aware of the ditch on the school's property, but had made minimal attempts to warn students and no attempt to fill the ditch. The student was injured and claimed that the school district, knowing of the hazard, did not take proper steps to protect him. The court ruled in favor of the student.[3]

An act of *commission* may be found in the case of a football player who passed out on the football field and was treated by school personnel for heat exhaustion instead of heat stroke. The student died as a result of the latter, as well as from the amount of time that the supervisors took before contacting the parents or seeking emergency aid. The court ruled in favor of the parents of the student.[4]

Malfeasance is an *illegal* act that should not be performed at all. It occurs when the individual acts *beyond the scope of duty*. A hypothetical case may illustrate the salient points best. Assume that a teacher paddles a student in the classroom even though school district policy prohibits a teacher from administering corporal punishment. The student is injured as a result of the punishment and brings charges against the teacher and others. The court would likely rule for the student since the act was illegal under school district policy.

Prerequisites for Negligence

For a successful negligence action, certain prerequisites must exist:

- The defendant must have a duty to the plaintiff.
- The defendant must have failed to exercise a reasonable standard of care in his/her actions.
- The defendant's actions must be the proximate (direct) cause of the injury to the plaintiff.
- The plaintiff must prove that he/she suffered an actual injury.[5]

Plaintiffs in actions addressing the school setting usually have little difficulty in proving that the defendant teacher or principal owes the student a duty. Actual injury and *proximate cause* are usually a matter of fact. The major point of contention, then, is whether or not the educator involved exercised a reasonable standard of care. For liability to be assessed under *proximate cause*, negligent conduct of school personnel must be the proximate or legal cause of the injury. Even in situations in which a recognized duty is breached by the failure to exercise a proper standard of care, liability will not normally be assessed if there is not a *causal connection* between the actions of school personnel and the injury.

Damages

When a court determines that an educator has been negligent, it often awards *damages* to the injured party. The purpose of this award is to make the plaintiff "whole again" and is designed to compensate the person who has suffered a loss. Normally, damages are measured in terms of money and can be categorized into three areas:

1. *Compensatory*—damages that are awarded in an effort to compensate the party for injury (medical expenses, court costs, attorneys' fees, and loss of income). Compensatory damages are often referred to as "actual damages."
2. *Exemplary*—damages awarded for the purpose of punishing the defendant for negligence. Exemplary damages are often referred to as "punitive damages."
3. *Nominal*—a small award granted when negligence has occurred but little loss or damage has been suffered.

Reasonable/Prudent Person and Foreseeability

To resolve the question of reasonable standard of care, courts use the model of a "reasonable and prudent person." This is a hypothetical ideal of human behavior that embodies the community's ideals and possesses all the special skills and abilities of the defendant. Court dicta provides this generic description: The defendant is not to be identified with any ordinary individual who might occasionally do unreasonable things; he/she is a prudent and careful person who is always up to standard. It is not proper to identify him/her with any member of the jury who is to apply the standard; he/she is rather a personification of a *community* ideal of reasonable behavior, determined by the jury's social judgment.

This abstract being, conceived in the law's imagination, performs under the question of *foreseeability*. If the educator could have, or should have, foreseen or anticipated an accident, the failure to do so may be ruled as negligence. The concept of foreseeability expects the educator to perform as a reasonably prudent person of *similar training and circumstances* should perform. This degree of care is based upon the standard equivalent of the age, training, maturity, and experience as well as any other related characteristics of the educator. The law does not require the educator to be able to see everything that might appear in the immediate future, nor do the courts require the educator to completely ensure the safety of students; however, courts do expect educators to act in a reasonable and prudent manner. If the ordinary exercise of prudence and foresight could have prevented an accident, courts have ruled educators to be negligent when they have not avoided a foreseeable danger to students, personnel, and patrons.

Examples of how the courts view foreseeability are illustrated by the following cases. A teacher's aide walked past a group of students just minutes before one child threw a rock and hit another student. No liability was assessed against the teacher's aide in this case because the court concluded that the aide had provided adequate supervision and had no reason to anticipate or foresee the event that caused the injury.[6] On the other hand, in a case where student rock throwing had continued for almost ten minutes before an injury occurred, the court saw foreseeability and found the supervising teacher liable for negligence.[7]

Unavoidable Accident

An *unavoidable accident* is defined as an event that occurs without fault, carelessness, or omission on the part of the individual involved. While expecting educators to display a high level of care in the performance of their duties, the courts recognize that "accidents happen when no negligence has occurred."[8]

Assumption of Risk

A common legal defense against negligence is based on the general legal theory of *assumption of risk* (no harm is done to one who consents). Although the consent may be expressed or implied, the legal theory is based upon one's ability to understand and appreciate the dangers inherent in the activity. "Even though the student voluntarily placed him/herself in a position of danger, the defense must show that the student understood the danger, had foresight in regard to the consequences and accepted the danger."[9] A more comprehensive description of assumption of risk can be found under the heading of "Athletic Liability and Spectator Safety" in Chapter 19.

Contributory Negligence/Causal Relationship/ Comparative Negligence

When an injury to a student is sustained as a result of the injured student's own negligence and this negligence is proved, then the student has contributed to his/her own injury. When a student "disregards the instruction, warning or advice of an educator, the student can be held liable for his/her own injury."[10] To counter a charge of *contributory negligence,* the student must establish a *causal relationship* between the negligence of the educator and the injury. The majority of states permit some recovery under the concept of *comparative negligence*. This legal doctrine prorates the damages to the degree of negligence determined by the court for each party found liable for negligence. The plaintiff might be found to be 50 percent negligent and the defendant the same. Most states bar recovery of any damages by plaintiffs who are 50 percent or more contributorily negligent.[11] While contributory negligence alone often bars any recovery by the plaintiff, the comparative concept requires that both the contributory negligence of the plaintiff and the negligence of the defendant be considered proportionately. A few states have a doctrine of "pure" comparative negligence in which the ratio is maintained regardless of the percentages. For example, a plaintiff who was found to be 95 percent contributorily negligent could still recover 5 percent of any award made by a jury.

Age of Plaintiffs

The *Rule of Seven* is often used to determine the liability for negligence. This legal doctrine requires the court to examine a student's age in determining negligence. Children are expected to exercise a degree of care for their own safety in proportion to their age, capacity, experience, and intelligence. Historically, courts have held that children from birth to age seven cannot be considered negligent under the law. Such a child does not realize or understand the degree of care that must be exercised to prevent injury to himself/herself. A teenager, on the other hand, is expected to have developed a general understanding of the care required for his/her own safety.[12]

Figure 18-1 demonstrates the relationship between duty and standard of care and the age of the student.

Common Conditions for Negligence

There are a number of different doctrines in the area of negligence. Those examined here represent the areas of concern that may be the most important to educators. The legal literature in the area of tort liability for negligence, specifically those cases involving educators, provides a list of some common conditions resulting in tort liability for negligence:

- Failure to provide adequate supervision
- Failure to aid the injured or sick
- Creation of further damage through misguided efforts
- Permitting students to play unsafe games
- Permitting use of defective equipment
- Maintaining attractive nuisances

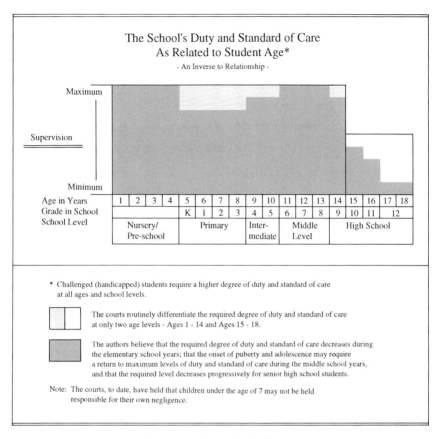

FIGURE 18-1 • *Age and Duty and Standard of Care*

- Failure to provide adequate instruction
- Failure to give adequate warning
- Entrusting dangerous devices to students incompetent to use them
- Taking unreasonable risks
- Improperly organized field trips

Figure 18.2 generally demonstrates the educator's risk of negligence in a school-related incident.

Intentional Torts

Although negligence cases are the norm in education tort litigation, it would be remiss not to mention intentional torts. An intentional tort is committed if a person, with or without malice, intentionally proceeds to act in a manner that

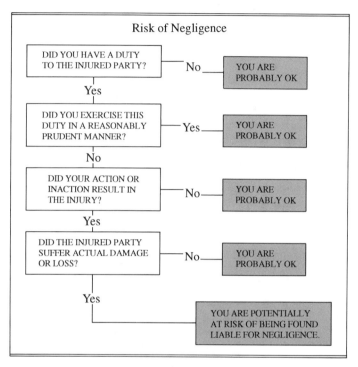

FIGURE 18-2 • _Risk of Negligence_

impairs the rights of others. Intentional tort actions in the education setting generally involve charges of assault and battery. Assault, simply defined, consists of an overt attempt to place another in fear of bodily harm; no actual physical contact need take place. However, when an assault is consummated with physical injury to a person, then battery has been committed.

In one case a student sustained a broken arm when a teacher shook him against the bleachers in the gym and then let him fall to the floor. The court found that the teacher's action was unnecessary to discipline the student or to protect himself.[13] In another case the court awarded damages to a 12-year-old student who claimed that a teacher used excessive force in discipline. The student suffered a fractured clavicle when the teacher threw him into a portable chalk board in the classroom and then pushed him into a wall in the hallway.[14]

School personnel may also initiate assault and battery suits against students, as witnessed in the case of a teacher who was physically attacked by a student outside the school building while attempting to escort the student to the school office for smoking. The court concluded that the student acted with malicious intent.[15] In another case where a student struck a teacher who was attempting to stop him from leaving the classroom, damages were awarded to the teacher.[16]

Endnotes

1. Hoseman v. Oakland Unified School District, No. 583092-9 (Cal. Super. 1986).

2. Gammon v. Edwardsville, 403 N.E. 2d 43 (Ill. App. Ct. 1980).

3. Libby v. West Coast Rock Co. Inc., 308 So. 2d 602 (La. Ct. App. 1975).

4. Magabgab v. Orleans Parish School Board, 239 So. 2d 456 (La. Ct. App. 1970).

5. WILLIAM PROSSER, LAW OF TORTS (4th ed.) (St. Paul, Minn.: West, 1971) p. 143.

6. Fagan v. Summers, 498 P.2d 1227 (Wyo. 1972).

7. Sheehan v. Saint Peter's Catholic School, 188 N.W. 2d 868 (Minn. 1971).

8. Clark v. Furch, 567 E.W. 2d 457 (Mo. Ct. App. 1978).

9. Everett v. Bucky Warren Inc., 380 N.E. 2d 653 (Mass. Sup. Ct. 1978).

10. Powell v. Orleans Parish School Board, 354 So. 2d 229 (La. Ct. App. 1978).

11. Connett v. Fremont County School District No. 6, 581 P.2d 1097 (Wyo. Sup. Ct. 1978).

12. Dailey v. Los Angeles Unified School District, 470 P.2d 360 (Cal. Sup. Ct. 1970).

13. Frank v. Orleans Parish School Board, 195 So. 2d 451 (La. Ct. App. 1967).

14. Sansone v. Bechtel, 429 A. 2d 820 (Conn. 1980).

15. Anello v. Savignac, 324 N.W. 2d 440 (Wis. App. 1983).

16. Garrett v. Olsen, 691 P.2d 123 (Ore. App. 1984).

CHAPTER NINETEEN

Duty and Standard of Care

Introduction and Foundations of Duty and Standard of Care

Scenario 19.1: Sam Cooke was a mentally challenged high school junior. While his actual age was 18, his tests showed him to have a mental age of 11. Sam was seriously burned during metal shop class when his shirt ignited as he stood with his back too close to the forge.

Points to Consider: Was the teacher liable for a breach of standard of care? Should we examine, in this case, Sam's actual age or his mental age? Might Sam be found to have contributed to his own accident?

Duty and Standard of Care Defined

In the previous chapter, negligence was defined as conduct that falls below the standard established by law for the protection of others against unreasonable risk or harm. Four elements must exist if a valid claim of negligence is to be sustained:

1. There must be a duty to protect.
2. There must be a failure to exercise a standard of care.
3. The conduct must be a proximate cause of the damage.
4. Actual loss must result.

Duty is an obligation that derives from the special relationship between the parties involved; that is, teacher/student, principal/teacher, principal/student. A failure to exercise a *standard of care* is determined by measuring the actual conduct against the conduct of a reasonable person. The standard of care is relative to the need and the occasion. What is proper under one circumstance may be negligent under another. When the court examines standard of care, it is concerned with the possibility of a breach of the duty between the educator and the student.

There is a duty of *due care* that the law recognizes one person owes to another. It requires a certain standard of conduct for the protection of others against unreasonable risks. One has a legal duty to act as an ordinary, prudent, reasonable person in the circumstances. Such duty can be specified by statute or as a matter of common law. The duty and standard of care imposed on school districts demand that the responsibility for protecting the safety of students and employees be accepted and fulfilled. School boards can fulfill a part of that responsibility through specific and consistently enforced regulations for the control and operation of schools.

Inherent Duty versus Assumed Relationship

There are two basic types of duty. The first type exists when the duty is *inherent* in the situation. This includes nearly every situation in which an educator has the responsibility to supervise a student. The second type of duty exists when a person voluntarily *assumes* or *creates* a relationship where no previous relationship existed. An assumed duty would exist when an educator acted in a way that would lead parents or students to *assume* that a supervisory relationship existed. For example, imagine a situation in which children regularly gather on school grounds long before the start of classes. The principal approves and is aware of the need for supervision, but does not provide any. If an injury occurs, the court might rule that the principal had assumed the duty of supervision by allowing the students to gather, and that if proper supervision had been provided, the injury might have been prevented. The court could hold the principal liable for any damages.

How the Courts View Duty and Standard of Care

In an Indiana case, the court commented:

What constitutes due care . . . of school children depends largely on the circumstances, such as the number and age of the students . . ., the activity in which they are engaged, the period for which they are left without supervision, the ease of providing some alternative means of supervision, and the extent to which the school board has provided and implemented guidelines and resources to insure adequate supervision.[1]

In Wisconsin, the state supreme court spoke to duty and standard of care when it remarked:

It does not seem inherently unreasonable to expect that teachers will be present in classes which they are entrusted to teach. This should not, of course, mean that a teacher who absents himself from a room is negligent as a matter of law. As this court said, the teacher's duty is to use reasonable care.[2]

A duty of care and a failure to perform that duty speak to the standard of individual conduct. In determining what that standard should be for educators and other school personnel, the California Supreme Court stated:

The standard of care imposed upon school personnel in carrying out this duty to supervise is identical to that required in the performance of their other duties. This uniform standard to which they are held is the degree of care which a person of ordinary prudence, charged with comparable duties, would exercise under the same circumstances.[3]

The following cases are illustrative of the duty and standard of care owed by schools.

A student was injured when a container labeled as floor wax but containing an inflammable liquid burst into flames during a physics class. A cause of action was maintained under a theory of failure to provide safe equipment. The court held that the school district ". . . owes a duty of ordinary care in providing equipment for student use."[4]

A principal failed to properly supervise the actions of the athletic director and football coach, who had organized a summer weight-lifting program for students trying out for fall football. Urged by the coach to maximize performance, the plaintiff, a 15-year-old student, fell while lifting a 250–300 pound weight. The plaintiff's injuries resulted in paraplegia. The principal was held to the standard of exercising reasonable supervisory power (setting a standard of due care) so as to minimize student injuries, and was found negligent.[5]

A 15-year-old student was injured in a wrestling match. The student had been in a wrestling class for approximately six weeks prior to the injury, during which time the wrestling instructor (who had little previous training in the techniques of wrestling) taught the class a number of maneuvers, some of which were potentially dangerous. On the day of the injury, the student was consistently paired off against boys heavier than himself. In addition, the instructor attempted to supervise two wrestling matches at one time. In considering whether the defendant school was guilty of negligence, the court identified as the applicable standard of conduct: "A teacher's superiority in knowledge and experience imposes responsibilities in his dealing with students which become an inherent element in measuring his compliance with the due care which is required of him."[6]

Using that as the standard, and comparing that standard against the facts, the court ruled that the possibility of negligence existed and that the coach had such a duty. The coach did not act in a reasonable manner commensurate with the particular circumstances.

A lack of ordinary or reasonable care under the circumstances was noted in the above cases. Liability results most often when school personnel fail to meet that reasonable standard of care while instructing, supplying equipment to, and supervising students.

Summary

The school and the personnel it employs owe a legal duty to protect students, employees and visitors from unreasonable risks of injury. The duty to meet a particular standard of care stems from three primary sources:

1. The duty may be inherent in the situation. Nearly every situation in which an educator engages has an inherent standard of care arising from it. These duties derive from the educator acting *in loco parentis,* acting as a professional, or acting as the administrator.
2. The voluntary assumption of an interpersonal relationship. A person who does not have a legal duty to meet a particular standard of care may incur one by voluntarily creating a relationship with someone else.
3. The duty may be required by statute.

Generally speaking, the school will owe a duty of ordinary care to all personnel, children, and adults involved in educational pursuits, academic or otherwise, if sponsored under the school's authority. This standard is based upon an objective test consisting of the standard of conduct demanded under the circumstances—that is, "the reasonably prudent person." The ordinary care standard takes into consideration the risk factor that may be apparent and the circumstances of the situation. The defendant's capacity, based upon age, intelligence, knowledge, skill, etcetera, to handle those circumstances is also considered in certain cases.

The Concept of Proper Instruction

Scenario 19.2: Bob Sullivan had wanted to be a cheerleader since he was seven and first attended a football game with his father. Bob practiced in his back yard every spare moment until he reached the seventh grade. He tried out for his junior high squad and was selected. He was a talented cheerleader and his stunts were outstanding. The next year, Bob made the high school squad easily and was eager to attend the first practice session in the new high school stadium, which had a hard, smooth artificial surface. Unfortunately, Bob was severely injured on the first day of practice. He had never worked on that kind of surface before and had no knowledge of the difference it would make to his balance.

Points to Consider: Were the school and cheerleading sponsor negligent in not providing instruction and warning about this surface? Was Bob partly responsible for his own injury?

Adequacy of Instruction and Instruction Defined

Cases involving various aspects of instruction frequently come before the courts. The most common complaint is that the student did not receive adequate instruction. In addition to providing inadequate instruction, school personnel have been found negligent in:

- Inadequately warning about the danger of a particular experiment, piece of machinery or equipment, game or exercise, or a facility or grounds problem
- Assigning activities beyond the skill level of students
- Deviating from the syllabus
- Assigning students activities when a known physical defect exists
- Not providing safety rules and/or regulations

The courts tend to favor those educators who have provided adequate instruction in the proper use of equipment and the proper methods of safety and who have warned students of the dangerous nature of any activity in which injury might occur. Failure to do either, instruct or warn, could be cause for establishing liability for negligence.

Education Malpractice

While the vast majority of improper instruction litigation falls within the categories previously discussed, the courts have heard a few education malpractice suits. In the past, with the exception of two nineteenth-century cases, almost all cases filed against educators for inappropriate instructional behavior that reached the appellate court level involved physical harm to the person rather than harm to the intellect.[7] However, in recent years our society has initiated litigation that tests *intellectual* harm, and while this chapter limits itself to physical harm, it is advisable for the prudent educator to be aware of this trend.

The issue of education malpractice has been judicially stalled to date; however, it is likely that when a strong case appears in a more receptive judicial climate, the results may be different than in past cases, where the courts have generally held to the dicta of the California Court of Appeals, which stated:

> *Unlike the activity of the highway or marketplace, classroom methodology affords no readily acceptable standards of care, of cause, or injury. The science of pedagogy itself is fraught with different and conflicting theories of how or what a child should be taught. . . . Substantial professional authority attests that the achievement of literacy in the schools, or its failure, is influenced by a host of factors which affect the student subjectively, from outside the formal teaching process, and beyond the control of its ministers. They may be physical, neurological, emotional, cultural, environmental; they may be present but not perceived, recognized, but not identified. [Holding schools accountable] . . . would expose them to the tort claims—real or imagined—of disaffected students and parents in countless numbers. They are already beset by social and financial problems which have gone to major litigation, but for which no permanent solution has yet appeared. The ultimate consequences, in terms of public time and money, would burden them—and society—beyond calculation.[8]*

Instilling Behavior to Protect from Danger

Authorities agree that instruction involves the teaching of a particular skill as well as instilling in the student the proper behavior for individual and class safety. The relationship between teachers and students in the area of instruction was defined by a Wisconsin court, as an example, when it stated:

> *The teacher occupies a position in relation to his pupils comparable to that of a parent to children. He has a duty to instruct and warn pupils in his custody of any danger which he knows or in the exercise of ordinary care ought to know . . . and to instruct them in the methods which will protect them from these dangers. A failure to warn students of such danger or to instruct them in the means of avoiding such danger is negligence.[9]*

Courts have said that educators are expected to select activities appropriate to the student's ability to perform and understand and should take into consideration the student's size, age, skill, condition, or special needs. When an activity entails risks to students, it is not sufficient merely to inform or warn of risks; students must also understand and appreciate the risks. Appreciation is influenced by factors such as experience, mentality, and the obviousness of the danger.

A fourteen year old boy who broke his arm when he fell from an apparatus during a gymnastics class alleged that the teacher had failed to provide adequate instruction and warning. The facts of the case showed, however, that the boy had been given instruction in the correct method of performing the stunt. That instruction had also included warnings about the danger of doing the activity incorrectly. Further, the boy had done the stunt several times and been corrected when it was not done properly. In ruling in favor of the teacher and the school, the court determined that sufficient instruction and warning had been provided the student.[10]

In another case the teacher did not provide adequate instruction or warnings appropriate to the activity. In this case the teacher required two high school boys to box several rounds. No instructions in the art of boxing or warnings of the danger involved in the activity were given to either participant. The court held the instructor negligent and liable when one of the boys suffered a fatal blow to his temple.[11]

A lack of ability was alleged when a junior high school girl was injured during a game of soccer. The rules of the activity, as shown in the syllabus, cautioned against allowing rough play and too many participants. The teacher had limited instruction to one 15-minute session preceding the activity. The teacher, in defending the short instructional period, stated that she believed that children were naturally skilled in running and kicking and did not need an extended session on such skills. The court ruled against the teacher, asserting that the preparation of students to participate in such an activity required more than a superficial assessment of skill in running or kicking. The court also held that the teacher's failure to follow the syllabus was negligent and the proximate cause of the injury.[12]

In similar litigation, negligent instruction was ruled when a teacher failed to follow state guidelines for conducting a physical fitness speed test by not instructing students to take necessary precautions,[13] and a student was injured.

Age and Condition of Participants

Educators have a responsibility to tailor required activities to the age and condition of students. When an 11-year-old girl was injured in a physical education class while attempting a head stand, the court ruled that the stunt was inherently dangerous for any young child to attempt and held the instructor liable for negligence.[14]

Another case involved a 17-year-old student who was injured attempting a gymnastic exercise. In attempting to do the exercise, the student had previously fallen a number of times. In addition, the student had a bad knee that "went out" at times. The student sustained a skull fracture when unable to properly execute the exercise. The court ruled that the condition of the student should have prevented the instructor from requiring the student to participate in such an activity.[15]

A teacher's failure to consider the history of a student's physical condition was alleged in the case of an eleven year old student who had previously suffered two broken arms. The teacher knew of the student's history and had been asked to excuse her from rough activities. The student was required by the teacher to participate in a rough activity, and the teacher was held liable when the student fell and broke her arm again.[16]

Equipment and Materials

One area of the education program that gives rise to frequent allegations of improper instruction is school activities that require the use of equipment. The following cases illustrate the thinking of the courts regarding educators' responsibilities in this area.

A thirteen year old student built a model volcano in his own home, then took it to school for a demonstration in the classroom as a science project. He was injured during an encore performance for his schoolmates at the bus stop on the periphery of the school grounds. Though the boy's father had helped him build his volcano, the student claimed that the school was negligent in supervision, instruction, and warning, since the project constituted academic homework. The court agreed and held for the student, citing improper instruction as well as improper supervision.[17]

Another court ruled in favor of the school when a student severed two fingers while operating machinery in the school shop class. In this case the student had failed a safety test on the operation of the machine and had been required to look up the answers. The student claimed the teacher was negligent in his failure to conduct a second closed-book test. The court ruled that the instruction and warnings given by the teacher were proper under the circumstances.[18]

In another case a student's misuse of a drill press resulted in a serious head injury to a classmate. The teacher had not instructed the students in the use of a specific drill bit, had not warned of dangers associated with its improper use, and was absent from the shop during the use of the drill. The court found the teacher negligent.[19]

While school personnel have a duty to provide appropriate instruction to protect students from unreasonable hazards, students must also act in a reasonable manner. School personnel will generally not be found negligent if students completely disregard the instructions and warning provided.

Age, Mental Abilities, and Appreciation of Risk

When a participant is inexperienced, the teacher is required to make a greater effort to communicate any risk. If the student is young but experienced, the student is held to assume those risks of which he/she is knowledgeable. Appreciation of risk is discussed in greater detail in the section of this chapter titled "Athletic Liability and Spectator Safety"; however, two examples will illustrate the basic concept.

In the first example an 18-year-old was injured on a trampoline while attempting to do a stunt. The student lost balance and fell to the floor, suffering serious and permanent injuries. The student was experienced on the trampoline and was practicing after class. Though the teacher required four spotters to prevent such an accident in class, at the time of the injury there was only one spotter. The court ruled that a proficient 18-year-old must exercise the same judgment and discretion regarding trampoline safety as a person of more advanced years.[20]

The second example illustrates that the appreciation of risks extends not only to young children but includes students who are mentally incapable of comprehending the situation. This case involved a mentally disabled student who drowned in a swimming area that had a sudden drop-off. Normally, the area was marked by a rope buoy line, which was not in position on the day of the accident. Instead, there was a sign warning "Swim at Own Risk." The court ruled that the student was unable to appreciate the dangers of deep water in a swimming area.[21]

Summary

School personnel are required to adequately instruct students before allowing them to participate in any activity that could result in injury. Instruction could be deemed inadequate, and therefore negligent, if a student is not warned of the dangers of a particular activity and has not been taught to appreciate such dangers. A teacher's failure to follow a required teaching syllabus may also be deemed negligent.

The Concept of Proper Supervision

Student participation in school-related hazardous activities requires a great deal of careful supervision by school personnel. The most prevalent forms of hazardous activities involve vocational training, experiments in chemistry and physics, physical education, playground activities, and athletic or intramural activities. Educator negligence in supervising such activities will generally be predicated upon a failure to instruct the student properly in the correct use of a dangerous instrument or to warn of the inherent dangers associated with an activity or experiment. The standard for conduct in this area continues to be that of a reasonable person in like circumstances.

Scenario 19.3:   Phil Lewis was struck in the eye by a bent nail that Clyde Moore had attempted to throw into a refuse barrel. The teacher was in the room.

Points to Consider: Would the teacher be liable for improper supervision? Is there an element of foreseeability?

Scenario 19.4:   Allen Gabler was eight years old when he was injured while playing with explosive chemicals he had found hidden in the bushes on the school grounds during morning recess. The chemicals had been placed there by two older students who served as lab monitors in a chemistry classroom. Such chemicals were routinely stored in a locked closet in the classroom to which the teacher had the only key.

Points to Consider: Does the school have liability for this incident? Does the teacher? Was there improper supervision of the student monitors? Was there a breach of security as well as duty and standard of care?

Supervision Defined

One of the most common allegations of negligence directed towards educators is that of negligent supervision. It is estimated that nearly one-fourth of negligence cases identify improper supervision as the primary or secondary cause of an injury. Courts recognize that it is impossible for educators to personally supervise every movement of every student every day, and that accidents will occur; no amount of supervision can completely prevent such an occurrence. Educators, however, are expected to exercise a reasonable degree and quality of supervision and to be physically in the general vicinity, fulfilling the responsibilities associated with the supervision assignment.

The presence of dangerous conditions is one of the key elements used to determine whether *general* or *specific* supervision is necessary. General supervision is required in situations where students are involved in activities that are not usually considered dangerous. Specific supervision is required when activities are unusually dangerous, or when the teacher is instructing an activity with which students are not familiar.

Risk Areas

Some areas in the educational setting have a greater risk of student injury associated with them than do others. These have been identified as physical education, playground and athletic areas, science classrooms, vocational shops, storage rooms, stage areas, and bus loading zones. It is essential that teachers and principals maintain a special awareness of the risks associated with these areas and provide such supervision as would be reasonable and prudent under the circumstances.

Responsibility to Supervise

When a classroom assignment is accepted by a teacher, or a principalship by a principal, that educator assumes the responsibility to supervise. The duty to supervise is comprehensive in scope, and some degree of supervision must be provided in all areas of the school where students are located at any time.

The test for determining negligent supervision is whether a reasonably prudent person, in the educator's place, should have reason to believe the situation presents the possibility of injury.[22] This does not, however, make the supervisor the ensurer of a student's safety. Fact patterns for the court to examine in negligent supervision cases vary with the situations that students, teachers, and administrators create. Although these patterns differ, certain questions appear repeatedly in the case studies and seem to bear heavily on the outcome. These questions include:

* Who are the defendants?
* Do they owe a duty of general or specific supervision?
* What is the plaintiff's age?
* Were the circumstances of the injury reasonably foreseeable?

Negligent supervision cases can be categorized by the negligent act or acts alleged in the plaintiff's petition to the court. These categories are failure to:

* Make and enforce rules
* Provide competent supervision
* Control crowds
* Provided appropriate postinjury treatment

The Establishment of Rules

School boards have the duty to establish rules for student safety and to enforce such rules. This duty is demonstrated by the following case, in which an 8-year-old student waiting for a school bus after school became involved in a scuffle. The student was pushed to the ground, and then struck in the head by another student riding a bicycle. There were no school board rules regarding riding a bicycle on the school grounds, even though a state statute required each school board in that particular state to establish rules and regulations regarding order and discipline. The court held that the school board was negligent in failing to adopt rules and regulations concerning bicycle use. In this same case the principal of the school was also found to be negligent in failing to maintain proper discipline and to provide proper supervision of the bus loading area.[23]

In the absence of board of education policy, principals have a duty to promulgate rules for their schools and, with teachers and other employees, the duty to enforce reasonable and lawful rules established for the safety of students and others. Schools must provide competent supervision in sufficient quantity to cover the supervisory needs of the situation.

Lack of Proper Supervision

Liability arising from supervisory activities is not limited to the failure to provide competent supervision. Situations occur when competent supervision has been provided but, for various reasons, the supervisor is absent when an accident occurs. Liability in such cases usually depends on the *foreseeability* of an accident. If the supervisor's presence at the time of the injury would not have prevented the injury, there likely will be no liability; however, if the accident was foreseeable and the supervisor's presence would have prevented the injury, the principal, teacher, or other school personnel may be subject to litigation. In one case, in which a student was injured in a physical education class while the teacher's attention was focused for an extended length of time in another area, the court ruled against the teacher in the resultant litigation.[24] The possibility of injury in a physical education class was deemed foreseeable.

In addition to foreseeability, courts also consider whether the supervisor's conduct was the proximate cause of the injury. Negligence is not present if proximate cause cannot be established. As an example, a principal left the playground during the noon hour recess to answer the telephone. While the principal was absent, a student was hit in the eye with a stone batted by another student. The court reasoned that the presence of a supervisor would not have prevented the accident, and that the principal's absence did not cause the accident.[25]

Specific Supervision

Establishing the standard of supervision is difficult. What may be adequate in one situation may not be so in another. When students are unfamiliar with an activity, or when an activity is unusually dangerous, specific supervision is required. The need for specific supervision is frequently related to the age of the student. In one case, a six year old student was injured at a construction site next to the elementary school where remodeling was being done. School officials knew of the potential dangers at the site, and although they had reminded students daily to stay away from the area, no other precautions to protect students were taken. The court found against the school, citing negligent supervision.[26]

General Supervision

Under normal situations, general supervision is all that is required. During playground time, general rather than specific supervision is usually adequate. Courts recognize this, as the following case demonstrates. A twelve year old student who was playing ball in the school yard during noon recess was injured by a rock thrown by another student. At the time of the incident there were about 170 students playing in the yard, with three teachers on duty to supervise. A negligence action was filed on the grounds that an unpaved area of the playground constituted an unreasonably hazardous condition. The case was dismissed on the basis that there was insufficient evidence to support the claim that the condition was hazardous, and the supervision at the time of the incident was adequate for the playground and the number of students using it.[27]

However, in another case an assistant principal was held liable for an injury sustained by a student. In this case a fight occurred during recess, and one student twisted the leg of another until it broke. At the time of the fight, there were over 100 students on the playground under the supervision of the assistant principal. Although the supervisor was in close proximity to where the student was injured, the court held that the administrator ". . . failed to use reasonable care and diligence in supervising the conduct of the students."[28]

Causal Relationship (Proximate Cause)

In order for negligence to be found, the supervisor's conduct must be shown to be the proximate cause of an injury. Whether or not a causal relationship exists can be seen in a case where a student was hit by a bat swung by another student. The teacher was standing 30 feet away, passing out milk, at the time of the accident. The court ruled in favor of the teacher, citing that the supervision was adequate, causal relationship was absent because the teacher was not directly responsible for the supervision of the students involved in the activity, and more supervision would not have averted the accident.[29]

Unattended Classroom or School Area

A difficult determination of proper or improper supervision occurs when teachers absent themselves from the classrooms for which they are responsible. The primary responsibility of a teacher is to provide supervision for the classroom. After a teacher's classes have been accounted for, secondary duties such as hall, cafeteria, or playground assignments may be assumed. Court dicta concerning this area of supervision demonstrate the importance of classroom supervision. In a New York case a trial court had entered a judgment against a teacher for negligence in leaving the classroom where a student injury occurred during the absence. A court of appeals reversed the verdict and found the teacher innocent of the charges; however, a dissenting justice took issue with the reversal and entered into the record the following statement, which is often noted in other cases of like nature. According to this justice:

> *When a large number of children are gathered together in a single classroom, without any effective control or supervision, it may reasonably be anticipated that certain of them may so act as to inflict an unintentional injury upon themselves or their classmates . . . the mere presence of the hand of authority and discipline normally is effective to curb this youthful exuberance and to protect the children against their own folly. On the other hand, it may reasonably be anticipated that the prolonged absence of such authority at the time when the children's activities are usually supervised will result in just such a situation as is demonstrated in this instant case.*[30]

In a similar case, the court stated: "It is necessary in order to constitute the absence of the teacher the proximate cause of the plaintiff's injury that it be reasonably inferred that, had the teacher been present, such assault would not have occurred."[31]

In a case where the justices could not find unanimously, the dissenting justice stated:

> *. . . To fix liability without other evidence to indicate a likelihood of serious disorder or any personal hazard arising if the teacher left the room unattended is not justified. While teenage school children are capable of free spirits, they are not hellions who require close custody on pain of disaster to one of them.*[32]

In a Maryland case, after a lengthy dictum that reviewed many cases dealing with teacher supervision, the court held that:

> *If a rule can be developed from the teacher liability cases, it is this: a teacher's absence from the classroom, or failure to properly supervise students' activities, is not likely to give rise to a cause of action for injury to a student, unless under all the circumstances the possibility of injury is reasonably foreseeable.*[33]

In a similar case of teacher absence from the classroom, the court indicated:

We are persuaded that foreseeability of harm to pupils in the class or at the school is the test of the extent of the teacher's duty to safeguard her pupils from dangerous acts of fellow pupils, and absent circumstances under which harm to her pupils might have been reasonably foreseen during her absence, that the teacher was not under a duty to remain with her class at all times or to provide other adult supervision at all times when she was absent.[34]

It may appear from the dicta cited above that school personnel walk a tightrope when it comes to absence from the classroom or from an activity area. However, the plaintiff must show, by a preponderance of evidence, that the defendant's act, or failure to act, was the factual and legal cause of the injuries. It is best that students be under some type of supervision at all times; however, educators who leave a classroom or play area momentarily unattended may not be liable for subsequent student injuries.

The Concept of Proper Maintenance

Scenario 19.5: Sally McCrory slipped and fell in her school lunchroom after stepping on spilled spaghetti sauce and suffered a severe sprain.

Points to Consider: Does the school owe the student the duty to use reasonable care to protect from injury? Is this incident a breach of such duty? Who was responsible for cleaning up the spill?

Scenario 19.6: Mr. Roberts's physical education class had been studying gymnastics for two weeks. They had just begun training on the pommel horse when he noticed a crack in one of the legs of the apparatus. Roberts decided that the crack was not serious and that nothing needed to be done. During instruction, Jerry Hall, a seventh-grade student, ran at the horse and placed his hands on the end of the unit. The leg collapsed and Jerry fell sideways striking another student. Both students sustained serious injuries.

Points to Consider: Is the school principal liable for any damages? Did the students assume the risk in this incident? Did the teacher exercise reasonable care? Was it the teacher's responsibility to maintain school equipment in his charge?

Like other entities, school districts have an obligation and common law duty to keep the school premises, including grounds, facilities, and equipment, reasonably safe and in good repair. Courts have awarded damages to students, parents, school employees, and visitors who have been injured as a result of defective conditions in school-owned property where school employees were aware of, or should have been aware of, hazardous conditions and did not take the necessary steps to repair or correct such conditions.

Nuisance Defined

Some courts draw a distinction between ordinary negligence and willful positive misconduct. In many instances the courts have held school districts liable for the maintenance of a nuisance. Increasingly, persons injured as a result of alleged failure of schools to maintain premises in a safe condition base their suits on "safe place" statutes that permit recovery against school districts if they maintain nuisances. Most courts hold that the fact that a public agency (i.e., school or school district) holds and manages property renders it accountable for damages that result in injury to a person or for damage to the property of others from mismanagement, willful positive conduct, or negligence.[35]

Under common law, people cannot press for an action in tort for a nuisance unless the plaintiffs can show that they were injured due to negligence. An example can be seen in litigation concerning school roofs, which have frequently been an attraction for children to climb. In one case the parents of a student killed in a fall from a school roof brought suit against the district for negligence, for maintaining an attractive nuisance, and for not preventing students from climbing to the roof. The student was one of three boys who, after leaving a school dance and being chased from the area, later returned to the school from a different direction and climbed up on the roof. The thirteen year old student fell from the roof and incurred injuries that resulted in his death. The court ruled in favor of the school.[36]

In another case, however, the court ruled in favor of a student, a young girl, who sustained an injury while watching a baseball game. While playing around an abandoned long-jump pit, she was frightened by a dog. She fell backward and cut her hand on a piece of broken glass in the pit that had been covered by sand. The girl presented evidence that the school knew of the dangerous condition as the school's janitor and school authorities had received written notification of the condition of the pit.[37]

The legal status of one who is injured is also important in deciding claims of nuisance. The general rule is nonliability for injuries suffered by an adult trespasser. Liability has been found, however, when the trespasser is a youth and circumstances provide an attraction, the danger of which cannot be perceived due to the age of the youth.

An *attractive nuisance* is seen by the courts as an unprotected, unguarded, unsafe condition that may attract a child to play. Schools can be held liable for allowing such a nuisance to exist. For example, a first-grade student arrived in the school yard before school and began swinging on the "monkey bars." Located adjacent to the bars was a tether ball pole about 10 feet in height. When the student reached the top of the bars, she grabbed the pole and attempted to slide to the ground. Attached to the center of the pole was a screw that protruded approximately 1 1/2 inches and lacerated the inside of the child's thigh when she slid over it. Among other claims, it was alleged that the location of the tether ball pole in such close proximity to the monkey bars provided an attractive nuisance for the student. The court agreed and ruled in favor of the child and her parents.[38]

Proper/Improper Maintenance

The courts have consistently held school district personnel liable for injury when they "knowingly" leave or provide a dangerous instrument exposed in a place likely to be frequented by children who, because of their age or other special condition, cannot realize or appreciate the danger. The age of the child and the child's ability to comprehend danger are always debatable issues in court, and there are a number of interpretations of age and ability when proper maintenance is litigated. For example, a boy was injured when he did not see a ditch and ran into it in an attempt to catch a ball. The school was aware of the ditch and had posted a notice on the school bulletin board that the ditch was there and could present a problem. The student claimed that the school was negligent in not providing a safe place to play. The court ruled in favor of the student because the boy was deemed incapable of appreciating the danger.[39]

In another case a student sustained serious injuries while playing among piles of dirt and sand on the school playground after school. The area was not fenced, and, prior to the incident, parents had complained to the school district concerning the dirt piles and "dirt fights" among children playing there. The court in this case concluded that the school district breached its duty to maintain the school grounds in a safe condition.[40]

Another case involved an older student. This student, while dressing for his physical education class, changed into his uniform and placed his clothing in an unused hallway storage area adjacent to the boys' locker room facility. Dressing and locker storage facilities were available in the locker room, but the student had no lock and chose to hide his clothing in the unused hallway in some shelving. When the student returned from his physical education class and began to look for his clothing, he stepped back on a piece of plywood from which some nails protruded. One of the nails pierced his foot, causing a painful injury. The wood had been placed in the hallway by a school employee. The court ruled against the school and for the student, citing improper maintenance caused by negligence.[41]

Buildings and Grounds and Preventive Maintenance

Schools owe a duty to the public to take all necessary positive steps to ensure that buildings and grounds are free of any potentially hazardous conditions. The following cases illustrate the courts' expectations in this regard.

In a New York case, snowmobilers collided with a snow-covered bench at night on a baseball field owned by the school district. The court ruled against the plaintiffs in this case, since they could not show that the bench was a dangerous instrument or that the school district was malicious in placing the bench in that area.[42]

The Utah Supreme Court ruled in favor of a woman who suffered injuries when she slipped and fell on an icy sidewalk leading to the side entrance of a school. The court held that the school district had the duty to maintain buildings and grounds in a reasonably safe condition and to remove dangers, and that "negligence was present."[43]

A Louisiana appellate court found a school district negligent in the case of a student who fell and injured his knee while running bases in a physical education class. The student claimed that the school was negligent because school personnel knew of a concrete slab that protruded about an inch above the surface of the ground on the path between two bases. The slab, the student claimed, constituted such a hazardous condition that it was a breach of the standard of care required of the school to allow it to exist on the playground. The court ruled in favor of the student.[44]

A student in New York stepped on some glass on an outside stairway and injured his foot. The student charged the school was negligent in allowing the glass to be present. The court ruled in favor of the student.[45] Another New York court, however, found a school was not negligent in a case in which a nine year old student had brought suit against the district and a school bus driver for damages allegedly resulting from an illness suffered by the student. The student had found a piece of unwrapped gum on the floor of the bus and chewed it. The gum was alleged to have been coated with phencyclidine (PCP), better known as "angel dust," a dangerous and potentially lethal drug. The student claimed that the school district and the bus driver were negligent in failing to properly maintain the interior of the bus and to properly supervise infants.[46]

Also in New York, a court ruled in favor of the parents of a student who was killed when a railing came loose around a platform in the school gymnasium. The parents of the student claimed that a nut and bolt were not in place to secure the railing, that the school had no program of preventive maintenance or inspection, and that such an incident was foreseeable since students were frequently seen hanging on the railing.[47]

A court also ruled in favor of a student in Connecticut who sustained injuries as a result of a fall on the school grounds. She fell while walking, at the direction of teachers, across an ice- and snow-covered sidewalk that was "uneven, slippery and defective." The student claimed that it was the school's duty to provide a safe place for students.[48]

Proper Maintenance of Equipment

A school district has the affirmative duty to exercise reasonable care not to provide equipment that it knows or has reason to know is dangerous for its intended use. Some jurisdictions have rephrased this standard of care, requiring an affirmative duty to supply effective equipment.

Although most defective equipment suits involve playground equipment, schools have been sued, for example, for supplying defective blankets, gymnastic apparatus, football equipment, playground toys, and hockey helmets. In one case an eleven year old girl was injured when she fell through a torn blanket and landed on the ground. The activity consisted of a student being tossed in the air from the blanket. The girl did not want to be tossed in the air, but was compelled to do so by the supervisor. She fell through the blanket, suffering permanent injuries. The court ruled that the school was negligent and liable for damages and cited defective equipment.[49]

Occasionally the nature of the subject matter being taught by the teacher requires students to use special apparatus in order for the students to gain the desired skills. Such devices may present a hazard to student safety, especially if improper equipment is used or if the equipment is not maintained in proper working order. The question of the teacher's responsibility, and ultimately the school's, has reached the court on several occasions. Teachers and others have been held responsible not only for the activities associated with a program, but also for not preventing accidents caused by the unsafe condition of equipment and facilities.

The increased use of and intricacy of equipment in today's educational programs require more care on the part of educators to avoid possible injury. As a result, courts view such care as a primary responsibility of schools and generally rule that schools have a duty to provide safe equipment and comprehensive instruction to ensure its proper use. Further, as the age of the school site or the student population or number of activities increases, the possibility is greater that defective equipment and unsafe conditions exist. Courts tend to favor the injured student or adult in cases where school officials know that dangerous equipment or unsafe facilities exist and still fail to remedy them. In a Pennsylvania case a football player was injured when he was sent into a game with a defective helmet. The player had informed the coach before the game that his helmet was broken, missing a face mask, and had a torn and defective chin strap. During a play his helmet was knocked from his head and he sustained serious injuries. The court ruled that the injury was a result of the coach's negligence in requiring the player to participate with defective equipment.[50]

Inspection of equipment and facilities has been defined by the courts as a general daily responsibility. Inspections must include the building and grounds; equipment, both fixed and movable; the floor; lighting fixtures; and seats. Teachers and principals must report to proper authorities any dangerous condition that needs to be corrected. Teachers and principals must modify programs to isolate hazards until proper corrections have been made.

Playground Areas

The majority of playground injuries occur when children fall from equipment and strike the underlying surface. Results of tests indicate that while they may require little maintenance or repair, surfacing materials such as asphalt do not provide injury protection from accidental fall impact and are unsuitable for use under playground equipment. The most suitable materials seem to be the more resilient surfaces such as bark, wood chips, or shredded tires. In school districts where such resilient surfaces have been installed, injuries from falls have been dramatically reduced.[51]

Litigation concerning playground equipment demonstrates the need for school districts to remove *entrapment* hazards such as swinging exercise rings or other *open* equipment in which body parts including the head can be placed. Other problem areas noted are ladders, protective barriers, and handrails. All should be designed so that they will not catch a child's clothing. Sharp points, corners and edges, pinch and crush points, and protrusions or projections should be covered or eliminated if possible. Each piece of playground equipment should have a "use zone" and should be spaced a safe distance away from its nearest counterpart. Written guidelines should be established and enforced for playground activities, and playground-related injuries monitored to determine if modifications are necessary to the guidelines or to playground equipment or grounds.

Summary

Liability for school districts, school administrators, and teachers can and does result from improper maintenance. Courts have found teachers and principals negligent when equipment has not been kept in proper repair. Courts have also ruled against districts that allow buildings and grounds to become so dangerous that personnel are injured. The educator will probably be found negligent if the educator:

- Knows or has reason to know that the equipment is, or is likely to be, dangerous for the use for which it is intended.

- Has no reason to believe that the potential users will be aware of the dangerous condition.
- Fails to exercise reasonable care to inform users of the dangerous condition or the facts that make it likely to be dangerous.

School districts have the affirmative duty to exercise reasonable care not to provide or to hold equipment or property that it knows or has reason to know is dangerous for its intended use.

The Concept of Negligence in Field Trips

Scenario 19.7:   A large group of eighth-grade students took part in a field trip to the city park. The trip included lunch at a restaurant across the street from the park. Teachers escorted the group across the relatively nondangerous street. A short time later, three students asked one of the teachers for permission to return to the park. Permission was given, with the teacher advising the students to be careful crossing back across the street. One of the students, 13 years old, mature for his age, and with no hearing or vision problems, was struck by a car.

Points to Consider: Was there negligence on the part of the teacher in this case? What would the teacher's level of duty be to the student as described?

Scenario 19.8:   Ms. Root often took her fourth-grade students on field trips. During a study of primates, she decided to take her students, with principal and parent permission, to the zoo. She led her students to the monkey island and proceeded to lead a discussion about primates. While looking at the animals, Beth, one of her students, was hit by an apple core thrown by one of the monkeys; she was injured in the eye.

Points to Consider: Were Ms. Root and the school safe from any liability because she had signed permission slips and waivers of liability for all of her students? Should Ms. Root have taken children of that age to a place as dangerous as a zoo? If Ms. Root had warned students of the possibility of being hit by an object thrown by a monkey, would she be safe from liability? Was Ms. Root's alleged negligence the proximate cause of Beth's injury?

Field Trip Defined

Field trips are school-related activities that take place away from school grounds. While such trips were once confined to locales within walking distance of the school building, today field trip activities involve thousands of miles of travel each year. The legal obligation of educators to exercise reasonable care and supervision of students so that they will not be at risk on such trips is the same as in any other site-based supervisory situation. Field trips, including athletic events, are merely extensions of the school.

The Assessment of Liability/Status of Students

The assessment of liability on field trips, where students are taken into unfamiliar situations, often turns on whether the students are on the premises solely for their own benefit, or whether the host organization derives some benefit from the visit. In general, three legal statuses of students are recognized by law:

1. Invitees, when the host organization has invited the group.
2. Licensees, when permission has been granted, upon request from the educator, to visit and/or perform.
3. Trespassers, when no permission has been granted to students to visit the premises. An example would be if, during a field trip, students decided on their own to visit a site without the permission or knowledge of the supervisor.

Invitees are due a higher standard of care than licensees. *Licensees* visit the premises at their own peril, since the permission to visit does not carry with it the same standard of care as in the case of invitees. *Trespassers* have little, if any, protection when on property without permission, unless it can be proved that the site was an attractive nuisance to the students due to their age and inexperience.

The educator must have full control of students during the time that they are away from the school. This includes the travel to and from the site or sites to be visited. The best approach for educators concerning safety and supervision on field trips is to treat all aspects of the trip with the same concern expected within the confines of the school and the school grounds.

Foreseeability and Warning

Schools have a duty to protect the health and safety of students while they are in their charge. Consequently, when students are injured, it is common to inquire whether the injury is due to a breach of this duty by a school employee.

If a student is injured while on a field trip, educators may find it possible to prove that reasonable care was taken if they can demonstrate that they visited the site prior to the trip in order to determine, in advance, that dangers might be involved, and that students were warned beforehand.

Waiver of Liability (Permission Slips)

Permission slips from parents are often required for field trips. While there may be certain public information or psychological advantages gained in obtaining signed releases, a waiver of liability does not completely protect the school or the teacher from court action. Students may still sue for injuries they incur. School districts cannot be absolved of their obligation toward students by a parental waiver or release. It may be that the waiver of the parent may affect only the liability arising from the act of taking the students on the trip itself. However, the above facts of law do not mean that some form of permission slip should not be used. To a certain degree the liability may be diminished with a signed document from a legal guardian granting permission to participate in the activity.

Errands

It is common practice for educators and other school employees to send students on errands for them. There is no legal authority for educators to use students in this manner. When a student is sent on a personal or school-related errand for a school employee and the student suffers an injury while on the errand, the legal question that arises is whether the school acted reasonably in sending the student on the errand. What constitutes reasonable action depends on the circumstances of each case. Also important is the fact that, while on an errand for the school employee, the student becomes an agent of the school and the liability for any damage done to, or caused by, the student falls on the school.

Transportation

The most common area of field trip litigation relates to transportation—both that which is provided by teachers or principals, and that which is contracted for, such as public or private bus service. When schools undertake to provide transportation service for students to or from any school activity, it is abundantly clear that the schools' duty of care regarding that transportation is at least equal to that owed on the school premises or to that owed by any public carrier.[52] When transportation is provided by independent contractors, duty and liability rest in them rather than with the school.

The issues of duty and proximate cause are not quite so clear, however, when schools play an intermediary role in organizing, arranging, or sanctioning the transportation of students by private vehicle. The issue of parental responsibility when driving on school-sponsored field trips was addressed in a case in which the court stated: ". . . the duty of care, and the liability for negligence which proximately causes injury to a student, shifts from the school to a parent who undertakes to provide transportation for school children other than his own."[53]

Where supplementary transportation to school activities is provided in vehicles operated by school personnel or by students themselves and is arranged or sanctioned by school officials, a school does not so easily avoid liability. Schools may be bound under the doctrine of *respondeat superior* with regard to their employees or by their duty to exercise reasonable care in the selection, approval and supervision of student cars and drivers.

Standard of Duty and Care

A general overview of the litigation involving field trip activities and transportation demonstrates the standard of duty and care inherent in this extension of the school's parameters.

A mentally challenged student member of a Special Olympics team was killed while walking with a group three blocks to a gymnasium. The student was accompanied by one teacher while another teacher followed in a car. The student ran into the street at a busy intersection and was struck by a car. The parents of the student claimed that the teachers were negligent by exposing the handicapped student to unreasonable and foreseeable risk of injury. The parents further claimed that the school failed to provide an adequate number of supervisory personnel and to select the safest route. The court found in favor of the parents.[54]

A point for educators to note is the age and the intellectual level of students involved in field trips. A student, 12 years old, left the premises of the school in the care of a college student who was employed by the school in a supervisory capacity. The parents of the student had given permission for the student to go on field trips with the child's teacher. Due to circumstances, the teacher was unable to attend and the college student volunteered, with the school's authorization, to take the students. During the outing the student was injured when the car collided with a disabled truck. The student claimed that the college student was acting outside of his scope of employment; therefore, the school was liable for injuries caused by negligence. The court found in favor of the student.[55]

A high school band member drowned in a hotel pool while on a trip with the band. The student dove into the water and minutes later was found at the bottom of the pool. Two chaperons who were supervising the pool activity gave immediate mouth-to-mouth resuscitation until an ambulance arrived. The parents of the student claimed negligence in failure to provide adequate supervision for their son, who did not know how to swim. The father, however, had given written permission to use the pool and did not inform anyone that his son could not swim. The court ruled in favor of the school, citing the age of the student, proper supervision on the part of the field trip sponsors, and negligence on the part of the father.[56]

A twelve year old student suffered a fatal injury when she stuck her head out of the bus window and was struck by a guy wire supporting a utility pole. The court ruled in favor of the school, citing the fact that the student was bright, alert, and intelligent and, as a result, contributed to her own negligence. In addition, the court noted that the supervisor and the bus driver had warned students not to place hands or other parts of the body outside windows when the bus was moving.[57]

The court in another case held a teacher responsible for the death of a student. The teacher allowed and made arrangements for students to ride in the automobiles of other students and for the drivers of the cars to receive gasoline for such trips at the expense of his school organization. The court noted that the school assumed a duty to perform its assumed role with reasonable prudence and foresight. The teacher negligently failed to consider the driver's reputation for recklessness or to ascertain the extraordinarily unsafe condition of the automobile in which the student was riding.[58]

In cases pertaining to breach of duty in field trips, lack of supervision is commonly demonstrated. An example is provided by a case that involved a teacher and six adults who took thirty-five elementary and preschool children to the beach. Four of the children climbed onto a large log and posed for a picture that the teacher took. With her back to the ocean, the teacher did not see the large wave that surged onto the beach. The wave caused the log to be lifted and the children fell off. When the water receded, the log settled on top of one child and crushed him. The court cited foreseeability and a breach of the duty to properly supervise and ruled in favor of the parents of the student.[59]

In another case, members of a senior class met at a city park on a Saturday to have pictures taken for the school yearbook. The school had approved the activity, and two teachers were assigned as supervisors. Two students received permission from the teachers to have their picture taken while on their motorcycles. In the course of the picture taking, a child walking nearby was hit by one of the motorcycles and injured. The court ruled in favor of the child and cited a breach of duty on the part of the teachers.[60]

Summary

Negligence in the classroom and in the school leaves the educator open to court action. The same is true on a field trip. Schools owe the same duty of care and supervision to take reasonable precautions to avoid foreseeable injuries to students who participate in mandatory field trips and excursions as would be owed to the students during the normal school day.[61] If schools authorize, sponsor, and encourage an extracurricular organization or activity that is of recognized general educational value and benefit, schools must exercise care and supervision.[62]

The Concept of Post-Injury Treatment

Scenario 19.9:   Connie Dixon, a tenth-grade student, was injured when she fainted and fell from the risers during an "under the lights" pre-performance choir practice. Because of the position of Connie's leg after the fall, the teacher and the principal believed Connie had suffered a fracture. They applied an inflatable splint, inflating the apparatus to the point that Connie's leg was straightened. An ambulance was called, but due to traffic did not arrive for forty minutes. By the time certified medical technicians looked at Connie's leg, gangrene had developed, and Connie lost her leg.

Points to Consider: Does the teacher have any liability for the original incident? Do the teacher and principal have any liability for the first aid attempted? Were they acting as "good Samaritans"? Was there any foreseeability?

Post-Injury Treatment Defined

A particularly disturbing problem at the time of an injury is the administration of first aid. The questions most often argued in the court are:

- Was there a duty to render first aid?
- Was the aid administered properly?
- What is the scope of treatment that may be administered?
- Was there a duty not to render treatment?

It appears that school officials have the duty to render first aid and the duty not to render anything more than first aid. Although educators are not authorized to provide general medical treatment to students, educators have a duty to administer emergency aid. The difficulty of post-injury treatment may be summed up with the generalization that educators are required to take appropriate steps in the case of an injury to a student, but may be held liable if an attempt is made to help too much or if they fail to do enough.

The American Red Cross defines *first aid* generally as the immediate and temporary care given the victim of an accident or sudden illness. Such action must be either to sustain the life of the injured person or to prevent further injury. In some states, "good samaritan" laws shield individuals providing treatment in emergency situations from liability. Because of the special duty of care required in the student–educator relationship, such laws would probably not indemnify school personnel from liability for unreasonable action. Courts have recognized that public policy considerations dictate an obligation to ensure that medical treatment given by a school is competently rendered.

The Duty of Post-Injury Treatment

Educators have a duty to provide some degree of medical assistance to injured students under their supervision commensurate with their training and experience. While courts do not expect educators to be physicians, they do expect people who work with children to be able to administer life-saving first aid whenever needed and to render the emergency care in a proper and prudent manner.

Although educators have the responsibility to implement acceptable and careful procedures, they cannot diagnose or treat injuries past the emergency state. When an emergency is indicated, educators are obligated to do the best they can relative to the amount of training and experience they possess. Either lack of action or unwise action may lead to an allegation of negligence against the educator.

Failure to Act versus Proper Action

The failure of an educator to administer immediate first aid that might have prevented the death of a student resulted in litigation when a student playing "hide and seek" during lunch recess shoved her arm through a glass pane on a door. As she pulled her arm out, the student received a deep cut in her arm. The young girl panicked and ran around the playground before being stopped by an older student. The teacher had left the area, and it was several minutes before the school nurse could be located and the bleeding stopped. The girl died later at the hospital because of excessive blood loss. The court felt that the teacher could have prevented her death by quickly stopping the flow of blood.[63]

As long as educators administer emergency care in a proper and prudent manner, the courts appear to favor the educator. A student was hit in the stomach while playing football. The teacher took him inside the dressing room, had the student lie down, and covered him with a blanket. Later, when the student went to the rest room, he found blood in his urine. The court ruled that proper and prudent care was given. The teacher had no indication of internal bleeding prior to the passing of the urine.[64]

The lack of immediate first aid, as well as the improper use of first aid, was the allegation of the parents of a football player who brought suit against a school after their son died of profound heat exhaustion. At the end of practice, about 4:20 p.m., the boy became faint and began to vomit after running "wind sprints." He was given a shower at room temperature and placed in a blanket. The coaches noticed the clamminess of his skin and his heavy breathing, but failed to take any other action. It was not until approximately 6:45 p.m. that the boy's parents were called, and they in turn contacted a doctor. Heat stroke was diagnosed, and the boy was taken to the hospital, where he died the next day. The court ruled that the death was due to the lack of immediate first aid after the first symptoms appeared, as well as the improper use of first aid.[65]

Unwise action may also lead to a charge of negligence against an educator. A football player was awarded damages when the coach failed to administer proper first aid. During a pre-season scrimmage, the player was initially injured when he was tackled. A grip test was used on the playing field to test for neck injury and/or possible damage to the spinal cord. The boy could move his hands, so he was carried by his arms and legs from the playing field by other players under the direction of the coach. The grip test was again administered at the sideline, but the boy was then unable to move his hands, arms, or legs. The court ruled that the boy became a quadriplegic because of a spinal injury resulting from his being improperly moved from the playing field to the sideline. The standard of care in this instance required the attention of a doctor and the use of a stretcher.[66]

In another case of improper first aid, two teachers forcibly held the injured hand of a student in scalding water for ten minutes. The treatment resulted in the development of blisters and permanent disfigurement of the hand. The student was hospitalized for almost a month. The court considered the treatment to be unreasonable and improper, even though the intentions of the teachers were directed toward the welfare of the student.[67]

A case of improper treatment was demonstrated when medical treatment was administered by students under the direction of the teacher. The plaintiff student had a pre-existing medical condition in one of his knees. The teacher directed incompetent and untrained students to attempt medical treatment of the knee; as a result, the plaintiff's knee was further damaged. The court ruled against the teacher.[68]

Administering Medication

See Chapter 14 for guidelines in this area.

Summary

The area of post-injury treatment is a difficult one in which to advise educators. Educators have a duty to provide some degree of medical assistance to an injured student. Courts, however, do not expect educators to possess the same knowledge as trained physicians. Educators cannot diagnose or treat injuries past the emergency state. When an emergency is indicated, educators are obligated to do the best that they can, relative to the amount of training and experience they possess.

Athletic Liability and Spectator Safety

Approximately seven million students are engaged in some type of interscholastic sport during the school year.[69] Thirty-six percent of secondary school football players incurred at least one injury during the 1988 season, 60 percent of which occurred during practice.[70] The National Athletic Trainer's Association totaled the football injuries during that season at 503,706 and noted that basketball and football alone were responsible during the 1987–88 school year for an estimated 705,000 injuries. When soccer, wrestling, track, gymnastics, and swimming were added, the total number was over a million injuries for the year.[71]

Although educators may be somewhat comforted by the available defense of assumption of risk if a participant is injured, an athletic participant may generally assume the risks inherent in a particular sport but not the risks resulting from educator negligence. In applying the concept of negligence specifically to school athletics, a major consideration is the duty educators owe to the participant. These duties are primarily to provide proper and adequate instruction and supervision, to provide and maintain safe facilities and equipment, to provide proper medical attention, and to reasonably select and match participants.

When an athletic injury occurs, educators often turn to the defenses of contributory negligence and assumption of risk for protection from liability. Of the two defenses, assumption of risk appears to be the most successful. However, assumption of risk does not have universal acceptance in the courts. In some states it been expressly abolished on the basis that reasonableness of conduct should be the basic consideration in all negligence cases. Nevertheless, if a school district or school employee has been negligent in duty and standard of care, neither defense will probably be upheld by a court. Students assume only the known risks inherent in a particular athletic activity.

Express assumption of risk, where students and their guardians sign waivers of liability for claims against the school district and school personnel for their negligence, are generally useless. While these waiver forms are contracts, minors can disavow most contracts at will. Waivers signed by parents, guardians, and adult students also are generally unenforceable because they are usually contrary to public policy.

Courts have also recognized that education institutions have a duty toward spectators. Even in states that provide government immunity, dangerous facilities fall outside of most immunity provisions. Spectators must be able to have confidence that physical structures, walkways, and other facilities are safe and well maintained. In addition, crowd-control procedures must be apparent, and appropriate first aid must be available.

In the context of athletic liability and spectator safety, educators have a duty to anticipate reasonably foreseeable dangers and to take precautions against their occurrence. An overview of litigation shows the following factors to be basic to liability prevention:

- Adequate instruction and warning to students and parents
- Adequate supervision of athletic participants and all other sports-related student organizations (i.e., cheerleaders, etc.)
- Proper equipment and proper maintenance of equipment
- Reasonable matching of participants
- Qualified athletic personnel and trained coaches
- Proper supervision, including formal evaluation, of adult personnel by administration
- Proper facilities and playing fields
- Proper health care, including the requiring of medical examinations
- Compliance with statutory guidelines, regulations, safety rules, and eligibility requirements
- Proper and safe transportation

Overall Summary of the Concepts of Tort Liability for Negligence in Education

An examination and review of the literature and selected litigation related to the area of tort liability provides the basis for the following summary statements:

1. The literature and judicial dicta recognize a critical need for educators to establish professional guidelines concerning appropriate educator behavior and professional standards against which an educator accused of inappropriate action can be judged.
2. Educators have been found financially responsible for their professional actions when an injured student or adult proved, to the court's satisfaction, that some inappropriate action of the educator or school district led to the student's or adult's injury.
3. Foreseeability of harm is a critical element in determining negligence in a given situation. Educators have been held liable for accidents that occur during their absence from the classroom or activity area if it could be anticipated that the educator's presence in the room or area would have prevented the accident.
4. Educators have been found accountable for their failure to take into consideration a student's special needs or limitations, abilities, age, and pre-existing medical conditions when making instructional or supervisory decisions.
5. Courts have recognized the difficulty of constantly supervising every student and have not held educators to be the absolute ensurers of each student's safety.
6. Courts have been cognizant of the burdens placed on educators when ruling on their liability; however, these burdens have not relieved

educators of the responsibility for their actions or inactions. Educators are responsible for any harmful consequences of their conduct.

7. The appropriateness of an educator's conduct in a given situation is measured by whether a reasonably prudent educator, with the skill and training expected under the circumstances, would have acted in a similar fashion under similar conditions.

8. Educators have been found liable for their selection, maintenance, and supervision of the use of instructional equipment if the educator's act.on in this regard was shown to be based upon poor judgment not expected of a professional educator.

9. Educators have been upheld by the courts for their attempts to provide post-injury first aid to injured students; however, the courts have not afforded protection for educators who attempted to deliver medical therapy or treatment that exceeded or fell short of rudimentary first aid procedures.

10. Educators have been found accountable on field trips for the same duty and standard of care expected within the confines of the school site.

11. Educators have not been found accountable for their instruction or supervision when the student was shown to have had adequate knowledge to complete the task assigned or the student knowingly assumed the risk inherent in the activity.

12. Educators can be held liable for assault and battery if they use excessive physical force with students.

13. Educators should be aware that students, parents, and others have an increasing tendency to bring the school into litigation.

Endnotes

1. Miller v. Griesel, 308 N.E. 2d 701 (Ind. Sup. Ct. 1973).

2. Civillo v. Milwaukee, 460 N.W. 2d 34 (Wis. Sup. Ct. 1967).

3. Dailey v. Los Angeles Unified School District, 470 P.2d 360 (Cal. Sup. Ct. 1970).

4. Ncilson v. Community Unit School District No. 3, 90 3d 243, 412 N.E. 2d 1177 (Ill. App. 1980).

5. Vargo v. Svitchan, 301 N.W. 2d 1 (Mich. Ct. App. 1980).

6. Stehn v. Bernard MacFadden Foundations, Inc., 434 F.2d 811 (Tenn. 6th Cir. 1970).

7. Stucky v. Churchman, 2 111, App. 548 (1878). *See also* Spear v. Cummings, 23 Pick. 224 Am Dec. 53 (Mass. 1839).

8. Peter W. v. San Francisco Unified School District, 60 Calif. Ct. App. 3d 814 (1976).

9. Laveck v. City of Janesville, 204 N.W. 2d 6 (Wis. Sup. Ct. 1973).

10. Savers v. Ranger, 83 A. 2d 775 (N.J. App. Div. 1951).

11. LaValley v. Stanford, 70 N.Y.S. 2d 460 (N.Y. App. Div. 1947).

12. Govel v. Board of Education in the City of Albany, 235 N.Y.S. 2d 300 (N.Y. Sup. Ct. 1962).

13. Ehlinger v. Board of Education of New Hartford Cent. School District, 465 N.Y.S. 2d 378 (App. Div. 1983).

14. Gardner v. State, 22 N.E. 2d 344 (N.Y. Ct. App. 1939).

15. Bellman v. San Francisco High School District, 81 P.2d 894 (Cal. Sup. Ct. 1938).

16. Luce v. Board of Education, 157 N.Y.S. 2d 123 (N.Y. App. Div. 1956).

17. Simmons v. Beauregard Parish School Board, 315 So. 2d 883 (La. App. 3rd Cir. 1975).

18. Miles v. School District No. 138, 281 N.W. 2d 396 (Neb. 1979).

19. Roberts v. Robertson County Board of Education, 692 S.W. 2d 863 (Tenn. App. 1985).

20. Chapman v. State, 492 P.2d 607 (Wash. Ct. App. 1972).

21. Brevard County v. Jacks, 238 So. 2d 156 (Fla. Dist. Ct. App. 1970).

22. Reynolds v. State, 207 Misc. 963, 141 N.Y.S. 2d 615 (N.Y. Ct. Cl. 1955).

23. Selleck v. Board of Education, 276 A.D. 263, 94 N.Y.S. 2d 318 (1949).

24. Armlin v. Board of Education, 36 A.D. 2d 877, 320 N.Y.S. 2d 402 (1971).

25. Wilbur v. City of Binghamton, 66 N.Y.S. 2d 250 (N.Y. App. Div. 1946).

26. District of Columbia v. Royal, 465 A. 2d (D.C. 1983).

27. Hampton v. Orleans Parish School Board, 422 So. 2d 202 (La. Ct. App. 1982).

28. Charonnatt v. San Francisco Unified School District, 133 P.2d 643 (Cal. Dist. Ct. App. 1943).

29. Nester v. City of New York, 211 N.Y.S. 2d 975 (N.Y. Sup. Ct. 1961).

30. Ohman v. Board of Education of City of New York, 300 N.Y.S. 306, 90 N.E. 2d 474 (N.Y. 1949).

31. Guyten v. Rhodes, 65, 163. 29 N.E. 2d 444 (Ohio App. 1940).

32. Gonzales v. Mackler, 19 A.D. 2d 229, 241 N.Y.S. 2d 254 (N.Y.S. 1963).

33. Segerman v. Jones, 256, 109, 256 A. 2d 749 (Md. 1969).

34. Carbon v. Overfield, 451 N.E. 2d 1229 (Ohio 1983).

35. WILLIAM PROSSER, LAW OF TORTS (4th ed.) (St. Paul, Minn.: West, 1971), p. 583.

36. Barnhizer v. Paradise Valley Unified School District No. 69, 599 P.2d 209 (Ariz. 1979).

37. Brown v. City of Oakland, 124 P.2d 369 (Cal. Dist. Ct. App. 1942).

38. Gibbons v. Orleans Parish School Board, 391 So. 2d 976 (La. Ct. App. 1980).

39. Libby v. West Coast Rock Co. Inc., 308 So. 2d 602 (La. Ct. App. 1976).

40. Monfils v. City of Sterling Heights, 269 N.W. 2d 588 (Mich. App. Ct. 1978).

41. Young v. Orleans Parish School Board, 391 So. 2d 11 (La. App. 1980).

42. Mattison v. Hudson Falls, 458 N.Y.S. 2d 726 (N.Y. App. Div. 1983).

43. Gurule v. Salt Lake City Board of Education, 661 P.2d 975 (Utah Sup. Ct. 1983).

44. Ardoin v. Evangeline Parish School Board, 376 So. 2d 372 (La. App. 1979).

45. Cooper v. Smith Town Central School District, 441 N.Y.S. 2d 553 (N.Y. App. Div. 1981).

46. Hatlee v. Oswego-Appalachian School District, 420 N.Y.S. 2d 448 (N.Y. Sup. Ct. 1979).

47. Woodring v. Board of Education of Manhasset Union Free School District, 435 N.Y.S. 2d (N.Y. A.D. 1981).

48. Lostumbo v. Board of Education of the City of Norwalk, 418 A. 2d 949 (Conn. Super. 1980).

49. Rook v. State, 4 N.Y.S. 2d 116 (N.Y. App. Div. 1938).

50. Martini v. Olyphant Borough School District, 83 Pa. D. & C. 206 (C. Lackawana County, 1953).

51. *See generally,* U.S. CONSUMER PRODUCT SAFETY COMMISSION, A HANDBOOK FOR PUBLIC PLAYGROUND SAFETY: GENERAL GUIDELINES FOR PLAYGROUNDS, EQUIPMENT AND SURFACING, vol. I and II (Washington, D.C.: Government Printing Office, 1987).

52. Raymond v. Paradise Unified School District, 218 Cal. App. 2d 1, 31 CAL. RPTR. 847 (1963).

53. Sharp v. Fairbanks North Star Borough, 569 P.2d 178 (Alaska 1977).

54. Foster v. Houston General Insurance Co., 407 So. 2d 759, 763 (La. App. 1981).

55. Brokow v. Black-Foxe Military Institute, 37 2d 274 P.2d 816 (Cal. Ct. App. 1951).

56. Powell v. Orleans Parish School Board, 354 So. 2d 229 (La. Ct. App. 1978).

57. Arnold v. Hayslett, 655 S.W. 2d 941 (Tenn. 1981).

58. Hanson v. Reedley Joint Union School District, 43, 2d 643, 111 P.2d 415 (Cal. Ct. App. 1941).

59. Morris v. Douglas County School District, 430 P.2d 775 (Ore. 1965).

60. Williamson v. Board of Education, 375 N.Y.S. 2d 221 (N.Y. App. Div. 1975).

61. Castro v. Los Angeles Board of Education, 54 3d 232, 126 CAL. RPTR. 537 (Cal. Ct. App. 1976).

62. Chappel v. Franklin Pierce School District, 71 426 P.2d 17. 471 (Wash. 1967).

63. Orgando v. Carquineu School District, 75 P.2d 641 (Cal. Dist. Ct. App. 1938).

64. Rickle v. Oakdale Union Grammar School District, 253 P.2d 1 (Cal. Sup. Ct. 1953).

65. Magabgab v. Orleans Parish School Board, 239 So. 2d 456 (La. Ct. App. 1970).

66. Welch v. Dunsmuir Joint Union High School, 326 P.2d 633 (Cal. Dist. Ct. App. 1958).

67. Guerrieri v. Tyson, 24 A. 2d 468 (Pa. Super. 1942).

68. O'Brian v. Township High School District 214, 73, 3d 618, 392 N.E. 2d 615 (Ill. Ct. App. 1979).

69. Carl L. Stanitski, *Common Injuries in Preadolescent and Adolescent Athletics,* SPORTS MEDICINE, vol. 7 (1989) pp. 32–33.

70. *Dimensions: High School Football Injuries,* EDUCATION WEEK, vol. 8 (1989), p. 3.

71. Sallie B. Zakariya, *Before the New Season Kicks Off, Get a Game Plan To Cut Sports Injuries,* AMERICAN SCHOOL BOARD JOURNAL, vol. 175 (1989), pp. 23–24.

CHAPTER TWENTY

The Principal as Risk Manager

Introduction to the Concepts of Risk Management

This chapter is designed to promote risk-management literacy specifically for principals. While the chapter examines districtwide risk-control methodology and issues related to district "exposures," effective principals see their schools from the district perspective as well as from the school-site viewpoint. A working knowledge of the components of risk management and the risk exposures inherent in school management provides principals with new tools to promote a safe environment for students, staff, and patrons. The primary goal of the school principal in risk management is safety and the reduction of exposures to liability.

Many educators believe that most accidents or incidents are people problems, not organizational problems, and therefore are not worthy of attention from the superintendent or school board. This perception has resulted in escalating insurance costs, unfavorable changes in coverage limits, and critical problems in securing liability coverage for school districts. The management of risk is an organization problem that currently, through unnecessary exposure to liability, costs school districts millions of taxpayer dollars for insurance coverage, litigation fees, personnel time, and damage awards—resources that could be more effectively used to educate children, upgrade curriculum and facilities, and recruit and retain quality personnel. School districts and other local government entities routinely retain insurance, reduce insurance, or self-insure in an attempt to prevent risk from becoming a financial burden to district taxpayers. It is not managerially possible for school districts to completely eliminate risk, nor is it fiscally prudent to insure all potential risk.

The primary task of school districts is to educate children, and many activities with varying risk are inherent in providing comprehensive educational experiences. Education litigation has demonstrated that our society has a heightened level of knowledge of personal and organizational liabilities when injuries occur and is aware that schools are not immune from liability. It is now commonly understood that schools, like any other public or private entity, cannot avoid accountability for their actions or inactions.

Traditionally, school districts have considered risk by looking backward. Just as in tort, this "hindsight" method of "damage control" has been shown, through the exorbitant cost of insurance and litigation, to be far less effective and less fiscally prudent than a well-planned, active program of risk anticipation and prevention. A risk-management program, fully developed and implemented, is, then, a pro-active approach to help school boards and district administrators use their best judgment to avoid potential litigation.

Insurance

Unfortunately, many school districts do little more than secure expensive insurance coverage to finance property and casualty losses and liability awards. A growing number of school districts, in an attempt to avoid escalating premiums, have begun to use their own financial capacity to retain or *self-insure* some of their loss exposures by financing these retained risks out of operating monies rather than transferring them to an insurance company.

Other school districts have self-insured by joining an insurance pool. Insurance pools are groups of school districts or municipalities that form a sponsoring unit, self-insure on a group basis, and purchase stop-loss insurance collectively. This option allows smaller school districts, unable to self-insure and still feel protected, to obtain the benefits available to a larger group at reasonable rates.

The majority of school districts still have some type of property and liability insurance. Property and liability insurance is usually divided into five classifications:[1]

1. Property insurance, which protects the insured against physical loss of, or damage to, owned property (financial protection against loss from fire, windstorm, and theft)
2. Income protection, which protects the insured from loss of income and extra expense resulting from physical damage to the insured's property or the property of others
3. Liability insurance, which protects the insured against claims for physical or emotional injury or property damage caused by negligence or imposed by statute or contract (transportation liability, worker's compensation, and contractual liability insurance)
4. Health insurance, which provides reimbursement of medical expenses caused by accident or illness and protects the insured against loss of income resulting from disability

5. Suretyship coverage, which offers a financial guarantee of the insured party's honesty or of its performance under contract or agreement (i.e., fidelity, construction, etc.)

The fact that school districts and their insurers pay millions of dollars each year in workers' compensation, liability awards, and unscheduled maintenance has begun to change the perception that insurance is the panacea for risk protection. Many school districts, in fact, have found that insurance carriers avoid unpredictable risk by canceling policies, refusing to renew them, or setting exorbitant rates. The supply of coverage is decreasing just as the demand for insurance is increasing. Such abandonment by their insurers, coupled with the realization by school districts that insurance is not the only answer to liability problems, has led to the emergence of a redesigned concept in the treatment of *hazards, exposures,* or *risks* districts face. Under this concept, commonly called *risk management,* insurance is thought of only as financial protection for unexpected failures in risk-management programs or for an unavoidable major catastrophe, not as the sole solution to all accidental loss.

The Concept of Risk Management

Risk management is a coordinated, effective pre-event and post-event response to a school district's liability exposures, developed through planning, organizing, leading, and monitoring a district's activities and assets. Risk management or risk control is generally defined as the process of minimizing accidental loss by anticipating and preventing the occurrence of unplanned events. In its broadest form, risk management embraces a wide range of interests in the education setting, including but not limited to:

- Student and staff safety
- Health
- Chemical safety
- Environmental affairs
- Property protection
- Contingency planning
- Security
- Transportation
- Third party liability
- Contractual liability

An overall examination of the types and frequency of litigation that have been brought against school districts demonstrates that these are the prime areas of potential exposure that need the leadership and monitoring available with a districtwide risk-management and liability-prevention program.

Risk management, as a concept, began in the insurance industry in the middle to late 1960s as a response to the increase in litigation. As insurance company exposure increased, and as claim and settlement costs began to climb, insurance managers evolved into risk managers.[2] Insurance companies began to develop strategies aimed specifically at avoiding litigation.

Because insurance underwriters must approve contracts before liability insurance is issued, underwriters are responsible for determining the probability of having to pay for a loss. They base this decision on the legal concepts and principles that a court would use in deciding what claims the insurer might be required to pay. A careful underwriter must first uncover all of a district's *exposures* (legal liability developed from an invasion of the rights of others); evaluate their potential for loss; and, finally, price them.[3]

As businesses realized that the cost of their insurance coverage depended to a large extent on their ability to reduce their exposure to risk, they began to assign an employee to perform the duties of a risk manager. The knowledge and ability of this employee to control or eliminate potential liability are very important factors in reducing the frequency and severity of loss.

Although risk management in education has not achieved the sophistication present in the private sector, it is becoming more widely practiced. An effective risk management plan, when implemented in a school district, is directed toward minimizing the risks of legal disruption in the operation of the district and its schools.

The Incorporation of Preventive Law and Legal Audit in Risk Management

School districts, in cooperation with their legal counsel, often include as a major component in their overall risk-management program the concepts and practices of *preventive law* and *legal audit*.

Preventive law is defined as a branch of law that endeavors to minimize the risk of litigation or to secure, with more certainty, legal rights and duties.[4] Preventive law emphasizes the importance of planning to avoid legal problems and their consequences should litigation ensue.[5] The components of preventive law include four basic levels:

1. Anticipation of legal challenges (foreseeability)
2. Evaluation of the legal merits of such potential challenges
3. Consideration of the policies (in effect or proposed) affected by such potential challenges

4. Implementation or modification, where appropriate, in response to the first three steps

To the extent that human behavior and the law are reasonably foreseeable, informed educators can predict certain legal risks and reduce their scope through policy, procedure, or practice. In those areas where the law is less certain, educators can at least evaluate risk and choose courses of action that are less risky than others.[6]

Legal audit is generally defined as a *professional* review of the legal affairs of the client (school district) done periodically and culminating in a summary report to management (superintendent and board of education).[7] Some of the advantages of legal audit are:

• The likelihood that significant, but preventable, legal problems will come to the attention of district administrators and the board of education is increased.
• The flow of information to district administrators and the board of education is increased, with the assurance that the parties are receiving accurate facts upon which to base preventive action.

The incorporation of the concepts of preventive law and legal audit into a comprehensive risk-management program helps school districts focus their attention on appropriate consultation and planning, rather than viewing insurance and litigation as the solution to all legal problems.

Risk Management at the School-District Level

The cost of an accident at school can be tallied by many means—insurance premiums today or direct compensation, replaced employees, unscheduled maintenance, and litigation awards tomorrow. Too often, school districts focus minimal attention on a cheaper and healthier way to pay for accidents—by preventing them.

Even after paying expensive insurance premiums, school districts are often faced with the additional costs of lawsuits for accidental injuries to staff members, students, visitors, and contract workers, not to mention property loss. Most school district accidents and losses can be avoided by greater attention to preventive maintenance, employee and patron training, security, safe school legislation, and better supervision—in other words, risk management. Many risk-management activities are things school districts already do at some level of efficiency: good supervision and maintenance; proper storage of chemicals and tools; attention to such substances as asbestos, lead, and radon; adequate security for people and property, and safety inspections for buses and other types of equipment. However, a comprehensive risk-management program coordinates and centralizes these activities—and plugs gaps in the system. For example, in the area of accident prevention, risk management focuses on preventing small, but expensive, accidents that occur frequently and big accidents that occur only rarely.

In general, risk management means becoming more serious about school district safety and security. Risk management provides an accountable means to document a district's standards of reasonable and prudent care in a potential lawsuit and guides the district into a rigorous and continuing examination of a district's operations to prevent or reduce injury, loss, or litigation.

Risk Management at the School-Site Level

Many school districts across the country are examining or implementing site-based management as a means to improve the delivery of effective educational services. Simply stated, site-based management places overall responsibility in the hands of building principals, who, working in close cooperation with teachers and representatives of the community, make the primary decisions regarding all phases of the educational program. The critical decisions concerning curriculum content and development, selection of instructional materials and methods, selection and supervision of faculty and staff, student management, budget planning and allocation, and resource and facilities management are made, under site-based prerogatives, by those most familiar with the specific educational needs of the students and the particular goals and priorities of the local community.

In developing site-based management programs, important questions for school district officials to consider are these: If a school district transfers much of the administrative operation and decision making from the district level to the school sites, is the district inviting problems in overall, districtwide risk management and liability prevention? Can a school district foresee and prevent some of the potential problems?

Traditional school district organization places the primary responsibility for risk management and liability prevention with central office administrators who determine, and supervise the implementation of, districtwide administrative policies and procedures. In recognition of the fact that it is the district as a whole that is legally accountable for safeguarding the rights and well-being of students and school personnel, such policies and procedures are generally subject to meticulous review by the school district's general counsel to assure compliance with all applicable legal principles.

As presently interpreted, site-based management implies modifications to the traditional model that could increase the district's potential liability. When the principal and the site-based management team are granted the authority to develop their own instructional program and effectively manage the school, there is an opportunity to shift the responsibility for developing administrative procedures and practices (if not overall policy) from central office administrators to principals. There is also the possibility that principals will be less closely supervised by central office administrators than in the past. Both situations suggest that principals will make more of the decisions that directly affect the quality and nature of supervision and instruction, student discipline, facility and equipment maintenance, etcetera. Unless principals are current and knowledgeable about basic education law and general risk-management policies and procedures, the opportunity for error and exposure will be increased, as well as the potential for litigation.

Though decision-making responsibility may shift from the central office to the school site, the liability for legal action does not. When a faculty or staff member commits an "error in judgment" or a principal violates "reasonable trust," the legal principle of *respondeat superior* (the master is responsible for the acts of the servant) may be applied, and an employee's alleged negligent performance of assigned duties commonly results in the school district's, as well as the individual's, liability for damages. While site-based personnel need not become experts in school law, they should recognize the circumstances surrounding potential litigation in order to avoid unnecessary risks and resultant law suits.

Summary

Risk management is an "AART." AART, an acronym derived from *Authority, Accountability, Responsibility,* and *Training,* is an ingredient essential for any risk program's success. Developing and sustaining a comprehensive risk-management program is not an easy task. The person who is selected to manage such activities has a tremendous responsibility. There is as much skill and AART needed in risk management as in any other administrative areas in a school district.

To create *authority,* an education organization's risk-management program requires the attention of the superintendent and board and ample resources. *Accountability* can be built into any program of risk management, with procedures and responsibilities clearly defined and individual managers and employees held accountable for successful implementation of the program. It should also be understood, and clearly stated in job descriptions, that *responsibility* for safety and health and loss control is a function for all school district employees.

An important element of risk management is the *training* of employees at all levels in a school district. By experience, many risk managers have recognized that in-depth, repeated inservice activities are central to fostering behavior conducive to controlling and managing risk.

Endnotes

1. Dennis R. Dunklee & Gerald C. Colleta, *Risk Control Is a Top Line Task for Bottom Line Executives,* EXECUTIVE EDUCATOR, May 1988, p. 17.

2. Linda J. Collins, *Lexicon of Risk Management Grows Along with Profession,* BUSINESS INSURANCE, Oct. 26, 1987, p. 42.

3. LARRY D. GAUNT, NUMAN A. WILLIAMS, & EVERETT D. RANDALL, COMMERCIAL LIABILITY UNDERWRITING, (Malvern, Penn.: Insurance Institute of America, 1982), p. 49.

4. A. Kennison, *By Way of Introduction,* 38 So. CAL. L. REV. 377 (1981).

5. K. Stampf, *Preventive Law and Continuing Education,* 38 So. CAL. L. REV. 381 (1981).

6. *See generally,* W. BEDNAR, NOLPE SCHOOL LAW UPDATE (Topeka, Kansas: National Organization on Legal Problems of Education, 1984), pp. 2–3.

7. *See generally,* L. Brown & E. Dauer, *A Synopsis of the Theory and Practice of Preventive Law,* LAWYER'S NOTEBOOK (American Bar Association, rev. 3rd, 1982), A3–16. *See also,* L. Brown, *Legal Audit,* 38 So. CAL. L. REV. 431 (1981).

CHAPTER TWENTY-ONE

The Knowledgeable Principal—Related Issues

As principals assume greater responsibility for site-based management, it is imperative that they expand their knowledge of three critical issues: workers' compensation, the principal's responsibility for managing chemical and material hazards, and crisis management. These three areas are commonly mishandled, leading to greater exposure to liability and poor employee and community relations.

Workers' Compensation

Many school district employees have responsibility for programs at several sites. Others have other responsibilities in addition to their school district employment. Some work into the late evening, and many travel to other communities on field trips or to participate in professional activities. Some serve as officers in state or national organizations or on community agency boards and commissions. Often they are called back to their offices or school sites after their normal working day has ended, or they find it necessary to report on weekends and holidays to prepare for upcoming activities. Schedules change frequently with little notice, and visiting in the homes of students and patrons is a common activity.

The scope of coverage of workers' compensation is of vital importance to school administrators, risk managers, and district insurers. School districts and principals should be familiar with their state's workers' compensation rules and regulations and should determine how the insurer might react to cases that are considered extraordinary. Each state has its own claim procedures. Individual state statutes cover such items as filing deadlines (statutes of limitations), employer verification of injuries, referees' decisions, and legal fees. A review of workers' compensation cases provides some classic cases of employee and attorney ingenuity in attempting to relate a specific injury to the workplace.

The following hypothetical scenarios are based on real cases. The cases have been reframed to demonstrate their effects on employees such as principals, teachers, and other school district personnel. Instead of "Points to Consider," these scenarios are followed by brief discussions outlining the major tenets of law that were used in deciding the case. These should help principals better understand the complexities of workers' compensation law and, at the same time, provide impetus for additional procedures that should be considered for a comprehensive risk-management program.

Scenario 21.1:   A school principal, as a voluntary member of the district's contract negotiating team, was required to attend the March 12th school board meeting. After school on that date, he assisted several P.T.A. members to prepare some backdrops for the upcoming school carnival. He left for home on his motorcycle quite late, intending to eat, shower, change his clothes, and go to the meeting. (He had not worn a suit to school that day, and a suit was required of all personnel attending a board meeting.) He was injured in a collision halfway between his school and his home.

Discussion: Workers' compensation would probably cover his injury. An injury suffered by an employee during his regular commute is compensable only if he was also performing a special mission for his employer. The employee's conduct is "special" if it is "extraordinary in relation to routine duties, not outside the scope of employment." Even though the employee was traveling home rather than between places of work, the trip was "reasonably undertaken at the request or invitation of the employer" and was a special mission.[1]

Scenario 21.2:   A classroom teacher, who also served as the district's supervisor of foreign languages, owned a computer and offered to use it to develop the master schedule for the district's foreign language program. Because her computer was a desk model, she did this work at home. She was killed in an automobile accident en route to the central office to deliver the schedule.

Discussion: Hazards encountered while commuting to and from work are normally not incident to employment and are not compensable. There are, however, exceptions to the rule: (1) "where the employer furnishes the means of transportation, or remunerates the employee; (2) where the employee performs some duty in connection with employment at home."[2] This teacher's death would probably be compensable under workers' compensation.

Scenario 21.3:   A community educator was injured when he was assaulted in his car immediately after leaving a school parking lot to go home from work. His car had been immobilized by students departing from the evening night school classes and was blocking traffic.

Discussion: This case seems to illustrate a noncompensable injury because the victim was undertaking a normal commute. However, "where the employment creates a special risk which extends beyond the boundaries of the employment premises, compensation will normally be allowed if the injury occurs within the zone of risk."[3]

Scenario 21.4: While attending an education conference in another state, a school district official fractured both of her heels in a fall. A sample of blood was drawn at the hospital. A doctor testified that the blood alcohol content revealed that she was intoxicated at the time of the accident.

Discussion: Workers' compensation would probably not cover this accident. Courts have ruled that "an employee can abandon employment by reaching an advanced state of intoxication. Any injuries suffered thereafter are not in the course of employment as the employee is no longer able to perform his or her job."[4]

Scenario 21.5: After completion of a night meeting held at one of the high schools, a district music teacher went to the weight room and began working out with weights. In attempting to lift a bar bell he seriously injured his back.

Discussion: "The employee was not engaged in those things which it should reasonably be expected an employee would do in connection with his duties. Unless the employee could demonstrate that his activity could be reasonably expected in connection with his duties, the court would not grant compensation."[5] If, however, "the employee could demonstrate that he regularly exercised at work which included weight lifting, and the employer was aware of and permitted such activities, the court would likely rule that the injury arose in the course of employment and was therefore compensable."[6]

Scenario 21.6: A high school teacher was stabbed by a former mental patient because the patient had seen the teacher talking after class with a student, the patient's former girlfriend.

Discussion: Some state workers' compensation acts do not cover injuries caused by the acts of third persons that are intended to injure the employee for personal reasons. However, "because the stabbing was incidental to the teacher's duties, and it arose out of his employment, the employee would likely be entitled to workers' compensation benefits."[7]

Scenario 21.7: A school principal was attending an out-of-town education conference that involved his staying in a motel. Following completion of the conference, he had dinner at a local restaurant. Leaving the restaurant, one of his companions was assaulted by someone unconnected with the conference. Attempting to assist the companion, the principal was himself assaulted and injured.

Discussion: The question here is whether the injuries sustained by the principal arose out of, and in the course of, his employment. In this scenario "there is no causal connection between the conditions under which the employee worked and the injury which arose. The employee's voluntary acts were the main cause of the injury."[8] His claim for workers' compensation benefits would probably be denied.

Scenario 21.8:   An elementary school teacher suffered injuries while she was participating in a softball game at a statewide teachers' association–sponsored conference. The district had paid her expenses to attend the conference on site-based management.

Discussion: The injury occurred during recreational activities rather than during the course of employment. In similar situations, courts have ruled that "if the injury did not occur on the employer's premises, the employer did not require or endorse participation in the game, and the employer obtained no tangible benefit, then there is no necessary relationship between the actions and the employer."[9] In such cases, claims have usually been denied.

Scenario 21.9:   A school district special education supervisor was on his way to visit a special education center in another city when he encountered a violent and unusual rainstorm with winds up to 100 miles per hour. When a tree fell on his car, his neck was broken, totally disabling him.

Discussion: Some courts have required that the accident must arise "both out of and in the course of employment" for an employee to be entitled to benefits under the provisions of workers' compensation. The term "arising out of" describes the accident and its origin, cause and character; the term "in the course of" refers to the time, place, and circumstances surrounding the accident. A claimant must establish both.[10] Here, the educator suffered an injury and it was in the course of his employment. However, the accident did not arise out of his employment. The risks the educator took were not inherent in his job but were risks to which the general public was exposed. This claim, unfortunately, would likely be denied.

The following real case, involving a teacher, is presented in more detail so that principals can see the "twists and turns" often found in workers' compensation cases. D. L. signed a teaching contract with a high school, including the responsibility of coaching football in the fall. Two months later, a college offered him the position of head basketball coach, a position he had long desired. An agreement was reached with the school board releasing him from his contract, subject to his continuing teaching duties until mid-September and finishing his season as head football coach.

D. L began undertaking both the college and high school duties, making four 100-mile trips per week. The stress of maintaining two jobs, both of which were inherently stressful, caused D. L. to develop a mental disorder for which he sought counseling. His condition deteriorated and he had suicidal thoughts. He was hospitalized, treated, and released, but then agreed to voluntary commitment. While sheriff's deputies were driving him to a hospital, he opened the car door and jumped out while the vehicle was moving at about 35 m.p.h., sustaining severe physical injuries.

D. L. filed for workers' compensation benefits, but was denied by the hearing officer. However, a trial court found his injuries compensable. Upon appeal, the court concluded that under the law of that jurisdiction, only injuries by accident arising out of and in the course of employment are compensable. Finally, the state supreme court held that a mental disability produced solely by mental stimuli or stress was not compensable under the state workers' compensation law.[11]

The Supreme Court of Mississippi, on the other hand, held, when an employee was found dead at a place where his duties required him to be during working hours, that there is a presumption that the death, even natural, arose out of and in the course of his employment if it cannot be proven that he was not engaged in his employer's business.[12]

The Principal's Responsibility for Chemical and Material Hazards

Scenario 21.10: Jane Jackson, the school custodian, prided herself on how clean she kept her school. She was a very neat person and did not like to have her supply room cluttered with old or outdated supplies. At the end of each school year, Jane collected any unused liquid materials and poured them down the drain of the sink in her supply room.

Scenario 21.11: Ron Brown had just been employed as a high school science teacher. When he looked in his science supply cabinet, he saw shelves of items that had long outlived their usefulness. All of these items had been ordered by previous teachers, and many containers had illegible or missing labels. There were also extremely large amounts of some chemicals that had been purchased in quantity to save money. There was no inventory sheet listing the contents of the supply cabinet.

Scenario 21.12:   There was very little space in the industrial arts area to store materials. Ed Summers, the auto mechanics teacher, saved the district money by regularly using his pickup truck to transport containers of used brake fluid, fuel oil, kerosene, motor oil, automatic transmission fluid, old batteries, and auto body repair products to a private landfill.

Scenario 21.13:   Ralph Sargent hated bugs, spiders, roaches, ants, wasps—it didn't matter, Ralph hated them At the elementary school where Ralph was head custodian, there was an ongoing war between Ralph and anything that flew, slithered, or crawled. Ralph had a two-stage plan for eradicating pests. First, he treated the school and its grounds with a chemical pesticide on a regular basis, regardless of whether or not any pests were seen, and, second, when a pest was reported to Ralph, he retreated the same areas with a double application of the same pesticide.

Points to Consider: Do most schools store significant amounts of hazardous materials? Are there regulations that govern the inventory, storage, and disposal of hazardous or polluting materials? What departments in the school or the school district are most likely to come into contact with toxic substances? Are individual schools responsible for complying with Occupational Safety and Health Administration (OSHA) standards?

When most people think of chemical hazards, they think of large industry. However, OSHA estimates that as many as 1,000 different hazardous chemicals, products, or materials are commonly found in elementary and secondary schools. Over 2,000 hazardous chemical accidents occur each year in schools and colleges in this country. A school district was sued for $50,000,000 when two middle school boys were injured in an explosion that occurred as the unsupervised students were mixing chemicals in a chemical storage room. In another case a 55-gallon drum that contained a chemical solvent exploded, severely injuring several students and an instructor. A school official explained that they thought the drum contained oil.[13] These and other recent events point to the need for schools to be come more aware of the dangers of hazardous materials.

The U.S. Environmental Protection Agency (EPA) considers a substance hazardous if it can catch fire, can react or explode when mixed with other substances, is corrosive, or is toxic. This definition includes many things that are commonly stored in school bathrooms, kitchens, science and art rooms, shops, office supply rooms, and janitor closets. Specific examples of hazardous materials found in typical schools include:

Kitchen areas: empty aerosol cans, aluminum cleaners, ammonia-based cleaners, bug sprays, drain cleaners, floor care products, furniture polish. metal polish with solvent, window cleaner, and oven cleaner.

Bathroom areas: toilet bowl and tile cleaner.

Industrial and vocational arts areas, art rooms, and janitor's storage: Antifreeze, automatic transmission fluid, auto body repair products, battery acid, brake fluid, car wax, diesel fuel, fuel oil, gasoline, kerosene, metal polish, motor oil, other oils, paint brush cleaners with solvent and TSP, aerosol cans, cutting oil, glue, paints, paint stripper, rust remover, turpentine, varnish, wood preservatives, fertilizers, fungicides, herbicides, insecticides, rat poison, and weed killer.

Science areas: A school's science and chemistry labs contain a large variety of toxic and potentially explosive materials.

Miscellaneous: Artist's paints and mediums, fiberglass epoxy, lighter fluid, mercury batteries and old thermostats, moth balls, photographic chemicals, lime, and swimming pool chemicals.

Federal Regulations

There are two sets of regulations governing chemical and material hazards in the schools—the OSHA Expanded Chemical Hazard Communication Standard[14] and the EPA's Emergency Planning and Community Right-to-Know Act of 1986. Schools are charged with carrying out these regulations.

Although OSHA's hazard communication standard was originally designed to protect workers who manufactured products containing hazardous chemicals, it was extended to include workers who merely use the products in their jobs. These standards require that employees be made aware of hazardous chemicals and that they have established safety precautions for the routine use of these chemicals, emergency procedures for handling them, and proper methods of disposal. Although school employees are more knowledgeable than they used to be, many are unaware of the potential dangers in cleaning, office, art, industrial, and vocational arts and science supplies. Schools are required by law to make sure that the presence of every chemical hazard is noted, that the labels on these products are adequate, and that a material safety data sheet is available for each.

In addition to the above-mentioned hazardous materials, the school environment can contain such health and environment dangers as pesticides, underground storage tanks, lead in water, unacceptable levels of radon gas, and asbestos exposure possibilities.

Pesticides

Although statistics on pesticide poisoning in schools are not available, there is a growing concern about the effect of pesticides that are used in and around schools. Reports of schools being closed because of unacceptable levels of carcinogenics have resulted in heightened concern by both professional and citizens. These concerns have resulted in the development of new concepts of pest management, which involve both nonchemical and chemical controls, known as integrated pest management (IPM).[15] The areas that have the highest potential for developing pest problems are food preparation facilities, dining and snack areas, and waste storage facilities. It is recommended that schools reduce the need for chemical pesticides, and thus reduce health dangers, by developing an IMP. This program should include:

• Monitoring, sanitation, and waste management
• Structural maintenance, physical barriers, and habitat modification
• Physical removal, traps, and biological controls[16]

Underground Storage Tanks

It is estimated that there are two to four million underground storage tanks containing petroleum products or hazardous substances in this country. Many of these tanks are under school property. The Hazardous and Solid Waste Amendments of 1984[17] set federal standards to regulate the storage and disposal of waste and the instillation of double liners, to monitor water, and to establish programs to regulate underground tanks. In 1988 the EPA established requirements for leak detection, leak prevention, corrective action, and financial responsibility for all underground storage tanks containing regulated substances.[18] Individual owners, directors, officers, and employees may be held responsible for the cost of cleaning up a leak and for compensating others for bodily injury and property damages caused by a such a discharge.

Lead

Any school built prior to 1977 may have paint that contains lead. The dust and chips from this paint can cause permanent impairment of a child's mental and physical development. Even low exposure has been linked to damage of the central and peripheral nervous system, learning disabilities, hyperactivity, impaired function of blood cells, impaired hearing, and shorter stature.[19]

An additional source of lead in schools is drinking water. Although lead may enter the water naturally from the ground where a well is drilled or from surface water from industrial or municipal sewage treatment plants, the most common source of lead in a school's drinking water is from the corrosion of lead pipe, solder, or fixtures. The Lead Contamination Act of 1988 requires the EPA and the states to develop programs to reduce the exposure of children to lead in school drinking water.

Other sources of lead in schools are:

• The powder pigments containing lead that can be found in paints
• Enameling materials and glazes for ceramics and the lead used in stained glass making
• Soldering, welding, grinding, and sanding lead-based painted surfaces[20]

Radon

Radon, a radioactive gas blamed for up to 40,000 cancer deaths each year, is becoming suspect as a cause for other kinds of illness as well. Because radon and its radioactive decay products are undetectable by our senses, people may not take this heath risk seriously. There is increasing concern about the radon levels in schools because studies have revealed that children may be more susceptible to harm from radon than adults. A 1989 EPA test of 130 schools in sixteen states found that 54 percent of the schools had at least one room where the radon levels exceeded the EPA recommended action level.[21]

Asbestos

Because it is noncombustible and an excellent source of heat and noise insulation, tens of thousands of tons of asbestos products were used in American elementary and secondary schools and colleges from 1946 until the early 1970s.[22] Buildings constructed in the 1960s are more likely to contain asbestos than are other buildings.[23] Unfortunately, when airborne asbestos fibers are inhaled, death or disablement may result. Medical evidence suggests that children face a greater risk of developing asbestos-related cancer than do adults.[24] Because of this health hazard, Congress enacted the Asbestos School Hazard Detection and Control Act of 1980.[25] The EPA enacted the Toxic Substance Control Act (TSCA) in 1976.[26] In 1983 the EPA published regulations that required local education agencies to inspect buildings, identify asbestos materials, and notify parents and employees of ways to minimize exposure to this hazard.[27] Federal funds were made available to schools in 1984 for asbestos abatement activities.[28] School officials must either remove the asbestos (permanent, but risks releasing fibers), or encapsulate or enclose it (less expensive, but has the potential for future hazards).

Disposal of Hazardous Chemicals and Materials

The improper disposal of hazardous wastes can cause problems for an entire community. Waste material can be explosive or highly flammable, corrosive, or poisonous to humans or wildlife. Waste water treatment plants are not designed to handle hazardous wastes, and just "dumping them down the drain" is one of the worst ways to dispose of unused chemicals. Hazardous wastes improperly disposed of in a landfill can pollute the environment though ground and surface water as well as through the air.

Environmental protective agencies near local schools can provide assistance in the disposal of waste materials.

Suggested Guidelines

The principal of each school should ensure that:

- A complete inventory exists of all hazardous materials in the school.
- The school is purged of all outdated and unlabeled materials.
- The school has an integrated pest management plan in order to minimize human exposure to toxic materials.
- The school district has a plan for leak detection in underground storage tanks and is equipped with devices to prevent spills or overflows. In addition, unused tanks should be removed or filled with sand to prevent a sudden elevation to the surface.
- Each school area is surveyed to determine the existence of lead-based paint on surfaces.
- Programs are instituted to test and contain lead where it occurs in the school environment.
- All rooms in the school on the basement level and ground level are tested for radon and all levels of the school are checked for airborne asbestos.
- All employees who come in contact with hazardous materials are informed of the hazards they may face.
- Employees are trained to identify and safely work with each type of hazard.
- The EPA's list of extremely hazardous chemicals is consulted to determine if any special reporting is required.
- EPA guidelines are followed for transportation and disposal of unwanted chemicals or materials.

Crisis Management

Scenario 21.14:   A tornado crushed a cafeteria wall, a boiler exploded, a fire erupted in the chemistry lab—tragic events like these and other human error or natural disasters highlight the critical need for schools and school districts to prepare for the unexpected.

Points to Consider: In case of a crisis, who is responsible for what? What kind of communication plan does your school and district have in place?

A *crisis* or emergency is a situation requiring immediate action, occurring unpredictably, or posing a threat of either injury or loss of life to school personnel or severe damage to property.[29] Emergency or crisis management has both pre-event (identification and analysis) and post-event (evaluation) goals. To achieve these goals, school districts should develop crisis-management plans tailored for particular potential emergencies. Crisis management assists the district to meet traditional education mandates of duty and standard of care and to comply with local and state laws. In addition, the inclusion of crisis planning in the overall risk plan provides for economy of operations.

Of special importance in crisis management is the pre-event goal of remaining prepared for prompt response to an emergency, emphasizing personnel safety whenever it conflicts with protection of property. Effective crisis planning integrates and coordinates school procedures with similar crisis plans at the municipal, county, and state levels. The post-event goals of crisis management emphasize organizational survival and continuity of operations. More specifically, in the wake of an emergency, crisis management seeks to save lives and to preserve property—to minimize the organization's actual losses of physical and human resources—so that normalcy can be restored promptly.[30]

When a crisis appears or is impending, a school district's response is critical. To safeguard resources, certain actions must be pre-planned so that responses to crises are prompt and effective. Effective crisis management protects the integrity of the *in loco parentis* responsibilities inherent in the education enterprise.

For everyone involved in a school district, crises are unsettling, stressful events. Constructive responses to such events require structure, order, and discipline. To achieve this goal, school districts should develop specific crisis management procedures, place such procedures in a readily understandable format (manual), and inservice appropriate personnel. The crisis-management manual should be disseminated to all site-based personnel. The following information is often included in crisis-management procedure manuals: the purpose, scope and organization of the manual; the structure of the crisis-management organization, including key contact personnel; evacuation instructions, including explanations of alarm signals and diagrams of exit routes; and communication procedures to be followed during and after the emergency.[31] In addition, school district plans should include:

- Sites of potential emergencies
- Appropriate responses to emergencies

- Arrangements for obtaining assistance from emergency service organizations and local government agencies
- Procedures for coordinating the use of district resources and personnel during emergencies
- Available district resources
- A system for informing all schools within the district of the emergency and for notifying parents or guardians
- Plans for taking the following actions, if appropriate: school cancellation, early dismissal, evacuation, and sheltering
- Pertinent information about each school—for example, enrollment and staffing information, transportation needs, etc.
- Procedures for obtaining advice and assistance from local government officials[32]

During a crisis, and immediately after, school districts need to preserve their standing in the community. To do so, they need effective communications with the media, employees, students, parents, and the community at large. Post-crisis communications should inform employees and patrons, as soon as possible, of the extent of losses caused by the crisis and should describe the school district's or school site's short- and long-term recovery plan. In any emergency situation the task of communicating is much simpler and more effective if the school district can report or forecast results that reflect the fact that the crisis has been well managed.

Endnotes

1. Jonathan A. Segal, *Goliath Had Rights Too,* HRMagazine (Society for Human Resources Management, Alexandria, Va.), Jan. 1990, p. 83.

2. Grenn v. Workers' Compensation Appeals Board, 232 Cal. Rptr., 465 (App. 2d. 1986).

3. Wilson v. Service Broadcasters, 483 So. 2d 1339 (Miss. 1986).

4. Parks v. Workers' Compensation Appeals Board, 660 P.2d. 382 (Cal. 1983).

5. American Safety Razor Co. v. Hunter, 343 S.E. 2d 461 (Va. App. 1986).

6. J.&W. Janitorial Co. v. Industrial Commission of Utah, 661 P.2d 949 (Utah 1983).

7. Aucompaugh v. General Electric, 490 N.Y. 2d 647 (A.D. 3d Dept. 1985).

8. Nasser v. Security Ins. Co., 724 S.W. 2d 17 (Tex. 1987).

9. Coneau v. Maine Coastal Services, 449 A. 2d 362 (Me. 1982).

10. Kempt's Case, 437 N.E. 2d 526 (Mass. 1982).

11. McGinn v. Douglas County Soc. Servs. Admin., 317 N.W. 2d 764 (Neb. 1982).

12. Lather v. Huron College, Sup. Ct. (South Dakota 1987).

13. M. Roll, *The OSHA Communication Standard and States Right to Know Laws,* School Business Affairs, vol. 56, no. 7, July 1990.

14. Title 29, C.F.R. subpart 2 of part 1910 (1910.1200).

15. S. Cooper, *The ABC's of Non-Toxic Pest Control,* SCHOOL BUSINESS AFFAIRS, vol. 56, no. 7, July 1990.

16. *Id.*

17. 40 C.F.R.

18. 40 C.F.R., parts 280–281.

19. S. Guyaux, *Lead Poisoning in Schools,* SCHOOL BUSINESS AFFAIRS, vol. 56, no. 7, July 1990.

20. *Id.* at 25.

21. Supplier Case Study, *Geomatrix Matting Helps Control Radon,* SCHOOL BUSINESS AFFAIRS, vol. 56, no. 7, July 1990.

22. The Attorney General's Asbestos Liability Report to the Congress prepared pursuant to Section 8(b) of the Asbestos School Hazard Detection and Control Act of 1980 (Aug. 1981), at ii, U.S. Department of Justice.

23. "EPA Issues New Asbestos Study," Wash. Post, Oct. 22, 1984, p. A19.

24. KRISTIN OLSEN, LEGAL ASPECTS OF ASBESTOS ABATEMENT, (Topeka, Kansas: National Organization on Legal Problems of Education, 1986), p. 1.

25. Pub. L. No. 96-270, 94 stat. 487 (1980).

26. 15 U.S.C. §§ 2601–2609 (1976).

27. 47 FED. REG. 23, 360 (1983).

28. Asbestos School Hazard Abatement Act, 20 U.S.C. § 4011 (1984).

29. Robert J. Rader, *Policy and Risk Management: Ties That Bind,* UPDATING SCHOOL BOARD POLICIES, vol. 21, no. 3 (March 1990), p. 1.

30. *See generally,* Curriculum of the IIA—Associate in Risk Management Curriculum, A.R.M. program, Insurance Institute of America, Malvern, Pennsylvania.

31. George L. Head, *Crisis Plans Insure Companies' Future,* BUSINESS INSURANCE, May 28, 1990, p. 39.

32. *Supra,* note 12 at 2.

Glossary

Selected Legal Terms and Amendments (abbreviated) to the United States Constitution

Absolute privilege Protection from liability for communication made in the performance of public service or the administration of justice.

Action A suit or lawsuit.

Adjudicate To hear the facts and settle a case in a legal proceeding.

Affidavit A written declaration under oath.

Appeal Asking a higher court to review the actions of a lower court in order to correct mistakes or injustice.

Appellant The party who appeals a lower court decision to a higher court.

Appellate court A tribunal having jurisdiction to review decisions on appeal from a lower court.

Assault the placing of another in fear of bodily harm.

Attractive nuisance Something that is threatening to young children because of their inability to appreciate its danger.

Battery The unlawful touching of another with intent to harm.

Burden of proof The duty of proving to a court that one's assertions are in fact the truth by showing clear evidence of the facts.

Brief Written argument presented by lawyers in court.

Certiorari A writ of review whereby an action is removed from a lower court to an appellate court for additional proceedings.

Civil action A judicial proceeding to redress an infringement of individual civil rights, in contrast to a criminal action brought by the state to redress public wrongs.

Civil right A personal right that accompanies citizenship.

Class action suit A judicial proceeding brought on behalf of a number of persons similarly situated.

Common law A body of rules and principles derived from usage or from judicial decisions enforcing such usage.

Compensatory damages   The actual losses suffered by a plaintiff, such as loss of income.

Concurring opinion   A statement by a judge or judges, separate from the majority opinion, that endorses the result of the decision but expresses some disagreement with the reasoning of the majority.

Consent decree   An agreement, sanctioned by the court, that is binding on the consenting parties.

Consideration   Something of value given or promised for the purpose of forming a contract.

Constitution   The supreme and fundamental law of a nation or state, establishing and prescribing the extent and manner of the exercise of sovereign powers.

Contract   An agreement between two or more competent parties that creates, alters, or dissolves a legal relationship.

Counterclaim   A demand by a defendant against a plaintiff.

Criminal action   A judicial proceeding brought by the state against a person charged with a public offense.

Damages   An award made to an individual to correct a legal wrong.

Decree   The judgment of a court.

Declaratory relief   A judicial declaration of the rights of the plaintiff without an assessment of damages against the defendant.

Defamation   False and intentional communication that injures a person's character or reputation.

Defendant   The party against whom a court action is brought.

De minimis   A violation that is so minimal as to not be worthy of judicial review.

Dictum (pl. dicta)   A statement made by a judge in delivering an opinion.

Discovery   Pre-trial procedures, such as depositions that allow each party to ascertain, within limits, the evidence of the opposing side.

Dismissal   Decision of a court not to hear a case.

Discretionary power   Authority that involves the exercise of judgment.

Dissenting opinion   A statement by a judge or judges who disagree with the decision of the majority of the justices in a case.

Due process   The fundamental right to notice of charges and an opportunity to rebut the charges before a fair tribunal if life, liberty, or property rights are at stake.

Duress   Unlawful coercion.

Eighth Amendment   Excessive bail shall not be required, nor excessive fines imposed, nor cruel and unusual punishments inflicted.

Ex post facto law   A law that retrospectively changes the legal consequences of an act that has already been performed.

Et al   "And others."

Felony   A class of serious crimes, as distinguished from lesser offenses called *misdemeanors*.

Fifth Amendment   No person . . . shall be compelled in any criminal case to be a witness against himself; nor be deprived of life, liberty, or property, without due process of law. . . .

First Amendment   Congress shall make no law respecting an establishment of religion, or prohibiting the free exercise thereof; or abridging the freedom of speech, or of the press; or the right of the people peaceably to assemble, and to petition the Government for a redress of grievances.

Fourteenth Amendment   No State shall make or enforce any law which shall abridge the privileges or immunities of citizens of the United States; nor shall any State deprive any person of life, liberty, or property, without due process of law; nor deny to any person within its jurisdiction the equal protection of the laws.

Fourth Amendment   The right of the people to be secure in their persons, houses, papers, and effects, against unreasonable searches and seizures, shall not be violated, and no Warrants shall issue, but upon probable cause, supported by oath or affirmation, and particularly describing the place to be searched, and the persons or things to be seized.

Governmental function   An activity performed in discharging official duties of a state or municipal agency.

Holding   A court's decision.

Informed consent   An agreement based on a full disclosure of facts needed to make a decision intelligently.

Injunction   A writ issued by a court prohibiting a defendant from acting in a prescribed manner.

In loco parentis   In place of parent; charged with rights and duties of a parent.

In re   "In the matter of"; concerning.

Invitee   A visitor by invitation, as distinguished from a trespasser.

Judgment   A decision of a court.

Judicial review   The power of a court to interpret the meaning of laws.

Jurisdiction   The right of a court to hear a case; also the geographic area within which the court has the right and power to operate.

Law   A system of principles or rules of human conduct; an enactment of a legislature.

Licensee   In tort law, a party permitted to enter property for his or her own purposes.

Liability   A legal obligation or responsibility.

Libel   Written defamation; published false and malicious written statements that injure a person's reputation.

Majority opinion   The opinion agreed on by more than half the judges or justices hearing a case; sometimes called opinion of the court.

Malice   Hatred; ill will; an intention to do an unlawful act.

Mandamus   A command from a court of law directed to a lower court, officer, or person ordering the court or individual to do some particular thing.

Mandate   A legal command.

Ministerial duty   An act that does not involve discretion and must be carried out in a manner specified by legal authority.

Misdemeanor   A minor offense usually punishable by fine or imprisonment in a facility other than a penitentiary.

Misfeasance   Improper performance of a lawful act.

Mitigation   The reduction in a fine, penalty, sentence, or damages initially assessed or decreed.

Moot   A question or dispute that is no longer viable, generally because the circumstances that caused the dispute no longer exist.

Negligence   The failure to exercise the degree of care that a reasonably prudent person would exercise under similar circumstances.

Nexus   A connection or link; in teacher employment issues, a rational connection between personal conduct and unfitness to teach.

Ninth Amendment   The enumeration of the Constitution, of certain rights, shall not be construed to deny or disparage others retained by the people.

Nonfeasance   Omission of performance in a required duty.

Opinion   A judge's statement of the decision reached in a case.

Plaintiff   The party initiating a judicial action.

Plenary power   Full, complete, absolute power.

Plurality   The prevailing opinion of an appellate court that is subscribed to by less than a majority of the participating judges. Concurring opinions by other judges cause the plurality to prevail.

Power   The expressed or implied authority to do something.

Precedent   A judicial decision observed as authority for subsequent cases involving similar questions of law.

Prima facie   "At first view"; a fact presumed to be true unless disproved by contrary evidence.

Probable cause   Reasonable grounds, supported by sufficient evidence to warrant a cautious person to believe that the individual is guilty of the offense charged.

Punitive damages   Money awarded to a person by a court that is over and above the monetary damage actually sustained.

Qualified privilege   Protection from liability for communication made in good faith, for proper reasons, and to appropriate parties.

Quasi   "As if"; a quasi-legislative act of a school board in formulating policy.

Remand   To send a case back to the original court for additional proceedings.

Respondeat superior   A legal doctrine whereby the master is responsible for the acts of the servant; i.e., a governmental unit is responsible for the acts of its employees.

Respondent One who makes an answer in a legal appellate proceeding; often used in place of *defendant*.

Search and seizure The discovery and confiscation of property belonging to a suspected offender.

Sixth Amendment . . . [T]he accused shall enjoy the right to a speedy and public trial, by an impartial jury . . . and to be informed of the nature and cause of the accusation; to be confronted with the witnesses against him; to have compulsory process for obtaining witnesses in his favor, and to have the assistance of counsel for his defense.

Slander Oral defamation; the speaking of false and malicious words that injure another person.

Standing A person's right to bring a lawsuit because he or she was directly affected by the issues raised.

Stare decisis To abide by decided cases; to adhere to precedent.

Statute An act by the legislative branch of government expressing its will and constituting the law of the state.

Summary judgment A court decision, prior to a full trial in a civil action, where the party moves and the court agrees that there is no genuine issue of material fact and that the moving party is entitled to prevail as a matter of law.

Tenth Amendment The powers not delegated to the United States by the Constitution, nor prohibited by it to the States, are reserved to the States respectively, or to the people.

Tenure A statutory right that confers permanent employment on teachers, protecting them from dismissal except for justifiable cause.

Tort A civil wrong, other than a breach of trust or contract, for which a remedy in damages is sought.

Trespass The unauthorized entry upon, taking, or interfering with the property of another.

Ultra vires "Beyond the power"; beyond the scope of authority of the corporate body.

Unilateral Action taken by one party only.

Vacate To set aside; to render a judgment void.

Verdict A decision of a jury on questions submitted for trial.

Vested Complete and fixed; not contingent.

Waive To renounce or abandon a right.

Writ A written order from a court requiring the performance of a specific act.

Table of Cases

Index